READING AND TEACHING
ANCIENT FICTION

WRITINGS FROM THE GRECO-ROMAN WORLD SUPPLEMENT SERIES

Clare K. Rothschild, General Editor

Number 11

READING AND TEACHING ANCIENT FICTION

Jewish, Christian, and Greco-Roman Narratives

Edited by

Sara R. Johnson, Rubén R. Dupertuis, and Christine Shea

Atlanta

Copyright © 2018 by SBL Press

All rights reserved. No part of this work may be reproduced or transmitted in any form or by any means, electronic or mechanical, including photocopying and recording, or by means of any information storage or retrieval system, except as may be expressly permitted by the 1976 Copyright Act or in writing from the publisher. Requests for permission should be addressed in writing to the Rights and Permissions Office, SBL Press, 825 Houston Mill Road, Atlanta, GA 30329 USA.

Library of Congress Cataloging-in-Publication Data

Names: Johnson, Sara Raup, 1966– editor. | Dupertuis, Rubén R., editor. | Shea, Chris, 1949– editor.
Title: Reading and teaching ancient fiction : Jewish, Christian, and Greco-Roman narratives / edited by Sara Johnson, Rubén René Dupertuis, and Chris Shea.
Other titles: Jewish, Christian, and Greco-Roman narratives
Description: Atlanta : SBL Press, 2018. | Series: Writings from the Greco-Roman world supplement series ; Number 11 | Includes bibliographical references and index. | Description based on print version record and CIP data provided by publisher; resource not viewed.
Identifiers: LCCN 2017060321 (print) | LCCN 2018008482 (ebook) | ISBN 9780884142607 (ebk.) | ISBN 9781628371963 (pbk. : alk. paper) | ISBN 9780884142614 (hbk. : alk. paper)
Subjects: LCSH: Classical literature—History and criticism. | Apocryphal books—Criticism, interpretation, etc. | Civilization, Ancient, in literature. | Literature—Study and teaching.
Classification: LCC PA3003 (ebook) | LCC PA3003 .R385 2018 (print) | DDC 880.09—dc23
LC record available at https://lccn.loc.gov/2017060321

Printed on acid-free paper.

Contents

Acknowledgments ix
Abbreviations xi

Introduction
    Richard I. Pervo† 1

Part 1: Early Christian Narrative

Desiring Women: Xanthippe, Polyxena, Rebecca
    Virginia Burrus 9

Madly in Love: The Motif of Lovesickness in the Acts of Andrew
    Christy Cobb 29

Trophy Wives of Christ: Tropes of Seduction and Conquest in
the Apocryphal Acts
    John W. Marshall 43

Unsettling Heroes: Reading Identity Politics in Mark's Gospel and
Ancient Fiction
    Scott S. Elliott and Eric Thurman 71

Narrative Pathology or Strategy for Making Present and
Authorization? Metalepsis in the Gospels
    Ute E. Eisen, translated by Sara R. Johnson 87

Part 2: Jews, Greeks, Romans, and Others

"And Also to the Jews in Their Script": Power and Writing in the
Scroll of Esther
    Donald C. Polaski 107

History Told by Losers: Dictys and Dares on the Trojan War
    Richard I. Pervo†..123

According to the Brothers: First-Person Narration in the
Testaments of the Twelve Patriarchs
    Brian O. Sigmon 137

A Tale of Two Moseses: Philo's On the Life of Moses and
Josephus's *Jewish Antiquities* 2–4 in Light of the Roman
Discourse of Exemplarity
    James M. Petitfils 153

Are Weeping and Falling Down Funny? Exaggeration in
Ancient Novelistic Texts
    Jared W. Ludlow...165

Grotesque and Strange Tales of the Beyond: Truth, Fiction,
and Social Discourse
    Gerhard van den Heever 179

Part 3: Pedagogies Ancient and Modern

Origen and Hypatia: Parallel Portraits of Platonist Educators
    Ilaria Ramelli..199

Teaching Fiction, Teaching Acts: Introducing the Linguistic
Turn in the Biblical Studies Classroom
    Shelly Matthews..213

Signature Pedagogies for Ancient Fiction? Thecla as a Test Case
    B. Diane Lipsett 233

Teaching Mimesis as a Criterion for Textual Criticism: Cases
from the Testament of Abraham and the Gospel of Nicodemus
    Dennis R. MacDonald 241

A New Subjectivity? Teaching Ἔρως through the Greek Novel
and Early Christian Texts
    David Konstan 251

Bibliography 261
Contributors 289
Ancient Sources Index 295
Modern Authors Index 305
Subject Index 309

Acknowledgments

This volume has been a long time coming—the last volume of collected papers from the Society of Biblical Literature's Ancient Fiction and Early Christian and Jewish Narrative (AFECJN) section came out in 2005—and accordingly there are many people to thank. Jo-Ann Brant, the principal editor of the previous volume, provided us with much sensible advice at the outset, while Chris Shea, who served as editor on both the previous volume and on this one, has been a continuous source of wise advice based on experience. Rubén Dupertuis, who came on as editor after Richard Pervo stepped down from the original editorial team, has rendered heroic service despite his many other responsibilities. Thanks to Billie Jean Collins and Bob Buller of SBL Press, both of whom encouraged and assisted us with the initial proposal. Earlier volumes of collected papers from the AFECJN section had appeared in the Symposium series, since discontinued, but Clare Rothschild, editor of the Writings from the Greco-Roman World Supplement series, welcomed our volume with open arms and has swiftly and efficiently seen us through to publication. Nicole Tilford, Production Manager, and Heather McMurray, Sales Manager, have capably managed the many technical details.

It was with deep sadness that we learned of the death of Richard I. Pervo on May 20, 2017, only a few weeks after the full manuscript was delivered into the hands of the series editor. In addition to being a pillar of the AFECJN section since its founding in 1992, attending every meeting and giving many a presentation, Richard was a key figure in the shaping of this volume from start to finish. He was originally a member of the editorial committee for the present volume, and even after his busy publication schedule and ill-health compelled him to step down, he often provided invaluable insights and advice, commenting on many of the papers at various stages along the way. There are few papers in this volume that have not been improved by his advice at some stage. One of his last acts was to contribute the promised introduction to this volume, which we dedicate to his memory. His cheerful and knowledgeable presence at future meetings of the AFECJN section will be sorely missed.

Sara Johnson, on behalf of the editorial committee:
Sara R. Johnson
Rubén R. Dupertuis
Christine Shea

Abbreviations

Ancient Sources

1 Clem.	1 Clement
1 Regn.	Dio Chrysostom, *De regno i* (*Or. 1*)
Ab urbe cond.	Livy, *Ab urbe condita*
Abraham	Philo, *On the Life of Abraham*
Act. diur.	Dares, *Acta diurna belli Troiani*
Acts Andr.	Acts of Andrew
Acts John	Acts of John
Acts Paul	Acts of Paul
Acts Pet.	Acts of Peter
Acts Thom.	Acts of Thomas
Anab.	Arrian, *Anabasis*
Ant.	Josephus, *Jewish Antiquities*
Anth. Pal.	Anthologia Palatina
Aug.	Suetonius, *Divus Augustus*
b.	Babylonian Talmud
Bib. hist.	Diodorus Siculus, *Bibliotheca historica*
Cels.	Origen, *Contra Celsum*
Chron.	John Malalas, *Chronographia*
Eccl. Rab.	Ecclesiastes Rabbah
Ep.	Jerome, *Epistle*
Eph. bell. Troiani	Dictys, *Ephemeris belli Troiani*
frag.	fragment
Gen. Rab.	Genesis Rabbah
Git.	Gittin
Hist.	Herodotus, *Historiae*
Hist. cons.	Lucian, *Quomodo historia conscribenda sit*
Hist. eccl.	Eusebius, *Historia ecclesiastica*; Socrates, *Historia ecclesiastica*

Il.	Homer, *Iliad*
Inst.	Lactantius, *Divinarum institutionorum libri VII*
Is. Os.	Plutarch, *De Iside et Osiride*
Jos. Asen.	Joseph and Aseneth
Leuc. Clit.	Achilles Tatius, *Leucippe et Clitophon*
Lives	Diogenes Laertius, *Lives and Opinions of Eminent Philosophers*
Math.	Sextus Empiricus, *Adversus mathematicos*
Metam.	Ovid, *Metamorphoses*
Midr. Num.	Midrash Numbers
Mor.	Plutarch, *Moralia*
Moses	Philo, *On the Life of Moses*
Nat.	Pliny, *Naturalis historia*
Num.	Plutarch, *Numa*
Od.	Homer, *Odyssey*
Pan.	Pliny, *Panegyricus*
Peregr.	Lucian, *De morte peregrini*
Phaedr.	Plato, *Phaedrus*
Poet.	Aristotle, *Poetica*
Praep. ev.	Eusebius, *Praeparatio evangelica*
Prot. Jas.	Protoevangelium of James
Prov. cons.	Cicero, *De provinciis consularibus*
Rab.	Rabbah
Resp.	Plato, *Respublica*
Ruf.	Jerome, *Adversus Rufinum libri III*
Sanh.	Sanhedrin
Serv.	Dio Chrysostom, *De servis (Or. 10)*
Sign. acut.	Aretaeus, *De causis et signis acutorum morborum*
Somnium	Lucian, *Somnium*
Symp.	Plato, *Symposium*
T. Ab.	Testament of Abraham
T. Benj.	Testament of Benjamin
T. Dan	Testament of Dan
T. Gad	Testament of Gad
T. Jos.	Testament of Joseph
T. Naph.	Testament of Naphtali
T. Sim.	Testament of Simeon
T. Zeb.	Testament of Zebulun
Tg. Neof.	Targum Neofiti

Tg. Ps.-J.	Targum Pseudo-Jonathan
Troj.	Dio Chrysostom, *Trojana* (*Or. 11*)
Ver. hist.	Lucian, *Vera historia*
Vir. ill.	Jerome, *De viris illustribus*

Modern Resources

AB	Anchor Bible
AHR	*American Historical Review*
ANF	Roberts, Alexander, and James Donaldson, eds. The Ante-Nicene Fathers. 10 vols. 1885–1887. Repr., Peabody, MA: Hendrickson, 1994
ANRW	*Aufstieg und Niedergang der römischen Welt: Geschichte und Kultur Roms im Spiegel der neueren Forschung*. Part 2, *Principat*. Edited by Hildegard Temporini and Wolfgang Haase. Berlin: de Gruyter, 1972–.
AOTC	Abingdon Old Testament Commentaries
BibInt	Biblical Interpretation Series
BLS	Bible and Literature Series
BZNW	Beihefte zur Zeitschrift für die neutestamentliche Wissenschaft
CBQMS	Catholic Biblical Quarterly Monograph Series
CNS	*Cristianesimo nella storia*
CP	*Classical Philology*
CQ	*Church Quarterly*
GR	*Greece and Rome*
GRBS	*Greek, Roman, and Byzantine Studies*
HThKNT	Herders Theologischer Kommentar zum Neuen Testament
IBC	Interpretation: A Bible Commentary for Teaching and Preaching
ICC	International Critical Commentary
JBL	*Journal of Biblical Literature*
JECS	*Journal of Early Christian Studies*
JFSR	*Journal of Feminist Studies in Religion*
JHS	*Journal of Hellenic Studies*
JJS	*Journal of Jewish Studies*
JQR	*Jewish Quarterly Review*

JRS	*Journal of Roman Studies*
JSJ	*Journal for the Study of Judaism in the Persian, Hellenistic, and Roman Periods*
JSNT	*Journal for the Study of the New Testament*
JSOTSup	Journal for the Study of the Old Testament Supplement Series
JTS	*Journal of Theological Studies*
LCL	Loeb Classical Library
LSJ	Liddell, Henry George, Robert Scott, and Henry Stuart Jones. *A Greek-English Lexicon*. 9th ed. with revised supplement. Oxford: Clarendon, 1996.
LXX	Septuagint
MT	Masoretic Text
MTSR	*Method and Theory in the Study of Religion*
NCB	New Century Bible
NovTSup	Supplements to Novum Testamentum
NPNF	Schaff, Philip, and Henry Wace, eds. *The Nicene and Post-Nicene Fathers*, Series 2. 14 vols. 1886–1889. Repr., Peabody, MA: Hendrickson, 1994.
NRM	new religious movement
NTAbh	Neutestamentliche Abhandlungen
NTApoc	Schneemelcher, Wilhelm, ed. *New Testament Apocrypha*. 2 vols. Rev. ed. English trans. ed. Robert McL. Wilson. Cambridge: Clarke; Loiusville: Westminster John Knox, 2003.
NTOA	Novum Testamentum et Orbis Antiquus
NTS	*New Testament Studies*
OTL	Old Testament Library
OTP	Charlesworth, James H., ed. *Old Testament Pseudepigrapha*. 2 vols. New York: Doubleday, 1983–1985.
P.Oxy.	Grenfell, Bernard P., et al., eds. *The Oxyrhynchus Papyri*. London: Egypt Exploration Fund, 1898–
P.Tebt.	Grenfell, Bernard P., and A. S. Hunt, eds. *The Tebtunis Papyri*. Vol. 2. London: University of California Publications, 1907.
R&T	*Religion and Theology*
RAr	*Revue archéologique*

RGRW	Religions in the Graeco-Roman World
SBLDS	Society of Biblical Literature Dissertation Series
SBLSymS	Society of Biblical Literature Symposium Series
SBLTT	Society of Biblical Literature Texts and Translations
SCS	Septuagint and Cognate Studies
SP	Sacra Pagina
SPhiloA	*Studia Philonica Annual*
SVTP	Studia in Veteris Testamenti Pseudepigraphica
TAPA	*Transactions of the American Philological Association*
TENTS	Texts and Editions for New Testament Study
TSAJ	Texte und Studie zum antiken Judentum
VC	*Vigiliae Christianae*
VT	*Vetus Testamentum*
WGRW	Writings from the Greco-Roman World
WGRWSup	Writings from the Greco-Roman World Supplement Series
WUNT	Wissenschaftliche Untersuchungen zum Neuen Testament
ZPE	*Zeitschrift für Papyrologie und Epigraphik*
ZTK	*Zeitschrift für Theologie und Kirche*

Introduction

Richard I. Pervo†

A quarter-century's involvement with the Ancient Fiction group tempts one to reflect on what has changed and where continuity blooms. The latter may be the more important category. Introductory questions consumed much of the energy devoted to the Christian Apocrypha and Jewish literature of the Hellenistic and Roman eras into the 1990s. Many of those questions remain unresolved. Some ignore them; others engage them with firm skepticism and limited passion. Literary attention to the apocryphal acts and the explosion of interest in ancient novels emerged at about the same time and with similar interests. Prominent among these was the social world portrayed by or reflected in the texts. Women were prominent in the stories and provided a fertile field for feminist studies. Classical studies had its canon, as did theology. The leading classical criteria were traditional and aesthetic. Orthodoxy and history were major bases for evaluating Jewish and Christian texts. The latter readily blended. If the canonical Acts was not historical, it did not belong in Scripture. In short, the study of ancient narrative over the last long generation has been a determined, willful violator of boundaries. We of Ancient Fiction welcome literary misfits and are perfectly content to treat the elite like misfits. Our seating charts would give a veteran protocol chief the vapors. We admire efforts to juxtapose a banal, multilayered entity like the Testaments of the Twelve Patriarchs with a sophistic Greek novel, fully knowing that their authors—if the former had one—would not appreciate the association. So nothing has changed.

Otherwise stated, nothing is the same. Because those engaged in Ancient Fiction are interested in texts, the group has accommodated a range of postmodern approaches, collaborators with postmodernism, and those who have never been moved to sample the fruit of the postmodern tree. Philological investment and skills vary, but philology still holds a seat of honor at the table. Sex and power have always been staples, but the former has become more complex and the latter possibly less so. Preservation of chastity has been the leaven of ancient fiction, whether until nuptial bliss and happily ever after or until the blissful hereafter. Chastity often reeks of sex. In this collection Virginia Burrus analyzes a compressed narrative that features only women, queerly enough. Burrus's critics might claim that her approach is perverse, but, if that charge is to be made, the proper target is the text. She also looks to similarities in feeling and function between ascetic practice and the conventional dangers, separation from nourishment and rest alongside separation from home and family. Christy Cobb looks at the hackneyed theme of lovesickness from the perspective of relations between men in the Acts of Andrew and *Leucippe and Clitophon* and, for a bonus, makes us current with medical thought on the subject—ancient medical thought. Her warrant is unimpeachable, for reflection on same-sex desire and the pursuit of enlightenment goes back to Plato (if not earlier). John W. Marshall takes up the inverse—some might again say perverse—trope of seduction in which apostles ruin young women destined for an honored and comfortable domestic life. Each of these essays explores the metaphor of erotics in religious conversion, the use of desire to describe pursuit of the holy. Our authors do not neglect possible subconscious aspects of religious desire, and one cannot be certain that the original authors were blind to them. The cultural distance provided by ancient literature offers good lessons in suspecting both overly concrete and excessively abstract interpretation. More on lessons later. Fiction's the name, power the game.

Marshall relates the seduction trope to various ancient depictions of conquest, mastery, and subjection. He proposes that one early Christian depiction of evangelism modeled itself on the Greco-Roman paradigm of gendered political control. This leads to reflection of the triumph of God—are the missionary successes depicted in the canonical Acts a variant of the same trope, and what about apocalyptic? The word *empire* was not common in the early years of Ancient Fiction; now it is ubiquitous. Our literature is a course in ancient empires: Egyptian, Persian, Ptolemaic, Seleucid, Attalid, Roman, Parthian, Byzantine, and Sassanid. Today no one need prefix *evil* to empire. Ancient narrative provides abundant material about different reactions to various empires in sundry times and diverse places among particular groups. Scott S. Elliott and Eric Thurman offer one approach to this complex phenomenon by looking at identity construction in Mark. Among their guides are some of the earliest examples of Greek prose fiction that sought to preserve national identity in the language of the imperial masters by, for example, narrating the glorious past. Their work is fruitfully informed by the contributions of postcolonial studies. That this mixture of modern theory and the rough ancient equivalent to comic books is illuminating indicates how complex Mark—a text admired fifty years ago for its lack of art and consequent claim to unvarnished tradition—really is.

Postmodernism has made the salient point that all (re)constructions of history amount to fiction, but this has not banished the questions of authorial intention and reader response. Donald C. Polaski takes up canonical Hebrew Esther. The longtime *Sitz im Leben* of the scroll has been carnivalesque, the Feast of Purim. Interpreters tend to find this an excellent choice. Polaski scrutinizes Esther's portrayal of the power of writing. All know, or once knew, about the inviolability of the laws of the Medes and Persians. What the king has had written, he has had written—except when it has been erased. Dethroning a symbol can enhance its status. This essay, with its astute analysis, enhances our awareness of the link between literacy and power.

A sizable number of scholars hold that if readers were expected to believe a text, it is either fact or fraud. Richard I. Pervo takes up the fictional accounts of the Trojan War attributed to Dares and Dictys. These come equipped with the conventional apparatus of authentication: eyewitnesses, personal diaries, and buried texts later unearthed. These were, in fact, marks of fiction, but their ostensibly factual claims prevailed, and Dares and Dictys were major resources for historians well into the Renaissance. Reception history and original intent may not coincide. Biblical studies does not contain all the advocates of this fallacy, but it has a very full share of them.

One device, first-person narration, sets the agenda for Brian O. Sigmon's probe into the Testaments of the Twelve Patriarchs. No fewer than six first-person narratives relate to Joseph's betrayal and sale into slavery. Sigmon studies these for their literary function, identifying three major aspects. His work both heightens appreciation of the literary character of the Testaments and provides models for similar works, including those within the various canonical collections. His essay should be read in the context of Ute E. Eisen's contribution.

The erudite Ilaria Ramelli transforms Socrates (the historian, not the philosopher) into a Plutarch. The historian Socrates wrote similar sketches of two representatives of the later Platonist tradition: Origen and Hypatia, both Alexandrian. She argues that the parallelism was intentional and supports this claim by identifying the qualities the subjects had in common. Socrates's audience was largely Christian; his point is difficult to miss. (Ironically, Origen's condemnation did nothing to elevate Hypatia's reputation; his opponents viewed the similarities as nails in Origen's theological coffin.) Since Hypatia is a blot upon the Christian conscience, it is a relief to find a Christian authority who could admire a virtuous pagan and lament her martyrdom. The portraits also show that late antique philosophical biographies suitable for propaganda and edification did not greatly differ whether their subjects were polytheist or Christian.

Two model portraits of Moses by Philo (*Life of Moses*) and Josephus (*Ant.* 2–4) lead James M. Petitfils to investigate the apparent influence of the ubiquitous Roman use of exemplary persons and their deeds. (This practice continued to influence elementary Latin textbooks used until at least the 1950s.) The utility of examples is apparent from its penetration into Greek literature written by Jews. Philo and Josephus constructed quite different portraits of Moses, but both found value in providing explicit examples of different virtues and qualities. If sustained in the continuing conversation, this proposal would be a strong instance of cross-cultural activity.

Exaggeration is one of the staples of humor. Because it is essentially universal in appeal, it is among the most readily detected forms of ancient humor. From Latin comedy come such types as the *servus currens* (dashing slave, often to get nowhere quickly) and the *miles gloriosus* (bragging soldier), both of whom could be transformed by Shakespeare and still make their appearance in broad comedy. Jared W. Ludlow selects the examples of hyperbolic weeping, crying out, and falling down in a survey of Tobit, Judith, and the Testament of Abraham. The last is quite humorous, Tobit somewhat so, but few read Judith for laughs. Ludlow seeks to identify literary clues that can signal that these usually distressing features are being given the comic touch. One of Ancient Fiction's missions over the years has been to identify humor in religious texts. Ludlow advances this project and relates it to the "vain fluctuating state of human empire."

The vast majority of those involved in the Ancient Fiction groups over the years have earned their daily bread by teaching, much of this in general or service courses. Ancient fiction belongs to our background interests, research that may be our true love. This collection includes four examples of ways in which background can make it to the front of a large class.

Those not engaged in pedagogy may be tempted to overlook these contributions, but not altogether to their advantage, for this material is useful for teaching *method*. Greek novels are easy to read, amusing or appealing in various ways to students, and not fraught with questions of religious status. Infallibility is not one of their attributes.

Shelly Matthews knows that one will not get far by warning students not to trust the canonical Acts. Through the use of a fictional parallel she begins leading them toward grasping the postmodern understanding of "history" in contrast to the modern and to appreciate that criteria may vary. Diane Lipsett finds the Acts of Paul and various theories about its composition and structure a useful means to engage students in the practices of criticism, to actually make them interested in it as well as in the history of reception that is still visible in the various witnesses.

Dennis R. MacDonald, who has largely developed a new genre of criticism, the study of mimesis in early Christian texts, shows how this tool can aid in the identification of an earlier recension. His example is the so-called Gospel of Nicodemus and the varying forms of the harrowing of hell. This sort of analysis is not novel, but by associating it with a specific discipline and an explicit method MacDonald has added weight to the argument. David Konstan does not have to wrestle with the descent into hell, but he has a suggestion for those who must or choose to venture into ancient sexuality: romantic novels are good places to begin. Although these novels represent a rather novel and individualistic understanding of love and marriage, they provide an apparently conventional introduction to what will become a different world. Similar cultures produced strikingly similar tales of lovers and martyrs. And, once more, students will enjoy them. Few of us would not relish the opportunity to sit in on Konstan's class.

The last two essays address formal topics. Gerhard van den Heever always gives thrill-seeking customers full satisfaction. His essays are roller-coaster rides after which the passengers will be permanently altered. His thesis is clear enough: systems of classification often reveal more about the culture and worldview of the classifiers than about the objects classified. One can do this with modern systems, but it will also work for illuminating antiquity. In so doing van den Heever moves from classificatory systems to the abundance of what we should call nonrealistic genres, the list of which is substantial. These two axes, classification and unrealistic genres, can work in tandem to sharpen the ideological profiles of the ancient world.

Ute E. Eisen jumps into the emerging exploration of narrative metalepsis. Those not familiar with the subject might suspect that it is a malady (for which a remedy is now available). In its basic manifestation, metalepsis was common in eighteenth-century novels. "At this juncture, dear reader, I should like to call your attention to a prior development heretofore unnoticed in this account …." When the actual author or the narrator intervenes in a narrative, there metalepsis can be found. In the broader sense metalepsis involves the blending or contamination of narrative voices and may come to resemble a sort of metonymy at the narrative level. (If metonymy is unfamiliar, it is a trope that substitutes cause for effect or vice versa. Advertising often exploits the former: if you wish to be handsome, rugged, and "manly," smoke Marlboros. In a cloudy corollary metonymy substitutes an attribute for the object: blue-collar workers belong on the factory floor supervised by office-dwelling suits. Narrative metalepsis has functions like these attributive metonymies.)

The basic phenomenon is well illustrated in the tale of the paralytic of Mark 2:1–12. Is this a healing story or an apophthegm focused on the pronouncement about forgiveness of sins? No example better serves teaching. One can see the seam. In verse 5a Jesus "says to the paralytic." Then follows the material about forgiveness until verse 10b, when "he says to the paralytic" reappears. Someone inserted the forgiveness discussion into the story and marked the interpolation with this repetition.

Eisen is not concerned with forms and editing. She notes that the return of the omniscient narrator in verse 10b is a metalepsis, describing the final product, the outfit on display rather than its previous condition and underpinnings. Many will think of the we-passages in Acts (and John). Equipped with this tool, attack the parable in Luke 16:1–9. Where does it end? Who is the κύριος in verse 8? The manager's master or Jesus? Those who have struggled to find meaning or utility in earlier papers on this subject will discover in Eisen an answer to their questions—if not their dreams. Metalepsis is about boundary violations, as is the Society of Biblical Literature's Ancient Fiction program unit.

Part 1
Early Christian Narrative

Desiring Women: Xanthippe, Polyxena, Rebecca

Virginia Burrus

Preserved in an eleventh-century Greek manuscript published in the late nineteenth century, with an English translation following swiftly,[1] the Acts of Xanthippe and Polyxena has received relatively little scholarly attention in the century and more that has passed since it first appeared in print. This neglect is due to the difficulty of establishing date and provenance, on the one hand, and to the work's apparent lack of either historicity or literary originality, on the other.[2] But perhaps this latter feature should provoke rather than discourage our interest. The Acts of Xanthippe and Polyxena not only models itself upon second- and third-century apocryphal acts of

---

I am grateful to Richard Pervo for his helpful suggestions and comments on this essay; I shall greatly miss his generosity, honesty, and humor. I also thank hosts and conversation partners at King's College London, Cornell University, and Ghent University, where I presented prior versions of this work.

1. Montague Rhodes James, ed., *Apocrypha Anecdota: A Collection of Thirteen Apocryphal Books and Fragments*, Texts and Studies: Contributions to Biblical and Patristic Literature, 2 vols. (Cambridge: Cambridge University Press, 1893, 1987), 1:43–85; note that James records corrections to this text in his second volume of *Apocrypha Anecdota*, 2:139–40. W. A. Craigie, trans., "Acts of Xanthippe and Polyxena" (ANF 9:205–17). Two other eleventh-century manuscripts and one fifteenth-century manuscript containing the Acts of Xanthippe and Polyxena have since been identified; see Eric Junod, "Vie et conduite des saintes femmes Xanthippe, Polyxène, et Rébecca (BHG 1877)," in *Oecumenica et patristica: Festschrift für Wilhelm Schneemelcher zum 75. Geburtstag*, ed. Damaskinos Papandreou, Wolfgang A. Bienert, and Knut Schäferdiek (Stuttgart: Kohlammer, 1989), 84–85.

2. As Max Bonnet sums up the main argument of James's introduction to his edition, "Il a fort bien démontré, en particulier, le manque d'originalité de cette composition, dont presque tous les éléments se retrouvent soit dans les Actes apocryphes des Apôtres, soit dans les romans grecs" ("Sur les Actes de Xanthippe et Polyxène," *Classical Review* 8 [1894]: 336).

apostles but also seems to delight in allusive play. Richard Pervo refers to "borrowing so sophisticated as to be arch."[3] The work's lack of originality manifests as a distinct style of creativity, in other words. The author lifts characters, plotlines, and episodes from the Acts of Paul and Thecla and of Peter, and most likely from the Acts of Andrew, Philip, and Thomas as well. These textual fragments are tweaked, recombined, and then mingled with elements drawn from the wider corpus of ancient novelistic literature, to produce what has been described as a "mosaic" or "genre hybride."[4] Such artful processes of textual dismemberment, displacement, and recombination are in fact characteristic of late ancient literature. As Marco Formisano puts it, "the texture of the tradition is used as the template for new creations that would be inconceivable without that form."[5] Since an anthology of apocryphal acts—our author's template—was circulating by the fourth century, current consensus places the Acts of Xanthippe and Polyxena between the fourth and the sixth centuries, without precluding a later date.[6] While we may not know exactly when or where it was written, this text sits comfortably in a late ancient literary context.

---

3. Richard I. Pervo, "Dare and Back: The Stories of Xanthippe and Polyxena," in *Early Christian and Jewish Narrative: The Role of Religion in Shaping Narrative Forms*, ed. Ilaria Ramelli and Judith Perkins, WUNT 348 (Tübingen: Mohr Siebeck, 2015), 162.

4. For the description of this literature as "mosaic," see James, *Apocrypha Anecdota*, 1:53. James argues that the author of the Acts of Xanthippe knew all of these works (*Apocrypha Anecdota*, 1:47–54). However, Junod finds the evidence for the Acts of Andrew, Thomas, and Philip less compelling (albeit not implausible) and emphasizes the Acts of Paul and Thecla as the single most significant influence on the Acts of Xanthippe ("Vie et conduite," 90–92). More recently, Jill Gorman has argued for the significant influence not only of the Acts of Paul and Thecla but also of the Acts of Thomas (Jill Gorman, "Reading and Theorizing Women's Sexualities: The Representation of Women in the *Acts of Xanthippe and Polyxena*" [PhD. diss., Philadelphia: Temple University, 2003], 27–60). Richard Pervo deems it certain that the author knew the Acts of Paul and Thecla and the Acts of Peter, probable that the author knew the Acts of Andrew and the Acts of Philip, and possible that the author knew the Acts of Thomas (Pervo, "Dare and Back," 169–76). For the description of this literature as "genre hybride," see Bonnet, "Sur les Actes de Xanthippe et Polyxène," 336.

5. Marco Formisano, "Toward an Aesthetic Paradigm of Late Antiquity," *Antiquité Tardive* 15 (2007): 283.

6. James considers mid-third century "a reasonable date," on the grounds that all of the apocryphal works apparently known to the author were in circulation by that point (*Apocrypha Anecdota*, 1:54). In his review of James's edition, E. N. Bennett

The Acts of Xanthippe and Polyxena is original in one respect, if no other: its plot pivots on an all-female romantic triangle. The featuring of female same-sex couples is, as far as I know, unprecedented within the corpus of ancient romances. Yet it is precisely the invocation of novelistic convention within an eclectically allusive and asceticizing Christian literary context that allows female homoeroticism to be represented, in this case. My essay aims to explore this paradox. It must be said that I am not the first to call attention to the homoerotic dynamics of our text. Jill Gorman addresses the topic in a chapter of her 2003 Temple University dissertation and in a closely related article, "Thinking with and about 'Same-Sex Desire': Producing and Policing Female Sexuality in the *Acts of Xanthippe and Polyxena*." As the title suggests, Gorman argues that the Acts of Xanthippe and Polyxena simultaneously "constructs female same-sex desire and commitment" and "condemns" it.[7] I am appreciative of Gorman's study, but we part company at the proposal that female homoeroticism is ultimately policed and condemned. The Acts of Xanthippe and Polyxena is queerer than that, as I hope to show.

I shall begin with a plot summary, since the text is not widely known. The narrative is fairly elaborate and divides into two distinct parts; the second may have been composed later, as a supplement to the first.[8] As we

---

suggests that James may have dated the Acts too early, basing his own argument on a close parallel between one of Xanthippe's monologues and an exegesis attributed to the fourth-century Apollinarius of Laodicea ("James, *Apocrypha Anecdota*," *Classical Review* 8 [1894]: 102–3). Following Bennett, Bonnet is inclined to believe the text "much less" ancient than the third century, noting the "extreme difficulty" that accompanies establishing a text transmitted only by a copyist for whom classical Greek is "an artificially preserved language"; it is "often almost impossible" to differentiate between a copyist's mistake and the language of the original author, who might in this case have composed the work as late as the eighth or ninth century, in an imperfectly classicizing Greek that imitates early Acts ("Sur les Actes de Xanthippe et Polyxène," 337, 340). Among more recent commentators, Junod dates the text to the fourth century or later ("Vie et Conduite," 91), Tibor Szepessy follows Schneemelcher in tentatively dating it to the sixth century ("Narrative Model of the *Acta Xanthippae et Polyxenae*," *Acta Antiqua Academiae Scientiarum Hungaricae* 44 [2004]: 318), and Richard Pervo considers a date between the fourth and sixth centuries most likely (Pervo, "Dare and Back," 162–66).

7. Jill Gorman, "Thinking with and About 'Same-Sex Desire': Producing and Policing Female Sexuality in the *Acts of Xanthippe and Polyxena*," *Journal of the History of Sexuality* 10 (2001): 417.

8. See Junod, "Vie et conduite," 101–3.

shall see, it is the second part that queers the plot, yet it builds on the first in crucial ways.

The first part conforms most closely to the generic expectations established by earlier apocryphal acts of apostles. Such works frequently contain episodes in which a nobly born woman is converted to a life of Christian piety and sexual asceticism by an itinerant apostle to whom she is powerfully drawn; both she and the apostle meet strong, even violent, resistance from her husband, who is typically the governor or ruler of the province; sometimes the apostle is martyred as a direct consequence; ultimately, however, the woman prevails and is able to continue with a life of celibacy.[9] Here, our heroine is one Xanthippe, the wife of a Spanish ruler named Probus. As we might anticipate, she becomes attracted to the ascetic message of an apostle—in this case, Paul—and refuses either to eat or to sleep with her husband. However, the tale exhibits some unusual features right from the start. Xanthippe's "conversion" is not provoked by a direct encounter with the apostle. Paul is initially far away in Rome when she learns of him through a slave who has heard the apostle preach while traveling on Probus's business. Upon his return to Spain from Rome, the slave falls ill (ἠσθένει) and grows lean (ἐλεπτύνετο) as he suffers from desire (ἐπιθυμία) for the absent Paul—the only physician who can heal his sickness, as he claims (1). Indeed, without Paul the slave proves incurable and, "carried off by illness, he ended his human life (κατέλυσε τὸν ἀνθρώπινον βίον)" (2)—an outcome that may recall homoerotic subplots in Greek romance novels in which the younger of two male partners dies tragically.[10] In the meantime, and somewhat mysteriously, Xanthippe catches the slave's disease; put otherwise, she imitates his example. Though she does not even know the name of the physician to whom the slave has referred (3), she is tortured by the pain of desire and is wasting away (κατατήκουσα)

---

9. I refer to these as "chastity stories" in an earlier study, *Chastity as Autonomy: Women in the Stories of Apocryphal Acts*, Studies in Women and Religion (Lewiston, NY: Mellen, 1987).

10. See David Konstan, *Sexual Symmetry: Love in the Ancient Novel and Related Genres* (Princeton: Princeton University Press, 1994), 26–30, and, more recently, John F. Makowski, "Greek Love in the Greek Novel," in *A Companion to the Ancient Novel*, ed. Edmund P. Cueva and Shannon N. Byrne (Chichester, UK: Wiley-Blackwell, 2014), 490–501. Note that here, as in other Christian works, it is not the master but the disciple who actively desires and is thus beset with love sickness. All chapter citations are given according to the text in James, *Apocrypha Anecdota*, 1:43–85. Translations here and elsewhere in this essay are my own.

from vigils and ascetic renunciations, we are told (2). Thus the novel opens with a triangulation of desire that is immediately aborted by the slave's death.

Probus is greatly distressed by Xanthippe's illness, by her refusal to share his bed, and by the fact that he cannot understand the cause of these dramatic changes in his young wife. Oddly, he does not seem to recognize what would be unmistakable signs of lovesickness for any ancient reader—loss of appetite, insomnia, mood changes, weight loss. When Paul arrives in the Spanish city (as he inevitably does), Xanthippe's heart pounds. Like the gospel woman who seeks healing from Jesus (Mark 5:27-28), she is filled with a yearning to touch the sweet-smelling hems of the apostle's garments (7). The seemingly clueless Probus responds by hurrying out to fetch the stranger, hoping that he can cure his wife. Upon first meeting Paul, Xanthippe throws herself to the ground and wipes his feet with her hair, imitating yet another gospel figure (John 12:3) (8). Despite this extravagant welcome, Paul hints that the time is not yet right for her baptism, because her husband has not yet been brought to the faith (9). Indeed, Probus subsequently becomes annoyed by the crowds visiting Paul in his home (an irritation presumably exacerbated by Xanthippe's unabated austerities), and he throws the apostle out of the house, locks Xanthippe in her room, and makes it clear that he does not expect to continue to be denied the pleasures of her bed (11-12). Undaunted, Xanthippe prays, to good effect, that Probus be overcome with sleep. As he slumbers, she sneaks out of the house to find Paul, bribing the porter, much like her narrative forerunner Thecla, who sneaked out of her mother's house to visit the same apostle in prison (Acts of Paul and Thecla 18). Having experienced both the fright of demons pursuing her with torches and lightning bolts and the thrill of a subsequent vision of Christ as a beautiful youth, Xanthippe finally reaches the apostle, who now baptizes her. Returning home, she has an even more intense visionary experience, following which she falls down, faint from lack of food and sleep. Meanwhile, Probus has had a disturbing dream that ultimately leads him to seek baptism from Paul as well—not, however, before Paul has clarified that he must renounce all fleshly desire.

The tension driving the plot would thus seem to be resolved by the arrival of Paul in Spain and his baptism of Xanthippe as well as Probus. However, the second part of the narrative reestablishes the circumstance of distance and desire. It does so by rather abruptly introducing the character of Polyxena, identified as Xanthippe's beloved younger sister, and by equally abruptly scripting her kidnapping by an enemy of her fiancé. At this point, the acts reads almost like a parody of ancient romance plots, as Polyxena repeatedly escapes from disastrous situations—abduction, shipwreck, attacking armies, wild beasts—only to be threatened yet again with rape and/or death. In the course of her adventures, she encounters the apostle Peter at sea and the apostles Philip and Andrew in Greece. The latter baptizes her along with a Jewish slave named Rebecca, whom they encounter at a well; a talking lioness adds further interest to the dual baptism scene. When Andrew subsequently refuses to accept the two women as companions on his travels, they head for the mountain where the lioness lives. Their journey is interrupted by a well-intentioned ass-driver, disciple of Philip, who offers to take them to the coast, where they can hope to board a ship for Spain. Although Polyxena disguises herself as a man, following the ass-driver's recommendation, the virgins are spotted by an inexplicably violent prefect, who seizes Polyxena; Rebecca is claimed by one of his soldiers but escapes. Polyxena initially evades rape by convincing the prefect's servants to tell him that she is sick. In the meantime, the son of the prefect, a crypto-Christian, attempts to help the girl flee, disguised in his clothes, in a second instance of what turns out to be ineffective transvestitism. But first, he tells Polyxena the story of Thecla—an artfully contrived scene, given that the reader will already have recognized that Polyxena is partly modeled on Thecla. Alas, the prefect learns of his son's plan and sentences both youth and maiden to fight wild beasts in the arena. When a fierce lioness docilely licks the soles of Polyxena's feet rather than attacking (another echo of the Acts of Paul and Thecla), the prefect is converted to Christ and releases both Polyxena and his son.

The narrative now abruptly switches to first-person voice, as one Onesimus (a Pauline associate whose name, appropriately enough, means "helpful")[11] discloses that he has received a revelation from God to take "two virgins and one youth" by ship from Greece to Spain; this is the only indication that Rebecca, who is not mentioned again by name, joins Polyxena and the prefect's son, who is also not mentioned again, on the journey back. More adventures ensue during an island stop-over, when "fierce and hardened men" attempt to capture the ever-alluring Polyx-

---

11. Onesimus is the subject of Paul's letter to Philemon and is also mentioned in the deutero-Pauline letter to the Colossians (4:7); see Pervo, "Dare and Back," 187. Note that Onesimus is synonymous with Onesiphorus, the name of a supporter of Paul who appears in both 2 Timothy (1:16–18, 4:19) and the Acts of Paul and Thecla (2–5, 23–26). Our author surely has one or both of these figures in mind.

ena; she leaps into the ocean while Onesimus and his crew defend her and subsequently haul her from the water. The novel ends with Polyxena's homecoming in Spain, where Xanthippe faints with joy at the sight of her—an instance of apparent death familiar from other ancient novels.[12] "But Polyxena, embracing [περιπλακεῖσα] her and kissing [ἀσπαζομένη] her for a long time, restored her to life," we are told (41). Xanthippe then relates to Polyxena how she has remained in her room for forty days, praying constantly for the preservation of Polyxena's virginity; she exclaims, "My beloved sister, having seen your face unexpectedly, I will happily die right now" (41).[13] From this point on, Polyxena, "fearing trials," remains safely by Paul's side, and both her former abductor and her former fiancé are baptized by the apostle.

As this synopsis suggests, the initial narrative unfolds the predictable love triangle between Xanthippe, her husband Probus, and the apostle Paul, modeling its plot on prior apocryphal acts of apostles. The latter part of the narrative has more in common, structurally, with non-Christian romance literature, emphasizing the travels, trials, separations, and ultimate reunion of two lovers; at the same time, it also incorporates many features from prior apocryphal acts. The dual influence of Christian acts and Greek romances has been recognized and highlighted since Montague James published his edition of the Acts of Xanthippe and Polyxena in 1893. Indeed, the Latin title that James gave the work seems designed to emphasize its affinities with apocryphal acts of apostles: "Acta Xanthippae et Polyxenae" is not, in fact, a translation of the title given by the Greek manuscript—Βίος καὶ πολιτεία τῶν ὁσίων γυναικῶν Χανθίππης Πολυξένης καὶ Ῥεβέκκας, or "Life and Conduct of the Holy Women Xanthippe, Polyxena, and Rebecca."[14] Βίος, or "life," is of course the conventional label for a hagiographical work, and πολιτεία, or "conduct," is virtually synonymous with "asceticism" in late antiquity. Both Eric Junod and Tibor Szepessy

---

12. See Pervo, "Dare and Back," 191–92.

13. Note that Gorman consistently reads Xanthippe as actually dying in this final scene. This interpretation is both idiosyncratic and unwarranted, it seems to me. Even less warranted is the conclusion that Xanthippe's death "perhaps reveals the author's greatest condemnation of the female same-sex bond"—a conclusion that is itself inconsistent with Gorman's prior claim that the "death kiss" privileges "a female same-sex relationship." "Same-Sex Desire," 427, 424.

14. The point is emphasized by Junod, who proposes that the shorthand "Life of Xanthippe" would be preferable to James's suggestion, if brevity is the point ("Vie et conduite," 83).

have pressed the point with regard to the implications for generic classification and, hence, literary interpretation, arguing that this work belongs at least as much to hagiography as to apostolic acts; it reflects, in effect, a strong reimagining of apostolic acts literature under heavy influence from "the genre of saints' and hermits' biographies."[15]

The women steal the limelight—even hog the title line—while the apostles suffer "narratological downgrading" as Szepessy puts it.[16] None of them is actually converted by an apostle, Szepessy notes further: as we have seen, Xanthippe hears mention of a "physician" from her husband's slave and somewhat inexplicably develops a passion for Christian faith, as if operating out of a strictly internal intuition; Polyxena learns of Christianity from Xanthippe, but once again very little information is supplied; and Rebecca, like Xanthippe, seems blessed with an intuitive knowledge of the truth. The apostles play merely supporting roles in the women's drama of conversion, primarily functioning as necessary agents of baptism.[17] The focus of the text is not, then, on the power of apostolic preaching and miracle working, as in other apostolic acts, but on the convert's interior, contemplative process of enlightenment, as performed with particular intensity in the nine highly rhetorical monologues that Xanthippe delivers in the first part of the text.[18] The other women also undergo their processes of conversion and enlightenment *"without any external help,"* as Szepessy emphasizes.[19]

For my purposes, it is important to add that internal enlightenment, as Szepessy describes it, goes hand in hand with ascetic practice and the intensification of both suffering and desire, whether it is Xanthippe's version—extreme fasting, vigils, and marital celibacy—or Polyxena's and Rebecca's version—displacement, physical danger, and the defense of threatened virginity. Each version inflects and interprets the other, so that ascesis is rendered more dramatic, drama more ascetic, so to speak. Desire

---

15. Szepessy, "Narrative Model," 318. See also Junod, "Vie et conduite," 104.

16. Szepessy, "Narrative Model," 323. Irene Dannemann also emphasizes the point that the apostles are relegated to the background and prove surprisingly ineffective even in their supportive roles; "Die Akten der Xanthippe, Polyxena und Rebekka oder: Drei Frauen und zwei Löwinnen," in *Kompendium: Feministische Bibelauslegung*, ed. Luise Schottroff and Marie-Theres Wacker (Gütersloh, Germany: Kaiser, Gütersloher Verlag-Haus, 1999), 754.

17. Szepessy, "Narrative Model," 323.

18. Ibid., 333.

19. Ibid., 337.

is stretched taut across distance and deferral, and lovesickness becomes as much an effect as a cause of ascetic practice.[20] Moreover—and this is crucial—desire is not merely oriented toward a transcendent object, as represented most resplendently by Xanthippe's visions of Christ as a beautiful youth "having around him trembling rays and under him an extended light on which he also walked" (15). It is also powerfully triangulated through human loves—but not, in this case, the *apostolic* ones we might expect.

Admittedly, Xanthippe's intense desire for the apostle Paul is strongly emphasized. However, her husband's response is not explicitly marked by jealousy, and he is won over to Christ with relative ease, so that even the first part of the acts reads more like a romantic novel and less like typical acts of apostles, as an ascetic marriage, following a period of temporary estrangement of wife and husband, is posited as the happy ending.[21] As Gorman has pointed out, this somewhat anomalous plot feature seems to reflect interest in promoting marital harmony even within asceticizing contexts, an interest that is resonant with concerns evident in other late ancient literature.[22] Narratively speaking, what is most significant, however, is the redirection of energy away from the apostolic love triangle, which begins to look more like a rather bland *ménage à trois*. This marital *ménage* is never effectively consummated, moreover: Xanthippe's preparations for a feast to celebrate Paul's baptism of her husband are interrupted by the appearance of a demon in the guise of an actor she knows; she hurls a lampstand at him and crushes his face. The plot is here slightly incoherent and the text may be corrupt, but the effect is to shadow the happy ending. (Has fleshly desire once again reared its ugly head?) The power of the first part of the narrative ultimately lies less with the affirmation of marriage than with the establishment of Xanthippe as the perfect *erastēs*, or lover, I

---

20. Gorman, following Theresa Shaw, rightly emphasizes the link between fasting and the quenching of sexual desire; however, she misses how fasting and abstinence intensify desire on another plane.

21. For similar instances of a converted husband, see the narrative of Drusiana and Andronicus in the Acts of John and Artemilla and Hieronymus in the Acts of Paul.

22. See Gorman, "Reading and Theorizing," ch. 2. Gorman is understandably suspicious of this defense of marriage, on feminist grounds. Irene Dannemann, also working from an explicitly feminist perspective, suggests that the acts might offer a positive revision of the married woman's role, exchanging house-keeping and child-rearing for a life of study, Christian community, and control over her sexuality ("Akten der Xanthippe," 751).

would suggest. The young matron is suspended in a state of intense longing sustained not only by demonic combat and heavenly visions but also by ascetic practices so stringent that they repeatedly bring her to the verge of death (e.g., 16, 18). Xanthippe's over-the-top desire remains a constant throughout the acts, but in the second part of the narrative its object shifts from Paul to Polyxena.

The intimate domestic scene in which Polyxena is introduced is marked by the absence of men: Probus has gone out to hear the word, presumably preached by Paul, and Xanthippe remains in her bedroom reading aloud from the books of the prophets while her sister Polyxena lies on the bed (ἐπὶ τῆς κλίνης). We are told that "Xanthippe loved [ἠγάπα] Polyxena exceedingly, because she was younger than her and beautiful of face" (22). The narrator adds, "Probus also loved her greatly," as if reasserting the priority of the marital bond, but the emphasis will remain on *Xanthippe's* love for Polyxena. The specification that she loves her so intensely because of her youth and beauty positions Polyxena as a typical *erōmenē*, or beloved, in a homoerotic dyad, albeit an *atypically* feminized dyad. As Xanthippe sits and reads, she has no way to know that the precious books that she has purchased from Rome for no less than seven hundred pieces of gold are prophesying the delectable Polyxena's future laments. Later, as the girl is being dragged away by her captors, she addresses the absent Xanthippe and recalls, "this evening you read, 'I looked to my right hand and beheld, but there was no one that knew me; flight perished from me and there is no one that seeketh out my soul' (Ps 142.4) " (23); later still, as she seeks refuge in the wilderness, she repeats, "Truly, my sister Xanthippe, you read about me, unhappy one, saying, 'I have suffered affliction and been utterly bowed down' (Ps 37.6)" (26). Evidently Xanthippe is reading not the prophets per se but psalms that prove prophetic.

While Xanthippe reads, Polyxena dreams. To be precise, she dreams that a dragon chases and devours her, and at this she leaps up, trembling. When she relates her dream to Xanthippe, she supplements it with the report that a beautiful youth whom she took to be the brother of Paul pulled her out of the dragon, which then disappeared. Xanthippe assures her that this signifies her baptism, which will rescue her from the dragon, and urges that she seek out Paul to administer the rite the very next morning. Of course, as it turns out, Polyxena's baptism will be much delayed, nor will it be performed by Paul (as the dream already hints); Xanthippe will not see her sister again until each has endured forty long days of suffering.

Xanthippe's love for Polyxena, their subsequent separation, and their final reunion thus provide the dominant structuring of the plot of the acts in its current bipartite form, overtaking and displacing the initial hetero-erotic triangle.[23] From this perspective, however, the ending of the acts appears decidedly enigmatic: in the climax of her joy at seeing Polyxena, Xanthippe pronounces herself ready to die on the spot; yet immediately thereafter we are told that Polyxena remains thenceforth with *Paul*. Why Paul? Has she forgotten that apostolic protection has not proved particularly effective in the past? Paul himself is off preaching the word when she is initially kidnapped; Peter, in an almost comical moment, simply says a prayer for her when his ship sails past the one in which she is held captive, diverting it from Babylonia to Greece; Philip, continuing the feeble apostolic relay team effort, rescues her when she is cast, half-dead, onto the shore of Greece but then promptly goes on his way "rejoicing," leaving Polyxena to flee an army of thousands marshaled by her initial captor; Andrew refuses to let Polyxena and Rebecca accompany him after he baptizes them; and a disciple of Philip sets out subsequently to help the two women but inadvertently brings about Polyxena's capture by the prefect and the women's separation. Only Onesimus, the temporary narrator, provides truly effective aid, and the convergence of savior with narrator is not uninteresting: it is the *plot* itself, ever the ally of divine providence in ancient novels,[24] that will save the women. Generic convention presses that plot toward reunion with the apostle, and a rationale is provided: Polyxena tells Paul that she fears that her afflictions were the result of her former irreverence toward the apostle; thus, she now remains with him, "fearing trials" otherwise. Yet there has been no prior mention of such irreverence, unless the mere fact of Polyxena's paganism counts as such. It is Xanthippe

---

23. As Gorman acknowledges, "In borrowing the structure of the Greek novel, in which a male and female couple are separated, endure hardships, and then experience reunion, the *AXP* creates the same bond between its female couple." It is puzzling to me, however, that Gorman goes on to interpret Polyxena's endurance of the very hardships to which novelistic heroines are typically subjected—above all, threats to virginity—as a sign that "the *AXP* disdains the bond between Xanthippe and Polyxena." It may well be that the "continual exchanging of Polyxena reveals an anxiety within the narrative over Polyxena's sexuality and a concern about who can best control it," but I would suggest that this is continuous with the romance genre and part of its excitement. "Same-Sex Desire," 423, 425.

24. As noted by Gorman, "Same-Sex Desire," 423. See also Pervo, "Dare and Back," 170: "Providence, not apostolic charisma, determines the outcome."

(not Paul) who has fasted and prayed for her for forty days unceasingly during those trials; it is Xanthippe (not Paul) to whom Polyxena has called out in her distress; it is Xanthippe (not Paul) whom Polyxena embraces and kisses upon her return to Spain. Her greeting to Paul is less erotic than simply submissive. Was it not Xanthippe to whom she was always returning?[25]

To get closer to an answer, we must take account of the novel's most significant subplot—the romance of Polyxena and Rebecca, which provides the final love triangle (or is it a *ménage à trois*?), the one still enshrined in the original Greek title of the text, featuring not two but three women. Having fled from a scene of battle in Greece, fearing that her abductor would capture her again, Polyxena is wandering in an area unpopulated by humans. She takes refuge for the night in a hollow in a tree, where she proceeds to lament her fate volubly: "I pass the night in deserts like a beast [ὡς θηρίον]. But the beasts live with others of their race [μεθ'ἑτέρων ὁμογενῶν], while I am left solitary, as not of one race with humankind [ὡς μὴ ὑπάρχουσα ὁμογενὴς ἀνθρώπων]" (26). In her loneliness, Polyxena experiences herself as a wild animal, no longer of the same *genos* or race as humans yet lacking even the companionship of other beasts. As it turns out, however, the hollow in which she has taken refuge is the den of a lioness, who returns from her hunting expedition in the morning; Polyxena is no longer alone, then. Trembling, she calls out, "By the God of Paul, O wild beast, have compassion on me and do not tear me apart until I receive baptism." The lioness responds by withdrawing to a distance, while continuing to gaze upon Polyxena: "she stared intently at her" (ἠτένιζεν εἰς αὐτήν). Polyxena then exits the den, and the lioness walks in front of her, leading her to the edge of the forest. Upon taking her leave, Polyxena addresses the lioness with gratitude, promising that the God of Paul will repay her kindness, and the lioness returns to her den (27).

Fortuitously, Polyxena immediately encounters the apostle Andrew and begs him to baptize her. Seeking water, they come upon a well. "And as the blessed Andrew stood at the well to pray, behold, a certain virgin named Rebecca from the tribe of Israel, brought to that country as a captive, came

---

25. Note that Dannemann interprets Polyxena as choosing "ein unverheiratetes Wanderleben mit Paulus und damit für eine Lebensform, die der von Thekla gleicht," also understanding Polyxena as leaving Xanthippe behind but taking Rebecca with her; this is a highly speculative reconstruction of the narrative's ending ("Akten der Xanthippe," 751).

to draw water at the well." This figure seems to have stepped straight out of the book of Genesis, where we read that another man, Abraham's slave, stood at a well and prayed (Gen 24:13), and "behold, Rebecca came out ... having a water-pitcher on her shoulders; and the virgin was exceedingly beautiful in appearance; she was a virgin; she knew no man" (Gen 24:15–16 LXX). Layered onto this Old Testament scene is one from the New: "And Jesus sat down by the well.... And a Samaritan woman came to draw water" (John 4:6–7).[26] While the New Testament scene might appear more resonant, in so far as Andrew is about to offer the "living water" of baptism, the language of the acts cleaves closer to the Old Testament passage: here again, our text is concerned more with the women than with the apostles. Rebecca, the beautiful virgin at the well, has been displaced from her Mesopotamian homeland to Greece, from her Israelite narrative to this Christian one. She detects in Andrew the appearance of a prophet and of one of the apostles (or simply, divine messengers); she herself was "once honored by prophets" but is now "insulted by idolaters," as she puts it, and she asks that Andrew "have mercy" on her and "call her," as he was sent to call sinners.[27] Traditionally known for her prophetic powers,[28] Rebecca has fallen on hard times; she would rather be saved by a Christian apostle

---

26. Oddly, Gorman mentions John 4 but does not note the significance of Gen 24 ("Same-Sex Desire," 422 n 22). Dannemann not only ignores the intertextual reverberations but proposes, with respect to Rebecca, that "über ihre Sexualität lesen wir nichts, sie ist aber als Sklavin sicher keine Jungfrau mehr" ("Akten der Xanthippe," 752); however, the text (like the biblical intertext) is very clear that Rebecca is a virgin, and ancient romance literature is full of examples of captive heroines who retain their virginity, against all odds.

27. The reference here appears to be to Matt 9:13: "But go and learn what this means: 'I desire mercy, not sacrifice,' for I have not come to call the righteous but sinners."

28. According to Gen. Rab. 67:9, all of the matriarchs were prophets, and among them Rebecca holds pride of place. Jubilees 25.14 refers to "the spirit of righteousness" descending into her mouth when she blesses Jacob, and both the Jerusalem Targum and Genesis Rabbah interpret Gen 27:42 to mean that the holy spirit tells Rebecca that Esau plans to kill his brother. Finally, Rebecca's words in Gen 27:45—"why should I lose both of you in one day?"—are interpreted as prophetic by the Babylonian Talmud, which recounts the deaths of Jacob and Essau, commenting, "At that moment the prophecy of Rebecca was fulfilled" (b. Sotah 13a). Might such traditions inform the Acts of Xanthippe, which associates Rebecca so closely with prophecy? She is able to recognize Andrew; she sees in him a prophet; and she names herself honored by prophets.

than dishonored by pagans. Andrew reassures the two girls: "God will care both for you, daughter, and for this stranger [τῆς ξένης]; now let both of you receive baptism, and be as of the same people [ὡς ὁμόεθνοι], praising God always" (29). Formerly Polyxena has felt herself outside the human *genos* in her solitude while being befriended by a lioness; now the gentile idolater is of one *ethnos* with a biblical Jew.

As Andrew is praying, the lioness runs up. "She stared intently at him [ἠτένιζεν εἰς αὐτόν]," we are told, just as she has previously gazed at Polyxena. "What does this beast want?" Andrew asks (30). Here the text takes a page from the Acts of Paul and Thecla, in which a fierce lion approaches Paul while he is praying and then throws himself at the apostle's feet. The apostle asks him, "Lion, what do you want?" The lion responds, "I want to be baptized" (Acts of Paul and Thecla 9). In the Acts of Xanthippe and Polyxena as well, the "beast" answers for herself, in a human voice. However, her concern is for Polyxena and Rebecca. The lioness explains that she has been impelled by Polyxena's prayer—presumably the prayer that she not be devoured before receiving baptism—and has come to entreat the apostle to confirm and instruct the two virgins in the Christian faith. Andrew baptizes Polyxena and Rebecca, as he was apparently planning to do anyway, and the lioness returns to the mountain. The apostle then urges the two women to comport themselves well in their sojourn and not to be separated from one another (ἀπ' ἀλλήλων μὴ χωρισθῆτε). Is *this* the instruction that the lioness has requested on their behalf? Polyxena vows, "We will follow you wherever you go [ἀκολουθήσομέν σοι ὅπου ἐὰν πορεύῃ]," in language that echoes simultaneously an anonymous disciple's pledge to Jesus (Luke 9:57: ἀκολουθήσω σοι ὅπου ἐὰν ἀπέρχῃ), Thecla's pledge to the apostle Paul (Acts of Paul and Thecla 25: ἀκολουθήσω σοι ὅπου δ' ἂν πορεύῃ), and Ruth's pledge to Naomi (Ruth 1:16 LXX: ὅπου ἐὰν πορευθῇς πορεύσομαι).[29] However, Andrew enjoins the women to remain behind as he continues on his way (30). The two are not to play disciples to his apostolic role, then, but rather to be Ruth and Naomi to one another. "Where shall we go [ποῦ πορευσόμεθα], sister?" asks Polyxena. "Let us depart for wherever you wish [ὅπου βούλει]," answers Rebecca, "so that my mistress does not send and separate [διαχωρίσῃ] us." Here the apostle's injunction

---

29. Pervo, "Dare and Back," 185 n. 88, calls attention to the reference to both Luke and the Acts of Paul and Thecla. Given Rebecca's Old Testament associations and the context of a friendship of two women, one a Jew and one a gentile, it seems to me not too much of a stretch to hear an echo of Ruth as well.

that the two not be separated is echoed in Rebecca's words. Now Polyxena takes the lead: "Come, let us depart for the mountain with the lioness," she proposes, to which Rebecca replies heartily: "It is indeed better for us to make our home with beasts and to die of hunger than to be forced by Greeks and idolaters to fall into the mire of marriage" (31). No marriage with men for these two virginal sojourners, then, but rather an unseverable bond between them, and a path laid out by a talking lioness who seems to see even more than she says.

As we have noted, their journey along that path is interrupted by an ass-driver who turns out to be a disciple of the apostle Philip; he intends to help them return to Spain but instead brings about their separation when Polyxena is carried off by the prefect.[30] Having escaped capture and rape herself, Rebecca takes refuge in the home of an elderly woman. There she weeps inconsolably: "Alas, my sister Polyxena…. See, I have been separated from you [ἐχωρίσθην ἀπό σου] and am again a captive"—a captive because exiled from her beloved, apparently—"but do seek after me (or: long for me) [ἐπιζήτησόν με], even if into the ages to come, my sister Polyxena." Rebecca's words once again recall the apostle's injunction that the two women not be separated. She tells the older woman that she suffers a "great and incurable pain in [her] heart." Meanwhile, Polyxena laments not her loss of Rebecca but the threatened loss of her virginity, as she is about to be led to the bed of the prefect (35). As we have seen, she evades the prefect's bed, only to be sentenced to the beasts. Yet among the beasts is another friendly lioness (or is it the same one?), whose intervention brings about Polyxena's release. When Onesimus's ship arrives to carry her back to Spain at long last, Polyxena is accompanied by Rebecca.

On the surface, this subplot seems to be not only unnecessary but even potentially troublesome to the main plot: the tale of Polyxena and Rebecca threatens to upstage that of Xanthippe and Polyxena, to put it simply. (The tale of Xanthippe and Paul and/or Probus does not stand a chance.) Part of the problem is that Rebecca fails to die, unlike Probus's slave or his male counterparts in the homoerotic subplots of non-Christian romances, which frequently end tragically with the violent death of the beloved. Then again, it is Polyxena, not Rebecca, who is the beloved in this tale. Surely,

---

30. Gorman sees this separation as a narrative judgment on "the failure of Polyxena and Rebecca to obey Andrew's command at their baptism" (Gorman, "Same-Sex Desire," 427). Yet romances typically introduce separation in such a way as to intensify desire, and moral agency is, equally typically, construed as extremely circumscribed.

we find ourselves wanting an account of Rebecca's reunion with Polyxena, at the very least. However, the narrator must remain silent on that topic, allowing Rebecca to fade into obscurity, as he steers us back to the story of Xanthippe and Polyxena: it is *their* reunion that is depicted with such poignancy and drama. Yet the power of that scene is largely carried by the energy of the narrative of Polyxena and Rebecca, I would suggest—a classic romance plot, not only because of the elements of travel, danger, and separation, but also because of the interest in mixed marriage.[31] One thinks of the Ethiopian Charikleia and the Greek Theagenes of Heliodorus's romance, of the gentile Aseneth and the Hebrew Joseph of the novel Joseph and Aseneth: "Fiction is heartily in favor of union with the stranger," as Margaret Doody has put it.[32] Gentile and Jew, foreigner and exile, Ruth and Naomi—Polyxena and Rebecca are baptized in the same well at the injunction of a talking lioness, instructed by an apostle never to separate from one another. This queer couple gives new meaning to sisterhood and thus allows us to read the relationship of Xanthippe and Polyxena differently, when we reach the final scene. Why should we assume that they too are not sisters through their love, rather than merely by birth?[33]

If the momentum of both the main plot and the subplot carries Polyxena toward Xanthippe rather than Paul, it may be more than the generic template of apocryphal acts of apostles that introduces ambiguity at the end. The logic of virginal eroticism may itself thwart a more satisfying conclusion. I have suggested that Xanthippe is the *erastēs*, Polyxena the *erōmenē*, in the terms of the active-passive model that pervades ancient understandings of eroticism. As Gorman notes, somewhat paradoxically Xanthippe also parallels the relatively passive male protagonists of the Greek romances, Polyxena the active and resourceful female protagonists.[34] Active in her desire, Xanthippe remains nonetheless stationary, scarcely leaving her bedroom, whether yearning for Paul or for Polyxena. The very

---

31. See my "Mimicking Virgins: Colonial Ambivalence and the Ancient Romance," *Arethusa* 38 (2005): 49–88.

32. Margaret Anne Doody, *The True Story of the Novel* (New Brunswick, NJ: Rutgers University Press, 1996), 103.

33. As Craig Williams notes, with respect to Latin literature, "the language and imagery of sibling love, like those of *amor* and *amicitia*, could be associated with a range of experience which could include the erotic" (*Reading Roman Friendship* [Cambridge: Cambridge University Press, 2012], 162).

34. Gorman, "Same-Sex Desire," 421–22.

intensity of her yearning, expressed in her eloquent prayers and her fasting and vigils, seems to draw the beloved ones to her. In their presence, her heart pounds; she falls to the ground; she is practically dead. In contrast, Polyxena, whose very name pronounces her a stranger in strange lands, is constantly on the run and in the midst of the action, from the moment that she is snatched from Xanthippe's bed; yet she remains mostly reactive toward the desires of others, focused above all on the defense of her virginity. Rebecca has beseeched Polyxena to seek after her, to long for her, even into the age to come; however, it is not clear that Polyxena's desire matches her own. For her part, Xanthippe embraces death in the climactic moment in which she once again lays eyes on her beloved sister, having fasted for forty days to bring her home safely; in a rare moment of warmth, Polyxena responds with embraces and kisses, but the moment seems to pass quickly. If Polyxena finally positions herself at Paul's side, it is not because this is where desire has drawn her but rather because this is where the unwelcome desire of other men may be deflected. The love of Xanthippe and Rebecca has secured her prize: Polyxena will not be caught in the "mire of marriage." Instead, she will remain suspended in her virginal allure—young, beautiful, and untouchable.

I confess that I wonder whether things might have turned out differently if Rebecca and Polyxena had made it back to the lioness's mountain—a promisingly heterotopic setting for a homoerotic romance composed along the lines of Longus's *Daphnis and Chloe*, as I imagine it, troubling distinctions of nature and culture, animal and human, active and passive. Later conveyers of the tradition seem to have followed a different trajectory of fantasy, however, extending the narrative of Xanthippe and Polyxena to include their subsequent careers as coevangelists (modeled on the story of Thecla) as well as their shared moment of death. According to the tenth-century Basilian Menology, which makes no mention of Rebecca, "both, teaching many the faith of Christ, were perfected."[35] More titillating is the sixteenth-century Spanish *Chronicle* published under the pseudonym of the late ancient historian Flavius Lucius Dexter, which not only records that "Xanthippe and Polyxena moved on to a better life" in the year 109, but also notes, for the prior year 108, that "Xanthippe and Polyxena her wife, the most blessed virgin, and her companion Rebecca, likewise a virgin, and Saint Onesimus, Saint Paul's disciple" made a trip

---

35. James, *Apocrypha Anecdota*, 1:43.

from Laminium to Toledo to consult Saint Eugenius (a Visigothic bishop transported to the early second century) and returned greatly cheered.[36] The framing "Xantippe et Polyxena eius uxor Virgo sanctissima et eius socia Rebecca, item Virgo" seems to sum up very nicely the female love triangle that drives and animates the "Life and Conduct of the Holy Women Xanthippe, Polyxena, and Rebecca," as I have tried to show—albeit a triangle that works narratively more through substitution or displacement than through rivalry, in the end.

So where does all of this leave us? In much ancient hagiographical literature, a Christ-oriented desire fosters dominantly homoerotic configurations with respect to male ascetics, heteroerotic ones with respect to female ascetics.[37] In the literary lives of male saints, the relationship of disciple to master, sometimes extended to the relationship of the author to his saintly subject, typically carries the erotic charge. In the lives of female saints, emphasis is typically on the status of the saint as bride of Christ, with focus on her death as the moment of erotic union with her heavenly spouse. Here too the relationship of author to saint can intensify the erotic dynamic, in this case a heteroerotic dynamic, authors of surviving ancient Lives of women being apparently exclusively male. Thus there might seem to be no place for the representation of female same-sex love of any kind in ancient hagiographical literature. However, we should hesitate before drawing such a conclusion. Elsewhere I have discussed Gregory of Nyssa's *Life of Macrina*, noting that female homoeroticism inflects representations of the domestic relationships of mother and daughter, nursemaid and child, mistress and slave, as these are carried over both literally and metaphorically into the affective intensities of a pedagogical community of ascetic women.[38] Here I have tried to show how female homoeroticism inflects not only the representation of women's relationships within a Christianized and asceticized domestic context—"sisters" in a bedroom—but also the transposition of those relationships into narratives of separation, trial, and reunion borrowed from the genre of romance.

---

36. Ibid., 1:45–46.

37. See Virginia Burrus, *The Sex Lives of Saints: An Erotics of Ancient Hagiography*, Divinations: Rereading Late Ancient Religion (Philadelphia: University of Pennsylvania Press, 2004).

38. Virginia Burrus, "Gender, Eros, and Pedagogy: Macrina's Pious Household," in *Ascetic Culture: Essays in Honor of Philip Rousseau*, ed. Blake Leyerle and Robin Darling Young (Notre Dame: University of Notre Dame Press, 2013), 167–81.

Pagan romances focus on a male-female couple, frequently also including subplots featuring male lovers, but rarely if ever female lovers. However, the asceticizing of eroticism allows the Acts of Xanthippe and Polyxena not only to feature the female lovers Polyxena and Rebecca in a subplot but also to displace the marital couple Xanthippe and Probus with the female couple Xanthippe and Polyxena in the main plot. It remains the case that the love of Xanthippe and Polyxena is doubly triangulated by the apostle Paul, who mediates Xanthippe's conversion in the beginning and protects Polyxena's virginity in the end; moreover, visions of beautiful young men appear to both sisters. Only the Jewish virgin Rebecca seems pure with respect to the desire of and for men. Indeed, Rebecca is finally the most elusive of the three. Is she not also perhaps finally the most alluring, in her biblical exoticism, her suffering endurance, her abiding love, and the hint of tragedy that clings to her? The plot of the romance—of any romance—has drained itself of interest when it reaches its happy ending. The conclusion of the Acts of Xanthippe and Polyxena may not be altogether satisfying,[39] but perhaps that is not such a bad thing. Xanthippe hovers joyfully on the threshold of death; Polyxena is suspended in her apostolically protected virginity; Rebecca has withdrawn from our sight, as has the lioness. Lacking consummation, desire is still in play, then—women desiring, desiring women.

---

39. Gorman goes so far as to conclude that the "*AXP*, in a move away from the Greek novel's structure, prohibits a stable reunion of the two female protagonists"; "the absence of a stable reunion at the conclusion of the *AXP* demonstrates a dissolution of the envisioned same-sex society it had momentarily produced" ("Same-Sex Desire," 427).

Madly in Love:
The Motif of Lovesickness in the Acts of Andrew

Christy Cobb

> For when I look at you for a moment,
> Then it is no longer possible for me to speak;
> My tongue has snapped,
> At once a subtle fire has stolen beneath my flesh,
> I see nothing with my eyes,
> My ears hum,
> Sweat pours from me,
> A trembling seizes me all over,
> I am greener than the grass,
> And it seems to me that I am a little short of dying. (Sappho, frag. 31)[1]

In this poem, Sappho perfectly illustrates the physical symptoms that often accompany the feeling of love. In antiquity, bodily reactions such as the inability to speak, nausea, insomnia, and anxiety are directly connected to the experience of falling in love. In addition to these effects, persons in love are often portrayed as manic (suffering from μανία) in antiquity. Because of these symptomatic differences, Peter Toohey has suggested that lovesickness in antiquity is represented in two ways: depressive and manic lovesickness.[2] Using Toohey's work on lovesickness, this essay explores

---

Special thanks to Virginia Burrus, who guided me as I worked through this interpretation, specifically as a student in her Ancient Novels seminar at Drew University in 2011.

1. David A. Campbell, trans., *Greek Lyric*, LCL (Cambridge: Harvard University Press, 1982), 79–81.

2. See Peter Toohey, "Love, Lovesickness, and Melancholia," *Illinois Classical Studies* 17 (1992): 265–86; Toohey, *Melancholy, Love, and Time: Boundaries of the Self in Ancient Literature* (Ann Arbor: University of Michigan Press, 2004).

the literary motif of lovesickness, seen particularly in the manic form, within the Acts of Andrew, a second-century Christian apocryphal text. I argue that the motif of lovesickness is used within this ascetic narrative to portray the erotic connection between two male characters: the apostle Andrew and his disciple Stratocles. I read the Acts of Andrew alongside two Greek novels, Achilles Tatius's *Leucippe and Clitophon* and Xenophon's *An Ephesian Tale*, both of which contain male homoerotic relationships in which one or both of the male partners exhibit symptoms of lovesickness specifically occurring when the love of the partner is threatened or lost. I suggest that the portrayal of the character as physically sick is an intentional narrative strategy functioning to show the depth of the love experienced between the two men. Moreover, I argue that attention to the manic symptoms of lovesickness reveals a reversal in the text, especially when compared to typical pederastic relationships in antiquity. As Andrew is the apostle, he is expected to be an *erastes*, or the older, more active lover, while Stratocles, the disciple, should be represented as an *eromenos*, the passive lover. Yet, in the Acts of Andrew, only Stratocles is portrayed as lovesick in the narrative, while Andrew is not struck with these same physical symptoms, an observation that inevitably undoes the traditional binary. In this way, the male homoerotic relationship found within the Acts of Andrew disrupts the pederastic binary and also allows for Andrew, the apostle, to retain his elevated status within the narrative, even in his erotic relationship with Stratocles.

In antiquity, lovesickness was described as a disease that medical doctors could diagnose through identification of a number of symptoms. Greek physicians such as Galen, Aretaeus, and Soranus outline the symptoms one should look for when diagnosing lovesickness, as will be described below. Using these medical texts along with representations of lovesickness found in literature, Toohey crafts a broad definition for the term in its many manifestations: "I take lovesickness (or love-melancholy, as it came to be known) as the product of *unconsummated* or perhaps unseasonably frustrated love."[3] Ultimately, Toohey argues that there are two types of lovesickness found within ancient literature: the depressed[4] and the manic lovesick patient. One can recognize the depressed lover through symptoms such as insomnia, lack of appetite, loss of weight, and taciturnity.

---

3. Toohey, "Love, Lovesickness, and Melancholia," 266 n. 6.

4. Though the term *depressed* is anachronistic, it is the term that Toohey uses in his study; therefore, it is also used here to aptly describe his thesis.

Though these symptoms of lovesickness might be more recognizable to the modern Western reader, this type of lovesickness was not the prevailing one used in antiquity. Instead the "dominant reaction to frustrated love in ancient literature" is the manic and frequently violent form, recognized by the erratic behavior of the lover, which will be described subsequently.[5]

A brief look at the way in which Greek medical writers describe the physical symptoms of lovesickness will help form the narrative guide through which I will read the Acts of Andrew.[6] Galen, for example, concluded that lovesickness was caused when a person fell in love (ἔρως).[7] In his treatise *On the Affected Parts*, Galen goes to great lengths to show that lack of sexual intercourse can be a cause for lovesickness. Providing future doctors with examples of symptoms, Galen writes, "Lovers might become emaciated, pale, sleepless, and even feverish."[8] Additionally, two Greek physicians, Aretaeus and Soranus, include the manic symptoms of lovesickness in their medical texts.[9] Aretaeus of Cappadocia states that lovesick patients often exhibit the typical symptoms of melancholy and also

---

5. Ibid., 266.

6. The work of Jacques Ferrand, a seventeenth-century French doctor, on lovesickness is relevant to this study for a number of reasons. First, Ferrand was the first physician to write an entire treatise completely dedicated to lovesickness. Second, Ferrand references the work pertaining to lovesickness of the ancient Greek physicians in detail. Finally, Ferrand lists the symptoms of lovesickness in a systematic way that many scholars, including Toohey, utilize in their writings on the ailment. See Jacques Ferrand, *A Treatise on Lovesickness*, trans. Donald A. Beecher and Massimo Ciavolella (Syracuse, NY: Syracuse University Press, 1990).

7. Stanley W. Jackson, *Melancholia and Depression: From Hippocratic Times to Modern Times* (New Haven: Yale University Press, 1986), 353.

8. Ibid.

9. Later medical writers referred to lovesickness using the Greek term ἐρωτομανία, meaning "love-madness." However, early Greek physicians employed a variety of terms to describe lovesickness, as these ancient writers were trying to determine the ailment of their patients. Though the ancient medical writers did not have a technical title for this ailment, they often referred to it as a disease (νόσος) that needed a cure. The Greek medical writers often mentioned lovesickness alongside the verb μελαγχολᾶν (to be melancholy), because the symptoms of the two conditions were similar. Apparently, Greek physicians would often diagnose a patient as melancholic when he or she was actually suffering from lovesickness. Because of this conflation, the Greek medical writers addressed this misdiagnosis in their writing so that future physicians would not make this mistake when treating patients. Since the Greek medical writers do not provide one term for this illness, I am utilizing Toohey's term *lovesickness* as well as his definition and categorization in order to explain the disease.

lists "desire to die" (ἔρανται δὲ θανάτου) as one of the symptoms (*Sign. acut.* 1.5).[10] Additionally, Aretaeus lists "irascible or prone to anger" (ὀργίλος) as a symptom (*Sign. acut.* 1.5). Soranus of Ephesus discusses lovesickness in a section on mania included in *On Acute and Chronic Diseases*.[11] Soranus helpfully describes the erratic tendencies of a person suffering from lovesickness. He writes, "It manifests itself now in anger, now in merriment, now in sadness or futility."[12]

The physical symptoms of lovesickness not only were included in the writings of the Greek medical writers, but also were found in the literature and poetry of antiquity, as exemplified by Sappho's poem included at the opening of this essay. Indeed, the writers of the ancient novels utilized lovesickness in their stories—in every novel the main characters and many minor characters experience moments of physical pain and anxiety as a result of their love for another person within the narrative.[13] In my reading of the Acts of Andrew, I will use the motif of lovesickness as a narrative guide to understanding the complex nature of the erotic relationship between Andrew and Stratocles.

The first instance where this motif is present is actually not within the relationship between Andrew and Stratocles but instead in the relationship between Stratocles and his servant, Alcman. The author describes Alcman as a young boy (παῖς) whom Stratocles loved dearly.[14] The word for "love" used here is στέργω in Greek, which is not typically used for sexual love. However, the author of the Acts of Andrew uses this word later on in the text, as we will see, in a context that is clearly erotic in nature.

---

10. Aretaeus, *The Extant Works of Aretaeus, the Cappadocian*, ed. Francis Adams (London: Sydenham Society, 1856), 299.

11. Soranus is best remembered for his work *Gynaecology*; however, for this study, his treatise on *Acute and Chronic Diseases*, preserved by Caelius Aurelianus through a Latin translation, is most helpful.

12. Caelius Aurelianus, *On Acute Diseases and On Chronic Diseases*, ed. I. E. Drabkin (Chicago: University of Chicago Press, 1950), 537–41.

13. Regine May, "Medicine and the Novel: Apuleius' Bonding with the Educated Reader," in *The Ancient Novel and the Frontiers of Genre: Fluid Texts*, ed. Marília P. Futre-Pinheiro, Gareth Schmeling, and Edmund Cueva, Ancient Narrative Supplementum 18 (Groningen: Barkhuis, 2014), 107.

14. Dennis R. MacDonald, *The Acts of Andrew and the Acts of Andrew and Matthias in the City of the Cannibals*, Texts and Translations 33, Christian Apocrypha 1 (Atlanta: Scholars Press, 1990), 326–27. Note: the Greek text and English translations, unless noted, will be from MacDonald's translation.

When Alcman becomes sick, "stricken by a demon," Stratocles hears of it, and he becomes very distressed, saying, "If only I had never come here but perished at sea this would not have happened to me! Friends, ... I cannot live without him."[15] Then Stratocles begins to act quite erratically. First, he "hit himself about the eyes," then he "became disturbed and unfit to be seen."[16] This narrative episode reveals the lovesickness, in the form of mania, experienced by the character Stratocles. At the fear of the loss of his love, Stratocles is irascible and disturbed and makes a statement indicating that he wants to die.

I suggest that the relationship between Stratocles and Alcman appears as a traditional pederastic relationship.[17] In Acts of Andrew, Stratocles is the *erastes*, grieving the impending loss of his *eromenos*, Alcman. The erratic behavior of Stratocles is expected for a grieving *erastes*, and Alcman's desire for Stratocles is not mentioned in the text, also typical for the role of the *eromenos*. Yet, when Andrew heals Alcman and the boy does not die, the relationship between Stratocles and Alcman seems to dissipate, as Stratocles turns his attention completely to the apostle Andrew. After serving as Stratocles's midwife during a conversion experience metaphorically represented through labor pains, Andrew stays up all night long teaching Stratocles, who is said to have abandoned his former philosophy in order to fully embrace Andrew's ascetic message.[18] The twist in this erotic subplot is that Stratocles, who was the *erastes* in his relationship to Alcman, now appears to have become the *eromenos* to Andrew, yet he retains an active, even excessive desire.

---

15. Ibid., 327.

16. Ibid.

17. In typical pederastic literature the boy (*pais/paidika/meirakion*) is referred to as the *eromenos*, the one being loved, while the older male was usually referred to as *erastes*, lover. See Kenneth James Dover, *Greek Homosexuality* (Cambridge: Harvard University Press, 1978); Michel Foucault, *The Use of Pleasure*, vol. 2 of *The History of Sexuality*, trans. Robert Hurley (New York: Vintage, 1985); Foucault, *The Care of the Self*, vol. 3 of *The History of Sexuality*, trans. Robert Hurley (New York: Vintage, 1988); William Armstrong Percy, *Pederasty and Pedagogy in Archaic Greece* (Urbana: University of Illinois Press, 1996); Percy, "Reconsiderations about Greek Homosexualities," in *Same-Sex Desire and Love in Greco-Roman Antiquity and in the Classical Tradition of the West*, ed. Beert C. Verstraete and Vernon Provencal (Binghamton, NY: Haworth, 2006), 13–62.

18. MacDonald, *Acts of Andrew*, 335.

Throughout the narrative, the erotic relationship between Andrew, the teacher, and his disciple Stratocles becomes obvious and is even noted by characters in the narrative. One of the servants of Aegeates, the antagonist of the narrative, vocalizes the erotic tension between Andrew, Stratocles, and Maximilla (another disciple of Andrew), which leads Saundra Schwartz to identify these three as involved in a "love triangle."[19] Yet, it is only when Andrew is condemned to die that the full depth of Stratocles's love is revealed, through his manic-lovesick behavior. This can be seen first through the words of Andrew as he interrogates Stratocles: "Why are you afflicted with many tears [δάκρυ] and why do you groan [στένω] out loud? Why do you despair [δύσθυμος]? Why your great grief [ἄλγος] and great sorrow [ἀνία]?"[20] Andrew continues questioning Stratocles in a discourse that Schwartz deems "laden with homoerotic imagery."[21] Moreover, several of these words in Andrew's speech indicate Stratocles's symptoms of lovesickness. The Greek word δύσθυμος, which Dennis MacDonald translates as "despair," has another meaning of "melancholy."[22] As mentioned previously, Greek medical doctors often conflated melancholy and lovesickness, since their symptoms were so similar. Additionally, the primary meaning of ἄλγος is "pain of body," suggesting the corporeal nature of Stratocles's pain.[23]

Following Andrew's speech, Stratocles continues to "weep and wail" (κλαίων καὶ ὀδυρόμενος) in his despair over the impending loss of his love.[24] In response, Andrew takes Stratocles's hand and assures him of his love saying, "I have the one I sought. I have found the one I desired. I hold the one I loved" (ἔχω ὃν ἐζήτουν· εὗρον ὃν ἐπόθουν· κρατῶ ὃν ἠγάπων).[25] Thus, although Andrew attempts to control Stratocles's highly emotional response, the apostle confirms his desire for Stratocles openly and directly. Yet, Stratocles continues to react physically to the anticipated loss of

---

19. Saundra Schwartz, "From Bedroom to Courtroom: The Adultery Type-Scene and the Acts of Andrew," in *Mapping Gender in Ancient Religious Discourses*, ed. Todd C. Penner and Caroline Vander Stichele (Leiden: Brill, 2007), 309.
20. MacDonald, *Acts of Andrew*, 380–81.
21. Schwartz, "From Bedroom to Courtroom," 310.
22. LSJ, s.v. "δύσθυμος."
23. Ibid., 57.
24. MacDonald, *Acts of Andrew*, 382.
25. Ibid., 382. Schwartz mentions that hand-holding might have been read in the ancient world as a seductive symbol, reminding the reader of the act of sexual intercourse ("From Bedroom to Courtroom," 297).

his love, as the text indicates that he is "groaning still louder and crying uncontrollably."²⁶ Through this manic type of reaction, Stratocles responds to Andrew in a highly erotic passage that I will quote here at length:

> Most blessed Andrew ... the words that came from you are like flaming javelins impaling me: each of them strikes me and actually blazes and burns with love [στοργή] for you. The sensitive part of my soul, which is disposed toward what I have heard, is tormented in that it presages with anguish (what will take place). For you yourself may leave, and I know well that it is good that you do so. But after this, where and in whom will I seek and find your concern [ἐπιμέλεια] and love [στοργή]? I received the seeds [σπέρμα] of the words of salvation while you were my sower [σπορεύς]; for them to shoot up and reproduce requires no one else but you, blessed Andrew.²⁷

Striking a remarkable resemblance to Sappho's poem quoted at the beginning of this essay, Stratocles's words seem more like those of a lover than a beloved, exceeding the expectations of *anteros*, or reciprocal love, as described in Plato's *Phaedrus*. As Schwartz puts it, "It is thus in Stratocles that Andrew's message is metaphorically consummated."²⁸ It appears in this farewell scene that the love between Andrew and Stratocles is mutual and reciprocated (albeit not entirely symmetrical), unlike the traditional *erastes*/*eromenos* relationship in antiquity, in which the *erastes*'s love is typically depicted as stronger.

As a result of this mutual love, and the threat of its demise, Stratocles reacts violently when executioners take Andrew away to be crucified. "He did not spare any of them but gave each a beating, ripping their clothing from top to bottom."²⁹ The text indicates that Stratocles was "furious" and "perturbed" and was murmuring under his breath as he tore Andrew away from the executioners.³⁰ This behavior is unusually violent for the character of Stratocles, who gave up his position fighting in the war in order to study philosophy. This specific circumstance provides the clearest example of the manic lovesickness experienced by the character of Stratocles, who is acting erratically and violently. Indeed, in the context of the narrative

---

26. MacDonald, *Acts of Andrew*, 382.
27. Ibid., 382–85.
28. Schwartz, "From Bedroom to Courtroom," 310.
29. MacDonald, *Acts of Andrew*, 386.
30. Ibid.

of the Acts of Andrew, Stratocles is a devoted, consistent character, except in the instances when a person whom he loves is in danger, and then he behaves unpredictably. Through this manic display of lovesickness, the traditional understanding of the teacher/disciple relationship is reversed. For in this text it is the *eromenos* who is reacting erratically as a result of the loss of his partner.

Yet this inconsistent behavior should not be viewed as altogether unusual. Indeed, MacDonald argues that the Acts of Andrew incorporates numerous literary elements from classical Greek writings, specifically the *Odyssey*.[31] MacDonald also shows the ways in which this early Christian narrative mimics Plato's dialogues. The inclusion of lovesickness, particularly in its manic form, located within the character of Stratocles, could be further indication of the author's reliance on Platonic dialogue. For instance, in *Phaedrus*, Socrates describes the madness associated with love as preferential and even desired:

> Such then is the tale, though I have not told it fully, of the achievements wrought by madness that comes from the gods. So let us have no fears simply on that score; let us not be disturbed by an argument that seeks to scare us into preferring the friendship of the sane to that of the passionate. For there is something more that it must prove if it is to carry the day, namely that love is not a thing sent from heaven for the advantage both of the lover and beloved. What we have to prove is the opposite, namely that this sort of madness is a gift of the gods fraught with the highest bliss. (Plato, *Phaedr.* 244b)[32]

Put elegantly by Plato, the form of love that is a gift from the gods, the highest form, manifests itself in madness. Thus, the mad love of Stratocles, the disciple, could be viewed as superior to the love of Andrew, his teacher.

I will now turn to the novels of Xenophon and Achilles Tatius, narratives that include examples of complex homoerotic relationships. First, in Achilles Tatius's novel *Leucippe and Clitophon*, the story of Clinias and Charicles provides a seemingly typical example of a homoerotic relationship involving lovesick behavior exemplified by the grieving partner.[33] In

---

31. Dennis R. MacDonald, *Christianizing Homer: The Odyssey, Plato, and the Acts of Andrew* (Oxford: Oxford University Press, 1994), 5.

32. R. Hackforth, trans., *Plato's Phaedrus* (Cambridge: Cambridge University Press, 1952), 58.

33. Greek and English references are from the following edition: Achilles Tatius,

the context of this narrative, Clinias, the cousin of the male protagonist, is immediately identified as the lover of Charicles. Charicles's age is not identified specifically, but he is always referred to in the text as a μειράκιον, meaning "boy" or "lad."[34] Clitophon teases his cousin because he is a "slave to the pleasures of Eros" when it comes to Charicles. Yet, the relationship is immediately threatened when Charicles's father arranges a marriage for him. As a result, Clinias becomes angry and launches into a tirade against the love of women. As Virginia Burrus observes, this speech "rehearse(s)— without clearly endorsing—traditional arguments for the superiority of pederasty over marriage."[35] After his lover's speech Charicles nonchalantly dismisses his worry about the arranged marriage, indicating that the gods will take care of it, and leaves for a horseback ride, a ride that ends tragically with the boy's gruesome death. Clinias, in shock at first, runs for the body of his love. Vocalizing his grief and guilt, Clinias is in true mourning over the loss of his lover: "At this news, Clinias was struck with utter silence for a considerable period; then, as if suddenly awakened from a swoon of grief, he cried out very pitifully and hurried to run to meet the corpse" (Achilles Tatius, *Leuc. Clit.* 1.13 [Gaselee]). As he arrives, Clinias is utterly distraught and reacts so violently in his grief that "none of the standers-by were able to refrain from tears" (Achilles Tatius, *Leuc. Clit.* 1.13 [Gaselee]).

Several scholars mention the pederastic nature of Clinias and Charicles's relationship.[36] David Konstan, for instance, suggests that this male pair is an example of a pederastic relationship and argues that Clinias is

---

Leucippe and Clitophon, trans. S. Gaselee, rev. ed., LCL 45 (Cambridge: Harvard University Press, 1984).

34. In fact, James Davidson argues convincingly that the term μειράκιον refers to a boy who is eighteen or nineteen years old; see James N. Davidson, *The Greeks and Greek Love: A Bold New Exploration of the Ancient World* (New York: Random House, 2007), 80.

35. Virginia Burrus, "Mimicking Virgins: Colonial Ambivalence and the Ancient Romance," *Arethusa* 38 (2005): 66.

36. In addition to David Konstan, Tim Whitmarsh also views this relationship as pederastic, but he indicates that it is mistaken to view the novels in "Foucauldian terms as symptomatic of a cultural shift away from a classical model of sexual relationships (promoting a phallocentric hierarchy between penetrated and penetrated, irrespective of the gender of the latter) towards a new, more symmetrical conjugal ethics" (*Narrative and Identity in the Ancient Greek Novel: Returning Romance* [Cambridge: Cambridge University Press, 2011], 161).

in the "dominant role."³⁷ Indeed, Clinias is described as an *erastes* by the novelist during the mourning scene (Achilles Tatius, *Leuc. Clit.* 1.14.1).³⁸ However, the following sentence complexifies this title as Clinias refers to Charicles as his "master" (δεσπότης) in his monologue of grief (Achilles Tatius, *Leuc. Clit.* 1.14.1).³⁹ The use of this title is suggestively opposed to the identification of Clinias as the *erastes*. Perhaps this discrepancy indicates the fluidity of the relationship between Clinias and Charicles. In this way, they can be seen as an example of a homoerotic pair that disrupts the typical pederastic relationship.

Xenophon's *An Ephesian Tale* contains the story of Hippothous and Hyperanthes, reported by Hippothous himself. When he was "young" (νέος), Hippothous fell in love with a "beautiful youth" (μειρακίου) named Hyperanthes (Xenephon of Ephesus, *Ephesian Tale of Anthia and Habrocomes* 3.2.2).⁴⁰ Hippothous approached Hyperanthes concerning his love, and the youth consented; thus an erotic relationship blossomed. Hippothous, madly in love, states:

> I first fell in love with him when I saw his tenacious wrestling in the gymnasium, and I lost control of myself. When a local festival with a nightlong celebration was held, I took that occasion to approach Hyperanthes and begged for his pity. The youth listened, promised everything, and took pity on me. The first stage of love's journey were kisses and caresses and many tears from me, and in the end we took an opportunity to be alone with each other, and the fact of our respective ages went unsuspected. We were together a long time, feeling extraordinary affection for each other, until some divinity took offense at our good fortune. (Xenophon of Ephesus, *Ephesian Tale of Anthia and Habrocomes* 3.2.3–4 [Henderson])

It is this "divinity" that is responsible for the threat to the relationship of these two men. As a result, Aristomachus, an older man, desires to have

---

37. David Konstan, *Sexual Symmetry: Love in the Ancient Novel and Related Genres* (Princeton: Princeton University Press, 1994), 28. See also Katharine Haynes, "Minor Male Characters," in *Fashioning the Feminine in the Greek Novel* (London: Routledge, 2003), 150.

38. καὶ ἦν θρήνων ἅμιλλα, ἐραστοῦ καὶ πατρός.

39. Ἐγώ μου τὸν δεσπότην ἀπολώλεκα.

40. Jeffrey Henderson, ed. and trans., "Xenophon of Ephesus: Anthia and Habrocomes," in *Longus: Daphnis and Chloe and Xenophon of Ephesus: Anthia and Habrocomes*, LCL 69 (Cambridge: Harvard University Press, 2009), 278–79.

Hyperanthes as his own. Aristomachus is "captivated" by Hyperanthes and attempts to seduce him, but the young man refuses, because of his love for Hippothous.[41] Yet, Hyperanthes is forced by his father to go to Aristomachus, which ultimately drives Hippothous mad. Acting out of manic love and passion, Hippothous stabs Aristomachus and kills him.[42] The two young lovers secretly escape together on a ship sailing to Asia. However, a storm hits their ship, and they capsize into the ocean. Hippothous swims alongside Hyperanthes, who ultimately drowns at sea.

Again, we find two men in an erotic relationship, revealed through symptoms of manic lovesickness, which resists the typical ideals of a pederastic relationship.[43] For instance, Hippothous and Hyperanthes are specifically said to be of the same age and seem to be of similar social status. Moreover, they are equal in passion and love for each other. After their mutual love is threatened, Hippothous is the one who reacts, like Stratocles, in a manically lovesick way. However, the lovesickness functions in this text to show the depth of the love of Hippothous, and even after such violent behavior, the two lovers are able to escape together, if only for a short time. Moreover, Aristomachus, the typical *erastes* figure, is killed in the narrative.

As we can see, the characters in these three narratives are dealing with the loss or the threat of the loss of their love. In the face of this possible calamity, they lose control and are portrayed as erratic and irrational. Both Stratocles and Hippothous engage in physical violence in the face of this threat, Stratocles beating Andrew's executioners and Hippothous murdering Hyperanthes's new lover. Clinias, having no one to blame, is stunned into silence and then moans and cries loudly. All three lovers display their emotions outwardly and experience great despair when their love is taken away from them.

Additionally, in all three homoerotic couples, glimpses of mutual love can be found. Yet, the relationship between Stratocles and Andrew is distinctive because of the clear hierarchal structure between the two. Certainly, Andrew and Stratocles first appear a traditionally pederastic relationship, as Andrew is the teacher and Stratocles the student. Yet, the erotic desire presented in the text disrupts this model, as both partners

---

41. Henderson, "Xenophon," 281.
42. Ibid., 283.
43. Konstan, notably, notes this as a homoerotic relationship in the novel but determines that it is ultimately "doomed" (*Sexual Symmetry*, 29).

desire each other and vocalize that erotic desire in the narrative. Moreover, in this story it is the *erastes* who dies and the *eromenos* who is grieving and stricken by lovesickness. As opposed to the typical *erastes* of the novel, who survives, Andrew is the one whose life is threatened. In the midst of this dramatic ordeal, Andrew is fully in control and is even portrayed as smiling while hanging on a cross. The idea of losing his love (or his life) is not threatening to Andrew, and it is this aspect of his characterization that makes Stratocles appear all the more lovesick in his actions.

Seen in this light, the motif of lovesickness illuminates the complexities of the apostle/follower relationship. By identifying the physical reactions of Stratocles, alongside similar distraught male lovers in the ancient novels, the motif of lovesickness becomes clear. Like that of Hippothous and Hyperanthes, Clinias and Charicles, the love of Stratocles and Andrew is presented as mutual, yet the lovesickness in each relationship is experienced by only one partner: it is the surviving lover who grieves manically. In the Acts of Andrew, however, the lover is still alive to witness the erratic behavior and even question it, querying the dramatic nature of Stratocles's reaction to this impending loss. In this aspect, a new facet of the apostle/follower relationship is revealed. The apostle, although an active lover, has his emotions under control, while the follower is the one madly in love. Through the motif of lovesickness, the erotic nature of Stratocles's relationship with Andrew surfaces, and the traditional binary is disrupted.

MacDonald refers to Andrew as a "Christianized Socrates," and perhaps this captures something of his erotic role as well.[44] Indeed, according to Alcibiades in the *Symposium*, his relationship with Socrates reversed the typical roles of *erastes* and *eromenoi*: "Accordingly I invited him to dine with me, for all the world like a lover [ἐραστής] scheming to ensnare his favorite [παιδικοῖς]" (Plato, *Symp.* 217c).[45] Alcibiades, who expected to lure Socrates with his beauty, finds instead that he has been seduced: "For when I hear him I am worse than any wild fanatic; I find my heart leaping and my tears gushing forth at the sound of his speech, and I see great numbers of other people having the same experience" (Plato, *Symp.* 215e [Lamb]). So Stratocles might have put it, yet the erotic dynamic of his relationship with Andrew is queerer still, less a reversal than an undoing of

---

44. MacDonald, *Christianizing Homer*, 301.

45. ἀτεχνῶς ὥσπερ ἐραστὴς παιδικοῖς ἐπιβουλεύων; trans. W. R. M. Lamb, "Symposium," in *Lysis; Symposium; Gorgias*, vol. 3 of *Plato*, LCL 166 (Cambridge: Harvard University Press, 1925), 225.

the traditional binary. The contrast is not between lover and beloved but between a lover who is lovesick and one who is not. Both are active lovers, yet the apostle still comes out on top.

Trophy Wives of Christ: Tropes of Seduction and Conquest in the Apocryphal Acts

John W. Marshall

The apocryphal acts of the apostles offer a pattern of interaction wherein females embrace chastity in response to apostolic preaching of sexual restraint. In the Acts of Paul the preaching of the apostle is summed up succinctly by Theoclea, the mother of a virgin betrothed: "fear one single God only, and live chastely" (Acts Paul 3.9 [*NTApoc* 2:240]).[1] A significant element of the dramatic action that ensues in the narrative proceeds from the social and/or sexual disenfranchisement of those in charge of the women who have listened to the apostles, most commonly husbands or fiancés but occasionally parents. That is to say, the woman's sexual activity is a ground of contest between the apostle of Jesus and the non-Christian man.[2] Considering more closely what is at stake in this conflict and what cultural resources inform the contours of this narrative trope is the purpose of this essay. The argument presented here is that traditional Roman ways of describing the domination of imperial rule formed an important template for Christian narrative description of the spread of the gospel through the preaching of the apostles.

---

1. Unless otherwise noted, quotations of the apocryphal acts use the translation and numbering scheme of Wilhelm Schneemelcher, *NTApoc* 2.

2. Virginia Burrus, *Chastity as Autonomy: Women in the Stories of the Apocryphal Acts* (Lewiston, NY: Mellen, 1987); Peter W. Dunn, "Women's Liberation, the Acts of Paul, and Other Apocryphal Acts of the Apostles: A Review of Some Recent Interpreters," *Apocrypha* 4 (1994): 245–62; David Konstan, "Acts of Love: A Narrative Pattern in the Apocryphal Acts," *JECS* 6 (1998): 15–36; Andrew S. Jacobs, "A Family Affair: Marriage, Class, and Ethics in the Apocryphal Acts of the Apostles," *JECS* 7 (1999): 105–38.

Three topics need to be addressed before proceeding: the coherence of grouping "the apocryphal acts," the scope of my claim of a Roman colonial model, and the relation of the present study to the history of scholarship. First of all, "the five great apocryphal acts" are not a natural corpus but attested first of all in the Manichaean circles.[3] François Bovon's cautions about divorcing this literature from other early narratives of the apostles and saints are apt.[4] Second, given the diversity within the corpus, I am not arguing that there is a single explanation of the role of women or of the influences on the various authors and contributors to the tradition. The debate and discussion over the meaning and function of the female characters in the apocryphal acts is extensive, and a claim of exclusive explanatory power is (rightly) unlikely to be accurate or persuasive (more below on scholarly analyses of female characters in the apocryphal acts). Moreover, my claim about the role of gender in Roman thinking about colonial domination is not meant to address all the female characters in the apocryphal acts. It is specific to the conflicts over chastity.

In his influential article on the formal and substantive relations of the apocryphal acts of the apostles and the canonical Acts of the Apostles, Bovon treats the "famous" love triangle of the apostolic hero, the elite woman and her sexual partner, only very briefly. He writes: "The famous triangle (conversion of a lady infuriates the husband who attacks the apostle) reflects a sociological reality of the Christian mission (see Justin Martyr, *2 Apology*)."[5] This article seeks to illuminate and to specify the first half of Bovon's statement concerning the love triangle and to provide an alternative to the second half, in which Bovon asserts the sociological reality of the phenomenon and claims that the literary trope simply reflects it.[6] It must be noted, and will examined be below, that the tri-

---

3. Wilhelm Schneemelcher, "Introduction: Second and Third Century Acts of the Apostles," in *NTApoc* 2:76.

4. François Bovon, "Canonical and Apocryphal Acts of Apostles," *JECS* 11 (2003): 167.

5. Ibid., 184.

6. This claim is made in more detail by Jan N. Bremmer, "Why Did Early Christianity Attract Upper-Class Women?," in *Fructus centesimus: Mélanges offerts à Gerard J.M. Bartelink à l'occasion de son soixante-cinquième anniversaire*, ed. A. Bastiaensen, A. Hilhorst, and C. Kneepkens, Instrumenta Patristica 19 (Dordrecht: Kluwer, 1989), 35-47. See, however, detailed criticism in Judith M. Lieu, "The 'Attraction of Women' in/to Early Judaism and Christianity: Gender and the Politics of Conversion," *JSNT* 21.72 (1999): 5.

angle almost invariably includes a dimension of class: the woman is an elite woman, her husband (or other patriarchal keeper) an elite man who is not only sexually jealous but also furiously protective of social class and of the continuance of the hierarchy of the social order. Regarding this triangle as a simple reflection of a sociological reality glosses over the complex relations of power inscribed in these narratives as well as the adroit deployment by early Christian writers of Roman techniques of wielding and expressing power.

These elements of the relationship—class, sex, and power—must be treated in order to more fully understand the love triangle that forms such a prominent motif in the apocryphal acts of the apostles. Each of these is undertreated in Bovon's characterization of the triangle. The early Christian trope of upper-class converts in conflict with magistrates and elite figures reflects several concurrent factors: the appetite for stories of the privileged, the presence of upper-class converts within the Christian movement,[7] and—the focus of this study—the Roman habit of using their conceptions of hierarchical gender relations as a mode of discourse to portray and consolidate their colonial domination.

Overwhelmingly, the non-Christian man with whom the apostle contends is an elite man. The apostles convert the wives of proconsuls, leading citizens, friends of the governor, concubines of the civic prefects, wives of the friends of the emperor or the king, or daughters and wives of kings themselves. This is no random, reflective, or representative sample of female conversion. While many scholars of the apocryphal acts have emphasized, and with some justification, the liberating potential of stories of chastity for women in the ancient world, it is also clear that the stories function to depict a contest among males in which the possession of sexual access to a woman, and an elite woman in particular, is a good over which men contend.[8] With varying degrees of explicitness, the apocryphal

---

7. For accounts of proportions of the rich and poor in early Christian communities, see Justin J. Meggitt, *Paul, Poverty and Survival* (Edinburgh: T&T Clark, 1998); Steven J. Friesen, "Poverty in Pauline Studies: Beyond the So-Called New Consensus," *JSNT* 26 (2004): 323–61; Walter Scheidel and Steven J. Friesen, "The Size of the Economy and the Distribution of Income in the Roman Empire," *JRS* 99 (2009): 61–91. Urban elites are grossly overrepresented in the apocryphal acts, as they are in much literary fiction of the ancient (and modern) world.

8. Kate Cooper, *The Virgin and the Bride: Idealized Womanhood in Late Antiquity* (Cambridge: Harvard University Press, 1996); Jacobs, "Family Affair"; Amy-Jill Levine, "Introduction," in *A Feminist Companion to the New Testament Apocrypha*, ed.

acts portray the apostles, or Jesus, as the new gatekeepers of converted elite women's sexual activity.[9]

Teresa Ramsby and Beth Severy-Hoven have argued that in Augustan Rome "the conquered were frequently figured as subordinate family members, often women."[10] I argue that a key pattern of depiction of the evangelized in the apocryphal acts corresponds to and finds its coherence in this larger Roman trope of articulating power through the portrayal of gender hierarchy. Joan Scott's cross-cultural claim that "gender is a primary field within which or by means of which power is articulated"[11] is an important generalization to which early Christianity does not form an exception.

The Pattern of the Apocryphal Acts

The narrative pattern in the apocryphal acts to which I am attending is distributed widely, though not evenly, among early Christian narrative literature focused on the apostles. Unresolved questions concerning date, provenance, and relative order plague the study of the apocryphal acts.[12] Lacking scholarly consensus on these matters, discussions of literary influence among the acts are difficult to pursue in any broadly persuasive manner. Moreover, the acts as we have them bear significant signs of cross-contamination in the process of transmission. This makes it nearly

---

Amy-Jill Levine and Maria Mayo Robbins (New York: Continuum, 2006), 1–17. More than most, Jacobs attends to class in his reading of the apostolic triangle. His contention, however, that the apocryphal acts are an instance of early Christian resistance to the class privilege of formal legal marriage seems inadequate to the virulence of the apostolic denunciation of bodily sexual activity.

9. It should be noted that the offense of sexual violence was highly enmeshed in systems of class and hierarchy. See John W. Marshall, "Sexual Violence: Roman World," in *Oxford Encyclopedia of Bible and Gender Studies* (Oxford: Oxford University Press, 2014), 2:360–66.

10. Teresa R. Ramsby and Beth Severy-Hoven, "Gender, Sex, and the Domestication of the Empire in Art of the Augustan Age," *Arethusa* 40 (2007): 44.

11. Joan W. Scott, "Gender: A Useful Category of Historical Analysis," *AHR* 91 (1986): 1069.

12. See discussion in Jan Bremmer, "Magic, Martyrdom and Women's Liberation in the Acts of Paul and Thecla," in *The Apocryphal Acts of Paul and Thecla*, ed. Jan Bremmer (Kampen: Kok, 1996), 57; Bremmer, "Women in the Apocryphal Acts of John," in *The Apocryphal Acts of John*, ed. Jan Bremmer (Kampen: Kok, 1995), 56; Bremmer, "Man, Magic, and Martyrdom in the Acts of Andrew," in *The Apocryphal Acts of Andrew*, ed. Jan Bremmer (Leuven: Peeters, 2000), 15–17.

impossible to trace within the acts corpus the development of the apostolic triangle motif. Thus the following survey emphasizes the breadth and intensity of the triangle rather than pursuing a claim about the development of the motif.

Acts of Paul

In many ways the motif is clearest in the Acts of Paul and especially in that portion of the Acts of Paul that may have circulated independently as the Acts of Paul and Thecla.[13] When Paul arrives in Iconium, he begins to preach his gospel of abstinence and resurrection. A young virgin, Thecla, betrothed to Thamyris, one of the leading citizens of the city and a friend of the governor, overhears Paul's preaching and undertakes to devote herself to the apostolic message and to the practice of chastity that Paul preaches, abandoning her planned marriage to Thamyris. The rage that ensues, not only from Thamyris but also from Thecla's mother, Theocleia, brings Thecla into conflict with the imperial authorities. The issue is not simply sexual jealousy (Thamyris) or the private potential loss of marriage-based alliances between elite families (Theocleia); the text clearly portrays the integrity of the social order as at stake. Thamyris brings civic authorities in a mob to confront Paul and shouts at him: "Thou hast destroyed the city of the Iconians, and my betrothed, so that she will not have me. Let us go to the governor Castellius!" (Acts Paul 3.15 [*NTApoc* 2:241]). Civic order depends on acceptable performances of gender roles.[14] Conversely, as we shall see, hierarchical gender arrangements are tools in imperial propaganda concerning the propriety of Roman rule. Moreover, what constitutes acceptable gender performance is deeply conditioned by social status.

The confrontation between Paul's gospel as portrayed in the Acts of Paul and the Roman order is evident in the direct conflicts with the governor that ensue and also through the adoption and deployment of the

---

13. Jeremy W. Barrier, *The Acts of Paul and Thecla: A Critical Introduction and Commentary* (Tübingen: Mohr Siebeck, 2009), 44; Glenn E. Snyder, *Acts of Paul: The Formation of a Pauline Corpus*, WUNT 2/352 (Tübingen: Mohr Siebeck, 2013), 101; Richard I. Pervo, *The Acts of Paul: A New Translation with Introduction and Commentary* (Eugene, OR: Cascade Books, 2014), 67, 81.

14. Ross S. Kraemer, "The Conversion of Women to Ascetic Forms of Christianity," *Signs* (1980): 299; *NTApoc* 2:220. At this point, Jacobs is surely correct that it is elite marriage that is in mind ("Family Affair," 110, 128).

tropes of Roman rule—not only the emblematic contest over elite women but also other means of representing colonial rule: the advent of the imperial envoy[15] and the portrayal of Paul's God as the deliverer of the goods that the emperor claimed to deliver (Acts Paul 7.2 [*NTApoc* 2:251–52]). The apostolic triangle motif is repeated in Antioch again with the cast of premier citizens, an elite man whose lust is frustrated, and an exclamation of the danger to the civic order (Acts Paul 3.26–43 [*NTApoc* 2:243–46]). The Acts of Paul ends with a confrontation between Paul and Nero that emphasizes the analogy between the spread of the gospel and the spread of imperial authority. Paul resurrects Nero's fallen cupbearer Patroclus, and Patroclus explains to Nero that he was resurrected by the power of the king of the ages who destroys all kingdoms (Acts Paul 11.2 [*NTApoc* 2:261]). Likewise Paul, after being beheaded, returns to haunt Nero and proclaim himself "God's soldier" (Acts Paul 11.6 [*NTApoc* 2:263]). The prominent trope of the apostolic triangle has its coherence within this larger pattern of mixture of both conflict between gospel and empire and analogy between gospel and empire.[16]

Acts of Peter

The Acts of Peter is distinctive among the apocryphal acts in the intensity with which it focuses on the apostle's conflict with a semi-internal enemy: Simon Magus. This focus on the contest with Simon necessarily reduces the prominence of the contest with a rival man in the apostolic triangle. Nevertheless, the Acts of Peter shows clearly the combination of analogy and conflict with the empire in several ways, including the apostolic triangle. Descriptions of Jesus as the one who "has broken all kingdoms" (Acts Pet. 8.24 [*NTApoc* 2:306]), and a miracle story in which a broken statue of Caesar is repaired by Peter to prevent reprisals against Marcellus, set

---

15. Trevor S. Luke, "The Parousia of Paul at Iconium," *R&T* 15 (2008): 225–51.

16. Monika Betz, "Die betörenden Worte des fremden Mannes: Zur Funktion der Paulusbeschreibung in den Theklaakten," *NTS* 53 (2007): 130–45. Betz emphasizes the transformation of Greco-Roman literary depictions of romantic love in the Acts of (Paul and) Thecla. The transformations are doubtlessly significant, but the underlying contest over control of a woman's sexual activity is a motif the Acts share with Greco-Roman romance. See Heike Omerzu, "The Portrayal of Paul's Outer Appearance in the Acts of Paul and Thecla: Re-considering the Correspondence between Body and Personality in Ancient Literature," *R&T* 3 (2008): 268.

the apostle in tension with the emperor even as other currents in the Acts of Peter strive to mitigate such a tension. The apostolic triangle returns in the conversion by Peter of the four concubines of Agrippa the prefect (Agrippina, Nicaria, Euphemia, and Doris) (Acts Pet. 8.33 [NTApoc 2:313]). Predictably, Agrippa rages. The episode is brief but functions as an introduction to the main event: Peter's conversion of the Xanthippe, the wife of Albinus the friend of Caesar (Acts Pet. 8.34 [NTApoc 2:313–14]). The rage of Albinus precipitates Peter's famous upside-down crucifixion. While conflict with Simon draws significant focus in the Acts of Peter, the conflict of the gospel in general and the representatives of imperial authority is signaled frequently, and the apostolic triangle's formulation of this conflict is absolutely clear in the conversions of the concubines of Agrippa and of Xanthippe.

Acts of John

In fragmentary remains of the Acts of John, the apostolic triangle is explicitly harmonious rather than conflictual in those portions of the original text that survive in the Christian tradition. John has preached a gospel of faithful continence to Drusiana. Andronicus, the husband of Drusiana, a Roman official (*praetor*), a leading citizen of Ephesus, appears initially in the text as unconverted, but after a substantial lacuna in the manuscript, he appears as a follower of the apostle in a continent marriage. On the basis of a backward-looking remark in Acts of John 63 that recalls Andronicus's intense jealousy and also the narratives of the Manichaean Psalm-book that imply Drusiana was imprisoned in a sepulcher for fourteen days of conflict between the apostle and Andronicus, Knut Schäferdiek concludes that a bitter conflict between John and Andronicus originally followed Drusiana's conversion.[17] Thus the primary triangle of the Acts of John clearly bore the significant marks of the type: the conversion and control of the elite woman and the conflict with the elite male. A subsidiary triangle repeats the conflict over Drusiana. When Satan possesses a man to fall into love/lust over Drusiana, she, by force of prayer, commits suicide rather than be responsible for the fall of another into adultery and incontinence (Acts John 63 [NTApoc 2:194]). Death, however, is insufficient to deter the possessed suitor, who begins a necrophilic defilement

---

17. Knut Schäferdiek, "The Acts of John," in *NTApoc* 2:163, 178.

of Drusiana only to be killed by a giant snake that appears unexpectedly in the sepulcher. At last, it is revealed that the possessed suitor is none other than Callimachus, a leading citizen of the Ephesians. The apostle proceeds to turn the horror into a win-win-win: first, by raising from the dead and converting Callimachus; second, by raising Drusiana from the dead; and third, by claiming victory in another triangular contest in which control of a woman's sexual activity was the emblematic prize representing the conflict of John's gospel and the status quo of the Roman city. This apostolic triangle is set in a narrative that Jan Bremmer notes gives greater prominence to the Roman-ness of the context than the Greek novels of the eastern Mediterranean do.[18] John arrives like the envoy of the emperor, greeted by the praetor of the city before he reaches the gates (Acts John 19 [NTApoc 2:172–73]), and preaches the "God whom every ruler fears" (Acts John 23 [NTApoc 2:174]). Agonism and analogy jointly characterize the treatment of empire and gospel in the Acts of John.

Acts of Andrew

In the Acts of Andrew, the other members of the apostolic triangle are Aegeates the proconsul and Maximilla. Given the fragmentary state of preservation of the Acts of Andrew, the initial contact between Andrew and Maximilla is missing. It is clear, however, that Aegeates's anger remains hot despite the slightly less polemical tone of the Acts of Andrew. Aegeates threatens to intensify his tortures of Andrew if Maximilla does not resume expected sexual intercourse with him (Acts Andr. 4 [NTApoc 2:129]). While the Acts of Andrew is less elaborate in the conflict, it is notably articulate in the relationship between the elite woman and the apostle. Speaking to Maximilla about Aegeates's rage, Andrew declares: "I rightly see in you Eve repenting, and in myself Adam being converted: for what she suffered in ignorance you to whose soul I direct my words are now setting right because you are converted" (Acts Andr. 5 [NTApoc 2:130]). By convincing elite women to relate chastely to the apostles, the apostles claim to undo the sin of Eve.[19] This endeavor to rectify the generative sin

---

18. Bremmer, "Women in the Apocryphal Acts of John," 53.
19. It should be noted, however, how closely the Acts of Andrew is aligned with the sexual morality of the wider culture when it comes to class. Maximilla's long-term strategy for living chastely with Aegeates is to force her maidservant Eucleia to act as a sexual imposter servicing Aegeates's sexual desires disguised as Maximilla. When the

of sexuality is entangled in a narrative that sets itself in conflict with the Roman empire. Combat metaphors are the primary manifestation of this combined agonism and analogy that permeates the text (Acts Andr. 2, 17 [*NTApoc* 2:126, 133]).

Acts of Thomas

The Acts of Thomas is very much oriented toward conflict between Thomas and ruling authorities. Though the action of the narrative is set beyond the eastern edge of the Roman empire, it continues the trope of conflict over elite women. Moreover, while there is no certainty in this matter, Edessa and eastern Syria are the prime candidates for the place of composition.[20] That is to say, its compositional environment is more securely acquainted with Roman discourses of colonial domination than are the areas in which the fictional text's action is set.

Early on in the narrative, Thomas is compelled by the king of Andrapolis to pray over the daughter of the king and her new bridegroom just before the king locks the newlyweds alone in the bridal chamber. Thomas has offered a flowery though ambiguous prayer, but after the doors are locked Jesus appears in the marriage bed in the form of the apostle Thomas and preaches a strident continence to the newlyweds, noting among other things that children are a grave trial and that "the majority of children become unprofitable, possessed by demons" (Acts Thom. 12 [*NTApoc* 2:344]). The newlyweds are persuaded and refrain from a sexual consummation of their marriage. The memorable wedding-night scene in the Acts of Thomas captures the apostolic preaching in a summary made by a miraculous appearance of Jesus himself: "Remember, my children, what my brother [the apostle Thomas] said to you, and to whom he commended you; and know this, that if you abandon this filthy intercourse you become holy temples, pure and free" (Acts Thom. 12 [*NTApoc* 2:344]). The conflict becomes explicit at the next morning's breakfast with the bride's parents. Pressed for explanations, the bride declares: "I have set at naught this man [her new husband], and this marriage which passes away from

---

ruse comes undone after many months, Aegeates has Euclia maimed and then fed to dogs and the other slaves who knew crucified. None of this action comes under criticism by the narrative voice of the text or by characters within it.

20. Jan Bremmer, "The Acts of Thomas: Place, Date, and Women," in *The Apocryphal Acts of Thomas*, ed. Jan Bremmer (Leuven: Peeters, 2001), 76.

before my eyes, because I am bound in another marriage. And I have had no intercourse with a short-lived husband, the end of which is remorse and bitterness of the soul, because I am yoked with the true man" (Acts Thom. 14 [*NTApoc* 2:344]). Though the bridegroom concurs, the king predictably rages and offers a bounty on the apostle's head. Thomas, however, sails away before the conflict can develop, having left the seed (or weed) of the gospel of continence in his wake.

Several episodes ensue with talking animals, demon lovers, tours of hell, and further adventures. Conflict with King Gundaphorus is a recurrent motif. Jesus is characterized as the invincible conquering military commander leading the apostles as his soldiers (Acts Thom. 39 [*NTApoc* 2:355–56]). The apostolic triangle reasserts itself as the means of discussing Thomas's triumph over King Misdaeus in the ninth act and following. Thomas converts Mygdonia—the wife of Charisius, kinsman of king Misdaeus—to chastity. Charisius is overcome with grief and anger, and enlists the king in his conflict with the apostle. After imprisoning Thomas, Charisius expects his wife back, proclaiming to her "both the gods and the laws give me the right to rule over thee" (Acts Thom. 114 [*NTApoc* 2:385]). Here the confluence of colonial ideology and gender ideology is complete; what is the ideology of colonialism but the rule of one group over another by right understood to be natural or divine?

Thomas raises the stakes by baptizing Mygdonia, after which she seeks out her estranged husband and forcefully rejects his entreaties to resume marital/sexual relations, describing her newfound devotion thus: "Thou hast seen that marriage, which passed away <and remains here (on earth)>, but this marriage abides forever.... That bed was spread <with coverlets>, but this with love and faith. You are a bridegroom who passes away and is destroyed, but Jesus is a true bridegroom, abiding immortal forever" (Acts Thom. 124 [*NTApoc* 2:389]). As the narrative progresses, Thomas also converts Tertia, the wife of King Misdaeus himself, to chaste loyalty to Jesus and the apostle. Vazan the son of Misdaeus soon follows (Acts Thom. 150–158 [*NTApoc* 2:398–402]). Though Thomas is eventually martyred by Misdaeus, the final victory belongs to the apostle when Misdaeus converts after using the dust of the bones of Thomas to exorcise a demon possessing one of his sons (Acts Thom. 170 [*NTApoc* 2:404–5]). The Acts of Thomas—though with very different theological concerns from, for example, the Acts of Paul—displays a vibrant continuation of the pattern of the apostolic triangle and portrays the gospel as a conflict of the reign of God with the reign of earthly realms and empires.

The emblematic trophy in all the apocryphal acts of the apostles is the woman whose patron is an elite man of the world, a trophy that Jesus, as the "true man," invariably takes (Acts Thom. 14 [*NTApoc* 2:344]).[21] Beyond Bovon's claim that this is a reflection of social reality,[22] it needs to be noted that it is a distortion of social reality in its overwhelming focus on elite men and women. The rest of this article is devoted to showing how the use of gender to portray domination reflects not an opposition between Christians and Roman power but an embrace and internalization of the gendered articulation of power that Rome developed.

The Pattern of Roman Depiction of Political Domination

The pattern that I see operative in the apocryphal acts—namely, the depiction of the spread of the gospel through the possession of elite women—derives its cultural cogency, its ability to make sense, from the wider Roman pattern of inflecting conquest with gender. The pattern I have in mind as a comparison to the apocryphal acts is well attested in the literary and material remains of antiquity and also in the attitudes to sex and gender that scholars have analyzed in the wake of the work of Michel Foucault.[23]

My claim is not that Roman representations of conquest were always through the possession of elite women, or that the focus on sexual renunciation in the apocryphal acts is always about conquest, but that gendered representation of conquered peoples was a prominent trope in Roman depictions of conquest and provides an important context within which to understand related motifs in the apocryphal acts. It is important to see the

---

21. See also Acts Thom. 124 (*NTApoc* 2:389), where Jesus is the "true bridegroom." Kraemer ("Conversion of Women," 300) describes the pattern well, although her analysis is guided by the explicit assumption that the pattern of conversion described is accurate. Her argument that the transformation of socio-sexual standards could have been a significant attractant of women to Christianity is well supported. The notion that elites were so prominent is demographically impossible and not part of Kraemer's argument.

22. Bovon, "Canonical and Apocryphal Acts," 184.

23. Michel Foucault, *An Introduction*, vol. 1 of *The History of Sexuality* (New York: Pantheon, 1978); David M. Halperin, "Is There a History of Sexuality?," *History and Theory* 28.3 (1989): 257–74; Amy Richlin, *The Garden of Priapus: Sexuality and Aggression in Roman Humor* (New Haven: Yale University Press, 1983); Simon Goldhill, *Foucault's Virginity: Ancient Erotic Fiction and the History of Sexuality* (Cambridge: Cambridge University Press, 1995).

reciprocal relationship between Roman understandings of gender, Roman imperialism, and Roman ethnographic thought. In 1963 Peter Brunt summarized the ethnographic and imperialistic relationship within this triangle, writing that "Romans divided the rest of mankind into 'subjecti' and 'superbi' and saw it as their mission" to vanquish as superiors. From this position, to deal with an enemy as an equal was "itself an offence."[24] It was a category error, according to Brunt, for Roman elites to imagine equality with other peoples.

In terms of sexual imagination, Roman conceptions of sexual relationships were similarly and deeply hierarchical, with no cognitive space for equality. The most prominent example of this was in the division of participants into an active partner and a passive partner. Love between equals was not a value conceived in Rome even when love was ideally mutual. Roman ideals of mutual love between men and women were conceived in coordination with rather than in tension with the superior position assigned to men in Roman thought. As many scholars have noted, this hierarchical conception of partners in a sexual relationship was a stronger constant than any particular gender distribution of parties to a sexual relationship.[25] Instead, for Romans, the hierarchy of active and passive partners in a sexual relationship was an abomination only if it conflicted with other canonical hierarchies in the Roman world, men over women, free over slaves, the propertied over the poor.[26] Again, equality is a category error in the realm of Roman sexual thinking, and Bernadette Brooten's chronicle of the deeply befuddled, or simply aborted, attempts of Roman males to imagine or account for female homosexual relationships shows how sex without ready penetration signaling hierarchy confounded the male imagination.[27]

The imagined naturalness of hierarchy in the sphere of sexual behavior had a close analog in the Roman conception of political relations.

---

24. Peter A. Brunt, review of *Die Aussenpolitik des Augustus und die augusteische Dichtung*, H. D. Meyer, *JRS* 53 (1963): 175.

25. Bernadette J. Brooten, *Love between Women: Early Christian Responses to Female Homoeroticism* (Chicago: University of Chicago Press, 1998), 303.

26. Halperin writes: "Sexual penetration was thematized as domination: the relation between the insertive and the receptive sexual partner was taken to be the same kind of relation as that obtaining between social superior and social inferior" ("Is There a History of Sexuality?," 260).

27. Brooten, *Love between Women*, 241.

Thus Cicero could encapsulate the natural givenness of Roman colonialism for himself by describing Syrians and Jews as nations "born for slavery" (*Prov. cons.* 10).[28] Here, Cicero sorts the variety of ethnicity in the empire into the continuum of supervision and servitude. The third side of this triangle of ethnicity, social domination, and gender that is my focus concerns the Roman use of gender as a conceptual category to represent conquest and to represent the domination of Romans over other ethnic groups.

Literary Sources

It is possible to see this nexus of gender, power, and conquest in various literary sources of the Roman world. Alexander's generals and their marriages to the princesses of Persia form an ancient historical instance of this motif and one that moves to the literary world in ancient history and fiction (Arrian, *Anab.* 7.4.4–5.6). In the literary realm, Aeneas's seduction of Dido puts the motif to work in Virgil's piece of imperial propaganda.[29] Treating the Latin epic as a genre, Alison Keith has emphasized the role of female characters as tools of representation in the dramatization of imperial rule. Tracing the very wide pattern of woman as land and man as the culture that masters nature, Keith observes that Lucretius crystallizes the gendered understanding of Roman power in a vision of "the interpenetration of Greek philosophical and Roman social hierarchies of order, including the subordination of nature to philosophy, *orbis terrarum* ('the inhabited world') to Rome, and woman to man."[30]

The strong scholarship on the gendering of Roman political thought makes it possible to turn relatively quickly to nonliterary sources. Moreover, nonliterary media were the primary means of communicating imperial ideology to a mass audience in the ancient world, and frequently nonliterary media inflected conquest and domination with gender.

---

28. Tradidit in servitutem Iudaeis et Syris, nationibus natis servituti.

29. Musa Dube Shomanah, *Postcolonial Feminist Interpretation of the Bible* (St. Louis: Chalice, 2000), 81–82; David Quint, *Epic and Empire: Politics and Generic Form from Virgil to Milton* (Princeton: Princeton University Press, 1993).

30. Alison Keith, *Engendering Rome: Women in Latin Epic* (Cambridge: Cambridge University Press, 2000), 41.

Iconographic Sources

One of the most compelling material depictions of Roman conquest understood as the possession of elite women comes from the Sebasteion of Aphrodisias. Discovered in 1979 by Kenan T. Erim, the Sebasteion at Aphrodisias offers an unrivaled window on elite provincial understandings of Roman domination.[31] Figures 1 and 2 illustrate the remains and a reconstruction of the Sebasteion. The Sebasteion was subvented by two prominent Aphrodisian families and contained a massive sculptural program that lined the passage to the temple of Aphrodite and the Theoi Sebastoi.[32] The topics of the relief sculptures ranged widely across Roman mythology and the imperial family. Two elements of the sculptural program are of significant interest to my argument: the north colonnade depicted the conquered nations of the Roman Empire through a series of statues of female figures, and the south colonnade offered specific depictions of the conquest of Britain by Claudius and of Armenia by Nero. The construction as a whole is a testament to ruling power—in the labor it concentrates, the materials it imports, the space it occupies and creates, the patronage it demonstrates, and above all the domination it depicts.

One of the primary sculptural programs of the north portico was the portrayal of subdued nations. According to R. R. R. Smith and Joyce M. Reynolds,[33] the material setting implies a total of approximately fifty nations. The nations were depicted through female figures and identified

---

31. On the discovery of the Sebasteion, see R. Naumann et al., "Recent Archaeological Research in Turkey," *Anatolian Studies* 31 (1981): 177–208; Kenan T. Erim, "Recentes decouvertes à Aphrodisias en Carie, 1979–1980," *RAr* 8 (1982): 167; R. R. R. Smith, "Simulacra Gentium: The Ethne from the Sebasteion at Aphrodisias," *JRS* 78 (1988): 50–77; Kenan T. Erim, *Aphrodisias: A Guide to the Site and Its Museum* (Istanbul: NET Turistik Yayınlar, 1990). More recently John Dominic Crossan and Jonathan Reed have discussed the Sebasteion as a strong example of imperial domination and the imperial cult (*In Search of Paul: How Jesus's Apostle Opposed Rome's Empire with God's Kingdom; A New Vision of Paul's Words and World* [San Francisco: HarperSanFrancisco, 2004], 16–23). See also Davina C. Lopez, *Apostle to the Conquered: Reimagining Paul's Mission* (Minneapolis: Fortress, 2008), 34–47. Lopez treats a similar set of Greek and Roman evidence as is treated here, though her orientation is focused on Paul rather than on the apocryphal acts.

32. R. R. R Smith, "The Imperial Reliefs from the Sebasteion at Aphrodisias," *JRS* 77 (1987): 90.

33. See nn. 31, 32, 34.

Fig. 1. Remains of Sebasteion. Photo by R. Ascough on behalf of the author.

Fig. 2. Reconstruction of Sebasteion. Image from Özgür Öztürk, "A Digital Reconstruction of Visual Experience and the Sebasteion of Aphrodisias" (MA thesis, Middle East Technical University, 2011), 100 fig. 43. Used by permission.

through inscribed bases. Currently six figures have been recovered as well as nineteen bases in whole or part. Reynolds has argued that the nations represent specifically the conquests of Augustus.³⁴ Figure 3 illustrates the ethnos Pioustae.

The nations in question include some well known—the Egyptians, the Cretans, the Cypriots—and others less commonly known in the study of early Christianity—the Trumpilini and the Pioustae. Smith notes the "impressive unfamiliarity" of the names of at least some of the nations—it is unlikely that these latter nations were known first-hand by Aphrodisians. Instead, they probably functioned as clichés of the exotic that represented the completeness of Augustan domination.³⁵ Also among the sixteen nations identifiable by their inscribed bases are the Judeans (see fig. 4).

Though there is no secure basis to connect any particular instance of the extant female statues with the Judean base, the pattern of making collective representations of conquered nations by means of a female figure is clear.

Fig. 3. Ethnos Pioustae. Photo by R. Ascough on behalf of the author.

Smith puts it thus: "The idea of personifications of peoples conquered in war seems distinctively Roman. They grew out of the Roman triumph, where defeated captives were led in procession. Art turned them into permanent memorials and into generalized female personifications."³⁶

---

34. Joyce M. Reynolds, "New Evidence for the Imperial Cult in Julio-Claudian Aphrodisias," *ZPE* 43 (1981): 317–27; Reynolds, "Further Information on Imperial Cult at Aphrodisias," *Studii clasice* 24 (1986): 109–17; Smith, "Simulacra gentium," 50.

35. Smith, "Simulacra gentium," 77.

36. R. R. R. Smith, "Myth and Allegory in the Sebasteion," in *Aphrodisias Papers:*

Of course, Roman art had many ways of representing conquered peoples, as monuments such as the Arch of Titus or the columns of Trajan and Marcus Aurelius demonstrate. Smith's repair to the triumph as an explanatory locus is helpful and accurate, but only partially so. Gender too must be part of the account. I would suggest that Smith's focus on female characters as "generalised ... personifications" points to the specific value that gender brings to the representation, namely, generalization within the Roman worldview: it expresses political hierarchy on the basis of normative Roman conceptions of gender hierarchy.

Fig. 4. Judean base. Photo by R. Ascough on behalf of the author.

A relief from the south portico of the Sebasteion, given in figure 5, shows the operation of two modes of hierarchy: size and gender. The relief combines the realism of captured prisoners, that is to say, the male figure in the upper left, with rounding out of the tale of domination in the very expressive figure of the captive woman on the lower left. Evidently, her hands are bound behind her back and her posture is one of abjection.[37] The two large figures are male: the nude idealized male Emperor and the togate Roman people or perhaps the Senate. Two further reliefs simplify the scene and more vividly exemplify the pattern. Figure 6, a relief from the north portico, depicts Claudius subduing Britannia. The inscription on a nearby base, "*Tiberios Klaudios Kaisar Bretannia*," makes the parties clear, as does the iconography of Claudius himself.[38] Perhaps even more vividly, a depiction of Nero subduing Armenia, figure 7, makes the trope

---

Recent Work on Architecture and Sculpture, ed. Kenan T. Erim and Charlotte Roueché, Journal of Roman Archaeology Supplement Series (Ann Arbor: University of Michigan Press, 1990), 95.

37. Smith, "Imperial Reliefs," 112–15.

38. Kenan T. Erim, "A New Relief Showing Claudius and Britannia from Aphrodisias," *Britannia* 13 (1982): 277; Reynolds, "New Evidence for the Imperial Cult in Julio-Claudian Aphrodisias"; Smith, "Imperial Reliefs."

Fig. 5. Captured prisoners. Photo by R. Ascough on behalf of the author.

Fig. 6. Claudius and Britannia. Photo by R. Ascough on behalf of the author.

clear. The inscription runs "~~Neroni~~ Klaudios Drousos Kaisar Sebastos Germanikos."[39] In the course of Nero's *abolitio memoriae*,[40] his name was erased from the corresponding base, but the image—idealized male figure emperor and subservient and sexually exposed female personification of a subject nation—was so readily understood, so general, so idealized, that there was no need to modify it in the erasure of the specificity of Nero. The particulars of the process of *abolitio memoriae* show how effectively generalized this trope of representation was in the empire.

Fig. 7. Nero and Armenia. Photo by R. Ascough on behalf of the author.

The classicists who have published the Sebasteion at Aphrodisias have made two observations that deserve emphasis. First, gender is a tool to undertake the generalization, normalization, and naturalization of colo-

---

39. Smith, "Imperial Reliefs," 117–18.

40. Timothy D. Barnes (*Early Christian Hagiography and Roman History* [Tübingen: Mohr Siebeck, 2010], 68) notes that the more commonly used term *damnatio memoriae* is a modern misrepresentation.

Fig. 8. Hadrianeum provinces. Photo by author.

nial domination. Second, though this model is strikingly attested in Aphrodisias, it is widely distributed in the Roman world.

Several statues now in the Capitolene museum have been identified as representations of the provinces from the Hadrianeum. Obviously, the Aphrodisias Sebasteion is chronologically prior, but the statues from the Hadrianeum are the most vivid witnesses to a tradition in Rome of representing conquered nations as women, and they were founded in the same period when the traditions found in apocryphal acts of the apostles were under intense development. Figure 8 illustrates four female figures widely identified as personifications of provinces. Building on earlier interpretations of the province as personifications, recent research emphasizes the two factors: the generalizing idealization of the figures and the foregrounding of the Roman military relationship to the provinces.[41] Interspersed between "nation" figures were "trophy" reliefs depicting the captured armor and weapons of conquered nations. In Jessica Hughes's words, "the placing of the personifications between the trophy reliefs would have suggested the nations' own status as conquered booty."[42] Quite literally, the figures were "trophy wives."

Moving from back to the time of the Aphrodisias Sebasteion, the famous *Prima Porta* statue of Augustus is known for the intensity of its

---

41. Jessica Hughes, "Personifications and the Ancient Viewer: The Case of the Hadrianeum 'Nations,'" *Art History* 32 (2009): 7. Hughes provides an up-to-date guide to the literature on the statues.

42. Ibid.

idealization of Augustan masculinity, and the readings of art historians such as Jocelyn M. C. Toynbee and others[43] make it clear that iconography of conquest on the cuirass employs the gendered personification of conquered provinces as an element of the wider traditional iconography of victory, that is, Venus, Mars, sea and land, and so on (see fig. 9). Beneath the left pectoral sits the conquered and personified Gaul, and beneath the right Hispania (figs. 10 and 11). The personification of conquered provinces as female fits within the *conventionality* of this iconography. Cuirassed statues were distributed all around the empire, and the iconographic grammar was consistent even when the execution was particular.[44] In the case of the *Prima Porta* statue, female personifications of Gaul and Spain decorate the cuirass under the imposing pectoral sculpting. These figures are identified by the conventionality of their iconography.[45]

Fig. 9. *Prima Porta*. Photo by author.

Parallel to these sculptural depictions of dominated women are the numismatic sources that are well known in the study of early Christianity and Second Temple Judaism. Coins with the Judea Capta reverse were issued under all the Flavian emperors for ten to fifteen years after the

---

43. Jocelyn M. C. Toynbee, *The Hadrianic School: A Chapter in the History of Greek Art* (Cambridge: Cambridge University Press, 1934), 32; Heinz Kähler, *Die Augustusstatue von Primaporta* (Cologne: DuMont Schauberg, 1959).

44. Judith Lynn Sebesta and Larissa Bonfante, *The World of Roman Costume* (Madison: University of Wisconsin Press, 2001), 193–96.

45. Toynbee, *Hadrianic School*, 82, 100; Ann L. Kuttner, *Dynasty and Empire in the Age of Augustus: The Case of the Boscoreale Cups* (Berkeley: University of California Press, 1995), 71, 84; Smith, "Imperial Reliefs," 88. See figs. 9–11.

Fig. 10. Hispania Photo by author.

Fig. 11. Gaul Photo by author.

Fig. 12. Judea Capta I. Courtesy Heritage Auctions, HA.com.

Fig. 13. Judea Capta II. Courtesy Heritage Auctions, HA.com.

conflict was concluded. Though there was some variation each time the type was reissued—the most obvious being the optional male representation of Roman power—the representation of the subject female figure of Judea is the most prominent constant in the series (see figs. 12 and 13). Though the Judean series is the best-known and most widely distributed Capta series in the ancient world, Germania and Armenia receive very similar treatment on coin issues (see fig. 14).[46] Armenia's repeated humiliation is adver-

Fig. 14. Germania Capta. Courtesy Heritage Auctions, HA.com.

---

46. Annalina Caló Levi, *Barbarians on Roman Imperial Coins and Sculpture* (New York: American Numismatic Society, 1952), 9–14; Keith Bradley, "On Captives under the Principate," *Phoenix* 58.3 (2004): 303; Shelagh M. Bond, "The Coinage of the Early Roman Empire," *GR* 4.2 (1957): 157; Janusz A. Ostrowski, "Personifications of Countries and Cities as a Symbol of Victory in Greek and Roman Art," in *Griechenland und Rom: Vergleichende Untersuchungen zu Entwicklungstendenzen und -höhepunkten der antiken Geschichte, Kunst und Literatur*, ed. Manfred Fuhrmann et al. (Tbilisi: Universitatsverlag Tbilissi in Verbindung mit der Palm & Enke, 1996), 268; Janusz A. Ostrowski, "Simulacra barbarorum: Some Questions of Roman Personifications," in *Akten des XIII Internationalen Kongresses für Klassische Archäologie Berlin 1988* (Mainz: von Zaben, 1990), 567; Milton Moreland, "Jerusalem Destroyed: The Setting

tised not only in the Sebasteion, the coins, but also in the Grand Cameo of France, where the province is personified as female and together with Parthia depicted in subjection.⁴⁷ Similarly, the Boscoreale cup—which in its primary face depicts Augustus receiving the orb of the world and a winged victory from Venus victrix—shows Mars Ultor leading a group of seven provinces all represented by women in the war god's train on the right side of Augustus. Africa, Gaul, Spain, and perhaps Asia are identifiable through the conventionality of their iconography (figs. 15 and 16).⁴⁸

One piece of material that articulates with particular clarity the role of gender in the representation of hierarchy is a bronze mirror from Corinth (fig. 17). It depicts personifications of Corinth and its colony Leukas. Both cities are personified, and although the usual patron of Corinth is Aphrodite and of Leukas Artemis, in the case of two cities Corinth is portrayed as male and its colony as female. Gardner suggests that "there can be little doubt that it is a copy of a more important work in sculpture or painting."⁴⁹ This is, according to Ostrowski, "the only known example in Greek Art where the city was represented as a male figure."⁵⁰ Again, when it was necessary to represent hierarchy, gender provided a broadly effective set of symbols for the task.

Such an investigation of the gendered personification of conquered provinces could be pursued at much greater length. Available for consideration are a personified Asia on a vase, Britannia in mosaic, Cappadocia in statue, Germania in relief, female cities in statuettes, the entire series of figurative provinces on the coins of Hadrian, the colossus of Porto Raphti—all of these definitely female personifications of conquered peo-

---

of Acts," in *Engaging Early Christian History: Reading Acts in the Second Century*, ed. Rubén R. Dupertuis and Todd Penner (Durham, UK: Acumen, 2014), 17–44.

47. See J. P. V. D. Balsdon, "Gaius and the Grand Cameo of Paris," *JRS* 26 (1936): 157; Luca Giuliani and Gerhardt Schmidt, *Ein Geschenk für den Kaiser: Das Geheimnis des grossen Kameo* (Munich: Beck, 2010), 26. Compare also the conquered peoples portrayed as female in the lower register of the *Gemma Augustea* in Tonio Hölscher, "Images of War in Greece and Rome: Between Military Practice, Public Memory, and Cultural Symbolism," *JRS* 93 (2003): 16.

48. Kuttner, *Dynasty and Empire*, 71–73.

49. Percy Gardner, "Countries and Cities in Ancient Art," *JHS* 9 (1888): 62–63. Gardner's nineteenth-century context of analysis does not bring gender to the forefront, yet still he notes that the meaning of the iconography is essentially political.

50. Ostrowski, "Personifications of Countries and Cities," 266.

Fig. 15. Augustus receiving globe. Photo from Antoine Héron de Villefosse, Edmond Rothschild, and Fondation Eugène Piot, *Le trésor de Boscoreale*, Monuments et mémoires publiés par l'Académie des inscriptions et belles-lettres 5 (Paris: Ernest Leroux, 1899), plate XXXI.

Fig. 16. Provinces in the train of Mars Ultor. Photo from de Villefosse, Rothschild, and Piot, *Le trésor de Boscoreale*, plate XXXII.

Fig. 17. Corinth and Leucas. Photo from Victor Duruy, *History of Greece and of the Greek People, from the Earliest Times to the Roman Conquest*, trans. M. M. Ripley (Boston: Estes & Lauriat, 1895), 2.1:130.

ple.[51] The figures of fourteen *nationes* or people at Pompey's theatre, those of Augustus's *Porticus ad Nationes*, the nations of the altar at Lugdunum, and figures of the nations carried in Augustus's funeral procession do not survive,[52] and literary testimonies that alert us to them do not spec-

---

51. On Hadrian's coins, see Schäferdiek, "Acts of John" (*NTApoc* 2:220); on Porto Raphti, see Cornelius Vermeule, "The Colossus of Porto Raphti: A Roman Female Personification," *Hesperia* 45 (1976): 67–76; on the various statues, see Gardner, "Countries and Cities in Ancient Art," 78–81; on the Germania Relief, see Ostrowski, "Simulacra barbarorum: Some Questions of Roman Personifications," 557.

52. On Pompey's theatre, see Ann L. Kuttner, "Culture and History at Pompey's Museum," *TAPA* 129 (1999): 356–49; Mark A. Temelini, "Pompey's Politics and the Presentation of His Theatre-Temple Complex, 61–52 BCE," *Studia Humaniora Tartuensia* 7 (2006): 1–14. On Augustus's *Porticus ad Nationes*, see Paul Rehak, *Imperium and Cosmos: Augustus and the Northern Campus Martius* (Madison: University of Wis-

ify gender. Even without pursuing each of these in detail, it may be said with confidence that figural depictions of conquered—"tribes, tongues, peoples, and nations," to use a New Testament phrase (e.g., Rev 7:9 and elsewhere)—were often women, and it was conventional to do so.

Conclusion

Thus equipped with a rich view of gender as a key grammar or means of which Romans articulated, and by implication justified, their dominance over subject peoples, we are in a strong position to return to the problem of the meaning and function of the "apostolic triangle." That triangular narrative formation—in which the apostle intervenes between an elite pagan husband and wife to control the woman's sexual activity and convert her to chastity—finds its coherence and function not in the prominence of a social phenomenon in early Christianity but in the cultural legibility of a rhetorical and narrative topos. The apostolic "soldier" who extends the dominion of the Christian God is portrayed in the acts literature as doing so within a culturally existing grammar of gender, hierarchy, and domination.

Appendix: Evangelism and the Gendering of Power

It is beyond the scope of a single article to present exhaustively the representations of gender-inflected conquest in Roman material culture. Let me return to the apocryphal acts only briefly and consider a key difference that my comparison should face. Namely, this: the narratives of the apostles highlight chastity as the mode of possession of sexual access. The fact that the apostles are not portrayed as making use of this access is of course significant to any reconstruction of early Christian sexual ideals, but I would contend that it does not create a significant disruption from the pattern of conquest symbolized by control of sexual access.

The Alexander Romance provides a helpful illustration here.[53] In the narrative of the romance, Alexander, after routing Darius at Issus in Cili-

---

consin Press, 2009), 101. On altar at Lugdunum, see Toynbee, *Hadrianic School*, 12; Kuttner, *Dynasty and Empire*, 84. On Augustus's funeral procession, see Smith, "Imperial Reliefs," 86; Ida Östenberg, *Staging the World: Spoils, Captives, and Representations in the Roman Triumphal Procession* (Oxford: Oxford University Press, 2009), 219.

53. For a fine treatment of basic questions regarding the Alexander Romance, see

cia, captures the mother, the wife, and the daughters of Darius. In the historical looseness of the romance, Roxanne is the daughter of Darius. The text takes pains to note that Alexander holds them as captives but that he treats them with respect, that is, does not have sex with them (1.41). For his part, Darius seems to assume that Alexander has taken his wife and daughters sexually, lamenting this in a letter to Alexander (2.10). Alexander, however, replies that nothing can undermine his prerogative to respect the captive women. The taking of sexual access that is expected of Alexander is made explicit when Darius offers somewhat attractive terms of surrender, and one of the generals of Alexander urges him to accept the terms and return the three generations of women, but only after having sex with them. Alexander demurs for the moment and rejects Darius's terms but declares that he, in the end, will take *everything* from Darius including his family (2.17). Finally, Darius, on his deathbed, surrenders to Alexander, and the emblematic act of this surrender is the gift by Darius of Roxanne to Alexander as wife, the trophy Alexander has held all along. Alexander accepts and informs Roxanne.

The Alexander Romance is instructive because it shows more than simple rapacity. It shows an ethic of restraint that also has no qualms about possessing a woman sexually. It shows both the conventional expectation of sexual possession as emblematic and symptomatic of conquest and also Alexander's modification of that expectation in relation to the Greco-Roman ideal of self-mastery. In the reassignment of Roxanne from the historical daughter of a Bactrian nobleman to the fictional daughter of Darius king of Persia, the text shows how narratively attractive it was to illustrate conquest through the possession of an elite woman and how much more attractive than veracity or historical accuracy.

The discourse of colonialism naturalizes the domination of one people over another, and the preeminent insight of postcolonialism is that there is nothing natural or given about such domination. The Roman discourse of colonial domination buttressed its understanding of colonialism by casting it in terms of those other relationships that humans are relentlessly tempted to read as natural in all its cultural particulars: the relationship between men and women.

Richard Stoneman, "The Alexander Romance: From History to Fiction," in *Greek Fiction: The Greek Novel in Context*, ed. John Morgan and Richard Stoneman (London: Routledge, 1994), 117–29.

Scott's description of gender as a "primary field within which or by means of which power is articulated" finds particular instantiation in the Roman discourse of imperial domination and in the apocryphal acts' description of the spread of the gospel.[54] Trevor Luke has captured this relationship by describing second-century Christianity as, among, other things, a "mode of participation in Roman imperialism."[55] The correspondence of Christian illustrations of the apostolic spread of the gospel with Roman representations of conquest illustrates how, in the apocryphal acts of the apostles, winning peoples for the gospel was articulated in the grammar of colonial domination.

---

54. Scott, "Gender," 1069.
55. Luke, "Parousia," 249.

Unsettling Heroes:
Reading Identity Politics in Mark's Gospel and Ancient Fiction

Scott S. Elliott and Eric Thurman

Third world texts ... necessarily project a political dimension in the form of national allegory: the story of the private individual destiny is always an allegory of the embattled situation of the public third-world culture and society.
—Fredric Jameson, "Third-World Literature in the Era of Multinational Capitalism"

[National hero romances are] the spiritual bread without which no proud people can stand the pressure of alien domination, and it is individual heroic figures in whom the feeling and longing of the masses come to a concentrated expression.
—Martin Braun, *History and Romance in Graeco-Oriental Literature*

I use *information* so as not to use *representation*—a word that ... seems to me hypocritical, an illegitimate compromise between *information* and *imitation*.... I believe there is no imitation in narrative because narrative, like everything (or almost everything) in literature, is an act of language.
—Gérard Genette, *Narrative Discourse Revisited*

National Hero Romance and Allegorical Identities

Nearly all of the novels from the late Hellenistic and early imperial periods come from the geographical and cultural margins of empire, and scholars have become increasingly attuned to the ways ancient authors self-consciously reimagine their cultural identities after the coming of imperial power represented by Alexander and Augustus. Central to the literary politics of many *popular* Greek novels, and therefore of particular importance for our reading of identity politics in Mark, is the reinterpretation of "individual heroic figures in whom the feeling and longing of the masses comes to a concentrated expression."[1] Classicist Martin Braun describes such figures as "national heroes" and calls the narratives recounting their exploits "national hero romances."[2] After Alexander, observes Braun, the peoples of the Hellenistic East experienced, as they had not under earlier empires, "political, economic, and moral oppression within the immediate grasp of the conqueror."[3] Under the "alien pressure" of Greek rule, a "consciousness of nationality" emerged among some indigenous peoples who articulated their "active moral resistance" to foreign domination through popular narratives centered around celebrated persons from the past. Such national heroes also frequently embodied the competition between indigenous people for claims to social preeminence under empire. Cultural differences and rivalries between peoples were crystallized in the literary accounts of these local figures.

Published in Germany in 1934 and translated into English in 1938, Braun's study reflects (somewhat obliquely) Europe's preoccupation with nationalism, race, and empire in the decades leading up to World War II. Significantly, Braun in some ways also anticipates an important contribution to recent discussions about postwar decolonization and (post)colonial literature, namely Fredric Jameson's controversial essay "Third-World Literature in the Era of Multinational Capitalism." Reading Braun with Jameson, we believe, adds a certain degree of theoretical insight into the relationship between individual literary characters and the social groups they are claimed to represent in colonial narratives, ancient and modern. Like Braun, Jameson draws attention to the way individual protagonists figure the social position of a larger constituency, specifically the "nation."[4] Jameson famously argues that "third world texts ... necessarily project a political dimension in the form of national allegory: *the story of the private individual destiny is always an allegory of the embattled situation of the public third-world culture and society.*"[5] Allegory in Jameson's

---

1. Martin Braun, *History and Romance in Graeco-Oriental Literature* (Oxford: Blackwell, 1938), 2.

2. Ibid., 1.

3. Ibid., 2.

4. Fredric Jameson, "Third-World Literature in the Era of Multinational Capitalism," *Social Text* 15 (1986): 69; Braun, *History and Romance*, 3.

5. Jameson, "Third-World Literature," 69, emphasis in original.

sense, we suggest, nicely describes the interpretive strategy animating Braun's (undertheorized) reading of "national hero romances," a heuristic category that has recently been expanded by some scholars to include a variety of early Jewish and Christian novelistic texts as well.[6] Not quite third-world novels, all of these popular Greek texts nevertheless emerge amid ancient cultures that lacked the kind of distinction between private and public characteristic of the first world on Jameson's reading. Moreover, Braun repeatedly details how popular legends surrounding mythical founding figures, usually kings or renowned warriors, are rewritten as romances that signify a people's social location under empire, occasionally even introducing "fictional" erotic entanglements into otherwise "historical" plots in order to further refract contemporary political conditions.

Pressing beyond this comparison, our aim here is to rethink the representational power of figurative characters such as Mark's Jesus. Writing into the events of the Judean revolt against Rome (according to the current scholarly consensus),[7] Mark, we suggest, presents Jesus as a national hero of sorts, the true Messiah who stands as a counterhero to the rebel messianic pretenders and who figures the contemporary experiences of Mark's community. Both Judean rebels and Roman ideologues appropriated the historical precedent of significant national heroes as part of their ideological strategies during and after the war. Likewise, we suggest, Mark mobilizes traditions of Davidic kingship as an act of resistance. Just as the authors of national hero romances reconfigure their inherited legends in creative response to the context of empire, so too Mark gives his kingship traditions some ironic transformations from the prologue to the passion narrative. Revolutionary nationalism is thereby subtly critiqued by Mark, while the political status of Israel is reconfigured in ways that prompt us

---

6. Marius Reiser, "Der Alexanderroman und das Markusevanelium," in *Markus-Philologie*, ed. Hubert Cancik (Tübingen: Mohr Siebeck, 1984), 131–64; Reiser, *Syntax and Stil des Markusevangeliums im Licht der hellenistichen Volksliteratur* (Tübingen: Mohr Siebeck, 1984); Mary Ann Tolbert, *Sowing the Gospel: Mark's World in Literary-Historical Perspective* (Minneapolis: Fortress, 1989), esp. 55–79; Lawrence Wills, *The Quest for the Historical Gospel: Mark, John, and the Origins of the Gospel Genre* (London: Routledge, 1997), 12, 16; Michael Vines, *The Problem of Markan Genre: The Gospel of Mark and the Jewish Novel* (Atlanta: Society of Biblical Literature, 2002), 14, 144; and Christine Thomas, *The Acts of Peter, Gospel Literature, and the Ancient Novel* (Oxford: Oxford University Press, 2003).

7. See, e.g., Joel Marcus, *Mark 1–8: A New Translation with Introduction and Commentary*, AB 27 (New York: Doubleday, 2000), 25–39.

to hold on to the concept of the "nation" used in the work of Braun and Jameson, but precisely as a form of collective identity to be further interrogated and unsettled. If the nation is an unstable construct, as postcolonial theorists have argued, then literary characters that stand in for the nation may be no less so; the same literary dynamics that set in motion the process of identification between literary character and social collective simultaneously unsettle any confidence in an achieved identity for either the hero or his people. Jameson himself suggests that "the allegorical spirit is profoundly discontinuous, a matter of breaks and heterogeneities, of the multiple polysemia of the dream rather than the homogeneous representation of the symbol."[8]

Drawing from Jameson's hints as well as from more recent postcolonial theory, what follows is a reading of the Markan prologue, where Jesus is first identified as a messianic national hero. Our reading will attend precisely to moments where the dynamics of literary characterization itself produce discontinuity and heterogeneity in the construction of Jesus as both a literary character and a figure for collective identity. We suggest that the very construct of a national hero is unsettled by virtue of its reliance on literary representation within narrative frameworks. Precisely because the hero is a literary character, a narrative figure, a discursive figuration, he may in fact be no hero at all—contrary to the enabling assumptions of many approaches to Mark's narrative.

To be a national hero, an icon of social identity, Jesus must somehow stand in for the people of God (as Mark imagines them), and the reader (as an imagined member of that people) must be able to identify with him. Many types of modern biblical scholarship—redaction and postcolonial approaches, for example—posit (usually in vastly different ways) some sort of connection between the gospel's depiction of Jesus and the (historical reconstruction of) the gospel's audience and context. Political readings in particular, such as Richard Horsley's recent work,[9] risk reducing the gospel to a transparent representation of Mark's culture and community. Ignored on this approach are the specifically aesthetic dimensions of representation, particularly the way language works to both enable and constrain characters. As we will try to show, characters in Mark, especially Jesus, are

---

8. Jameson, "Third-World Literature," 73.

9. See, e.g., Richard A. Horsley, *Hearing the Whole Story: The Politics of Plot in Mark's Gospel* (Louisville: Westminster John Knox, 2001); Horsley, *Jesus and Empire: The Kingdom of God and the New World Disorder* (Minneapolis: Fortress, 2003).

not clear reflections of a social movement in the recent past; nor are they simply figures for the situation of a social group and that group's imagined identity in Mark's present. As narrative constructs, national heroes like Jesus stand at the intersection of political and literary modes of representation, modes that intersect dialectically, productively, and problematically.

Narrative critical readings of Mark's Gospel, too, often argue that the (ideal) reader closely identifies with the character of Jesus. Frequently it is argued that the reader's point of view is aligned with the perspective of both the narrator and God, establishing a firm evaluative viewpoint of Jesus. By focusing exclusively on the mechanics of narratives, however, literary readings, such as the work of David Rhoads,[10] risk abstracting the gospel from any historical context. From the perspective of this false transcendence, characters like Jesus risk being stripped of the political ideologies through which they are constructed. Literary characters like Mark's Jesus, we stress, are unavoidably political constructs precisely because narrative language is always bound up with, thought not reducible to, the ideological struggles of a particular historical moment.

Positioning ourselves within the space of these equally but differently reductive interpretive moves, we are interested precisely in the literary dimension of Mark's politics. Especially interesting to us is the way the narrative dynamics of characterization problematize any unambiguous notion of Mark's political stance, while at the same time refusing any apolitical reading. Political and literary orders of representation come together in Mark's Gospel, but they do not easily cooperate. Throughout the prologue, Jesus is interpellated into the urgent hope of contemporary messianic ideology. To be interpellated, as Marxist critic Louis Althusser famously described the process,[11] is to be pulled into a larger structure of social meaning through an act of language, in this case an act of naming, that surreptitiously determines the self-understanding of the one so addressed. Jesus's appellation as God's Son then is the consequence of his interpellation by a messianic ideology, by which he is also transformed from an individual peasant at the Jordan into a national subject.

---

10. See, e.g., David Rhoads, Joanna Dewey, and Donald Michie, *Mark as Story: An Introduction to the Narrative of a Gospel*, 2nd ed. (Minneapolis: Fortress, 1999).

11. Louis Althusser, "Ideology and Ideological State Apparatuses," in *Lenin and Philosophy and Other Essays*, trans. Ben Brewster (New York: Monthly Review Press, 1971), 121–76.

Yet the ideological construction of Mark's Jesus as a political subject, which takes place through language, is also the construction of a literary character. The status of Mark's Jesus as a literary character, we suggest, at once enables and complicates his status as a political subject because narratives as such lack the power to be representative—politically or aesthetically. Writes Gérard Genette, "A narrative can only *inform*—that is, transmit meanings. Narrative does not 'represent' a (real or fictive) story, it *recounts* it—that is, it signifies it by means of language."[12] Put simply, narrative is not transcription; it is διήγεσις. "Whether fiction or history, narrative is a discourse; with language, one can produce only discourse."[13]

Like all literary heroes, then, Jesus is first of all an *object* of the narrative: he is apprehended always and only from within the language of the text; he is altogether incapable of escaping the discursive plot in and through which he is conscripted. As narrative theorist Michael Roemer contends, since stories are always already completed before they begin and thus are told only in retrospect, the characters therein are never really free. Plot is an exterior aspect, "a manifestation of 'forces' that are beyond the reach of the figures."[14] Characters enter a plot that is already in play before their arrival and that continues once they are gone. Although heroes may appear to overcome and escape the challenges they face in the story, they never escape the plot itself. Constrained by the narrative, a literary character like Mark's Jesus may lack the ability to be politically representative. Whereas a national hero must function in a mimetic fashion, there may be in fact no imitation in narrative (i.e., not in the classical sense) because narrative is an act of language. Consequently, Mark's Jesus may lack the subjectivity and agency necessary to function as a true representative. Taken together, these points strongly suggest that the reader's identification with Mark's Jesus is far from unproblematic, as our review of the gospel prologue will highlight.

---

12. Gérard Genette, *Narrative Discourse Revisited*, trans. Jane E. Lewin (Ithaca, NY: Cornell University Press, 1988), 42–43.

13. Ibid., 101.

14. Michael Roemer, *Telling Stories: Postmodernism and the Invalidation of Traditional Narrative* (Lanham, MD: Rowman & Littlefield, 1995), 42.

The Markan Prologue

Mark 1:1–15, which "is essential as a basis for the entire narrative [of Mark]," according to Stephen Smith,[15] should lay the necessary groundwork for establishing Jesus as the expected and longed-for Messiah, that is, the representative hero. However, when we look closely, we find that the passage instead confronts us with a series of knots, perplexities, and entanglements that have as their cumulative effect the destabilization of the very thing they seek to construct: namely, a (purposeful) beginning that qualifies a narratively figured character as a representative stand-in, a delegate, an envoy. The narrator's effort to establish the narrative by weaving it into historical and theological time is indicative of Mark's desire to imitate and re-present an actual reality, to connect literary and political forms of representation. Mark aims to begin the story in medias res so as to suggest that the "imagined community" founded by Jesus does not come into being ex nihilo. Mark asserts that *this* Messiah and *this* community *authentically* lay claim to the myths of Israel's origins. Later, when the Markan Jesus warns his disciples about the deceptive claims made by pseudo-messiahs, who may in fact have been Judean rebel leaders, the urgency of this narrative move becomes even more apparent. Since this pericope functions to ground the story that follows, the instability inherent in the initial characterization of Jesus becomes even more troublesome for reading Mark's messiah as a political allegory.

The text opens with an ambiguous beginning: "the beginning of the gospel" (RSV). Commentators have long recognized the interpretive uncertainty here: Does the opening phrase signify the narrative itself or its content? What interests us is the way in which the two possibilities overlap, each conditioning, determining, and qualifying the other. By making the narrative simultaneously both a report about and the message of Jesus, the narrator takes the first step toward eliminating the distance between the narrative and the act of narration. By doing so, he draws attention away from the narrator's presence. The political implications of the term *gospel*—originally meaning "good news of victory from the battlefield"—lend immediate support to our reading of the text as a national hero allegory. Writing into the events of the Judean revolt,

---

15. Stephen H. Smith, *A Lion with Wings: A Narrative-Critical Approach to Mark's Gospel* (Sheffield: Sheffield Academic, 1996), 96. See also Eugene Boring, "Mark 1:1–15 and the Beginning of the Gospel," *Semeia* 52 (1990): 451–71.

Mark usurps the primary sense of *gospel* and gives it a paradoxical and nearly parodic twist throughout his narrative: the good news recounts an alternative way of the Lord that unfolds as nothing less than the way of a Roman cross taken up by Jesus of Nazareth, herald of the "empire of God" (1:15; 10:32–34). In sum, the gospel of Jesus Christ is that the victory of the empire of God comes through the willed vulnerability of Jesus, and Mark anticipates that the discourse of this paradoxical gospel will exceed the frame of his story and even rival the scope of Roman dominion as it reaches "all the nations of the world" (13:10). Jesus here is at once the speaking subject of an anti-imperial discourse as well as the linguistic object spoken into being by a discursive narrative. Identifying with this national hero, it would seem, means being drawn to a figure whose agency is complicated and compromised by the unsettling intersection of political and literary orders.

In 1:1, the narrator continues the introduction, naming Jesus as "Christ, the Son of God." Roland Barthes equates the "process of nomination" with the act of reading itself: "To read is to struggle to name, to subject the sentences of a text to a semantic transformation."[16] He describes the transformation as erratic: "it consists of hesitating among several names."[17] Here Jesus himself is read and doubly named by the narrator prior to his actual introduction: the one from Nazareth of Galilee who comes with many to be baptized by John already has been transformed into an icon of Israel's restoration, the Messiah. With the textual apparatus in the Greek Testament itself bearing witness, this act of naming of Jesus in fact hesitates between two names. The tradition itself seems reluctant to nominate Jesus as the Son of God, though it also seems to find a single name, connected to a singular people, to be insufficient: "Son of God" itself may signify both Israel's divinely appointed king and more broadly Greek traditions of divinized heroes.

By being named as the Messiah, Jesus is also already distinguished from those whom he would lead and represent to the world. Formally, this distance is marked by the narration of a separate arrival of Jesus at the Jordan River. Like "the whole of Judean countryside and all of the people of Jerusalem" (1:5), Jesus goes to be baptized by John (1:9), though his proleptic nomination sets him apart as their (as yet unrecognized) leader,

---

16. Roland Barthes, *S/Z: An Essay*, trans. Richard Miller (New York: Hill & Wang, 1974), 92.

17. Ibid.

the "more powerful" one (1:7) anticipated by John's work of baptism and the words of prophecy.

Despite being little more than a hint at this point in the text, the presence of crowds throughout the narrative highlights some of the tension produced by the attempt to construct and represent a collective identity. Always depicted *only* as an undifferentiated group, the crowds dramatize the ambivalence surrounding the definition of any identity by shifting throughout the narrative between being attracted to and repulsed by Jesus as the embodiment of their collective desire. Beginning with the scene at the Jordan, then, we may see the paradox at the intersection of political and literary or discursive forms of representation: to represent others, Jesus must be both typical and distinct, both from the people and removed from them.

At his baptism Jesus is (again) constructed through language, summoned by a divine speech-act that simultaneously produces him as a national subject, a messianic hero, and as a literary object, a character who is directed by a providentially plotted story. Doubling the initial naming made by the narrator, "a voice from heaven" hails Jesus as the beloved Son. With this imagery Mark arguably evokes the nationalist discourse of Judean rebels who lay claim to David's dynastic legacy; he may also subtly underline the strategic reversal of that discourse by anticipating victory precisely through the sacrificial vulnerability of God's "beloved." As noted above, Jesus is addressed by *the* figure of divine authority and interpellated into the urgent hope of contemporary messianic ideology. Jesus's appellation as "Son of God" follows from his interpellation by a messianic ideology, by which he is also translated into a national subject.

With the voice from heaven comes the Spirit, and the Spirit violently drives Jesus into the wilderness in a move that foreshadows so many instances in the gospel where individual autonomy and agency are compromised, especially by demonic possession. Together the episode of the baptism and the temptation prefigure, in a paradoxical fashion, the manner in which Jesus has been drawn into a messianic ideology and embodies its material existence in his nomination. Violently cast out into the wilderness, Jesus here begins his service to the empire of God in a manner that seems to undermine his capacity to act. This effect is not only demonstrated by the Spirit's unimpeded control of Jesus but also reinforced by the narrative itself with repeated notices that everything that happens to Jesus happens "as it is written."

The importance of this scene for our argument should not be missed because it prefigures the subjugation of characters to their narration, anticipating Roemer's argument. As a literary character, Jesus lacks the freedom necessary to function seamlessly as the foundation of a group identity. The forces he stands against within the framework of the plot are beyond his reach as a narrative figure. He enters a plot that is already in play before his arrival and that continues once he is gone. Now, lest we slip into the maelstrom of an age-old debate over whether character is subordinate to plot or vice versa, we should substitute *narrative* for Roemer's notion of *plot*. Only in this way does Roemer's analogy hold up, namely, that narrative itself (i.e., rather than *stories*) reflects the human condition. "We know our control is tenuous at best," writes Roemer, "and that, despite all progress, we remain beholden for our existence to processes and occurrences we cannot command."[18]

Given how the Markan text has already interpellated Jesus, positioning him as a national hero in service to a messianic ideology, this scene is not simply mimetic (i.e., representative) of reality (e.g., of Jesus's real baptism). Nor is it a simple typology according to which Jesus's experience stands in a one-to-one correspondence with the experience of Israelite prophets of the past. Rather, the *form* of the scene itself mimics the specific social conditions of empire and resistance. As a literary character and a colonial subject, Jesus is conscripted, written into a subject position that complicates his agency: his opposition to Rome is channeled through the vector of national ideology; he is virtually pressed into the service of the coming empire of God by the divine Spirit; and providence itself has predetermined he will give his life for that empire. Nearly possessed by the Spirit, Jesus remains possessed by the plot. Neither simply a national hero nor a figure for collective identity, as Mark's Messiah Jesus also figures the narrative production of the national subject itself.

The Markan Passion Sequence

Betrayal and Arrest

The literary construction of Mark's Jesus as a national subject reaches new levels of intensity in the passion narrative, where the collective import of the character's agency is both compromised and ironically reaffirmed as the plot reaches its inexorable conclusion in the death of the would-be libera-

---

18. Roemer, *Telling Stories*, 47.

tor (14:1–15:39).[19] Yet again, his subjectivity is both predetermined by the politics of empire, reflected above all in his Roman crucifixion, and prefigured by the power of narrative discourse, reflected now in the increasing, and increasingly self-conscious, allusions to "Scripture" (γραφα, "as it is written"). Earlier, for example, the Markan Jesus proclaimed that he would be put to death by his enemies (8:31; 9:31; 10:32b–34), despite the fact that he was God's Messiah, by stressing in an abstract way the divine necessity of what *must* happen to him. Now, at his final meal and a final moment of prayer before his arrest, he speaks knowingly of the providential power of written discourse.

"The Son of Man will go just as it is written of him" (14:21), he says in the context of announcing his forthcoming betrayal by one of his own. The announcement itself draws attention to the harsh constraints language imposes on human agency by underlining both the divine inevitability and moral culpability of Judas's actions: "but woe to that one by whom the Son of Man is betrayed! It would have been better for that one not to have been born" (14:21; see Pss 41:10, 55:10–11).[20] As Judas approaches with the arresting party a short while later, the Markan Jesus describes his own fate in strikingly similar terms that, again, combine an act of agency with an awareness of how Scripture circumscribes that the autonomy of that act. "Get up, let us be going" (14:42), he says as he goes to meet the arresting party, only to conclude with a rebuke as he surrenders: "Day after day I was with you in the temple teaching, and you did not arrest me. But let the scriptures be fulfilled" (14:49). Tellingly, these moments of self-conscious reference to Scripture, which present a messianic subject nearly powerless to bring messianic salvation on his own terms, bookend perhaps the most intense scene of conflicted subjectivity in the gospel, a moment constructed with numerous references to scriptural discourse, the prayer in

---

19. On irony, see Jeremy Camery-Hoggatt, *Irony in Mark's Gospel: Text and Subtext* (Cambridge: Cambridge University Press, 1992). On Jesus as a would-be liberator executed by agents of and collaborators with Roman rule, see Horsley, *Hearing the Whole Story*, 109–20.

20. John Donahue and Daniel Harrington (*The Gospel of Mark*, SP 2 [Collegeville, MN: Liturgical Press, 2002], 394) note the references to the Psalms, which add to the sense of tragedy they see here. On complex characterization of Judas as a moral subject in the canonical gospels, see now Holly J. Carey, "Judas Iscariot: The Betrayer of Jesus," in *Jesus among Friends and Enemies: A Historical and Literary Introduction to Jesus in the Gospels*, ed. Chris Keith and Larry Hurtado (Grand Rapids: Baker Academic, 2011), 249–68.

Gethsemane: "Abba, Father, for you all things are possible; remove this cup from me; yet, not what I want, but what you want."[21]

Jesus before the Council

As the arresting party takes the Markan Jesus to the high priest and the hastily assembled council of "all the chief priests, the elders, and the scribes," the image of a national hero wholly contained by the preordained power of others continues but does not last. In fact, as the passion narrative becomes layered in verbal and dramatic ironies, perhaps the most ironic aspect is the construction of Jesus as the divinely chosen messianic leader not despite but because of his increasingly eroded messianic agency.[22] Paradoxically, the national subject ultimately will be produced by the very forces that would oppose and constrain him, in this case the "chief priests and the whole council" who "were looking for testimony against Jesus to put him to death" (14:55). Whether or not this trial accurately reflects the legal procedures of the historical Sanhedrin in the first century CE, the scene is, as commentators routinely note,[23] a travesty of justice, since the council is looking for a predetermined conclusion, a certain framing of the subject as a real threat to the nation he ostensibly claims to represent. So it is with deep irony that the narrative depicts the council of the most important and powerful men of the nation. Not only do they fear a peasant preacher as a threat to their well-established authority, but also they seem nearly powerless to condemn him despite being ruthlessly corrupt.

Indeed, they are only able to render a verdict when Jesus incriminates himself (14:60–64), an act filled with dramatic irony: the supersecret Son of God finally reveals the truth about himself, only to be doubted by those

---

21. On the use of the Psalms here, see Donahue and Harrington, *Gospel of Mark*, 406–13. For a comparative reading of the construction of subjectivity in Mark's passion narrative and similar scenes in the ancient romance, see Eric Thurman, "Novel Men: Masculinity and Empire in Mark's Gospel and Xenophon's An Ephesian Tale," in *Mapping Gender in Ancient Religious Discourses*, ed. Todd Penner and Caroline Vander Stichele (Leiden: Brill, 2007), 185–230.

22. For another reading of irony in this scene, see now Tom Shepherd, "The Irony of Power in the Trial of Jesus and the Denial by Peter—Mark 14:53–72," in *The Trial and Death of Jesus: Essays on the Passion Narrative of Mark*, ed. Geert van Oyen and Tom Shepherd (Leuven: Peeters, 2006), 229–45.

23. See, e.g., Donahue and Harrington, *Gospel of Mark*, 419–29.

who should know better.²⁴ Here, again, the text dramatizes the link between written discourse and subjectivity, only this time in a new way, as a means of enabling, not simply compromising, heroic agency. Silent during the false testimonies made against him, Jesus answers the one direct question about his identity as "the Messiah, the Son of the Blessed." "I am," he says, "and you will see the Son of Man seated at the right hand of the Power, and 'coming with the clouds of heaven'" (14:62). Weaving together a messianic psalm (Ps 110:1) and an apocalyptic vision (Dan 7:13), Jesus here is not merely subjected to scriptural models; he is being actively constructed by the narrator as one constructing his identity out of written discourse, casting himself as the exalted national hero who (someday) will subjugate his enemies as they have subjugated him. The power of Scripture is thus revealed to be both productive and destructive at the same time.²⁵

Jesus before Pilate

Pilate's exchange with Jesus in Mark 15:2–5 further illustrates the precariousness and instability of Jesus's agency. Already bound, Jesus is led away and handed over to Pilate by those seeking confirmation of their judgment, thereby obligating Pilate to the course of action they wanted but were powerless to enforce. It reflects, therefore, an effort on the part of characters to control what they ultimately cannot: the very discourse that conscripts them.

Pilate asks whether Jesus is "the king of the Jews," and Jesus answers cryptically, Σὺ λέγεις (15:2), which is commonly translated "You say so." Jonathan Schwiebert points out that narrative-critical interpretations of this passage have either read Jesus's words in a manner that suggests he could have just as well said nothing at all or else in a way that actually undermines Mark's plot and his characterization of Jesus. Schwiebert, therefore, proposes that we take the statement as a question rather than an assertion.²⁶ The respective statements of Pilate and Jesus share syntactical

---

24. Ibid., 423, 428.
25. On the use of the Hebrew Scriptures in Mark's passion narrative, see Mark Goodacre, "Scripturalization in Mark's Crucifixion Narrative," 33–47, and Jocelyn McWhirter, "Messianic Exegesis in Mark's Passion Narrative," 69–97, both in Oyen and Shepherd, *Trial and Death of Jesus*.
26. Jonathan D. Schwiebert, "Jesus' Question to Pilate in Mark 15:2," *JBL* 136 (2017): 937–47.

parallels; Jesus's reply is introduced with the formula Mark typically uses with questions; and, most significantly for the purposes of this chapter, Jesus's responding to Pilate's question with one of his own is consistent with the strategy Mark assigns the character of Jesus throughout the narrative and especially in these final chapters, wherein Jesus uses questions, silence, and ambiguity to escape entrapment (see, e.g., 11:27–33; 12:13–17; 14:55–61).[27] Reading Jesus's response as a question makes explicit what has been implicit all along: Jesus's identity and function as a national hero are not grounded in any essence or assertion but inextricably interwoven in the fibers of their discursive construction and forever beholden to the reader's response (see 8:27, 29).

Pilate does not recognize or accept Jesus's reply as an answer, and so, following an outburst of accusations from the chief priests, "Pilate asked him again, 'Have you no answer?'" (15:3–4). But this time he is met with outright silence; the narrator scripts no further dialogue for his protagonist. Jesus is both silent and silenced, and the result is speechlessness on the part of Pilate himself (15:5). After the charade of a prisoner's release, wherein Jesus stands passively by while he is put on display to the crowds, Jesus is "handed over" (15:15) with no further word.

Mockery, Crucifixion, and Death

As he is led before an entire cohort of Rome's finest, Jesus's verbal predictions of suffering and death turn into narrative discourse. Consequently, his descent into abject subjectivity is measured by the number of times he is represented as the passive object of verbs of violence and abuse (see, e.g., Mark 15:16–20, 24–25, 29, 31, 32). The intense mockery is intended to deny his agency as a liberator who, alone, could lead the nation back to political autonomy and moral authority as a messianic ruler. Yet there is a deep irony in the soldiers' ascription to him of a title and a role ("Hail, King of the Jews!") that he never asserted for himself but was instead assigned to him by another figure with the power to name and hence control subjects, namely, God, who represents the implied author's own point of view and power to conjure reality with words. Indeed, a focus on the interrelationship between language and power in narrative reveals uncomfortable

---

27. Schwiebert notes the exception to the pattern in 14:62 but argues that the terms of both the question and Jesus's reply are in line with reliable statements of Jesus's identity (that is, as God's Son) made elsewhere in the gospel (1:1, 11; 9:7; 12:6).

analogies between divine and imperial characters in this and other ancient narratives, as postcolonial interpretations have taught us.[28]

When the Roman soldiers finish abusing Mark's hero, we learn that "they crucified him, and divided his clothes among them, casting lots to decide what each should take" (15:24). Mysteriously, and mercifully, the excruciating details of crucifixion are left unwritten, but its effects are subtly symbolized well enough by the desire to divide up Jesus's clothes. The spectacle of crucifixion in Roman society displayed for all to see the shattering of the criminalized subject as a capital penalty for transgressing Roman authority. To the extent that his dress marks him as a man and a Jew, the division of Jesus's clothes by Roman soldiers represents the division of his social identity by the Roman colonial administration. Yet this scripted scene of Jesus being denuded of any subjectivity at all is, ironically, also the scene in which a new subjectivity emerges from the play of literary discourse, especially the discourse of Scripture. Verbal and dramatic irony reach the height of their intensity with Pilate's inscription of the charge against Jesus ("King of the Jews") and with the derisive taunts of his enemies and antagonists ("Let the Messiah, the King of Israel, come down from the cross now, so that we may see and believe").[29]

What they say about Jesus is true, though they are scripted precisely so that they cannot understand how. Intended to mock his pretensions, the remarks instead unwittingly gesture to his status as a national hero—king and Messiah—and to the paradoxical process by which the whole narrative has made him into such: "He saved others; he cannot save himself." Indeed, this scene is almost a metaphor for how any subjectivity, any active sense of the self, is only gained through the process of being subjected to discourse, which in this case especially includes the discourse of Scripture, whether it be that of the Hebrew Bible or of Mark's own gospel.[30]

---

28. See Mary Rose D'Angelo, "Abba and 'Father': Imperial Ideology and the Jesus Traditions," *JBL* 111 (1992): 611–30; Tat-Siong Liew, *The Politics of Parouisa: Reading Mark Inter(Con)textually* (Leiden: Brill, 1999), 103–32; Stephen D. Moore, *Empire and Apocalypse: Postcolonialism and the New Testament* (Sheffield: Sheffield Phoenix, 2006), 24–44.

29. See also Thurman, "Novel Men," 218–25.

30. Horsley, *Hearing the Whole Story*, 231–53, questions the legitimacy of a "messianic" reading of the Hebrew Scriptures by the evangelist, in part on the grounds that the evangelist is not primarily a literary interpreter of Scripture at all but rather a performer of a popular and largely oral tradition of Israelite history and heroes. Among other problems, however, this view runs against the everyday sense of γραφαί as "writ-

Jesus's final words—"My God, my God, why have you forsaken me?"—not only explicitly quote Ps 22:1 but implicitly signal how threads from the Psalms and other Hebrew Scriptures have been artfully woven together to stage this, the climatic scene in Mark's narrative.[31] Importantly, they do so by scripting the behavior and subjectivity of Jesus himself as he speaks. Misunderstood by some of the bystanders, he is not misunderstood by the reader, who by now knows enough to read between the lines of the text and to hear not the voice of one waiting to be saved or of one who has given up in defeat before his enemies but of the one whose paradoxical victory in defeat produces that foreordained subject scripted from the beginning of the narrative to which the reader has also submitted: "The beginning of the good news of Jesus Christ, the Son of God" (Mark 1:1).

Conclusion

Our reading of Mark's narrative has attempted to highlight that the linguistic construction of Jesus as Israel's Messiah is at once an aesthetic and ideological representation. Literary and political orders of representation are brought together in the figure of the national hero, but in a manner far more complex than is usually assumed, a manner that exceeds the control of an author. The very nature of the medium called on to construct the hero (i.e., narrative) leaves the collective identity for which he stands in a precarious position, one that is always uncertain, unsettled, and unstable precisely because it is built on a literary figure.

---

ings" that seems assumed and nowhere explicitly challenged in the narrative. It is our contention that, whatever his attitude toward a literate, elite culture might be, the evangelist himself participates in that culture to a greater extent than Horsley allows.

31. Again, see the essays by Goodacre and McWhirter in Oyen and Shepherd, *Trial and Death of Jesus*.

Narrative Pathology or Strategy for Making Present and Authorization? Metalepsis in the Gospels

Ute E. Eisen
Translated by Sara R. Johnson
Dedicated to Peter Lampe, on his sixtieth birthday

A first reading of *The Life and Opinions of Tristram Shandy, Gentleman*, by Laurence Sterne, from the middle of the eighteenth century, presents curious features. For instance, numbered chapters appear in muddled order, the typography contains spidery lines or omissions in the form of long asterisks, and ultimately the reader is asked to close the window of the protagonist, Mister Shandy, and put him to bed. Such narrative phenomena surprise, irritate, or even shock us. Should we regard them as narrative pathology or narrative strategy? If strategy, what are the forms, implications, and effects of it? And does this strategy occur in early Christian literature?

Until 1972 the phenomenon had not yet been given a precise name in the scholarly literature.[1] This was first achieved by Gérard Genette, who called it "métalepse narrative" and thus interpreted a concept from classical rhetoric in an original fashion.[2] He defines metalepsis as "any intrusion by the extradiegetic narrator into the diegetic universe (or by

---

This paper was originally submitted in German, was translated by me (SRJ) at Eisen's request, and was subsequently revised in English by Eisen for additional clarity in communicating her ideas.

1. For a survey of the literature and a terminological guide, see Sonja Klimek, *Paradoxes Erzählen: Die Metalepse in der phantastischen Literatur* (Paderborn: Mentis, 2010), 17–72.

2. On the conceptual history of metalepsis see Ruurd Nauta, "The Concept of 'Metalepsis': From Rhetoric to the Theory of Allusion and to Narratology," in *Über die*

diegetic characters into a metadiegetic universe), etc., or the inverse."³ Genette emphasizes that this involves a paradoxical contamination between the level of narration and the level of story, which are separated by "a shifting but sacred frontier between two worlds, the world in which one tells, the world of which one tells." ⁴ In other words a transgression of borders takes place, and interventions occur, sometimes from top to bottom (top down) and sometimes from bottom to top (bottom up). This "produces an effect of strangeness that is either comical … or fantastic."⁵ Already Jorge Luis Borges, who termed this narrative strategy "reflections" (*Spiegelungen*), had drawn far-reaching conclusions: "Such reflections suggest that if the figures of a fiction can also be readers and spectators, we, their readers and viewers, might be fictitious."⁶

Such conclusions resonate strikingly in an age of postmodern and virtual worlds. It is increasingly difficult to avoid the suspicion that one is "just a figure in a gigantic media conspiracy."⁷ While Genette in his earlier work still offers a quite simple definition of metalepsis, this changes in his essay *Métalepse: De la figure à la fiction* (2004).⁸ Here he expands his study of metalepsis beyond narrative texts to examine the ways it is employed in paintings, theater, film, and television. A good example from the art world is the painting *Escapando de la crítica* (1874) by Spanish artist Pere Borrell del Caso. It is a late example, following the pattern of the Dutch portraits of the seventeenth century, in which the figure in the painting

---

Grenze: Metalepse in Text- und Bildmedien des Altertums, ed. Ute E. Eisen and Peter von Möllendorff (Berlin: de Gruyter, 2013), 469–82.

3. Gérard Genette, *Narrative Discourse: An Essay in Method*, trans. Jane E. Lewin (Ithaca, NY: Cornell University Press, 1980), 234–35.

4. Ibid., 236.

5. Ibid., 235.

6. "Solche Spiegelungen legen die Vermutung nahe, daß, sofern die Figuren einer Fiktion auch Leser und Zuschauer sein können, wir, ihre Leser und Zuschauer, fiktiv sein könnten." Jorge Luis Borges, "Befragungen," in *Gesammelte Werke*, trans. Karl August Horst, vol. 5.2 (Munich: Hanser, 1981), 57. Unless otherwise specified, all translations of quotations from German are by Sara R. Johnson.

7. "Nur eine Figur in einer gigantischen medialen Verschwörung zu sein." Achim Hölter, "Das Eigenleben der Figuren: Eine radikale Konsequenz der neueren Metafiktion," in *Komparatistik: Jahrbuch der Deutschen Gesellschaft für Allgemeine und Vergleichende Literaturwissenschaft 2007*, ed. Christiane Dahms (Heidelberg: Synchron, 2008), 42.

8. Gérard Genette, *Métalepse: De la figure à la fiction* (Paris: Editions du Seuil, 2004).

steps over the painted frame and thus crosses the boundary into the world of the observer.[9] Genette characterizes such phenomena as transgressions that defy logic. He ultimately applies them to the grammatical subject of narratives. Every narrative that presents itself as an "I-narrative" is already regarded by him as a prime candidate for metalepsis. Above all, he now incorporates the phenomenon of feedback between extratextual reality and the textual world. Examples of this are when actors are so closely identified with the roles they have played that they are no longer accepted by their audience in any other role, or when spectators accost an actor in the street and even insult him or her because she or he embodies a role that has incurred their disgust. These are far-reaching indications of the powerful effect of fiction, and they demonstrate how strikingly fictions affect human perception.

The phenomenon of narrative metalepsis is not confined to modern literature; even in Genette one finds occasional glimpses from the literature of antiquity. Irene de Jong published a groundbreaking initial investigation of the subject in 2009.[10] In 2011, at an international conference on narrative metalepsis in ancient discourse, examples from ancient literature and art were brought together: Akkadian, Egyptian, Hebrew, and rabbinic literature; the art of the archaic Greek world; pagan Greek literature from the classical, Hellenistic, and Roman imperial periods; and Roman historiographical literature as well as early Christian literature.[11] The conference demonstrated that the phenomenon is so widespread and pervasive that it suggests the existence of fundamental metaleptic sensitivities in ancient literature. Ute E. Eisen and Peter von Möllendorff give an elementary definition of the phenomenon: "Metalepsis is a vertically oriented transgression and interaction of entities of different levels of representation in a work of art."[12]

---

9. For more examples of metalepsis in other works of art, see Klimek, *Paradoxes Erzählen*, 73–116.

10. Irene de Jong, "Metalepsis in Ancient Greek Literature," in *Narratology and Interpretation: The Content of Narrative Form in Ancient Literature*, ed. Jonas Grethlein and Antonios Rengakos (Berlin: de Gruyter, 2009), 87–115.

11. The conference took place February 4–5, 2011, at the Justus-Liebig-Universität Gießen in Germany. See the collected papers published by Eisen and von Möllendorff, *Über die Grenze*.

12. "Die Metalepse ist eine vertikal gerichtete Grenzüberschreitung und Interaktion von Instanzen differenter Ebenen der Darstellung im Kunstwerk." Eisen and von Möllendorff, "Zur Einführung," in Eisen and von Möllendorff, *Über die Grenze*, 1;

Narrative metalepses are met in different forms and intensities, concern different aspects, and generate different effects:

(1) The most direct manifestation of metalepsis is the apostrophe,[13] meaning a direct address that either takes place from the extradiegetic narrator top down or (in the case of the second form, see below) from a character bottom up.

(2) The second form of apostrophe, from a diegetic character bottom up, occurs when "characters announce the text in the text," which has metatextual implications.[14]

In modern literature these two forms of metalepsis destabilize the realism of the story, while in ancient literature the reverse can be observed: it enforces the status and authority of the speaker (narrator or character). The effect is that "for an instant, the distinction between the—temporal and spatial—universes of the narrator and the narrated world collapses,"[15] and the impression of simultaneity, immediacy, and authenticity arises. Crucial moments of story and discourse can be highlighted by this metaleptic strategy.

(3) A less direct and more widely used form is the blending of narrative voices and worlds.[16] In the case of blending narrative voices, the speech has double relevance, that is, a metaleptic process of blending together the speech of a character and the narrator. It is ambiguous and leads to a subtle blending of narrative worlds.

It has the effect that the speech or performance of either a character or the narrator gains a subtle double relevance for both worlds, the world of the discourse and the story world. The effects are similar to those of the apostrophe but less obvious and more subtle.

(4) The intensity of narrative metalepsis can be navigated by loose end technique or fade-out, which we define as a metalepsis that is not marked

---

see also Eisen, "Metalepsis in the Gospel of John—Narration Situation and 'Beloved Disciple' in New Perspective," in Eisen and von Möllendorff, *Über die Grenze*, 318–21, and 320 for an illustration concerning the levels of representation.

13. For more information, see de Jong, "Metalepsis," 93–97; and Eisen and von Möllendorff, "Einführung," 5, with references to further contributions.

14. De Jong, "Metalepsis," 98–99; Eisen and von Möllendorff, "Einführung," 5.

15. De Jong, "Metalepsis," 96.

16. For more information, see de Jong, "Metalepsis," 99–106; and Eisen and von Möllendorff, "Einführung," 5.

with an endpoint.[17] This metaleptic technique provides for a sustained and intensified blending of narrative worlds.

(5) The intensity of metalepsis furthermore depends on duration and impact. Temporary metalepsis is traditionally called rhetorical, while on the other hand prolonged metalepsis with impact on the plot or the discourse is termed ontological metalepsis.[18] Whereas a rhetorical metalepsis only "opens a small window that allows a quick glance across levels,"[19] a window that closes after a few sentences, the ontological metalepsis shows the narrator physically present in the story or a character performing on the level of discourse.

(6) Metalepsis concerns inter- and metatextual as well as medial aspects, which are to be found in metaleptic strategies that, with narrative sophistication, reflect and simultaneously enact the textuality and the transmission of their own narratives.[20] Metaleptic functions mediate between textuality, orality, and autopsy, and enhance the authority and credibility of the narrator or a character.

(7) Concerning functional aspects and effects of metalepsis, it can be observed that in ancient literature metalepsis is intended not to disturb and destroy, as in modern literature, but rather to intensify the illusion of reality and contribute to mimetic stabilization.[21] Metaleptic interventions top down or bottom up as well as the blending of narrative voices evoke with greater or lesser intensity the impression of the immediacy or the simultaneity of the separated worlds. We want to term this as a strategy for

---

17. For loose end technique, see Siegmar Döpp, "Metalepsen als signifikante Elemente spätlateinischer Literatur," in *Über die Grenze*, ed. Eisen and von Möllendorff, 441. For fade-out, see De Jong, "Metalepsis," 106–13; see also Eisen and von Möllendorff, "Einführung," 6.

18. Marie-Laure Ryan, *Avatars of Story* (Minneapolis: University of Minnesota Press, 2006), 207; see also Eisen and von Möllendorff, "Einführung," 6.

19. Ryan, *Avatars*, 207.

20. See Eisen and von Möllendorff, "Einführung," 6–7.

21. For the functional aspects and effects of metalepsis, see ibid., 8. De Jong, "Metalepsis," 115, emphasizes that in ancient literature metalepsis is "for the most part serious (rather than comic) and … aimed at increasing the authority of the narrator and the realism of his narrative (rather than breaking the illusion)." See the collection of examples from different ancient literatures in the volume by Eisen and von Möllendorff, *Über die Grenze*. For a modern comparison, see the epic theater of Bertolt Brecht, where the act of calling attention to the stage setting makes it clear to the audience that they are watching a play.

making present (*Vergegenwärtigungsstrategie*). By this strategy the credibility and authenticity of the narrator or characters are stabilized, which in turn authorizes the whole narrative.

In what follows, examples of metaleptic strategies in early Christian literature that are found in the Gospel of Mark, in Luke-Acts, and in the Gospel of John will be examined and conclusions drawn.

Metalepsis in the Gospel of Mark

Metaleptic strategy can be detected at the beginning of the second chapter of the Gospel of Mark in the scene of the healing of the paralytic (Mark 2:1–12).[22] The reader is puzzled by the speech of the character Jesus (vv. 8–11). It is introduced by the formula (v. 5) "he said to the paralytic" (λέγει τῷ παραλυτικῷ) and followed by the statement "Child, your sins are forgiven" (τέκνον, ἀφίενταί σου αἱ ἁμαρτίαι; v. 5).[23] The words are repeated two more times in his reaction to the scribes' objection to his forgiving sins (vv. 9, 10). Jesus says (v. 9): "Which is easier, to say to the paralytic, 'Your sins are forgiven'" (τί ἐστιν εὐκοπώτερον, εἰπεῖν τῷ παραλυτικῷ· ἀφίενταί σου αἱ ἁμαρτίαι), and then says in his statement about the Son of Man followed by the repeated introduction formula from verse 5 in verse 10: "'But so that you may know that the Son of Man has authority on earth to forgive sins'—he said to the paralytic—" (ἵνα δὲ εἰδῆτε ὅτι ἐξουσίαν ἔχει ὁ υἱὸς τοῦ ἀνθρώπου ἀφιέναι ἁμαρτίας ἐπὶ τῆς γῆς—λέγει τῷ παραλυτικῷ). How can the sudden change of grammatical person in verse 10 be explained?

Rudolf Pesch appropriately observes in his commentary on Mark 2:10: "The narrator steps out of his distant role and speaks directly commenting through the mouth of Jesus before linking back through a repetition of verse 5 λέγει τῷ παραλυτικῷ (prepared in v. 9 εἰπεῖν τῷ παραλυτικῷ) to the miracle story, which now is used as a proof."[24] Despite this he offers form- and source-critical explanations: the autonomous miracle story (vv. 1–5, 11–12), he argues, was later enlarged by the debate about the forgiveness of sin and the Son of Man (vv. 6–10). Pesch supposes that the sudden use

---

22. David du Toit, "Entgrenzungen: Zu metaleptischen Strategien in der frühchristlichen Erzählliteratur," in *Über die Grenze*, ed. Eisen and von Möllendorff, 294–97.

23. Biblical translations follow, with small modifications, the NRSV.

24. Rudolf Pesch, *Einleitung und Kommentar zu Kap. 1,1–8,26*, vol. 1 of *Das Markusevangelium*, HThKNT 2.1 (Freiburg: Herder, 1980), 160.

of the phrase "Son of Man" is here intended as a christological title derived from later early-Christian tradition, reflecting Jesus's ministry from the perspective of death and resurrection.[25]

In the actual debate about reading the gospels as consistent narratives it is more appropriate to explain verse 10 in terms of narrative strategy. Narratalogically it can be analyzed as a blending of narrative voices and as speech with double relevance. Through metaleptic strategy, the speech about the Son of Man gains a programmatic function. It is introduced with "so that you may know," includes the affirmation "that the Son of Man has authority on earth to forgive sins," and continues with an abrupt change of the addressee: "he said to the paralytic." From a metaleptic point of view, the address in the second-person plural can be interpreted as an address with double relevance: the words are spoken by Jesus, but at the same time it can be interpreted as the narrator's speech. Through this narrative strategy of blurring the lines between intra- and extradiegetic narrative, the statement is doubly addressed and authorized. Theologically it is probably no coincidence that this strategy is introduced in the context of the first mention of the term "Son of Man," with its shocking christological implications, in this case his proclaimed authority to forgive sins, an authority traditionally attributed only to God. The narrator gives the reader, in the mouth of Jesus, instruction and orientation to understand Jesus's further enigmatic use of the term "Son of Man" in the third person throughout the gospel.[26] Moreover, the strategy has a conceptual significance: "The narrator uses the apparent break in syntax as a literary way of getting the reader's attention and thus draws attention to his lasting presence (as reader and interpreter) in the text.... In this way he prepares us for each instance in which, without comment, he exchanges the voice of narrator for the voice of the actor."[27]

A second example of metalepsis in the Gospel of Mark is the parenthetical address to the reader in the apocalyptic speech of Jesus (Mark

---

25. See ibid., 158–60.

26. The fourteen references to the "Son of Man" in the Gospel of Mark are all found in Jesus's mouth (Mark 2:10, 28; 8:31, 38; 9:9, 12, 31; 10:33–34, 45; 13:26; 14:62; 24:21, 41).

27. "Der Erzähler nutzt den scheinbaren Bruch in der Syntax als literarisches Aufmerksamkeitssignal und macht somit nachhaltig auf seine (die Lektüre steuernde und deutende) Präsenz im Text aufmerksam.... Er bereitet so jene Erzählerkommentare vor, in denen er ohne expliziten Hinweis die darstellende gegen eine kommentierende Stimme tauscht." Du Toit, "Entgrenzungen," 297.

13:14).²⁸ It is certainly the most prominent passage in the New Testament that can be classified as an apostrophe bottom up. The carefully staged scene depicts Jesus together with four of his disciples, Peter, James, John, and Andrew, on the Mount of Olives, and a simple question from Peter opens the way for Jesus's detailed reply, which also concludes the scene (Mark 13:3–37). Jesus's answer takes the form of an apocalyptic speech to his disciples. In passing, there occurs an apostrophe: "let the reader understand" (Mark 13:14). This passage has long posed a riddle for exegetical scholarship and invited source criticism. The intrusion has been interpreted as a holdover from an apocalyptic discourse, which was inadvertently left in place when the discourse was incorporated into the imagined speech of Jesus. It can more plausibly be interpreted as an instance of metalepsis. It is one of the few shocking instances of metalepsis in the New Testament, in that it brings the mediated nature of Jesus's speech directly before the readers' eyes. Readers know that they are not hearing Jesus's words directly from his own mouth but rather a speech transmitted through a narrator; but the conventional taboo on bringing direct attention to this fact is here broken. The diegetic Jesus shows himself to be conscious of the later written transmission of his words and speaks to the reader from the bottom up. This defies logic, because it awkwardly transgresses the seemingly sacred boundary between the diegetic and the extradiegetic world. Fictitious orality and factual writtenness abruptly collide in the way in which the speech is crafted and instruct the reader how to understand the speech as a whole. The repeated use of the imperative "beware" (βλέπετε, Mark 13:5, 9, 23, 33) now points to a blurring of the boundary between the two audiences (disciples and readers). Likewise, the traditional formula with which Jesus's speech and the scene conclude gains new depth: "And what I say to you I say to all: Keep awake" (γρηγορεῖτε, 13:37; also 13:35; 14:34, 37). These indications can be interpreted as a metaleptic loose-end technique within the speech of a dramatic character with which the scene ends (13:37).

What are the effects of such a metaleptic strategy? The words of the diegetic Jesus are *made present (vergegenwärtigt)* for the reader for a moment. The figural proclaiming of the text within the text²⁹ in the form of an apostrophe produces a sense that the narrated events and the actual experience of the reader are occurring simultaneously, and the gap

---

28. With Matt 24:15, Luke 21:20 omits the apostrophe.
29. De Jong, "Metalepsis," 98–99.

between past and present becomes fluid. Through this narrative strategy past and present blur together into a consecutive whole, and a sense of quasi-immediacy is generated.

Metalepsis in Luke-Acts

Luke-Acts is introduced by an explicit and self-aware I-narrator (Luke 1:1-4; Acts 1:1), distinct from the other canonical gospels.[30] He informs his no less explicit addressee, the "most excellent Theophilus," about his goals and the nature of his work, with the use of a narrative "I" in the prefaces to both books (Luke 1:4; Acts 1:1). The narrator himself remains anonymous, but he confidently places his work in the context of competitive literary production ("Since many have undertaken to set down an orderly account of the events that have been fulfilled among us," Luke 1:1) and makes the sources transparent ("just as they were handed on to us by those who from the beginning were eyewitnesses and servants of the word," Luke 1:2). Thus he emphasizes his way of investigating more carefully and in a more orderly manner ("after investigating everything carefully from the very first, to write an orderly account for you," Luke 1:3), in comparison with earlier narratives that are suggested to be less reliable. He establishes himself as a careful and reliable historian—albeit not an eyewitness. Finally, he formulates his theological goal, the proof of the truthfulness (ἀσφάλεια) of the doctrine, in which his addressee, Theophilus, was educated (Luke 1:4). Following this impressive opening statement, which seeks to guide the reader's understanding of the text, the narrator retreats into the background.

The four relatively short we-passages in Acts become then all the more perplexing (Acts 16:10-17; 20:5-15; 21:1-18; 27:1-28). These passages, too, have often been interpreted by scholars from a source-critical viewpoint as the remnant of a we-source. But when we compare the we-passages with the preface, we can interpret them as examples of metalepsis top down, where the narrator, who has already positioned himself explicitly as extradiegetical and not as an (intra)diegetical eyewitness, abruptly and without warning becomes the companion of his own diegetic actor, Paul. The sudden transgression of the extradiegetical narrator into the narrated

---

30. For further information, see Ute E. Eisen, *Die Poetik der Apostelgeschichte: Eine narratologische Studie*, NTOA 58 (Göttingen: Vandenhoeck & Ruprecht, 2006), 63-99 (summary on 95-99).

world makes the world of the narrative and the narrated world for some moments permeable, evoking the simultaneity of the separate worlds of the narrative. This metalepsis is *temporary and without any relevance for the plot* and thus can be termed as rhetorical, but it enhances the authority of the narrator—not only as careful historian but now also as eyewitness of Paul—and intensifies the experience of the reader. Through this strategy the window to the narrated world is open for only a short time, but with the profound effect that the entire Lukan narrative gains increased credibility and authority from this logic-defying metalepsis.

If we look back at the preface, it stands out all the more starkly, in light of the use of metalepsis in Luke-Acts, how carefully the narrator endeavors to distinguish his own work from that of the "many" others who have attempted to capture a narrative of the events. The preface serves to justify and to give authority to both books that follow. The metaleptic strategy in the second book (Acts) intensifies the self-stylization of the narrator in the first book (Luke). Following his eloquent self-introduction at the beginning of his narrative in the first book, to which he explicitly alludes at the beginning of the second book, he inserts himself—against his general proclamation that he gained the material from eyewitnesses but not his own eyewitness experience—into the narrated world briefly several times in the second half of the second book. This paradoxical manner of staging the narrative and guiding the reader's interpretation of it has exercised a powerful effect. To this day, his role as an eyewitness of Paul's travels continues to be debated, and this has generally lent greater authority to the whole two-volume work.

Also in the Lukan parables metaleptic strategy can be observed.[31] To the extent that the voices within the narrated world cannot be clearly attributed to a speaker, one can observe the strategy of the blending of narrative voices, for example in the parable of the great banquet (Luke 14:16–24), which the Lukan Jesus narrates. According to the parable, a man prepares a feast, and when he sends his slave to invite the guests to attend, they all make excuses to decline. The slave reports this to his master, who becomes enraged. He orders his slave to invite first the poor and the lame and then whomever he can find in the streets. Within the fictitious speech of the master to his slave, there occurs at the end an abrupt switch of the addressee from singular to plural: "For I tell *you* [pl.]" (v. 24). As far as

---

31. On this, see further du Toit, "Entgrenzungen," 298–302.

this formula is typical of Jesus's speech in the Gospel of Luke, the formula here suggests a blending of narrative voices—the voice of the master in the parable and the voice of Jesus in the gospel. Through this speech, with its double relevance, the narrative planes blur together, and a sense of simultaneity arises between the separate worlds within the narrative. The events of the story of the parable become intertwined with the events of the main narrative, the listeners of Jesus's parable are directly addressed from within the world of the parable, and the readers are invited to identify with the listeners in the main story, which is consistent with the application-oriented nature of the parable form.

Metalepsis in the Gospel of John

Unlike any of the other canonical gospels, the Gospel of John is distinguished by a fundamental metaleptic disposition. This is shown in what follows by the example of the Nicodemus scene and the figure of the beloved disciple.[32]

First, metalepsis can be analyzed in the conversation between Nicodemus and Jesus (John 3:1–21). The scene opens with a scant characterization of the person of Nicodemus, who is introduced as a Pharisee and a leader of the Jews (3:1). We are further told that he came to Jesus by night and spoke to him (3:2). There ensues a dialogue between the two that is clearly dominated by Jesus.

In this dialogue there occur some anomalies in the change of the addressee. In the speech of Nicodemus, who according to the narrator had come alone, it says (3:2): "Rabbi, we know that you are a teacher who has come from God." The first-person plural at this point can still easily be understood to refer to the Pharisees as a group, to whom Nicodemus belongs and in whose name he seems to speak, for at this point in the narrative of the Gospel of John there have not yet been any confrontations between Jesus and the Pharisees or any other members of the Jewish leadership, a circumstance that changes later in the narrative. A few verses later, however, there occurs a much greater anomaly in Jesus's reply, which puzzles the attentive reader. The Johannine Jesus quite suddenly speaks in the first-person plural. He begins his speech with the typical

---

32. On this and what follows, see further and with additional examples Eisen, "Metalepsis."

"very truly, I tell you" (3:3) and continues by referring to himself in the first-person plural, addressing a second-person plural audience (3:11): "We speak of what we know and testify to what we have seen; yet you [pl.] do not receive our testimony." In the following sentence the speaker Jesus changes back to the logical singular ("I"), but the addressee still remains in the plural (3:12).

In the scholarly literature there has been much speculation about this baffling we-passage in the speech of the Johannine Jesus. The most frequent explanation of the *crux interpretum* is the assumption that the Johannine church is here erroneously made to speak, in the *pluralis ecclesiasticus*, most likely as a survival from an earlier literary source. It seems more appropriate to understand this we-passage as a metaleptic strategy. Contrary to the two-volume work of Luke, the we-passage here marks not the sudden intrusion of the extradiegetic narrator into the narrative but a blending of narrative voices—the voice of Jesus and the we-narrative of the Johannine framing narrative (John 1:21). The speech of Jesus thus gains a double relevance. In a flash, the sacred boundary between the extra- and intradiegetic worlds fuses into a present reality. Jesus and the we-group suddenly appear as a common witness and thus speak as a collective to those Pharisees and readers who are in danger of refusing to accept their testimony.

The narrative voice of the framing narrative of the Johannine gospel a few times speaks as a collective "we" (John 1:14, 16; 3:11; 21:24). This also makes it possible to identify the unexpected "we" in Jesus's speech (John 3:11)—so unlike the usual and emphasized "I" of the Johannine Jesus—with the voice of the we-narrative. The blending of narrative voices in the speech of Jesus highlights the address to Nicodemus as a member of a group within the diegetic universe, a group that is early in the story characterized as posing inappropriate questions: "Are you a teacher of Israel, and yet you do not understand these things?" (v. 10).

It is striking that the paradoxical use of "we" in Jesus's speech ends abruptly after only seven words, but Jesus continues to speak to the addressee in the plural (vv. 11–12). In this way Jesus's speech continues to have a double relevance—for Nicodemus and for the readers. So it is not surprising that Nicodemus vanishes from the scene, which ends with Jesus's speech. The metaleptic staging of the speech, which contemplates fundamental existential questions—it deals with "the things of heaven," with the "Son of Man," and the "Son of God," and with nothing less than the future of this world—pushes the reader to identify with it.

The speech of Jesus in the Nicodemus scene is only one example of the subtle character of direct speech in general—and in the New Testament, extended speeches are characteristic of the Gospels of Matthew and John, as well as Luke and especially Acts. For direct speech can be interpreted as "a deliberately delimiting strategy ... in which the boundaries of the narrated world and the narrative world are leveled out by the ambiguity of the textual references."[33] Narratology has long described how marked direct speech reduces the distance of the reader to what is narrated.[34] Through metaleptic strategy, this effect is intensified still further.

The narrative "we" appears at three other points in the Johannine narrative. In the prologue (John 1:1–18) the credo of the narrative is set forth: "And the Word became flesh and lived among us, and we have seen his glory, the glory as of a father's only son, full of grace and truth" (v. 14). It continues in the passage about John the Baptist: "From his fullness we have all received, grace upon grace" (v. 16). In these verses the narrative voice is articulated as a collective entity, which functions as a witness to "grace and truth." By fusing this "we" in the speech of Jesus in John 3:11 with the voice of Jesus himself, the world of Jesus and the narration of it collapses into a single present tense that "speaks," "knows," and "testifies" (v. 11), what we term a strategy for making present.

The we-voice appears one last time in the Gospel of John at the end of the narrative with a momentous piece of information (John 21:24a): "This is the disciple who is testifying to these things and has written them, and we know that his testimony is true." It reveals nothing less than the author of the gospel, who has literally testified to and written this gospel in truth (v. 24b). In this way the "we" refers to the beloved disciple, who not only acts in the preceding last scene of the gospel (John 21:1–23, esp. v. 7) but is also the topic of the final word of both characters and narrator (21:20–23). The we-voice in verse 24 thus functions as a witness to the eyewitness, the "beloved disciple" (John 13:23, 25; 19:35; 20:30; 21:20, 24), of the witness par excellence, Jesus (John 1:18). The complex narration of the Gospel of John as a whole is characterized by a graded process of testifying to the truth (John 1:14; 21:24).[35]

The beloved disciple, whom the reader has previously met only as a character within the narrated world, is revealed as witness, transmitter,

---

33. Du Toit, "Entgrenzungen," 309.
34. See Eisen, *Poetik*, 110–21, especially 117–18.
35. For more information see Eisen, "Metalepsis," 323–30, especially 330.

narrator, and author of the gospel, as the "Evangelist im Evangelium."[36] This revelation at the end of the Johannine gospel comes as a shock, especially on the first reading, and casts the entire narrative in a new light. It invites the reader to read the gospel again to learn more about this disciple, who camouflages himself as extradiegetic narrator. The credibility and authority of the gospel is assured and vouched for through the metaleptic interweaving of the extradiegetical narrator and the eyewitness testimony of the very same beloved disciple.

Who is this enigmatic disciple, "whom Jesus loved"? The narrator—if we are to follow John 21:24, he is identical with the beloved disciple— mentions him(self) a total of five times (13:23; 19:26; 20:2; 21:7, 20). In four important scenes he stands on the stage of the narrated world. He is first introduced "as the one who reclined on Jesus's bosom" (ἦν ἀνακείμενος ... ἐν τῷ κόλπῳ τοῦ Ἰησοῦ, John 13:23) at the Last Supper, a description that is three times emphasized in the gospel (13:23, 25; 21:20). This position of intimacy recalls with similar words Jesus's intimacy with the Father ("who is in the bosom of the Father," ὁ ὢν εἰς τὸν κόλπον τοῦ πατρός, John 1:18). On the second occasion, the beloved disciple appears as the only male disciple to stand beneath the cross. The dying Jesus assigns to him a new position, which is to remain by the side of his mother, Mary (19:27). In this same scene he serves as a witness to the death of Jesus and to the details that Jesus did not have his legs broken like the other men who were crucified with him but had a lance thrust through his side by one of the soldiers (19:33–34). Aside from the theological reasons for this observation, from a narratological viewpoint it evokes a heightened sense of reality. The narrator himself comments on this scene in the form of an aside to the reader (19:35): "He who saw this has testified so that you also may believe. His testimony is true, and he knows that he tells the truth."

It is only against the background of the reader's knowledge of John 21:24 that the meaning of this address to the reader in 19:35 becomes clear. The testimony of the beloved disciple is framed as an autopsy and placed in the context of proving the truth. The narrator speaks of the beloved disciple as a character in the narrated world in the third person, without revealing that he himself is identical with this character (21:24). Through this strategy the narrator can, on the one hand, assume the position of an omniscient

---

36. Franz Overbeck, *Das Johannesevangelium: Studien zur Kritik seiner Erforschung* (Tübingen: Mohr, 1911), 409.

narrator who has inside knowledge of the mind of Jesus, the disciples, and other characters in the story, and is not subject to the restrictions placed on the knowledge of an I-narrator. On the other hand, he subtly demands the authority of an eyewitness and intimate disciple of Jesus, one who was explicitly "beloved" by Jesus. The act of narrating and the witnessing of the narrated world merge into one present tense in this subversive metaleptic strategy. With Josef Blank, the Johannine theology can be described as a "theology of making present" (*Vergegenwärtigungstheologie*).[37]

Within the Johannine narrative, we meet the beloved disciple a third time as he races with Peter to reach the empty tomb (20:1–10). He is faster than Peter but generously allows Peter to enter the tomb first (vv. 6–8). Nevertheless, he is the first of the two to recognize the significance of the tomb, since he "believed" (ἐπίστευσεν, v. 8). It is all the more confusing, in light of the reader's knowledge of John 21:24, when the narrator declares in a distancing third-person voice: "for as yet they did not understand the scripture, that he must rise from the dead" (John 20:9). Does the narrator, who was one of the two disciples, wish to indirectly make it clear to the reader that at the point of discovering the empty tomb, he "believed" but he "as yet … did not understand" (οὐδέπω γὰρ ᾔδεισαν, v. 9)? Is he quietly allowing his readers, by way of narrative strategy, to participate in his own learning process?

The form of the metaleptic strategy in the speech of Jesus to the disciple Thomas is less complex (John 20:29): "Have you believed because you have seen me? Blessed are those who have not seen and yet have come to believe." The blessing in the second part of verse 29 can be interpreted as a blending of narrative voices, the voice of Jesus and the voice of the narrator. Again, this strategy makes the diegetic universe permeable to the reader, who can identify with the blessing. It also forms the transition to the narrator's speech: "Now Jesus did many other signs in the presence of his disciples, which are not written in this book. But these are written so that you may come to believe that Jesus is the Messiah, the Son of God, and that through believing you may have life in his name" (20:30–31). For a second time, the narrator speaks directly to his readers ("so that you may come to believe," v. 31; so already 19:35). He again speaks as an objective reporter about the signs that Jesus performed before the disciples, with-

---

37. Josef Blank, *Das Evangelium nach Johannes*, 2nd ed., Geistliche Schriftlesung: Erläuterungen zum Neuen Testament für die geistliche Lesung 4.2 (Düsseldorf: Patmos, 1986), 24.

out letting it be known that he himself was one of them. The alert reader knows better.

The fourth and last scene in which the beloved disciple stands on the stage of the narrated world deals with the appearance of the risen Jesus at the Sea of Tiberias (John 21:1–23). It is also the final scene of the gospel. Some of the disciples of Jesus are working on the lake, and the risen Jesus appears at the shore, talking to them without their recognizing him (20:4). Only after a successful fishing haul does the beloved disciple recognize him and confess to Peter: "It is the Lord!" (ὁ κύριός ἐστιν, 21:7). Does the narrator imply that the very beloved of Jesus did not immediately recognize the risen Jesus, just as he did not entirely understand events before? The metaleptic strategy makes the step-by-step process of coming to understand "the truth" transparent, inviting the reader to identify with that process.

In the Gospel of Mark and in Luke-Acts metaleptic strategy remains *rhetorical*. In the Gospel of John an ontological metalepsis can be detected because the narrator is physically present in the story as the character of the beloved disciple. Even at the very end of the story the question of the origin and the whereabouts of the beloved disciple is raised within the narrated world. Peter speaks in his last dialogue with the risen Jesus about the beloved disciple (John 21:21) and asks Jesus: "Lord, what about him?" Jesus answers Peter (v. 22): "If it is my will that he remain until I come, what is that to you?" Jesus's answer is gruff and off-putting. What this cryptic speech about the beloved disciple means is nowhere made clear. Only one thing is certain: the beloved disciple travels like an undercover agent between the worlds. To this the we-voice (John 21:24) testifies, making the witness of the beloved disciple and the narrator of the gospel all the more authentic, credible, and believable.[38]

Conclusion

It could be said that early Christian literature displays metaleptic strategies, if not to say metaleptic sensitivities. In exegetical scholarship, the passages referred to above have long been treated as examples of narrative pathology and analyzed in the horizon of a source-critical paradigm. But narratology opens up perspectives to decipher puzzling textual phe-

---

38. For a critique of the historicizing interpretation of this textual strategy by Martin Hengel, see Richard Bauckham, "The Beloved Disciple as Ideal Author," *JSNT* 49 (1993): 21–44.

nomena in terms of narrative strategy and to focus on their functions and effects.

Metaleptic strategies break down the boundaries between (narrative) worlds, mediating between them. They make possible the crossing of boundaries, the interaction and the subversion between worlds. This evokes the impression of immediacy and simultaneity, with the effect of making present (*vergegenwärtigen*). The dissolution of distinct narrative levels has, above all, the effect of stabilizing the authority of the narratives, including the credibility and authenticity of their narrators and selected characters.

In New Testament narratives,[39] the smooth blending of narrative voices prevails over the direct and shocking effect of metalepsis. Speeches with double relevance promote quasi-immediacy, which is intensified through the use of loose-end technique. In a sublime manner, it bridges the "the broad and ugly ditch"[40] between the worlds.

Metalepsis, especially in Luke-Acts and more intensely in the Gospel of John, accumulates metatextual functions and seeks to mediate between textuality, orality, and autopsy. Their attempts to prove truth can be traced directly back to the tripartite conception of the truth content of narrative speech (truth, probability, invention), which is already characteristic of classical Greek epic. The two-volume work Luke-Acts and the Gospel of John show themselves to be particularly anxious to anchor the truthfulness (Luke 1:4) and the truth (John 1:14, 17, and elsewhere) of their narratives in a multilayered textual manner. The credibility of their books and their truth claims, which is being put to the test, is assured by quasi-eyewitness testimony. Metaleptic strategies as a whole are suitable to create smooth and trustworthy transitions between the postulated orality and the literary product, between past and present. They serve not, as in modern literature, to break the illusion of reality, but rather to help form the illusion in the sense of the trustworthiness of what is narrated through the medium of the book, implicitly in the Gospel of Mark and explicitly in Luke-Acts and the Gospel of John.

---

39. For more examples see Eisen and von Möllendorff, *Über die Grenze*, and in particular the contributions of du Toit, Eisen, and Spittler in the named volume.

40. Gotthold Ephraim Lessing, "On the Proof of the Spirit and of Power," in *Philosophical and Theological Writings*, ed. and trans. H. B. Nisbet (Cambridge: Cambridge University Press, 2005), 83–88, here 87.

Part 2
Jews, Greeks, Romans, and Others

"And Also to the Jews in Their Script": Power and Writing in the Scroll of Esther

Donald C. Polaski

> As some day it may happen that a victim must be found, I've got a little list—I've got a little list.
> —W. S. Gilbert and A. S. Sullivan, *The Mikado*

If there is any biblical text that seems destined to become fodder for Gilbert and Sullivan, it is the scroll of Esther: incredible reversals play out in the context of an "overblown, pompous, over-bureaucratized" imperial administration.[1] As Adele Berlin puts it, Esther is a farce, a "burlesque" of the imperial court.[2] Other scholars have noted parallels between Esther and Mikhail Bahktin's notion of carnival.[3] For example, Kenneth Craig points to numerous marks of carnivalization in Esther: reversals, feasting, the "open market," "pregnant death," crowns, masks, fools, collective gaiety. Thus for Craig, Esther is "unofficial"—it resists, inverts, and

---

1. Jon Levenson, *Esther: A Commentary*, OTL (Louisville: Westminster John Knox, 1997), 12.

2. Adele Berlin, *The JPS Bible Commentary: Esther* (Philadelphia: Jewish Publication Society of America, 2001), xix: "the burlesque of the Persian court provides the setting for the farce."

3. See Kenneth Craig, *Reading Esther: A Case for the Literary Carnivalesque*, Literary Currents in Biblical Interpretation (Louisville: Westminster John Knox, 1995); Yona Shapira, "A Postmodernist Reading of the Biblical Book of Esther: From Cultural Disintegration to Carnivalesque Texts" (PhD diss., SUNY Stony Brook, 1996), 93–215; J'Annine Jobling and Alan Roughley, "The Right to Write: Power, Irony, and Identity in the Book of Esther," in *Sacred Tropes: Tanakh, New Testament, and Qur'an as Literature and Culture*, ed. Roberta Sterman Sabbath, BibInt 98 (Leiden: Brill, 2009), 317–33; and Jonathan Grossman, *Esther: The Outer Narrative and the Hidden Reading*, Sifrut 6 (Winona Lake, IN: Eisenbrauns, 2011), 233–39.

subverts official discourse. It opposes oppression and a fixed social order through the unofficial and powerless pair, Esther and Mordecai.[4]

In this paper, I wish to examine the ways that the construction of imperial authority as carnivalized might interact with the ways writing is constructed in the text.[5] In Esther, as in the discourses of the Persian and Hellenistic empires, writing serves as a means of power. Empires enforce written laws, keep written records, sponsor propagandistic inscriptions, and write lists, lists that determine death and life. As such a means of official power, we would expect writing to be exposed to parody and reversal in Esther. Craig says as much: "Just as 'the authoritarian word' does not allow any other speech that would interfere with it, so official culture attempts to constrain unofficial culture. The authoritarian word in Esther is 'the law,' and carnival transgresses such laws. Indeed, carnival is anti-law."[6]

Yet Esther also assumes that imperial writing has a great deal of power. In Esther the imperial court presumes its writing ("the laws of the Medes and the Persians") to be immutable (1:19), and the book nowhere mocks that claim.[7] In this text, Purim, the exercise of carnival, is established by imperial writ (9:20–32). The scroll of Esther itself thus takes on the characteristics of an imperial edict.[8] In a very real sense, the scroll of Esther *is* imperial writing.

So just how complete is the carnival in Esther? Esther could be literature resisting the official. Or Esther's playfulness might exist only to naturalize the imperial order; thus it would be an *anticarnival*. To approach

---

4. Craig, *Reading Esther*, 30. On reversals, see Levenson, *Esther*, 8: "The theme of the whole book is summed up in two Hebrew words—*nahăpok hû*, 'the reverse occurred.'"

5. *Text* here refers to MT Esther. All translations are drawn from the NRSV.

6. Craig, *Reading Esther*, 52.

7. The immutability of Persian law appears here, Esth 8:8; Dan 6:8, 15; and in Diodorus Siculus, *Bib. hist.* 17.30. There is no evidence that such a requirement was part of actual imperial procedure. See Michael V. Fox, *Character and Ideology in the Book of Esther*, 2nd ed., Studies on Personalities of the Old Testament (Grand Rapids: Eerdmans, 2001), 22.

8. While its basis in an imperial edict is historically unlikely, Purim, a calendrical innovation not found in the Torah, does seem to have required its own high-powered textual justification. The colophon at the conclusion of LXX Esther claims that the scroll of Esther (F:11) was brought to Egypt as an "authentic" "letter about Purim" (ἐπιστολὴν τῶν Φρουραι) by certain officially connected persons from Jerusalem.

these difficulties, I will first look at humor in the scroll, laughter being a key locus of subversion in the carnivalesque. Then I will look at the ways subjects are constituted in writing in Esther, especially the figures of Esther and the Jews.

Writing for Laughs: A Trip to the Archive

Archives are a key to imperial power. They allow the empire to define its own past, to define its courses of action, and to keep track of all those things vital to proper administration.⁹ In the scroll of Esther's trip to the archives, though, we see an inversion. We end up laughing at the records.

The imperial archive appears in the context of the king's insomnia: "On that night the king could not sleep, and he gave orders to bring the book of records [ספר הזכרנות], the annals [דברי הימים], and they were read to the king. It was found written how Mordecai had told about Bigthana and Teresh, two of the king's eunuchs, who guarded the threshold, and who had conspired to assassinate King Ahasuerus" (Esth 6:1–2). It should be noted, first, that the archival record, ironically enough, is incomplete; it is defective. Esther's role in alerting the king, explicit in 2:22, has apparently not been written down. She has vanished.¹⁰ Moreover, a name seems to have been misspelled. Where the archives call one of the conspirators "Bigthana" (בגתנא), the earlier story records him as "Bigthan" (בגתן, 2:21). We as readers may have better information than the Persian book of annals. At the very least we are left wondering about the real name of a royal assassin.

Second, the imperial archive here functions as a way to avoid action, not as the basis on which to take action. The king desires sleep, so he wants to hear archival texts. If the king's power manifest in the drunken excesses of the banquet hall has failed, and the king's power manifest in the harem has failed, perhaps the king's power manifest in writing will do the trick

---

9. On the power of archived records in the Achaemenid Empire, see Cameron B. R. Howard, "Writing Yehud: Textuality and Power under Persian Rule" (PhD diss., Emory University, 2010), 49–62, and works cited there. Howard coins the evocative phrase "Persian hypertextuality" to describe the empire's approach to writing (63).

10. This omission maintains Esther's secret identity, as there is no permanent reminder of Esther's collusion with Mordecai. The whole matter is odd and bespeaks administrative incompetence. See Fox, *Character*, 40.

and give the king a good night's sleep.[11] Imperial records are here exposed for what they so often are: boring, droning prose.

But the royal archives, far from being mocked, end up disclosing the king's inability to master imperial power. The king has forgotten an obligation, has not acted properly, although he was present when Esther and Mordecai exposed the plot, and the whole business was carefully (or not so carefully) recorded. Here is the mockery one would expect at a carnival. The king, along with his scribes, is the butt of the joke. But the written records, despite missing details and inspiring slumber, survive. In the end, writing compels the king's action to set matters right.[12]

Erasing Vashti

At the opening of the book, Vashti, the queen, refuses the king's summons to present herself, setting off a long discussion concerning imperial law (דת) and the destabilizing effects of its flouting.[13] Memucan, one of those "well versed in דת" (Esth 1:13), suggests that word of Vashti's deed will spread like wildfire in women's unofficial oral discourse. But it can be contained via an immutable text:

> If it pleases the king, let a royal order [דבר־מלכות] go out from him, and let it be written [ויכתב] among the laws [בדתי] of the Persians and the Medes so that it may not be altered, that Vashti is never again to come before King Ahasuerus; and let the king give her royal position to another who is better than she. So when the decree made by the king is proclaimed throughout all his kingdom, vast as it is, all women will give honor to their husbands, high and low alike. (1:19–20)

---

11. Lewis B. Paton (*A Critical and Exegetical Commentary on the Book of Esther*, ICC [Edinburgh: T&T Clark, 1908], 244) claims that the use of the participle נקראים to describe the reading of the text is periphrastic, indicating the reading was of long duration, perhaps lasting all night. That would simply increase the humor here: the reading drones on, hour after hour, until dawn and the mention of the assassination plot coincide.

12. Mieke Bal ("Lots of Writing," *Semeia* 54 [1991]: 90) notes that Ahasuerus's response is to act "that justice be done to the writing."

13. For a full account of how Vashti is and is not erased in the book of Esther, see Timothy K. Beal, *The Book of Hiding: Gender, Ethnicity, Annihilation, and Esther* (London: Routledge, 1997), 15–28.

Memucan's advice is simple: tell everyone Vashti is gone, and they will get the message. But the king cannot seem to make the move from oral to written with anything like accuracy. Instead of following Memucan's advice, he issues a ridiculous edict directing that men must be masters of their households: "[The king] sent letters [ספרים] to all the royal provinces, to every province in its own script and to every people in its own language, declaring that every man should be master in his own house" (1:22).[14] The joke is yet again on the king. A man who was singularly inept in maintaining authority in his own palace uses writing to cover his inability. Official discourse, immutable written law, is a faulty and laughable representation of the original idea.

Unlike the archive above, immutable law is not quite the victim of parody.[15] The king, unable to control his own household, mandates all men to control theirs. This is a silly assertion because of the king's obvious incapacity, not because the king is overstepping his bounds. But the king's power to mandate conduct via written edict is not in question. The empire's writing covers every province and each ethnic group and is expressed in every language.[16] In this case, the content—what is written—reveals, ironically, the king's lack of control.[17] So while the king's power may be taken in jest, his means of expressing his power, the written edict, is still incontestable.

Indeed, whatever the king writes about Vashti, it is effective. Vashti, who will not be summoned by the king's oral call, is made subject to the king's writing. The king decrees (נגזר עליה, 2:1) that she vanish, and she does.[18] In case there was any doubt, the story then proceeds to tell us how

---

14. Berlin (*Esther*, 20) claims that the edict itself is not cited but that the notice in Esth 1:22 summarizes the effect of Memucan's legislation. Fox (*Character*, 23), however, presumes that "the decree is not exactly what Memuchan called for."

15. Beal (*Hiding*, 23–28) captures the power of writing here, referring to Vashti's removal as a process of "writing out" or "exscription."

16. The verse finishes with the problematic phrase "and speak the language of his own people" (Esth 1:22, trans. Berlin). This phrase is omitted in the Greek versions and is not translated in the NRSV. It may suggest the male heads of household are being singled out to receive the communication in their vernacular speech (Berlin, *Esther*, 20–21). If so, this phrase would underscore the edict's overstated, almost histrionic, quality.

17. A similar ironic slippage occurs in 1:8, where the king's law "was that there should be no law" (Levenson, *Esther*, 46).

18. While Vashti could easily delight in this fate (Levenson, *Esther*, 51–52), and it would add one more humorous wrinkle to the story, it makes no difference to the

beautiful virgins of the empire are subject to the king's bureaucracy, which will summon them, classify them, and subject them to extensive treatments, all according to the law of the women (כדת הנשים, 2:12).[19] They are no longer addressed as representatives of differing national or ethnic groups (2:3) but simply as women, subjectified by cosmetic processes, the evaluative stare of the eunuchs, and the king's embrace.[20] Despite parodic excess here, writing functions to express imperial authority and account for ethnic difference.[21]

Hearing versus Seeing: Writing as the Preferred Option

Haman, in his plot against the Jews, assumes the power of writing. It has a universal role, constraining all ethnic difference. With one exception, it seems: a "certain people" in the provinces has different laws (דתיהם, 3:8). Thus, in Haman's way of thinking, this people cannot keep the king's דת. The king must not let this people alone. Haman's solution is to write in a way that applies just to this people, an edict for their destruction (יכתב לאבדם, 3:9).[22] Haman immediately follows this proposal with mention of monetary payment. The king allows Haman to keep the money, as well as to do as he pleases with this people (3:11).

---

argument. Writing effectively defines Vashti as its subject, against her will or not. As Beal (*Hiding*, 27) notes, "*gazar* is the most literal Hebrew equivalent for *exscription*."

19. Carol Bechtel (*Esther*, IBC [Louisville: John Knox, 2002], 32) emphasizes the importance of the term דת here, claiming that this shows "a general impression of obedience to Persian law." Paton (*Esther*, 178) explicitly adds writing to the process, claiming it would require various written records.

20. Beal, *Hiding*, 36–37. Note also that the text appears to claim that Hegai "changes" Esther (וישנה, 2:9) in some way. For more discussion of the possible use of a root שנה to indicate promotion, see the views of James L. Crenshaw ("The Expression *mî yōdēaʿ* in the Hebrew Bible," *VT* 36 [1986]: 279), who favors that reading, and J. A. Emerton ("The Meaning of *šēnāʾ* in Psalm CXXVII 2," *VT* 24 [1974]: 27), who sees little advantage to that reading.

21. Berlin (*Esther*, 27) points to the extreme length of the cosmetic treatments as comic exaggeration, while Levenson (*Esther*, 61) sees here a critique of the empire's "self-indulgent body culture."

22. Haman neatly obscures his own agency by using the passive voice here, perhaps suggesting that writing has a power all its own, without regard for who the author might be. This remains a temporary position, since Haman will eventually use the king's signet ring to mark the text with imperial authority.

One wonders whether the king is aware of what he has done. Like other scholars, I suggest the king has misheard Haman.[23] When Haman says אבד, "destroy," the king hears עבד, "to be a slave." In the king's view, then, the recalcitrance of this "certain people" will be resolved by enslaving them. Haman's mention of money afterward—which might be the offer of a huge bribe—could support this version of events in the king's mind. This oral process allows Haman to play a "rhetorical trick" on the king.[24]

The process of writing will be subject to no such ambiguities. The story emphasizes this by going into great detail about the writing process, including the scribes (3:12), the familiar claim to universality (3:12; see 1:22), the use of the king's signet ring (3:12), and the promulgation of a copy of the document (פתשגן הכתב להנתן דת, 3:14). The edict is a bureaucratic masterpiece, clearly delineating who will be killed and when, while piling up words: "to destroy, to kill, and to annihilate [ולאבד] all Jews" (3:13).[25] Haman's destructive pun commends writing as more accurately encoding power. Here, the letter kills.

This is not to say that, even in this grim scene, there is not parody involved. Haman's plot relies on the king's illiteracy or alliteracy. If the king were capable of reading Haman's edict or had the desire to have it read to him, the plot would have been a nonstarter. Persian emperors were often illiterate, so we can hardly blame Ahasuerus for being so.[26] But his alliteracy, his utter disinterest in imperial paperwork (except as a sleep aid), parodies imperial power. The edict, correctly written, exposes the king's lack of control of oral language, while also asserting the absolute, unquestionable, and immutable power of the written word.

Writing is and is not implicated in Esther's reversals of imperial, official culture. Writing may be so linked to official actions that it is parodied. It is

---

23. Sandra Beth Berg, *The Book of Esther: Motifs, Themes and Structure*, SBLDS 44 (Missoula, MT: Scholars Press, 1979), 101–2; Bechtel, *Esther*, 42–43.

24. Bechtel, *Esther*, 43.

25. The detailed process here may serve as a kind of overkill, with the stacking up of synonyms speaking to "the totality of the slaughter" (Levenson, *Esther*, 73). The use of the Persian loan term *patšegen* is a somewhat more subtle evocation of Persian power.

26. Regarding Darius I, Muhammed A. Dandamaev and Vladimir G. Lukonin claim that "he, like the majority of ancient oriental kings, was obviously illiterate, as can be seen from his own statement that, after the [Behistun] inscription was completed, it was read to him" (*The Culture and Social Institutions of Ancient Iran*, trans. Philip L. Kohl [Cambridge: Cambridge University Press, 1989], 282).

part of the bloated and ineffective imperial bureaucracy. But, in a very real sense, it escapes carnivalization. No matter how silly the imperial court or its king appear, writing encodes imperial power in ways that the scroll of Esther leaves unquestioned.

We have already seen that imperial writing covers all provinces and peoples. It "accounts for" ethnic difference as it goes out "to every province in its own script and to every people in its own language" (1:22; see 2:3; 8:9). Even when it parodies royal pretensions (1:16–22, etc.), imperial writing invites subject peoples to realize their status as the subject of imperial discourse.[27] To examine this process in Esther, we will first focus on Esther as she becomes enmeshed in imperial writing, then on the Jews as a whole, watching how writing encodes power by producing Jewish subjects.[28]

Esther as Subject

The first edict in the scroll of Esther does not seem to touch Esther in any real sense. In Memucan's formulation, the decree will only affect married couples: "all women will give honor to their husbands, high and low alike" (1:20). So Esther is outside its compass. The king's expansion of this to the broader claim "every man should be master in his own house" (1:22) would affect Esther, as she is a woman in her cousin Mordecai's house. Yet Esther has already chosen to obey Mordecai like a master; she has already been made a subject by Mordecai.[29] We are informed later that Esther conceals her Jewish identity on Mordecai's orders, since she "obeyed Mordecai

---

27. The focus here is on the subject as produced socially. The Jew is created as subject not only by being made subject to imperial law but also by becoming a subject of the empire's discourse, an object of the empire's interest. So Esther, even when she is an acting subject, is not simply an individual taking action. She represents a whole process of imperial subjectification. For a more psychological approach to Esther as subject, see Joshua A. Berman, "Hadassah Bat Abihail: The Evolution from Object to Subject in the Character of Esther," *JBL* 120 (2001): 647–69.

28. Jobling and Roughley ("Right to Write," 318) note this nexus between writing and identity: "Identity is ironically stabilized as authoritative through access to the written word, which in the Book of Esther both produces and guarantees them."

29. Here Esther, as subject of the family, becomes (by extension) a Jewish subject. She is at least enough aware of her Jewish subject status for Mordecai to order her to keep it hidden (2:10)

just as when she was brought up by him" (2:20). Her obedience is obviously pre-edict.

But imperial commands soon affect Esther. The king commands beautiful young virgins should be sought for him (2:4). This "edict" (דת) results in Esther's being placed in the harem.[30] So Esther is simply one of "the women" (2:3, 8), an initially undifferentiated mass from the various provinces, all of whom are summoned to be subjects of the empire. In short, Esther's journey as a colonial subject has begun.[31]

Yet this journey is anything but simple. Esther's identity, her status as a subject constructed by Jewish family power, is not eliminated by the edict.[32] The king's law can force Esther to do all sorts of things she may or may not wish to do, but her identity remains in flux. The king's edict gives her a universal identity (one of the beautiful women of the empire), and then increasingly specific roles until she is queen of all Persia (2:17). But this new identity does not erase her old identity.[33] The king may summon

---

30. Though not explicitly written, presuming this law was written makes a great deal of sense. This law, like the written edict in Esth 1, has pretensions to universal effect and involves provincial officials (2:3). If that is the case, then the harem is constituted by royal writing, enforcing a (written?) "law of the women" that defines the treatment of the women's bodies, and (perhaps) relying on record keeping (Paton, *Esther*, 178; and David J. A. Clines, *Ezra, Nehemiah, Esther*, NCB [Grand Rapids: Eerdmans, 1984], 289).

31. According to Louis Althusser, ideological state apparatuses constitute subjects by interpellating them, or calling them forth. Althusser (*Lenin and Philosophy* [New York: Monthly Review Press, 1971], 74) explains the process this way: if you are walking down the street and a police officer addresses you, when you turn around and acknowledge him, your self-consciousness has been constructed in some way by that interaction. You have been assigned a role, and you have accepted it. In the case of Esther, she is being hailed as a subject in a colonial context: the empire is calling her name and assigning her an identity, a status as subject. For a brief introduction to interpellation as part of Althusser's work, see Robert P. Resch, *Althusser and the Renewal of Marxist Social Theory* (Berkeley: University of California Press, 1992), 208–13.

32. This doubled nature of Esther as subject relates well to Homi Bhabha's concept of ambivalence. For Bhabha, colonial subjects are never simply collaborating with the empire or resisting it. Rather, their relation to the empire is constantly fluctuating. For more information, see Bill Ashcroft, Gereth Griffiths, and Helen Tiffin, *Post-Colonial Studies: The Key Concepts*, 2nd ed. (London: Routledge, 2007), 10–11, and the works cited there.

33. Berman ("Hadassah," 650) points to a shift in Esther's identity at 2:17: "She enters the king's palace as the daughter of Abihail, as the adopted daughter of Mor-

her—interpellate her—by name (ונקראה בשם, 2:14), but Esther has a name, Hadassah, in reserve.³⁴

Haman's edict changes matters, but not immediately. The edict goes out "to the king's satraps and to the governors over all the provinces and to the officials of all the peoples, to every province in its own script and every people in its own language" (3:12), but a copy seems not to have made it to the harem.³⁵ Esther clearly demonstrates her lack of knowledge of the edict in her attempt to have Mordecai change out his sackcloth, just after the narrator has told us that "wherever the king's command and his decree came, there was great mourning among the Jews, with fasting and weeping and lamenting, and most of them lay in sackcloth and ashes" (4:3).

Perhaps the royal court assumes that the women in the harem no longer have their own script or language, those distinctions having been removed by the universalizing effect of the summoning edict (2:3) and the law of the women (2:12). Thus the women in the harem seemingly evade being subject to this order. The harem is not a "people" possessing its own script and language. Rather, it is rendered as the very image of the supposedly transnational empire, an invitation to a different kind of colonial subjectivity.

Mordecai must make Esther aware of an edict that defines her differently. If she is to lobby the king on behalf of her people, she must identify herself as a part of that people. This means she must take on her role as fully subject to imperial writing, inhabiting the space of the colonial subject differently. Where her Jewish identity was held earlier not to be governed by writing—she can evade the universalization of the harem edict—here Mordecai must undo that, since now Jewishness is established by edict.

Mordecai thus sends a written copy of the decree (פתשגן כתב־הדת) with the verbal request she intervene with the king (4:8); the oral register is not enough.³⁶ Mordecai's action here corresponds almost exactly with

---

decai. But she will emerge from those chambers with a new designation: *Esther, the king's wife.*" But the shift is, for Berman, only a part of a long process of negotiating her identity both as a Jew and as the king's other, a process the book never resolves (653).

34. Linda M. Day (*Esther*, AOTC [Nashville: Abingdon, 2005], 52) also sees the ambiguity here: "the action of summoning Esther 'by name' is thus an act of both revelation and concealment."

35. Bechtel (*Esther*, 46) notes the possibility of mockery here: "In spite of the fact that the edict's content is being proclaimed far and wide by the king's state-of-the-art courier service, the news has not spread within the palace walls themselves."

36. Bechtel (ibid., 47) suggests that Mordecai sends a written copy to remove the chance that Esther, like Ahasuerus, would confuse עבד with אבד.

Haman's action in sending the written edict (פתשגן הכתב להנתן דת, 3:14), representing imperial power effectively acting through writing. His action makes Esther the addressee of the edict, breaking the harem's universality. When once eunuchs instructed her on how to be an imperial subject in the harem (2:8–9, 15), now the eunuch Hathach instructs her in a new style of colonial subjectivity.[37]

Esther, though, responds by claiming to be subject to a different imperial law. Going before the king unbidden is a universally held offense: "there is but one law—all alike are to be put to death" (4:11).[38] This law assigns all persons a place and structures the way they know themselves (after all, everyone knows this law). Only the king can interpellate, can call forth a subject. The empire finds any other way unthinkable. Only the king's golden scepter can invite persons to a different understanding of themselves, a redefinition that is by its nature temporary. There is no permanent or ongoing release from this law.

In reply, Mordecai simply reiterates Esther's special subject status created by Haman's edict. Esther's dilemma is that she is now doubly subject. She has been summoned to the harem and to the gallows; she is covered by, called forth by, two decrees that do not necessarily agree. Esther's identification with the Jews—she will be joined with them in fasting—will then allow the king's power to be demonstrated, in wrath or mercy.[39] Esther has now claimed her role as a doubled, contradictory colonial subject, and immediately Mordecai obeys her orders.

At this point, דת disappears from the scroll, and כתב as well, except for a cameo appearance in the archival reading (6:2). Both words reappear later, where Esther and Mordecai write their own edicts, subjecting all peoples and provinces to certain demands.

---

37. Esther here is being reinscribed as a colonial subject, not, as Levenson (*Esther*, 80) would have it, making the transition from "a self-styled Persian" to a "reconnected Jew."

38. There is some evidence the Persians regulated access to the king this way. See Berlin, *Esther*, 44–45, citing Herodotus, *Hist.* 3.117–119.

39. Berman ("Hadassah," 656) claims that "in calling for a new fast, Esther is embarking on a mode of behavior that is paradigmatically Jewish, and in so doing she joins ranks with her fellow Jews." It is worth noting that imperial writing draws forth this Jewish identity. By identifying with Jews, Esther makes herself subject to another imperial edict, inhabiting another space in colonial discourse.

Jews as Subjects

Haman accuses the Jews, identified as a "certain people," of having a different law than the king. This is a situation that the king cannot let rest. Writing, the ability to make a law, must be controlled by the empire. Writing by any other author is a dire threat. Haman's answer to this threat is, logically enough, to write an edict. This edict will make this people take up their rightful position within imperial discourse. While this edict seeks to destroy the Jews, it seeks at the same time to constitute them as an imperial subject, to interpellate or summon them.

The detailed yet urgent narration emphasizes the ideological importance of this project. Harking back to the beginning of the story, the edict is "written to the king's satraps and to the governors over all the provinces and to the officials of all the peoples, to every province in its own script and every people in its own language" (3:12; see 1:22). Writing must account for ethnic difference; it must be universal. Yet there is a slippage here. While the Jews are certainly the subject of the edict, it is unclear whether the edict is addressed to them. Does it make sense to assume imperial writing addresses everyone here?

If the Jews receive their own copy of the edict, it would be foolish strategy but perfect ideology. Imperial writing must go to everyone. Presumably imperial writing so thoroughly manifests power that it will succeed, despite giving so much warning and time to the Jews![40] If the Jews do not receive their own version of the edict, it could simply be good strategy.[41] Why would Haman *want* to inform the victims of the plot? But if this is the strategy, it fails. Mordecai learns what has been done (4:1), as do all Jews when the edict arrives in their respective provinces (4:3). So either Haman's attempt to keep the Jews from knowing failed, or he simply included them in the addressee list—edicts have to go to everyone.

Jewish reaction to the edict is swift. Mordecai and all Jews (except Esther and any other Jews in the harem) mourn, fast, weep, and lament. The Jews do not use the copious amount of time between the edict's issuance and 13 Adar to plot resistance. If they did plan to resist, they would

---

40. Paton (*Esther*, 209) assumes that the Jews would not necessarily know about the plot: "If the Jews had been warned a year in advance of their impending destruction, they would have found means to escape."

41. While Bechtel (*Esther*, 75) thinks it "incredible" that the Jews had been left off the list, she claims that the explicit mention of Jews in 8:9 seems to imply just that.

show they disregard an imperial writ. This would prove Haman's assertion true—this *is* a people that sets itself over against imperial authority (3:8). By failing to plan resistance, they show respect for imperial writing and assume it controls their destiny, absent divine intervention.[42] But showing this deference also points to the edict's essential falsity: this people is a people just like other subject nations and does not merit death. Their death would be a macabre parody of imperial power.

One Jew, Mordecai, does resist after a fashion, realizing that appeal to the king via Esther is the only route that resists without questioning imperial authority. Esther rightly perceives that the continued existence of her people is a matter of royal will: "If I have won your favor, O king, and if it pleases the king, let my life be given me—that is my petition—and the lives of my people—that is my request" (7:3).

These hints that Jews constitute themselves within imperial writing are worked out more fully in Mordecai and Esther's edict in chapter 8, a piece of writing that neatly parallels Haman's.[43] Mordecai gains the power to write, just as Haman had, by receiving the king's signet ring (8:2; see 3:10). Esther is, however, the driving force behind the edict. Esther first asks that Haman's text be erased. The king, for once showing a grasp of imperial power, denies the request.[44] Texts are much harder to eliminate than people are; the late vizier's immutable written orders must stand. Haman himself was dispatched by writing (עם־הספר, 9:25), but his edict cannot be nullified by writing. It can only be "overwritten": the only solution is to write more immutable edicts (8:9–14; 9:14–15, 20–23, 25, 29–32). From here on the imperial carnival becomes a bulk-mailing exercise.

The king orders Esther and Mordecai together to write "with regard to the Jews" (כתבו על־היהודים, 8:8). This time, the Jews are explicitly mentioned in the process of writing and delivery. Since this process is a very close repeat of the process by which Haman sent his edict (3:10–15), the

---

42. It seems that the Jews wait on an edict before they begin to plan resistance (8:9–11). Here is another hyperbolic claim regarding imperial power and writing: "The notion that people will refrain from acting in self-defense unless they have royal permission may be another comic element" (Levenson, *Esther*, 111).

43. Bechtel (*Esther*, 73–74) and Fox (*Character*, 101–4) provide a chart of the parallels between the two.

44. It is interesting that the king mentions the need to write more edicts before he mentions that he cannot withdraw the prior edict. He thus provides a solution to an as-yet-unnamed problem. Such a move allows the interview to focus on the power of writing from beginning to end.

explicit mention of Jews is even more striking: "An edict was written, according to all that Mordecai commanded, to the Jews and to the satraps and the governors and the officials of the provinces from India to Ethiopia, one hundred twenty-seven provinces, to every province in its own script and to every people in its own language, and also to the Jews in their script and their language" (8:9). Jews are listed with various officials, and they count as both a people with their own language and a province with their own script. The Jews have taken their place in the context of Ahasuerus's massive 127-province empire (1:1); they have their own script included in the imperial scribal machinery.[45] They are exceptional not only in their own law but also in their solicitude for imperial writing. It is no wonder that, as one subject people defined by special imperial writing, other peoples could fear them but also identify with them: "In every province and in every city, wherever the king's command and his edict [דבר־המלך ודתו] came, there was gladness and joy among the Jews, a festival and a holiday. Furthermore, many of the peoples of the country professed to be Jews [מתיהדים], because the fear of the Jews had fallen upon them" (8:17).[46] Perhaps they wish to be "written in" to Jewish identity, lest they be "written out" of the empire.

The battle of 13–14 Adar indicates that the Jews keep the king's law, as do all others. Everyone waits for months for the imperially appointed day of rioting. It is no wonder the king is unconcerned about casualties in Susa; the whole violent business is under the control of imperial legislation. A second day of mayhem needs its own edict (9:13–14). Thus the first edict, not entirely effective, is simply the first step in more writing to cover the world or, in this case, at least Susa. This rioting is no revolution. Writing controls resistance. Here paper not only wraps rock but is useful against scissors as well.

Yet at one point the Jews demonstrate ambivalence regarding imperial writing (and, indeed, Jewish writing). Mordecai, following the language of Haman's edict, directs that the Jews are to "plunder" the "goods" (ושללם לבוז) of their enemies (8:11; see 3:11). But the narrator makes abundantly

---

45. Berlin (*Esther*, 76–77) claims that "by saying that the Jews of the Persian Empire retain their own language, the verse [8:9] signals that the Jews have preserved their Jewishness," but she fails to note that that language is now an explicit part of imperial writing/imperial discourse.

46. "Earlier, to be identified as Jewish was to be marked for death; now for some Persians it seems to have become a matter of 'to Jew or die'" (Beal, *Hiding*, 103).

clear that the Jews did not despoil their opponents, violating Mordecai's edict. We are told three times, using identical phrases, that the Jews did not touch the plunder (ובבזה לא שלחו את־ידם, 9:10, 15, 16). The narrator leaves the Jews' motives uncertain. They might wish to represent themselves (or the narrator might wish to represent them) as having a higher ethical standard than others.[47] Or perhaps the Jews could be adopting imperial ideology's privileging of property over human life.[48] This final suggestion brings us back to a central problem: the Jews are here negotiating a relationship with the empire and its claims. So we might expect them to express ambivalence regarding their construction in imperial discourse.

The Jews certainly claim their role in the empire by responding to being hailed as a people having their own language and script, one worthy of the direct address of the empire. They will, in general, follow the script the empire has dictated for them: they are made subject by Mordecai's edict as much as, if not more so, than by Haman's.[49] But even with a fellow Jew controlling imperial writing, there is a still a moment of uncertainty, a denial of the written.

Conclusion: Writing a Carnival

Perhaps because of the Jews' ambivalence, the story of Esther now exhibits "a kind of pedantic furor."[50] Esther and Mordecai single out the Jews as subjects and write to establish Purim. Mordecai writes down an account of the events and sends it to "all the Jews who were in all the provinces of King Ahasuerus, both near and far" (9:20). Another letter then appears, also enjoining the observance of Purim, which Esther seems to have written (9:29). More letters then are sent "to the one hundred twenty-seven provinces of the kingdom of Ahasuerus" (9:30) ordering Purim

---

47. Clines, *Ezra, Nehemiah, Esther*, 323. At the very least, the author may wish us to understand these Jews are better than King Saul, who kept loot against divine command (Berlin, *Esther*, 85, and many others).

48. Itumeleng J. Mosala, "The Implications of the Text of Esther for African's Women's Struggle for Liberation in South Africa," *Semeia* 59 (1992): 135–36.

49. Howard ("Writing Yehud," 185) claims that Mordecai here becomes "a new royal recorder, but for the history and future of the Jews … scripting his own fate and the fate of his people." While rightly emphasizing Mordecai's role as subjectifying the Jews, Howard fails to note that Mordecai's role is part and parcel of his imperial role. He now crafts all the groups in Persia; he has mastered all languages.

50. Ibid., 186.

observance, along with "regulations concerning their fasts and their lamentations" (9:31). Finally, in case we had missed the point, the narrator relates: "The command of Queen Esther fixed these practices of Purim, and it was recorded in writing [ונכתב בספר]" (9:32).

In the scroll of Esther, writing covers ethnic and other differences, accounting for them; it is a universalizing practice. Thus the reversals, the carnivalization, occur within writing, that exceedingly official practice. Reversals and parody cannot unseat the universal role of writing, only the persons who get to write. As Esther and Mordecai show, to get to write one must be a subject of writing. In the carnival that is the scroll of Esther, Esther and the Jews are made subject; this journey occurs along with the displacements of carnivalization. Purim is a carnival at the behest of imperial authorities, authorized by imperial means. If not for the skilled scribes of Susa, the transgressive, unofficial excesses of the carnival would not be. Esther's Purim party requires an engraved invitation.

History Told by Losers: Dictys and Dares on the Trojan War

Richard I. Pervo†

Were people expected to believe this? That question reverberates around the corners and through the crevasses of scholarly reflections about ancient popular narrative. Were the implied readers to identify Esther or 3 Maccabees or the Acts of Paul as fictions? Declarative answers notwithstanding, authorial intentions are difficult to discover. Implicit motives are probably best not pursued. One may posit that the authors of the Gospel of Mark and the Alexander Romance, for example, wished to have their narratives accepted (whatever that means); to contend that their purpose was deceit is to supply a dubious moral coloration.

An indisputable fact is that readers were quite prepared to take much fiction as fact. One cannot judge the inaccuracy of a book by its reception. An object of this paper is the exploration of that gap between definite fiction and perceived history. Antiquity holds no patent on this phenomenon. Few who work in historical disciplines cannot recount the exasperating experience of dealing with persons who prefer the account of some novel to the findings of critical historiography.

The *Trojan War Diary* (*Ephemeris belli Troiani*), issued under the name of Dictys of Crete, and "Dares the Phrygian's" *History of the Fall of Troy*, as it is called, or better, *The Trojan War Day by Day*, are, particularly the latter, prime examples of fiction accepted as fact.[1] For those in the Christian West who wanted to learn about the Trojan War during

---

1. The edition of *Ephemeris belli Troiani* used is Werner Eisenhut, *Dictys Cretensis*, 2nd ed. (Leipzig: Teubner, 1973). The original title of Dares's work is probably *Acta diurna belli Troiani*, as indicated by §44. See Gerlinde Bretzigheimer, "Dares Phrygius: Historia ficta; Die Präliminarien zum Trojanischen Krieg," *Rheinisches Museum* 151 (2008): 365–99, 366 n. 6, who refers to Willy Schetter, "Beobachtungen zum Dares

and beyond the Middle Ages, Dares and Dictys were the preferred and reliable sources. The impact of their work on Medieval and Renaissance literature was substantial. I mention only the vastly popular *Le Roman de Troie*,[2] and, of course, Chaucer's *Troilus and Criseyde* and Shakespeare's *Troilus and Cressida*.[3] For well over a millennium these two accounts of the Trojan War were history. This is a pretty good run.[4] Only for the past two and a half centuries have they been relegated—perhaps re-relegated is preferable—to the realm of fiction. This status cannot simply be attributed to the lack of competition, since the Ilias Latina, a short hexameter paraphrase, remained a standard school text until the high Middle Ages.[5] One major reason for their appeal was the apparently factual character of these two texts.

Dictys survives in six brief Latin books, the sixth of which is an epitome of four in the original that treated the *nostoi* of the heroes. The existence of a Greek original has been established by papyrus finds (which indicate

---

Latinus," *Hermes* 116 (1988): 94–109. The edition used is Ferdinand Meister, *Daretis Phrygii De Excidio Troiae Historia* (Leipzig: Teubner, 1873). This wants replacement.

2. Helen Waddell summarizes the section beginning at 1.2.45: "Homer was a clerk marvelous, says Benoît de Sainte-More; there was not much that Homer did not know. Sallust, too, Sallust was a clerk marvelous, and Sallust had a nephew, Cornelius Nepos, who was also a great clerk, and lectured at Athens. And one day when he went to look in an *armoire* for a book on grammar, before his lecture, he found instead a diary written by a Trojan called Dares, who was shut up in Troy all through the siege, who also was a great clerk but a fighter too. And of course it is better to believe Dares than Homer, who was born by his own showing a hundred years after Troy was burnt, and had his facts only by hearsay: but all the same Homer was a great clerk" (*The Wandering Scholars: The Life and Art of the Lyric Poets of the Latin Middle Ages* [Garden City, NY: Doubleday, 1961], xv).

3. This statement is especially true of Dares, *Acta diurna belli Troiani*. See Gilbert Highet, *The Classical Tradition: Greek and Roman Influences on Western Literature* (New York: Oxford University Press, 1949), 50–55. Highet characterizes Shakespeare's play as "a dramatization of part of a translation into English of the French translation of a Latin imitation of an old French expansion of a Latin epitome of a Greek romance" (55). For more detail in a broader context see Howard Clarke, *Homer's Readers: A Historical Introduction to the "Iliad" and "Odyssey"* (Newark: University of Delaware Press, 1980).

4. On the dates of these works see below.

5. On this abbreviated epic adaptation in 1,070 hexameters, see Marco Scaffai, "Aspetti e problemi dell' 'Ilias Latina,'" *ANRW* 32.3:1926–42. Ernst Robert Curtius (*European Literature and the Latin Middle Ages*, trans. Willard R. Trask [New York: Harper, 1962], 49) says that it was "normative." See also 56 and 261.

that the Latin translator improved the style of the original).⁶ The original appeared at some point between 66 and 200 CE, probably in the second century.⁷ The Latin translation is logically assigned to the fourth century.⁸ Dares's *Acta diurna belli Troiani* occupy a single book of forty-four chapters and may have been inspired by Dictys. The evidence somewhat favors a Latin original for this work.⁹ Although shorter and duller in appearance, Dares exhibits more deviation from the conventional (Homeric) accounts of the Trojan War.

Both take the form of an unpretentious soldier's diary rather than the fulsome periods of a professional litterateur. This style exudes the appearance of authenticity. In his tract on historiography Lucian reviews some writings on the Parthian War of 162–165. One of these was a "plain journal" (ὑπόμνημα ... γυμνόν) "such as a soldier or craftsman or merchant might have put together as a record of daily events" (Lucian, *Hist. cons.* 16 [author's trans.]). Lucian viewed documents of this sort as excellent raw material for a competent historian. Such resources were exactly what the good Dictys and Dares provided. In modern terms the argument would be that the works are too unpretentious to be inauthentic, that is, so wanting sparkle and art that they must be true. Dares wins whatever prizes are to be awarded in this category.

Both offer generous samples from the repertory of the wardrobe of credibility (*Beglaubigungsapparat*). Here Dictys will nudge out his rival, for he includes nearly the entire array. According the preface¹⁰ the Cretan Dictys went to war in the forces of Idomeneus and Meriones, who commissioned him to prepare a history. He arranged for this work, nine volumes written on wooden tablets in "Phoenician," to be buried with him. Why his efforts were not given to the authorities or otherwise published

---

6. The papyri are P.Tebt. 268 and P.Oxy. 2539. For the texts, see Eisenhut, *Dictys Cretensis*, 134–40.

7. See Stefan Merkle, "The Truth and Nothing but the Truth: Dictys and Dares," in *The Novel in the Ancient World*, ed. Gareth Schmeling, rev. ed. (Leiden: Brill, 2003), 563–80, 578.

8. The terminus ante quem for the Latin Dictys is Dracontius, *De raptu Helenae* (late fifth century). John Malalas knew and used the Greek Dictys in the mid-sixth century. He shows no knowledge of Dares.

9. Bretzigheimer ("Dares Phrygius: *Historia ficta*") presents the data and argues for a Latin original (392–97).

10. The preface is evidently original. The Latin translation intended to replace this with a prefatory letter. Both survived.

or, for that matter, how the discoverers learned of his will, is not revealed. "In the thirteenth year of Nero's rule" an earthquake shattered the tomb and revealed the metal box containing these memoirs. Some shepherds—one thinks of the discoverers of the Dead Sea Scrolls and of the Nag Hammadi library—happened upon this box, which they opened, expecting treasure.[11] Discovering writings in a strange alphabet—as it seemed to illiterate shepherds—they dutifully conveyed their disappointing find to their owner, one aptly named Eupraxides. Recognizing the script, he presented them to the governor, Rutilius Rufus, who abandoned his post to convey Eupraxides and the tablets to Rome. Nero knew Phoenician when he saw it and had the texts rendered into Greek. Why not Latin, one might ask, but never mind. Eupraxides was rewarded with both gifts and Roman citizenship, while the Greek library got the books.

Benighted as they may have been in some fields of learning, ancients knew about dreadful revelations ensconced within hidden books.[12] Some of these were as exciting in their own way as reports of the extrication from fanatically secured Vatican archives of a document revealing, for example, that Jesus was romantically involved with Mary of Magdala, who was, as he well knew, a female impersonator and double agent for the Roman occupation. To revert to the subject, Numa Pompilius, the legendary organizer of Roman religion, also had books buried in his tomb.[13] These emerged some four hundred years later, as the result of excessive rainfall (Plutarch, *Num.* 22) or agricultural activity[14] when Publius Cornelius and Marcus Baebius were consuls (181 BCE). In due course the newly discovered scrolls, which were in excellent condition, were brought to the attention of the Senate and condemned to be burned.[15]

The underlying tale evidently regarded these documents as confessions that Numa had concocted the entire apparatus of Roman cultic practice. So Lactantius, whose source was either Livy or an authority with

---

11. Although described as "little" (*arcula*), a box containing nine rolls on bark would have been fairly substantial.

12. On the phenomenon see Wolfgang Speyer, *Bücherfunde in der Glaubenswerbung der Antike*, Hypomnemata 24 (Göttingen: Vandenhoeck & Ruprecht, 1970), 43–124.

13. For the accounts see Livy, *Ab urbe cond.* 40.29.3–14; Pliny, *Nat.* 13.84–87; Plutarch, *Num.* 22; Lactantius, *Inst.* 1.22. Livy is the most circumstantial.

14. Digging, Lactantius; plowing, Livy.

15. On book burning in antiquity see Richard I. Pervo, *Acts: A Commentary*, ed. Harold W. Attridge, Hermeneia (Minneapolis: Fortress, 2009), 480–81.

the same perspective, assumed. An alternative, almost certainly secondary, was that the texts were Pythagorean and destroyed because of political hostility to this philosophy.[16]

Despite the differences among them, all reports agree that the books were interred with Numa, discovered at a precise date, investigated by the praetor Petilius, and judged by the Senate. This story exhibits the basic pattern: an old buried book comes to light centuries later, on a specific date. Its authenticity is confirmed by the approval of the ruling authority.

Another discovery permitted recovery of Antonius Diogenes's *The Wonders beyond Thule*.[17] The tale found a home on two sets of cypress tablets, one of which was placed near the tomb of Dinias at the time of his death. A letter from one Balagrus to Phila, the daughter of Antipater, revealed that a soldier reported finding burial vaults in Tyre following capture of the city. In them was a cypress box with appropriate directions. Thus Alexander learned of this story, which had thereafter to be transcribed and interpreted. Note the need for translation and the role of the monarch in the process. Before leaving the neighborhood of Tyre it is worth recalling Philo of Byblos, who around 100 CE allegedly rendered the ancient work of the putatively Tyrian Sanchuniathon from Phoenician into Greek.[18]

The final example of this fictional finesse comes from the (Latin) Apocalypse of Paul.[19] In the consulate of Theodosius Augustus the Younger and Cynegius (388), a respected (*honoratus*) man living in Tarsus, in a house once owned by Paul, received a revelation from an angel directing him to explore the foundations of his house and publicize the subsequent discovery. Since the recipient was skeptical, the angel had to make three visits. Prodded into action, the gentleman discovered a marble box. He was

---

16. Plutarch sees nothing objectionable in associating Numa with Pythagorean thought. Livy views it as erroneous. Both mention Valerius Antias.

17. This is based on the summary of Photius, *Bibliotheca* 166, 1111a–b. See John R. Morgan, "Lucian's *True Histories* and the *Wonders beyond Thule* of Antonius Diogenes," *CQ* 35 (1985): 475–90, esp. 481.

18. See Harold W. Attridge and Robert A. Oden Jr., *Philo of Byblos: The Phoenician History; Introduction, Critical Text, Translation, Notes*, CBQMS 9 (Washington, DC: Catholic Biblical Association, 1981).

19. See Hugo Duensing and Aurelio de Santos Otero, in *NTApoc* 2:716–17. The Latin text consulted here is the Latin text in Montague Rhodes James, *Apocrypha Anecdota: A Collection of Thirteen Apocryphal Books and Fragments*, Texts and Studies: Contributions to Biblical and Patristic Literature (Cambridge: Cambridge University Press, 1893), 1–42.

afraid to open it and took it to a judge, who had it sealed and forwarded to the emperor Theodosius. When opened the box contained the revelation subsequently presented and a pair of shoes worn by the apostle on his missionary journeys. Theodosius had a copy of the text made and transmitted the original to Jerusalem.

The story of the apocalypse's discovery contains standard features, such as a precise date and the place of the monarch, as well as different elements. Instead of discovery through natural event or unrelated human activity, the hand of Providence is patent.[20] Since Paul's tomb was known (i.e., believed) to be in Rome, a relic of the second class, his shoes, had to serve in place of the body. The motifs exhibit some fluidity, but recurrent features can be identified. This rapid survey has shown that in the Greco-Roman world the theme of the buried book served a number of functions. Those who were willing could believe such stories, as the accounts of Livy, the Elder Pliny, and Plutarch indicate.

Dares abstains from this particular theatric but quite compensates for his oversight with a prefatory epistle written by Cornelius Nepos to Sallust.[21] Nepos had what some graduate students of a certain ilk might consider a bit of good fortune. In the course of his study he came upon[22] the autograph of Dares's account of the Trojan War, which document he promptly and accurately rendered into Latin.

In 1.13 Dictys presents a delayed preface in which he states that his report on events leading up to the conflict derives from Ulysses. The balance derives from personal observations. Dictys proclaims his devotion to accuracy.[23] The assertion of *autopsia*, eyewitness participation, conforms to one of the most important criteria for ancient history. Its value

---

20. Earthquakes, rains, and, for that matter, plowing could be the result of divine initiative, but the angelophany removes any doubt.

21. Cornelius Nepos was no master of periodic style, and the *Lives* have many historical errors and exaggerations. See Edna Jenkinson, "Nepos—An Introduction to Latin Biography," in *Latin Biography*, ed. Thomas A. Dorey (New York: Basic Books, 1967), 1–15. The author did not make any evident qualitative distinctions between Sallust and Nepos. Irony increases with the apparent imitation of Sallust throughout. See Stefan Merkle, "News from the Past: Dictys and Dares on the Trojan War," in *Latin Fiction: The Latin Novel in Context*, ed. Heinz Hofmann (London: Routledge, 1999), 158.

22. The verb *inveni* could be a joke, as it may mean "invent." See Bretzigheimer, "Dares Phrygius: *Historia ficta*," 371.

23. Eorum ego secutus comitatum ea quidem, que ante apud Troiam gesta sunt,

is manifest in Diodorus Siculus's preface to his universal history, where he can characterize himself as an αὐτόπτης (*Bib. hist.* 1.4.1), although he must concede that this applies to geographical sites. After exhibiting this qualification Diodorus moves to his next step: narration of the origins of the gods, the universe, and the human race. Returning to the more modest Dictys: at the close of book 5 he reiterates his claim of active participation in the conflict and his use of interviews with people who were present at other events (5.17).[24] Dares includes a similar *sphragis* (44).

In addition to their presence on the scene, both of these authors exude the potent aroma of rationalism. The gods exist but restrict themselves to godly acts, abstaining from hand-to-hand combat with mortals and other unseemly intrigues. Divine detachment is the order of the day. Dictys at 2.30 reports the arrival of a "terrible plague," the same that erupts at the opening of the *Iliad*, with appropriate caution: "Whether this was due to the wrath of Apollo, as everyone thought, or to some other cause, was uncertain."[25] At 6.10 Dictys offers three explanations for the disappearance of Himera. This is the standard posture of the historian, who will provide both a natural and a supernatural explanation for events and leave conclusions to the audience, fulfilling the obligations of pious tradition while demonstrating their critical virtue.[26]

The marriage celebration for Peleus and Thetis came to be called "the banquet of the gods" because the participants used divine nicknames for one another (Dictys, *Eph. bell. Troiani* 6.7). To the utter and crushing disappointment of those nurtured on the story of the Trojan horse Dares coldly states: "At night, *Polydamas* said, they must lead the army to the Scaean gate—the one whose exterior was carved with a horse's head." Rationalism required—and requires—no defense, in so far as history is concerned.

By more or less all ancient and most modern criteria these accounts possess both the ring of accuracy and the qualifications of reliability. They are the rugged jottings of actual combatants innocent of the trappings of deceiving rhetoric; here one sees pristine journals uncontaminated

---

ab Ulize cognita quam diligentissime rettuli et reliqqua, quae deinceps insecuta sunt, quoniam ipse interfui, quam verissime potero exponam.

24. See also 6.10.

25. Translated by R. M. Frazer Jr., *The Trojan War: The Chronicles of Dictys of Crete and Dares the Phrygian* (Bloomington: Indiana University Press, 1966), 55.

26. See Herodotus, *Hist.* 2.3-4; Philo, *Mos.* 1.163–180; Josephus, *Ant.* 2.347–348; Arrian, *Anab.* 1.26.

with stories of wounded goddesses and seduced gods.²⁷ The truth is that they are fictions. If one is to propose a working principle it will be that suspicion should increase in direct proportion to the elaboration of the *Beglaubingunsapparat*.

A corollary to this is the fallibility of first-person narration. While insufficient to prove falsehood, in certain contexts this mode generates concern. Dictys utilizes the first person more than thirty times.²⁸ This form is supposed to be a residue of an unedited diary. As is well known, similar arguments have arisen in discussion of the "we" that intermittently permeates the narrative of Acts.²⁹ First-person narration is characteristic of later texts in the New Testament, where it serves as a mark of inauthenticity, such as John 21:24 and 2 Pet 1:16–21.³⁰ In the various pseudepigrapha and Christian Apocrypha first-person narration flourishes.³¹

Granting that the *Ephemeris belli Troiani* and the *Acta diurna belli Troiani* are fictions, questions remain. One is whether the readers were expected to accept the prima facie evidence for authenticity; that is, were these works frauds? Or, conversely, were readers expected to identify them as fictitious? Were they to be received as veracious accounts of the Trojan War? As fictions, might they be called novels? If they were primarily amusements, did they have any evident serious purposes?

That these stories could command credence and did so is indisputable. The argument from the fact of acceptance to authorial intent is fallacious. Equally uncertain is the construction of an implied reader. A case for Dares might be advanced on the grounds that his report of a discovery sends a strong signal of fictionality, but books were (and are) found in graves, and the stories about Numa showed that such tales could command belief.

---

27. For examples of modern critics who appeal to rugged style as proof of historical accuracy, see Richard I. Pervo, *Dating Acts: Between the Evangelists and the Apologists* (Santa Rosa, CA: Polebridge, 2006), 334–37.

28. Dares, however, avoids it.

29. Pervo, *Acts*, 392–96.

30. This observation is valid even when the "we" may be that of the believing community, the creedal "we," as it were.

31. See Harm Reinder Smid, *Protevangelium Jacobi: A Commentary* (Assen: Van Gorcum, 1965), app. 3, 176–78. For examples from the Christian Apocrypha, see Rosa Söder, *Die apokryphen Apostelgeschichten und die romanhafte Literatur der Antike* (Stuttgart: Kohlhammer, 1932), 211–15.

In his *Somn.* 17 Lucian addresses similar questions. The cock that serves as narrator allows that he was, in an earlier incarnation, Euphorbus, who had fought at Troy and suffered death at the hands of Menelaus. This creature is the ideal witness for revealing whether Homer was truthful. At that time the later poet was, the cock discloses, a camel in Bactria. Epic tends to exaggerate. Ajax, for example, was not as large as stated, nor was Helen so beautiful. She did have a pale complexion and a long neck, as befitted the daughter of a swan, but she was scarcely a day younger than Hecuba. And Achilles? Since he fought on the other side, Euphorbus did not come into contact with that hero, but he did kill Patroclus.[32] Author, context, and content make it unlikely that readers would take any of this seriously. The cock was, like Dictys and Dares, a foot soldier in the conflict and carefully avoids assuming omniscience. He, too, "demythologizes" Homer.[33] One can perceive in this brief exchange a number of the issues confronted in contemporary criticism of Homer, the very issues Dictys and Dares so successfully address.

The eleventh oration of Dio of Prusa (*Trojana*), which would demonstrate that Troy was not captured, is clearly a stunt. The speech nonetheless exhibits many of the criticisms lodged against Homer in antiquity.[34] If Homer's stories about the gods are indefensible, the attempt to explain them as allegory creates an a fortiori argument for not taking what is said about mortals literally.[35] Dio is also attentive to the problems of omniscient narration revealed in reports of private conversations among gods and Hera's seduction of Zeus, which took place under a cloud (19–21). The gaps in Homer's narration and his wily evasions when in a tight spot are

---

32. Contrast Homer, *Il.* 16.805–817.

33. On Euphorbus see also Ovid, *Metam.* 15.160–175; Flavius Philostratus, *Heroicus* 26.17; 33.39, 41; 42.1–2; 43.3 (in the edition of Jennifer K. Berenson MacLean and Ellen Bradshaw Aitken, *Flavius Philostratus: Heroikos*, WGRW 1 [Atlanta: Society of Biblical Literature, 2001]). See further, Diogenes Laertius, *Lives* 8.4. Pythagoras claimed to be a reincarnation of this man.

34. See Richard Hunter, "The Trojan Oration of Dio Chrysostom and Ancient Homeric Criticism," in *Narratology and Interpretation: The Content of Narrative Form in Ancient Literature*, ed. Jonas Grethlein and Antonios Rengakos (Berlin: de Gruyter, 2009), 43–62.

35. Allegorical interpretation as a means of managing the difficulties of venerable and authoritative texts was also rejected by Marcion, who, in this regard, conforms to the critical spirit of his era.

highly revelatory. Still worse, Homer did not write in chronological order (24–30). The last is a failure that both Dictys and Dares would correct.

Hector's attack on the Greek fleet (Homer, *Il.* 8; Dio, *Troj.* 11.88–90) is, however, valid narration. There Homer wrote as would Dares and Dictys. "For here," says Dio, "there is no Aeneas snatched away by Aphrodite, no Ares wounded by a mortal, nor any other such incredible tales."[36] This is the criterion for "true events … [that] resemble actual occurrences."[37] The second phrase is the very definition of fiction, that which possesses verisimilitude.[38] In justification for epic techniques Dio says that epic was popular literature, intended for the masses (οἱ πολλοί) and the uneducated (ἰδιῶται). This might be taken to imply that critical standards were not required in popular writing.[39] Behind Dio's amusing criticism possibly lurks a certain anti-Roman sentiment.[40]

Early in the reign of Alexander Severus, Flavius Philostratus wrote his *Heroicus* (*Heroikos* in transliteration).[41] This dialogue involves a gardener (see John 20:15) who tends the tomb of the hero Protesilaos, an early Greek casualty of the Trojan War. For his good services this rustic enjoys the company of the hero, who notes Homer's sins of omission and commission (e.g., §24). The poet deserves all praise for his art, but this skill should not lead readers to ignore his prejudices. This mode of criticizing Homer is reminiscent of the attempts of teachers of today to convince students that compelling and authoritative texts may not be historically

---

36. Dio Chrysostom, *Serv.* 11.90, trans. J. W. Cohoon, *Dio Chrysostom*, vol. 1, LCL (Cambridge: Harvard University Press, 1932), 513.

37. Ibid. See also the following note.

38. For ancient attempts to identify and define fiction, see, for example, Niklas Holzberg, "The Genre Novels Proper and the Fringe," in Schmeling, *Novel*, 11–28, esp. 11–18. A typical definition of "fiction" (πλάσμα) is expounded by Sextus Empiricus (c. 200 CE) in *Math.* 1.263–269: fiction is narration of events that resemble what has happened, i.e., what is credible on general grounds.

39. Dio Chrysostom opens with the ironic comment: "I am nearly certain that while all people are difficult to teach, they are easy to deceive" (*1 Regn.* 1.1 [Cohoon]).

40. See Philostratus, *Heroicus* 138–139 and below.

41. For a brief introduction see Ewen Bowie, "Philostratus: Writer of Fiction," in *Greek Fiction: The Greek Novel in Context*, ed. J. R. Morgan and Richard Stoneman (London: Routledge, 1994), 181–99. For a full study with text and translation see MacLean and Aitken, *Heroikos*. (The year 2014 witnessed the sudden and lamented death of Ellen Aitken. R.I.P.) Pages xlii–xlv examine date and authorship. For its cultural importance note Glen W. Bowersock, *Fiction as History: Nero to Julian* (Berkeley: University of California Press, 1994), 68, 111–13.

true.⁴² The development of a critical mind may be a common feature of these critiques of Homer.⁴³

Without delving further into these critical thickets, it is apparent that Dictys is immersed in the critique of Homer that flourished in the period from the last quarter of the first century through the first quarter of the third, although criticism was not restricted to that era. Dictys appears to have been a bit more coy about signaling his fictionality than the examples reviewed. A provisional conclusion is that neither the work of Dictys nor that of Dares was concocted as a fraud, nor did the authors go out of their way to signal readers that the texts were fiction. In modern terms this was good verisimilitude. One may also ask whether those of even a moderate education believed that new records about the Trojan War could possibly emerge. Dio is well aware that Homer was a poet and that poets wrote fiction. To criticize epic for omniscient narration is to denounce poetry for being poetry.

It is true, on the other hand, that most ancients believed that the Trojan War was historical.⁴⁴ This remains true for many. Less than 150 years ago Heinrich Schliemann could read Homer the way fundamentalists read Genesis—and he was rewarded for his beliefs. One enduring approach to legendary material has been to delete whatever seems miraculous or otherwise unduly improbable and accept the residue as fact. Its faithful companion, illustrated above by Dares's treatment of the wedding of Peleus and Thetis, is to recategorize events in rational terms. In short, various means for retaining the baby while disposing of the bathwater have long histories.⁴⁵ These two books could quite justifiably be read as reconstructions of history based on Homer. Mere chronicles they are not.

Both of these accounts have literary qualities, including plotting and structure, as numerous studies in the last few decades have demonstrated.⁴⁶ Stefan Merkle shows that Dares books 1–5 exhibit a sound dramatic

---

42. See the essays on pedagogy in this volume, e.g., the contribution of Shelly Matthews (who was one of the initial translators of the *Heroicus*), along with MacLean and Aitken, *Heroikos*, xi.

43. For the development of a moral critical facility for reading epic see Plutarch, *Mor.* 17d–37b.

44. See Bowersock, *Fiction*, 9.

45. In fact, these approaches are more likely to preserve the bathwater.

46. See, for example, the work of Stefan Merkle, including, "*Troiani belli verior textus*: Die Trojaberichte des Dictys und Dares," in *Die deutsche Trojaliteratur des Mittelalters und der frühen Neuzeit: Materialien und Untersuchungen*, ed. Horst Brun-

arrangement, in which the several sections alternate scene and summary.⁴⁷ A major force in the plot is the love of Achilles for Polyxena, a daughter of Hecuba, whom he encountered at a ceremony in the temple of Apollo. "When Achilles by chance turned his gaze on Polyxena, he was struck by the beauty of the girl. The longer he remained there, the deeper his passion grew. Finding no relief, he returned to the ships and, after several days of increasing torment, sent for Automedon and laid bare his heart."⁴⁸

This is a Hellenistic account of love at first sight, the woman first glimpsed at a religious ceremony. It would be entirely appropriate in a romantic novel.⁴⁹ Unromantically, Achilles is treacherously assassinated in that same temple (4.11), in the manner of Julius Caesar.⁵⁰ All in all, heroes who love women do not do well in these stories.⁵¹

Heroes do not do well in general, as Gerlinde Bretzigheimer establishes in her study of Dares's characterizations.⁵² War is not, both of these ancient authors argue, character building, nor is it all rousing adventure and crackling action. These two books are eloquent expressions of anti-

---

ner (Wiesbaden: Reichert, 1990), 491–522; "'Artless and Abrupt?' Bemerkungen zur 'Ephemeris belli Troiani' des Diktys von Kreta," in vol. 3 of *Groningen Colloquia on the Novel*, ed. Heinz Hofmann (Groningen: Forsten, 1990), 79–90; "News from the Past: Dictys and Dares on the Trojan War," in *Latin Fiction*, ed. Hofmann, 155–66; "Telling the True Story of the Trojan War: The Eyewitness Account of Dictys of Crete," in *The Search for the Ancient Novel*, ed. James Tatum (Baltimore: Johns Hopkins University Press, 1994), 183–96; "Truth," 563–80; Bretzigheimer, "Dares Phrygius: *Historia ficta*"; Bretzigheimer, "Dares Phrygius: Transformationen des Trojanischen Kriegs," *Rheinisches Museum* 152 (2009): 63–95.

47. Dares makes use of such conventional novelistic techniques as surprise, retardation, and parallelism. See Bretzigheimer, "Dares Phrygius: *Historia ficta*," 382.

48. Ac tum forte Achilles versis in Polyxenam oculis pulchritudine virginis capitur. Auctoque in horas desiderio, ubi animus non lenitur, ad naves discedit. Sed ubi dies pauci fluxere et amor magis ingravescit, accito Automedonte aperit ardorem animi.

49. E.g., Chariton, *Callirhoe* 1.1.5. Dares also reports love at first sight (27). Unlike the romantic novels, this account lacks symmetry. Readers learn nothing about any feelings Polyxena might have regarding Achilles. On Achilles's romantic attachments see Ben E. Perry, *The Ancient Romances: A Literary-Historical Account of Their Origins* (Berkeley: University of California Press, 1967), 355 n. 1.

50. See Dares, *Act. diur.* 34, who also reports a treacherous attack in the temple of Apollo. For a similar story see *Heroicus* 52.

51. Merkle, "Truth," 569 n. 11. He shows how Dictys has evidently transformed the story of Polyxena to meet his literary objectives.

52. Bretzigheimer, "Dares Phrygius: Transformationen." See her analysis of the characters of Hector (70–75) and Achilles (76–86).

war sentiment. Dictys, in particular, expounds what military writers call "replication," bluntly: you become what you fight. The plot is familiar to Americans: a peaceful people is compelled by barbarian aggression to go to war. By the end Greeks are acting like barbarians, a phenomenon also unfortunately familiar to Americans. Hector dies in an ambush. He and all but one of his companions are killed. The exception is one of Priam's sons, who is sent back to report the news, minus the hands that Achilles has chopped off. "Achilles was being driven to bestial acts, first by the slaughter of his most hated enemy, and then by his lasting grief for Patroclus" (Dictys, *Eph. bell. Troiani* 3.15).[53] The brutal treatment of the brave, badly injured Amazon Penthesilea would shame many barbarians (4.3).[54] Insofar as Achilles died for love, the story is sentimental. In its presentation of the horrors of war, it is realistic. The mixture may seem unlikely, but it is characteristic of much popular literature.[55]

Dares's account of the war is "sterile and bleak."[56] Readers are constantly aware of the number and horror of casualties, a point pressed home by the closing statistics, which state that 866,000 Greeks perished and 676,000 Trojans (*Act. diur.* 44). The most characteristic event of the war is the truce that will permit burial and recovery.[57] The literary function of these truces is to fill up the chronological gaps.[58] By introducing periodic and sometimes very lengthy truces Dares is able to stretch out the conflict to "ten years, six months, and twelve days" (44).[59] The author further illuminates an element of revisionist efforts. The critical historian of today would dismiss Homer's ten-year siege as impossible for an alliance of petty kings, but Dares rationalizes, and thereby canonizes, it.

These two stories about the Trojan conflict are fictions; not, of course, complete inventions of their writers, but accounts based on various traditions as well as authorial contributions. Such techniques are comparable to those used in other ancient historical novels, such as the *Cyropaedia* and

---

53. The adjective is *ferox*. See also 1.7; 3.10, 17, 23; 4.12; 5.6.

54. The narrator describes it as a punishment "postremae desperationis atque amentiae." To be sure, she was a woman and had no business fighting, but still....

55. Excepting, of course, the Greek romantic novels, which have more sentiment and less realism.

56. Bretzigheimer, "Dares Phrygius: Transformationen," 64.

57. E.g., Dares, *Act. diur.* 22, 23, 25, 26, 29, 31, 32, 34.

58. See Merkle, "Truth," 581.

59. The statistics on casualties and the precise chronology are examples of verisimilitude.

the Acts of Paul. The modes of characterization, attention to structure, and techniques for plotting are quite comparable to the methods observable in various ancient novels. They are better described as novels in journal form, a genre still recognized (a venerable example is Daniel Defoe's *Journal of the Plague Year*), than as false history, although ancients were not so likely to have posed this dichotomy in so many words.

Should the products of Dictys and Dares be seen as "spoofs,"[60] entertainments comparable to that of Dio of Prusa? This judgment requires more than one qualification. Whatever serious purposes Dio may have had are not immediately evident. These two books, on the other hand, are patent and vigorous critiques of war. Those who fight barbarians become barbarians. Since Rome had been engaged in conflicts with barbarians for centuries by the time Dictys and Dares were out in Latin editions, their sentiments could have not been very reassuring for the patrons of empire. "Mere entertainment" Dictys and Dares are not.

The final, and perhaps the most important in this context, question is that of the implied original readers. That these authors were believed is indisputable. If, as seems likely, they did not intend to deceive, were they willing to be believed? The most sophisticated and critical of readers can have been expected to know fiction when they saw it, but such readers became increasingly thinner on the ground in the course of antiquity and are far from an overwhelming majority in the modern West. My conclusion is that pursuit of the answer to this question is not very rewarding. Writings *were* believed, and ancient authors knew this.

Attempts to read authors' minds or make definitive judgments about the critical skills of implied readers will not produce substantial advances in the study of ancient literature. If one were to evaluate Dictys or Dares solely on the known reactions of readers, they would be judged literary frauds, since reactions of disbelief are absent. That conclusion is almost certainly erroneous. Belief in the accuracy of their contents does not transform historical fiction into history, regardless of the duration of that belief and the honored status of some of its proponents.[61]

---

60. This is the term used by John Morgan in "Make-Believe and Make Believe: The Fictionality of the Greek Novels," in *Lies and Fiction in the Ancient World*, ed. Christopher Gill and T. P. Wiseman (Austin: University of Texas Press, 1993), 209.

61. Those not advised of its fictional character would be likely to regard Defoe's *Journal* as historical. It is based on historical stories and is more circumstantial than the diaries of Samuel Pepys, for example.

According to the Brothers: First-Person Narration in the Testaments of the Twelve Patriarchs

Brian O. Sigmon

Introduction

The purpose of this paper is to show the importance of first-person narration in ancient pseudepigraphical literature by demonstrating its impact on the story of Joseph's sale into slavery in the Testaments of the Twelve Patriarchs. The Testaments of the Twelve Patriarchs contains multiple first-person narratives relating to Joseph's sale, each of which has a different narrator. The work therefore provides a unique opportunity to compare first-person accounts and to see the ways in which first-person narration influences the shaping of the story and its function in each testament.

I will begin this study by comparing narrative material related to the selling of Joseph in the Testaments of Simeon, Zebulun, Dan, Gad, Joseph, and Benjamin, with an emphasis on their first-person narrative presentation. I will then analyze the role that first-person narration plays in these passages based on the insights that emerge from comparing them to one another. This analysis will reveal that the impact of first-person narration in these passages is most keenly felt in three ways: (1) it gives the reader a focused and penetrating *perspective* on the story, but this perspective is also limited in many respects; (2) it contributes strongly to the development of the narrator's *character*, which is both in-depth and one-sided; (3) it promotes within the reader either trust or mistrust of the narrative based on the *reliability* of the narrator. In all of these respects, the literary device of first-person narration plays a crucial role in shaping how the story of Joseph's sale is to be read and interpreted in each testament where it appears.

First-Person Narratives of the Selling of Joseph

As will be readily acknowledged, the narrator and the mode of narration have an impact on the meaning and reading of a text. Shlomith Rimmon-Kenan notes the integral role that the narrator can play in the reader's understanding of a narrative work; she argues that the way a narrator participates (or not) in a story, the degree to which the narrator's presence is felt by the reader, and the reliability of the narration all impact the overall communication of the story.[1] Shimon Bar-Efrat argues likewise, giving a picturesque description of the narrator's impact:

> We see and hear only through the narrator's eyes and ears. The narrator is an a priori category, as it were, constituting the sole means by which we can understand the reality which exists within a narrative. The nature of this reality, and the essence of the narrative world, with its characters and events, and, above all, their significance, is entirely dependent on the narrator, through whom we apprehend.[2]

The Testaments of the Twelve Patriarchs provides a unique opportunity to compare first-person narratives of the same event within a single work,[3] allowing us to see how the various first-person narrators impact the story in different ways. If the narrator is indeed our sole means of entering the

---

1. Shlomith Rimmon-Kenan, *Narrative Fiction: Contemporary Poetics* (London: Routledge, 2002), 95.

2. Shimon Bar-Efrat, *Narrative Art in the Bible*, trans. Dorothea Shefer-Vanson (Sheffield: Almond, 1989), 13–14.

3. John Collins notes that the history of this work's composition is much disputed (*The Apocalyptic Imagination: An Introduction to Jewish Apocalyptic Literature*, 2nd ed. [Grand Rapids: Eerdmans, 1998], 133–34), as does Robert Kugler, who provides a concise summary of the differing viewpoints on the issue (*The Testaments of the Twelve Patriarchs*, Guides to the Apocrypha and Pseudepigrapha [Sheffield: Sheffield Academic, 2001], 31–38). But based on the structure of the Testaments of the Twelve Patriarchs and the common ethical concerns between them, Hollander and de Jonge conclude that the Testaments are a single literary composition, despite the fact that the author used older sources (Harm W. Hollander and Marinus de Jonge, *The Testaments of the Twelve Patriarchs: A Commentary* [Leiden: Brill, 1985], 27, 47). I follow their position that the Testaments are Christian texts, most likely from the second half of the second century CE (ibid., 82–85). At any rate, in their present form the testaments make up a single work, and its twelve speeches, including their narrative portions, are presented together and should be read alongside one another.

world of the story, as Bar-Efrat describes, then we have an opportunity in the Testaments of the Twelve Patriarchs to analyze multiple such entry points in the story of Joseph's sale into slavery. The Testaments of Simeon, Zebulun, Dan, Gad, Joseph, and Benjamin all contain narratives relating to the sale of Joseph, and each of these narrators presents the material in a different way, with different emphases, attitudes, and perspectives. Some, like the Testaments of Simeon and Zebulun, contain much information directly related to this story, while the Testaments of Benjamin and Dan contain only a few verses. Whereas Zebulun focuses primarily on the event itself, Simeon, Dan, and Gad focus largely on the attitudes and motivations behind their actions. Joseph narrates what happened immediately after the brothers sold him, but this material bears a relationship to the event itself.

The Testaments of the Twelve Patriarchs presuppose the biblical account of Joseph being sold into slavery (Gen 37). The patriarchs who narrate this story do not unfold the narrative as if for the first time, but rather as if they are reflecting on a story with which their audience is already familiar. Simeon, for example, does not offer an exposition in his version but begins with his motivations and then moves on to the sale of Joseph while he is away (T. Sim. 2.5–9). Likewise, Zebulun first refers to the event as τὴν ἄγνοιαν ἥν ἐποίησα ἐπὶ τοῦ Ἰωσήφ, "what I did to Joseph in ignorance," and τὸ γενόμενον, "what had been done" (T. Zeb. 1.5). Dan simply speaks of τῇ πράσει Ἰωσήφ, "the sale of Joseph" (T. Dan 1.5).[4] All of these references leave significant gaps that would puzzle the reader unless he had prior knowledge of the story. For this reason, it is helpful to keep in mind the biblical account found in Gen 37.[5] Below, I offer a brief summary of the content pertaining to Joseph's sale in each of the testaments.

Simeon's narration of the sale of Joseph is found in T. Sim. 2.6–13, with further information appearing in 4.1–3. It is highly focused on Simeon himself, communicating his motivations for wanting to kill Joseph, as well as his reactions and emotions as the story takes place. Simeon begins by recounting his jealousy (ζῆλος)[6] of Joseph in their youth, identifying their

---

4. Translations are from Testaments of the Twelve Patriarchs come from *OTP* 2:782–828, unless otherwise indicated.

5. Extrabiblical literature accounts for some, though not all, of the variations between this story in Testaments and in the biblical text. For Simeon as being especially hostile to Joseph, see Tg. Ps.-J. Gen. 37:19, Tg. Neof. Gen. 49. For Dan and Gad as hostile to Joseph's family, see Jos. Asen. 24–28 (Kugler, *Testaments*, 45–46, 67–68).

6. The Testament of Simeon uses both ζῆλος and φθόνος to convey Simeon's atti-

father's greater love for Joseph as the reason for his hatred and desire to kill his brother (2.6–7). While Simeon and Reuben were away, Joseph was sold into slavery by Judah (2.8–9). Reuben, who wanted to return Joseph to their father, was dismayed, but Simeon was furious with Judah for five months because he had allowed Joseph to live; it is implied that he wished to kill Judah, although God prevented him from doing so (2.10–12). Simeon eventually repented after God caused his hand to become withered (2.13), and the sorrowful and repentant Simeon accepted full responsibility for Joseph's betrayal (4.1–2).

Zebulun's narrative is less confined to emotion and reaction than Simeon's, although it also relates some of the narrator's thoughts and feelings. Zebulun provides a lengthy narrative of Joseph's sale, longer than the other version in the Testaments and more descriptive of the event itself. His narrative is found in T. Zeb. 1.5–4.13. Zebulun begins by differentiating himself from his brothers, saying that he committed the sin against Joseph in ignorance and only concealed the matter from Jacob because of a pact with his brothers and the threat that anyone who broke it would be killed (1.5–6).[7] His love for Joseph is felt throughout Zebulun's account. Simeon and Gad were the chief aggressors against Joseph, but Zebulun was moved to pity when Joseph begged for mercy (2.2–5). Joseph even hid behind Zebulun when his other brothers were coming after him (2.6). Zebulun also states that he did not receive any of the money acquired through Joseph's sale but that all the other brothers did and used the money to buy shoes (3.1–2). When Joseph was sold, Reuben became grieved and worried about what he would tell his father, running after the merchants with the money (4.5–7).[8] The brothers followed Dan's suggestion of dipping

---

tude. Although this use of two different terms may reflect two different strata in the text, it is simpler to conclude that the author just uses ζῆλος and φθόνος synonymously, similar to their use in 1 Clem. 3–6 (Kugler, *Testaments*, 45). See also Hollander and de Jonge, *Testaments*, 109–10.

7. Naphtali depicts himself similarly in his Testament (T. Naph. 7.2–4) and therefore seems to side with Zebulun here. I have not included his testament in my analysis because the reference is brief and incidental and because his position is so close to that of Zebulun. Including Naphtali's version in this analysis would therefore add nothing to the insights gained from those of the Testament of Zebulun with respect to first-person narration.

8. Kugler sees Reuben's reaction as one in which he is primarily concerned with saving his own reputation before Jacob rather than one of genuine concern for Joseph (Kugler, *Testaments*, 65).

Joseph's coat in goat's blood and giving it to their father (4.7–10), although Simeon wanted to cut up the coat with his sword because of his persistent anger that he had been unable to kill Joseph (4.11).

Dan's narrative is like that of Simeon in that it is focused on the narrator's emotions and attitude toward Joseph. Dan's account, found in T. Dan 1.4–9, is shorter than Simeon's and much shorter than Zebulun's, and it presents a highly secretive narrative of Dan's desire to kill Joseph—a desire that seems to have been hidden from his brothers. Dan begins his account with a confession of how he had rejoiced over Joseph's death—apparently Joseph's actual death, after all the brothers have gone to live in Egypt[9]—as well as over Joseph's sale into slavery. This gladness was due to the fact that Jacob loved Joseph more than his brothers (1.4–5). Dan speaks of an evil spirit that kept encouraging him to kill Joseph, referring to it several times and by many names (1.6–8).

Gad's narrative of Joseph's sale is found in T. Gad 1.4–2.5, and in it Gad gives a vivid account of how he came to hate Joseph. Gad contrasts Joseph's weak and delicate nature with his own, characterized in the opening verses as brave and strong (1.1–5). While Gad was in the fields killing wild animals and protecting Jacob's sheep (1.3), Joseph was at home because he was faint from the heat (1.4). At home, Joseph told Jacob that the sons of Zilpah and Bilhah were killing and eating the best animals of the flock (1.6). Gad, however, asserts his innocence, maintaining that Joseph had his facts wrong and had given a slanderous report to Jacob; this fact motivated Gad's hatred of Joseph (1.7–9). Gad joined Judah in selling Joseph to the Ishmaelites for thirty pieces of silver (2.2–3), but the two kept ten silver pieces for themselves and told their brothers the price was twenty (2.3).

The Testament of Joseph is longer than the others I have mentioned so far, but although it contains much narrative material (T. Jos. 3.1–9.5; 11.2–16.6),[10] very little of it relates to the story of when the brothers sell him into slavery. The first block of narrative material (3.1–9.5) deals with Joseph's trials with the Egyptian woman after he is already in Egypt. The second section, however, concerns Joseph's experience immediately after he is sold by his brothers and is therefore relevant to our discussion. The chief issue pertaining to my analysis is Joseph's repeated assertion that he was a slave and not the son of a free man—a departure from the biblical

---

9. This is how Kugler reads the account (ibid., 68), although another possibility is that Dan speaks of a figurative "death" with reference to Joseph being sold.

10. Ibid., 80; Hollander and de Jonge, *Testaments*, 362.

account in which Joseph protests his innocence to those with him in the prison (Gen 40:14–15).[11] The Ishmaelites questioned him right away, and Joseph told them that he was a slave from a household; he did this because he wanted to preserve his brothers' reputation and not disgrace them (T. Jos. 11.2). Joseph did this even in the face of his captors' strong skepticism (11.3), and he did it again when Pentephres questioned him, even though it led to Joseph being whipped (13.6–9). This all occurred while the other characters were well aware that Joseph was lying (see 12.2; 13.1, 9; 14.3–4; 15.3); Joseph thus worked very hard to convince them that he was a slave, being motivated by brotherly love and a desire to preserve his brothers' reputation.[12] Finally, he similarly withheld the truth concerning the amorous advances of Pentephres's wife (9.4) as well as the eunuch who stole money from her (16.6), so as not to disgrace either of them.[13]

The final narrative pertaining to the sale of Joseph in the Testaments of the Twelve Patriarchs is in the Testament of Benjamin (T. Benj. 2.1–5). In this testament, Benjamin speaks of seeing Joseph again after the whole family had joined him in Egypt. Benjamin tells how Joseph asked him what the brothers had told Jacob after they sold him. Benjamin replied that they had put blood on Joseph's coat, presented it to their father, and let him draw conclusions for himself (2.1–2). In response, Joseph briefly gives an alternative narration that Harm W. Hollander and Marinus de Jonge translate as follows: "True, brother, but, when the Ishmaelites took me, one of them stripped me of my coat and gave me a loincloth, scourged me and told me to run. And when he went away to hide my garment, a lion met him and killed him."[14] They interpret this to mean that, according to

---

11. George W. E. Nickelsburg, "Introduction," in *Studies on the Testament of Joseph*, ed. George W. E. Nickelsburg, SCS 5 (Missoula, MT: Scholars Press, 1975), 6.

12. Hollander and de Jonge, *Testaments*, 364–65.

13. Jean-Daniel Kaestli, "L'usage du Narratif dans le Testament de Joseph," in *Narrativity in Biblical and Related Texts*, ed. George J. Brooke and Jean-Daniel Kaestli (Leuven: Leuven University Press, 2000), 206. On this interpretation of Joseph's silence with regard to the Egyptian woman's advances, see Harm W. Hollander, *Joseph as an Ethical Model in the Testaments of the Twelve Patriarchs*, SVTP 6 (Leiden: Brill, 1981), 37.

14. Hollander and de Jonge, *Testaments*, 414. They base their translation on the Greek text taken from Marinus de Jonge, *The Testaments of the Twelve Patriarchs: A Critical Edition of the Greek Text* (Leiden: Brill, 1978), 168: Ναί, ἀδελφέ· καὶ γὰρ ὅτε ἔλαβών με οἱ Ἰσμαηλῖται, εἷς ἐξ αὐτῶν ἀποδύσας με τὸν χιτῶνα ἔδωκέ μοι περίζωμα, καὶ φραγελλώσας με εἶπε τρέχειν. ἐν δὲ τῷ ὑπάγειν αὐτὸν κρύψαι τὸ ἱμάτιόν μου, ὑπήντησεν

what Joseph told Benjamin, the brothers did not dip his coat in blood but found it that way and may have actually believed that he had been eaten by an animal. They note that the use of Ναί ... καὶ γάρ shows Joseph's essential agreement with Benjamin but with a slight modification according to his own story.[15] Thus, Joseph appears to have been trying to avoid disgracing his brothers to Benjamin by saying they had not actually lied.[16] Here we see two levels of narration at work: one in which Benjamin narrates a conversation he had with Joseph in Egypt, and one in which Joseph narrates what happened immediately after he was sold. The latter level of narration is situated inside the former; Benjamin is thus the overarching narrator, but within his story Joseph narrates a story of his own.[17]

First-Person Narration: An Analysis

As one can see from the foregoing summary of each patriarch's narrative about the sale of Joseph, a variety of versions of the story emerge. In some respects these versions agree with one another, such as in the fact that Simeon was particularly hostile toward Joseph in the Testaments of Simeon (T. Sim. 4.2) and Zebulun (T. Zeb. 2.1). At other points, however, they disagree, as when Dan suggests deceiving their father in the Testament of Zebulun (T. Zeb. 4.7–10), but all the brothers seem to think Joseph has actually been killed by an animal in the Testament of Benjamin (T. Benj. 2.3–5). Many of these differences and similarities illuminate the impact of the narrator on the story that is being told, as I will demonstrate below. The areas in which this influence is most evident are the perspective of the first-person narrator, the development of the narrator as a character in the story, and the narrator's reliability.

The narratives of Dan and Gad demonstrate the perspective that first-person narration brings to their stories. As stated above, the Testa-

---

αὐτῷ λέων καὶ ἀνεῖλεν αὐτόν (T. Benj. 2.3–4). Kee, translating Charles's text, gives the following translation: "Yes, brother. When they stripped off my shirt and gave me to the Ishmaelites, they gave me a loincloth, beat me, and told me to run. One of them who had whipped me was met by a lion and it ate him. So his partners were terrified and kept me under a looser rein" (H. C. Kee, "The Testaments of the Twelve Patriarchs," in *OTP* 1:825).

15. Hollander and de Jonge, *Testaments*, 416.
16. Ibid.
17. On multiple levels of narration, see Rimmon-Kenan, *Narrative Fiction*, 93–95.

ment of Dan is focused on the narrator's hidden and deeply felt emotions toward Joseph. Dan often refers to the evil spirit that kept encouraging him to kill Joseph, mentioning it three times in as many verses (T. Dan 1.6-8).[18] This spirit spoke of Dan's equality as one of Jacob's sons and told Dan that if he would kill Joseph then Jacob would love Dan (1.6-7). Dan, led by this spirit, was persuaded that he should suck the blood of Joseph as a leopard sucks the blood of a goat: ὡς πάρδαλις ἐκμυζᾷ ἔριφον, οὕτως ἐκμυζήσω τὸ Ἰωσήφ (T 1.8). As he narrates, Dan exhibits a strong inward focus, so that his narrative is almost psychological in nature. It is less an account of selling Joseph into slavery than of hatred's unseen growth inside of Dan. First-person narration allows for deep penetration into Dan's thoughts and emotions, because it allows the reader to see these things from the perspective of the character who experiences them. The account reads like a confession, with the narrator (Dan) opening for the reader a door into his own mind. By sharing Dan's perspective on his own powerful emotions, the reader feels them and reacts to them on a fundamental level.

Gad's narrative of Joseph's sale similarly illustrates how first-person narration can impact perspective. In this passage, Gad contrasts Joseph's character with his own, saying that Joseph is a weakling while Gad is powerful. Furthermore, Gad narrates what actually happened that led to Gad's hatred of Joseph: Joseph had given a slanderous report to Jacob concerning Gad (T. Gad 1.6-9). Gad, being himself a participant in the story, sees things from the level of the story rather than from above it. His narration of Joseph's character is filtered through his view of himself, and the reader, who shares this perspective, becomes drawn more fully into the story as well. The reader is invited to compare the character of Joseph with that of the narrator because the narrator himself does so. This shared perspective causes the reader to identify with Gad and to be sympathetic toward him to a certain degree; the reader is able to see Gad's side of the story and sees a small measure of justification for Gad's attitude and actions. Yet it also makes Gad's hatred of Joseph more intensely felt and more visibly present for the reader, and this leads to a stronger reaction to it on the reader's part. The reader feels Gad's hatred more intensely and therefore condemns

---

18. Dan refers to this spirit in the following ways: πνεῦμα τοῦ ζήλου καὶ τῆς ἀλαζονείας, "the spirit of jealousy and pretentiousness" (T. Dan 1.6); ἕν τῶν πνευμάτων τοῦ Βελιάρ, "one of the spirits of Beliar" (T. Dan 1.7); and τὸ πνεῦμα τοῦ θυμοῦ, "the spirit of anger" (T. Dan 1.8).

it more readily. This serves Gad's purpose elsewhere in his testament of warning his relatives about the pitfalls of hating one's brother (3.1–5.2).[19] From the narration of Dan and Gad, it is clear that first-person narration draws the reader into the story, allowing the reader to share the narrator's perspective and to see things from inside the narrative.

If first-person narration provides the reader with a focused and intimate perspective on the story, it also provides a limited one. As one can see by comparing the narratives in the Testaments, a first-person narrator can entirely miss certain details. All of the other patriarchs who narrate this story, for instance, make no comment on Dan's feelings of anger toward Joseph. Dan's narrative offers a reason why: in that account, Dan's anger appears to be a secret anger, one that he keeps inside him (ἐν καρδίᾳ μου) and that does not show through his actions (T. Dan 1.4). While a third-person narrator would have some knowledge of Dan's thoughts and could communicate them to the reader,[20] a first-person narrator other than Dan himself does not have access to this. Were it not for Dan's own narrative about his feelings toward Joseph, this information would not be available to the reader.

Similarly, we know from Gad's narrative that Gad and Judah sold Joseph for thirty pieces of silver but kept ten for themselves and only showed twenty to their brothers (T. Gad 2.3). The other narrators betray no knowledge that this has happened. It was an action rather than a thought of someone's heart, yet it was a secret action that took place behind the other brothers' backs. Again, a third-person narrator would have access to such information, whereas the first-person narrators of this story (other than Gad) do not.[21] We see from these examples that first-person narration creates a limited perspective on the story in which not all of the information is available to the narrator. Zebulun, for instance, simply does not know that Gad has taken money and that Dan secretly hates Joseph. This automatically narrows the perspective on the story that Zebulun's narrative provides for reader.

---

19. Kugler, *Testaments*, 75.

20. Bar-Efrat affirms not only that this information would be available to a third-person narrator but that in the biblical narratives the narrator frequently exploits this information for the purposes of characterization (Bar-Efrat, *Narrative Art*, 18–22). I would still maintain, however, that first-person narration gives the reader a window into the narrator's own thoughts in a way that third-person narration cannot.

21. Ibid., 17.

As first-person narrators, Joseph's brothers can also give erroneous interpretations of objects or events, since they are fallible human beings who react emotionally and intellectually to the story they narrate. This is hinted at in the Testament of Gad, where Joseph wrongly interprets Gad's actions in eating a lamb that has been harmed by a bear. Gad kills and eats the lamb because it is too weak to live, but Joseph erroneously tells Jacob that his brothers are simply eating the best sheep of the flock (T. Gad 1.6–8).

The possibility for misinterpretation is demonstrated more strongly in Simeon's and Zebulun's differing interpretations of Reuben's reaction on seeing that Joseph had been sold. In both versions, Reuben returns to find that Joseph had been sold while he was away, and Reuben is visibly distressed. Simeon's narrative takes this distress at face value, describing Reuben as being "sorrowful" (λυπέω) because Reuben wanted to restore Joseph to their father (T. Sim. 2.10). Zebulun, however, seems to have a different interpretation; in his version, Reuben's mourning seems to be due to the fact that he did not know how they would explain Joseph's absence to their father.[22] According to Zebulun, Reuben reacted in this way because he was concerned for himself and the consequences of the brothers' actions rather than for Joseph's well-being.

Both interpretations of Reuben's reaction have a clear function in their respective narratives. Simeon's narrative focuses on his jealousy of Joseph and how this led to a desire to kill his brother. Within this context, Simeon uses his elevated portrayal of Reuben in contrast with his own reaction to Joseph's sale, in which he becomes angry with Judah for five months for allowing Joseph to live and likely wants to kill Judah (T. Sim. 10–12). Reuben's reaction of concern for Joseph brings into relief Simeon's own reaction of murderous anger (2.11), and this in turn allows Simeon to develop further his message against envy and jealousy throughout his testament.[23] Zebulun's portrayal of Reuben likewise contrasts with his own character;

---

22. This is Kugler's interpretation of Zebulun's version, with which I agree (Kugler, *Testaments*, 65). Reuben's mournful words are focused on himself and on Jacob's probable reaction ("How can I look my father in the face?"), and Dan's response echoes Reuben's concerns: "Do not weep; do not mourn, for I have found what we should say to our father, Jacob" (T. Zeb. 4.5, 8).

23. Hollander and de Jonge, *Testaments*, 114. Exhortation against jealousy is widely recognized as the key theme of Simeon's Testament. See Kugler, *Testaments*, 44, and Hollander and de Jonge, *Testaments*, 109–10.

while Zebulun's weeping and protection of Joseph reveal genuine love for his brother (T. Zeb. 2.4–6), Reuben cares only for how Jacob will react.[24] Zebulun becomes a model of brotherly love in contrast to Reuben, an example of merely superficial concern. Both Zebulun's and Simeon's interpretations of Reuben affect their own characterization and the paraenesis with which their characters are associated (Simeon with envy, Zebulun with mercy and compassion). Limitations on the first-person narrator's perspective occur in the narrator's interpretations of events as well as in the information to which the narrator has access. Such limitations affect the way each brother presents information to the reader and how he uses it in his narrative.

The first-person narrator's impact on these stories is not only affected by the narrator's perspective but also by the development of the narrator's character. The character's effect on narration was just demonstrated in the analysis of Simeon's and Zebulun's interpretations of Reuben's reaction to Joseph's sale; Zebulun's morally superior characterization caused him to see Reuben's reaction negatively, while Simeon's admitted guilt caused him to see Reuben's reaction positively. Yet, because the narrator is not only an observer of the story but also a participant in it—with actions, motivations, reactions, and emotions—first-person narration itself impacts the development of the narrator's character. For one thing, the united perspective that the reader shares with the narrator automatically makes the narrator a central character in his version of the story, whereas he might be a peripheral character in other versions. Zebulun, for instance, receives no mention in the versions of the other testaments, but in his own version he is a key advocate for Joseph against the other brothers. This centrality makes it all the more important to pay attention to the characterization of the first-person narrator within the story.

One effect that first-person narration has on the narrator's characterization is that it provides depth and intensity to the character that might not otherwise occur. Thus, there are vivid descriptions of Gad's hatred of Joseph (mentioned above) as well as Simeon's. In the latter case, this is conveyed strongly by Simeon's portrayal of his reaction to Joseph's sale. Not only do we see that he reacted angrily against Judah, but it is implied that he wanted to kill him, and we are told that his hatred lasted for five months (T. Sim. 2.11–12). Another narrator, Zebulun, also conveys Sime-

---

24. Kugler, *Testaments*, 65.

on's anger, in this case by depicting his desire to cut up Joseph's coat (T. Zeb. 4.11–12). Zebulun's characterization of Simeon, however, lacks the sense of introspection and reflection that one sees through Simeon's account. Zebulun characterizes Simeon by portraying his actions, whereas Simeon characterizes himself through first-person descriptions of his own emotions and desires.

First-person narration also allows for reflection on the development of Simeon's character over time. Simeon's description of his hatred for Joseph occurs from the perspective of later repentance, so that he provides judgment on his thoughts and actions based on the change of heart that he has had. This leads him to accept full responsibility for the sale of Joseph (T. Sim. 4.2). Again, the fact that the reader sees this happen through Simeon's own eyes allows the reader to see into his character on a deeper level than might otherwise be the case. The reader is taken along for the ride, so to speak, journeying with Simeon as he repents of his hatred for Joseph. As another example of characterization through first-person narration, the reader can better experience the conflict in Zebulun's character between fear of telling Jacob the truth and the desire to do so, motivated by love for Jacob and for Joseph (T. Zeb. 1.6–7). Through the close and focused perspective that Zebulun, as a narrator, provides on his character, the character himself emerges with subtlety, depth, and multiple dimensions.

As first-person narration allows for a more nuanced and introspective development of the narrator's character, however, it also leads to a one-sided development of some characters. An excellent example of this is the character of Joseph, who in his own testament is a model of endurance, brotherly love, and a restrained tongue. Gad's narration of Joseph, however, adds an entirely different dimension to Joseph's character. From Gad's account, we see that Joseph is not a completely innocent victim but gave a false report to Jacob concerning Gad (T. Gad 1.6–8). As Hollander notes, this portrayal of Joseph even prevents him from serving as an ethical model in the Testament of Gad, a role that he receives in many of the other testaments.[25] Aspects of Joseph's character emerge in Gad's narration that Joseph does not mention. Joseph, who in his own narrative remains silent in order to preserve his brothers' reputation, tattles on his brothers to their father and tarnishes their reputation in Gad's account. Furthermore, while in Joseph's narrative he endures the advances of the Egyptian

---

25. Hollander, *Joseph as an Ethical Model*, 57.

woman as well as the lashes of his master, in Gad's narrative Joseph is delicate and unable to endure the labor as a shepherd in the field (T. Gad 1.4). Gad's narrative about Joseph may be no less one-sided than Joseph's own, but the point remains. When first-person narration occurs, the attitude with which the narrator's character is presented to the reader is none other than the character's own. Although this provides a detailed and nuanced view of the narrator's character, it provides a subjective one as well.

A third and final point at which one may study the first-person narrators in the Testaments of the Twelve Patriarchs is with respect to their reliability. Rimmon-Kenan describes reliable and unreliable narrators in this way: "A reliable narrator is one whose rendering of the story and commentary on it the reader is supposed to take as an authoritative account of the fictional truth. An unreliable narrator, on the other hand, is one whose rendering of the story and/or commentary on it the reader has reasons to suspect."[26] In other words, a reliable narrator is one the reader can trust to present the truth as the implied author intends it, and an unreliable narrator is one the reader cannot trust. Rimmon-Kenan also notes that limitations of knowledge, personal involvement in the story, and a faulty system of values are major sources of a narrator's unreliability.[27] If the narrator is known to have limited knowledge of the story being narrated, or if the narrator has a clear stake in the story or a moral stance that conflicts with that of the implied author,[28] the narrator should be mistrusted as representing the truth the implied author wishes to convey. I have shown above that the narrators in the Testaments of the Twelve Patriarchs do have limited knowledge and are personally quite involved as characters in the story. The reader is not unjustified in questioning the narratives they present. For instance, does the fact that Zebulun does not see Dan's secret anger toward Joseph, or Gad and Judah hiding a third of the money from Joseph's sale, make him an unreliable narrator? How well does he represent his brothers' motives in selling Joseph if he does not perceive Dan's inner intentions or Gad's deception and greed? Or, how might Gad's perceived justification at being angry with Joseph skew his narration of what happened when he

---

26. Rimmon-Kenan, *Narrative Fiction*, 101.
27. Ibid.
28. Rimmon-Kenan views the value system of the narrator in terms of its agreement or disagreement with that of the implied author. As she says, "If the implied author does share the narrator's values then the latter is reliable in this respect, no matter how objectionable his views may seem to some readers" (ibid., 102).

ate the lamb that had been harmed by the bear? Is he as innocent, and is Joseph as guilty, as Gad asserts in his narrative? The reader must answer such questions, sometimes unconsciously, and those answers will impact how the reader approaches the rest of the narrative.

With respect to the implied author's moral stance, Joseph's brothers are reliable. Every narrator except Joseph presents himself as repentant over what happened to Joseph, even Zebulun, to the degree that he sees himself as in the wrong (T. Zeb. 1.5). Joseph, having been the victim of these actions, does not need to repent; his continuing virtue is attested in his own testament and in those of his brothers.[29] The attitude of repentance that the brothers have implies that these narrators are reliable, since based on their repentance they exhort their audience to virtues that mirror those of the implied author.[30] Furthermore, confession strongly suggests narrative reliability. The reader is inclined to believe Simeon when he confesses his murderous attitude toward Joseph. For one thing, the reader knows that Simeon would be disinclined to speak falsely in a way that makes him appear evil. For another thing, the reader knows from Zebulun's account that Simeon actually was one of the aggressors against Joseph. Another example is Dan, who confesses his hatred of Joseph in his heart. Although his confession is unverified in the other accounts, the reader is inclined to believe him on this point, and it is therefore implied that Dan is reliable as a narrator of his own emotional story. The same is true for Gad, who confesses to having secretly kept ten pieces of silver along with Judah after Joseph was sold. Although none of the other narrators mention this, the reader does not doubt that Gad is telling the truth. So, while limitations of knowledge or personal involvement may show some of the brothers to have a certain amount of unreliability, their moral stance is not a major source of unreliability for the brothers.

---

29. Hollander has demonstrated Joseph's status as an "ethical model" within this work, showing that he is "a good example for his own sons," "an illuminating example in some of the other Testaments," and "a representative of the author's ideal of man" (Hollander, *Joseph as an Ethical Model*, 93).

30. Because ethical exhortation is the chief concern of the Testaments (see Hollander, *Joseph as an Ethical Model*, 6–12), we may reasonably consider the direct exhortations that the patriarchs pass on to their sons as the virtues that the author wishes to convey to his audience. Within the text, these exhortations are largely based on the biographical material that each patriarch narrates (Hollander and de Jonge, *Testaments*, 31–32).

Joseph's narrative presents a problem, however. His reliability does not coincide with his moral agreement with implied author. Joseph certainly embodies the virtues that the implied author wishes to uplift, both in Joseph's own narrative and in that of his brothers.[31] In all of the testaments that narrate the story of Joseph's betrayal, Joseph emerges as a model of brotherly love, one of the prime virtues in the Testaments of the Twelve Patriarchs.[32] In Joseph's own narrative, however, Joseph exhibits this virtue by lying about his true identity in order to preserve the reputation of his brothers. In doing so, he shows himself to be untruthful and thus potentially untrustworthy as a narrator of events. The fact that he also withheld the truth about the eunuch's theft strengthens this possibility (T. Jos. 16.5–6). Although these actions occurred in the past, the reader wonders whether Joseph still protects others' reputations in this way, especially since his virtuous character emerges when he does so. Hollander has even described Joseph's desire to hide the truth for the benefit of others as a "central characteristic of Joseph's attitude."[33] The cumulative effect is to undermine Joseph's reliability as a narrator.

We also see Joseph's unreliability as a narrator in the Testament of Benjamin, where Joseph is a secondary narrator rather than the primary one.[34] As stated above, Joseph's narrative in the Testament of Benjamin suggests that his brothers had found his bloody garment rather than dipping it in blood themselves, which helps to preserve his brothers' reputation in Benjamin's view.[35] Joseph's version of events here is cast in doubt since it contradicts not only the biblical account of the brothers' actions (Gen 37:23, 31–33) but the narrative in the Testament of Zebulun as well (T. Zeb. 4.8–13). Thus, although Joseph is a morally upright narrator according to the implied author, he is also an unreliable secondary narrator in the Testament of Benjamin and a primary narrator of questionable reliability

---

31. Hollander, *Joseph as an Ethical Model*.
32. Hollander and de Jonge, *Testaments*, 44. See also Walter Harrelson, "Patient Love in the Testament of Joseph," in Nickelsburg, *Studies on the Testament of Joseph*, 32. Harrelson argues that Joseph embodies the chief virtue that will enable God's people Israel to thrive in the world, namely, their commitment to one another in love.
33. Harm W. Hollander, "The Ethical Character of the Patriarch Joseph: A Study in the Ethics of the Testaments of the XII Patriarchs," in Nickelsburg, *Studies on the Testament of Joseph*, 70.
34. See Rimmon-Kenan, *Narrative Fiction*, 93–95.
35. Hollander and de Jonge, *Testaments*, 416.

in his own testament. This unreliability exists not in spite of his status as a model of brotherly love but because of it.

Conclusion

By comparing the various first-person narratives of the story of Joseph being sold into slavery in the Testaments of the Twelve Patriarchs, I have demonstrated the impact that first-person narration has on each of these narratives. This impact manifests itself in three key areas. First of all, the first-person narrator has an intimate and personally focused perspective on the story. This allows the narrator to draw the reader in, and it allows the reader to see the story from the perspective of one of its participants. The result is often narration with a great depth of emotional involvement, as in the case of the narratives of Dan, Gad, and Simeon. At the same time, however, first-person narration limits the narrator's perspective, and details of the story can be missed entirely or wrongly interpreted, such as Dan's secret hatred of Joseph or Reuben's reaction of distress when Joseph is sold. Second, first-person narration gives the author a powerful tool for developing one of the story's characters, namely the narrator. Because the reader shares the narrator's perspective on the story, the reader can infer the narrator's character by the emotions and attitudes with which he speaks or which he confesses. This also has its problems, however, since Gad's characterization of Joseph suggests that Joseph's self-characterization in his own narrative may be one-sided. Finally, the reliability of the narrator is achieved through repentance and the exhortation of virtue. While the brothers do have limited knowledge and are highly involved in the story they narrate, their expressed repentance shows them to be in line with the implied author's values and thus reliable in that respect; they are especially reliable at those points at which they confess to a wrongful act. Moral uprightness, however, does not guarantee narrative reliability, as can be seen in the case of Joseph. Although he is a model of virtue in the testaments, his very virtue causes him to narrate unreliably in order to preserve the reputations of others.

A Tale of Two Moseses:
Philo's *On the Life of Moses* and Josephus's *Jewish Antiquities* 2–4 in Light of the Roman Discourse of Exemplarity

James M. Petitfils

Introduction

In a panegyric to the emperor Trajan, Pliny the Younger underscores, "example is what we need more than command.... Men learn better from examples, which have the great merit of proving that their advice is practicable" (Pliny, *Pan.* 45.6).[1] Less then a century earlier, Philo of Alexandria seems to share similar pedagogical presuppositions as he deploys his Moses as a "well-wrought picture, a piece of work beautiful and godlike, a model for those who are willing to copy it" (*Moses* 1.158–159).[2] Are these corresponding sentiments regarding the moral utility of example simply a coincidental overlap in the pedagogical approaches of two ethnically distinct thinkers writing in the Roman Mediterranean, or does this similarity suggest something more? While much has been written tracing the interplay between Greek and Jewish culture in the eastern Mediterranean, this article will consider the presence of popular *Roman* leadership mores and discursive strategies discernible in the work of Philo of Alexandria and Flavius Josephus.[3]

---

1. Pliny the Younger, *Letters and Paegyricus*, trans. Betty Radice, LCL (Cambridge: Harvard University Press, 1969).

2. All English translations of *Moses* 1–2 in this essay will rely on F. H. Colson, trans., *On the Life of Moses*, LCL (Cambridge: Harvard University Press, 1935).

3. In tracing specifically Roman cultural forms, I seek to, in the words of Annette Reed, "move beyond the all-too-common appeals to an undifferentiated

I will begin by introducing the form of the Roman discourse of exemplarity as well as a key characteristic of ideal Roman leadership popularly celebrated in this discourse. The balance of the article will then explore the degree to which Josephus and Philo respectively deploy the distinguishing elements associated with the discourse in their narrative portrayals of Moses. Reading these accounts in such a light, I hope to move beyond an identification of exclusively elite cultural influences and trace their appropriation of discursive habits and leadership presuppositions operating even in the Roman populace.

Narrative Form of the Roman Discourse of Exemplarity

Over the past two decades, a number of works have emerged in the field of classics exploring the formal and informal cultural mechanisms involved in the creation and transmission of historical memory and morality in the various strata of Roman society.[4] One noteworthy area of agreement

---

'Greco-Roman' culture in research on early Judaism" ("The Construction and Subversion of Patriarchal Perfection: Abraham and Exemplarity in Philo, Josephus, and the *Testament of Abraham*," *JSJ* 40 [2009]: 188). For additional studies investigating Josephus in his Roman context, see Mary Beard, "The Triumph of Flavius Josephus," in *Flavian Rome: Culture, Image, Text*, ed. A. J. Boyle and W. J. Dominik (Leiden: Brill, 2003), 543–58; Steve Mason, "Flavius Josephus in Flavian Rome: Reading on and between the Lines," in *Flavian Rome*, ed. Boyle and Dominik, 559–90; Mason, "Figured Speech and Irony in T. Flavius Josephus," in *Flavius Josephus and Flavian Rome*, ed. Jonathan Edmondson, Steve Mason, and James Rives (New York: Oxford University Press, 2005), 244–88; and Erich Gruen, "Polybius and Josephus on Rome," in *Flavius Josephus: Interpretation and History*, ed. Jack Pastor, Pnina Stern, and Menahem Mor, JSJSup 146 (Leiden: Brill, 2011), 149–62. With respect to recent works on Philo and Roman culture, see Maren Niehoff, *Philo on Jewish Identity and Culture*, TSAJ 86 (Tübingen: Mohr Siebeck, 2001); Niehoff, "The Symposium of Philo's Therapeutae: Displaying Jewish Identity in an Increasingly Roman World," *GRBS* 50 (2010): 95–117; and Niehoff, "Philo and Plutarch as Biographers: Parallel Responses to Roman Stoicism," *GRBS* 52 (2012): 361–92. For a review of the few twentieth-century works dealing with Philo and Rome, see Niehoff, *Philo on Jewish Identity*, 6–7.

4. See Karl-Joachim Hölkeskamp, "*Exempla* und *mos maiorum*: Überlegungen zum kollektiven Gedächtnis der Nobilität," in *Vergangenheit und Lebenswelt: Soziale Kommunikation, Traditionsbildung und historisches Bewusstsein*, ed. Hans Joachim Gehrde and Astrid Möller (Tübingen: Narr, 1996), 301–38; Uwe Walter, *Memoria und Res Publica: Zur Geschichtskultur im republikanischen Rom*, Studien zur alten Geschichte 1 (Frankfurt am Main: Verlag Antike, 2004); Teresa Morgan, *Popular Morality in the Early Roman Empire* (Cambridge: Cambridge University Press, 2007);

arising in these studies is the importance of "example" in popular Roman education and socialization.[5] In Rome, both elites and nonelites would regularly encounter their carefully emplotted Roman leaders in everything from memorable stories repeated in public orations or deployed during one's domestic education, to public funerals, on coins, or in statuary and other forms of monumental architecture. In short, *exempla* functioned as preferred rhetorical vehicles of the *mos maiorum* (way of the ancestors), and this preference for example over precept was embraced by "all of Roman society, from the loftiest aristocrats to the humblest peasants, laborers, and slaves."[6]

Matthew Roller, perhaps the most influential scholar exploring this phenomenon, outlines the main features of the Roman discourse of exemplarity, a cultural conversation that he claims "exposes what Romans from the late Republic onward took to be the normal or normative way in which social values were established and instilled, deeds were done and evaluated accordingly, and social reproduction occurred."[7] He identifies four interacting narratological components comprising this discourse: (1) action, (2) audience, (3) commemoration, and (4) imitation.[8] The *action* on display in a particular narrative, spectacle, or monument is "held to be consequential for the Roman community at large" and is "regarded as embodying (or conspicuously failing to embody) crucial social values."[9] The primary *audience* viewing the action "place it in a suitable ethical

---

Peter Scholz, *Den Vätern folgen: Sozialisation und Erziehung der republikanischen Senatsaristokratie* (Berlin: Verlag Antike, 2011); and Matthew Roller, "Exemplarity in Roman Culture: The Cases of Horatius Cocles and Cloelia," *CP* 99 (2004): 1–56.

5. Teresa Morgan includes the *exemplum* as one of a handful of genres that served as "vehicles for popular morality" (*Popular Morality*, 6). Uwe Walter makes a connection between the popularity of this pedagogical approach and its easily digestible nature (*Memoria*, 44–45). See Scholz, *Den Vätern*, 26, 32, 89–126.

6. Roller, "Exemplarity," 6.

7. Ibid., 4. He continues his study of Roman exemplarity in two articles, "The Exemplary Past in Roman Historiography and Culture: The Case of Gaius Duilius," in *The Cambridge Companion to Roman Historiography and Culture*, ed. Andrew Feldherr (Cambridge: Cambridge University Press, 2009), 214–30; and "The Consul(ar) as *exemplum*: Fabius Cunctator's Paradoxical Glory," in *Consuls and "Res Publica": Holding High Office in the Roman Republic*, ed. Hans Beck et al. (Cambridge: Cambridge University Press, 2011), 182–210.

8. Roller, "Exemplarity," 4–5.

9. Ibid. 5.

category ... and judge it 'good' or 'bad' in that category."[10] The *commemoration* of the action can appear in forms as diverse as a textual witness, a statue, a title, or even an exposed scar. Such commemoration encourages secondary audiences to evaluate the exemplary action "in full knowledge of what the primary audience thought."[11]

Roller describes the implicit (and at times explicit) mandate for imitation: "any spectator ... whether primary or secondary, is enjoined to strive to replicate or to surpass the deed himself, to win similar renown and related social capital."[12] In sum, according to Roller, "looping through its four operations, then, exemplary discourse produces and reproduces the actors, deeds, judging audiences, monuments, and values that collectively constitute this way of knowing self and past in relation to one another."[13] Having introduced the pedagogical vehicle of Roman exemplarity, I will briefly review a characteristic component of its popular moral freight.

Preferred Moral Content in Roman Leadership *Exempla*

The leadership virtues most frequently celebrated in *exempla* and exemplary displays in Roman antiquity relate to the bravery and martial prowess of Rome's ancestors. In his *Memorable Doings and Sayings*—the best extant collection of ancient *exempla*—Valerius Maximus clearly prefers this "chief glory and mainstay of Roman empire" (2.7.praef.) more than any other virtue.[14] One anecdote illustrates particularly well the weight Valerius, and many in Roman society, placed on such *virtus*:

> The earth subsided in the middle of the Forum leaving a sudden huge chasm. An oracle was given that this could only be filled with what made the Roman people's greatest strength. This Curius, a young man of the noblest spirit and lineage, interpreted it in the sense that our city chiefly

---

10. Ibid.
11. Ibid.
12. For each structural element described below, see ibid., 4–5.
13. Roller, "Exemplary Past," 217.
14. After graphing the distribution and frequency of the main topics covered in the *Memorable Doings and Sayings*, Morgan concludes, "No single conventional virtue in Valerius' collection is provided with as many exempla as courage" (*Popular Morality*, 137). All English translations of Valerius Maximus will rely on Shackleton Bailey, trans., *Memorable Doings and Sayings*, 2 vols., LCL (Cambridge: Harvard University Press, 2000).

excels in valour [*virtute*] and arms. Wearing his military decorations he mounted his horse, dug in spurs, and drove him head-long into that abyss. On top of him all the citizens vied with one another in throwing down grain in his honour, and the ground in no time regained its former condition. (5.6.2)[15]

Beyond this representative account, Valerius's collection positively abounds with *exempla* involving the "valour and arms" of the Roman ancestors.[16]

In addition to such literary *exempla*—frequent fixtures of popularly consumed oratory—the paradigmatic martial prowess of Rome's leaders was further broadcast to audiences of all social stripes in monumental architecture. One prominent example of the use of statues, inscriptions, and architecture to advertise military accomplishment is Augustus's forum. The Forum Augustum featured a temple to Mars Ultor, a central statue of Augustus on a triumphal chariot, and showcased a veritable "Hall of Fame of distinguished Roman ancestors ... beginning with Aeneas and Romulus."[17] In a dedicatory edict, Augustus explains one of the forum's purposes, namely, to provide *exempla* by which the citizens of the empire could judge his own rule (Suetonius, *Aug.* 31.5). The glorious complex possessed particular potential with respect to advertising *exempla* since it was a setting for daily life (including popular spectacles) rather than a space solely reserved for elite ritual.[18] Its influence, moreover, was not limited

---

15. See Livy, *Ab urbe cond.* 7.6. Reflecting its popularity and popular accessibility, see Valerius Maximus, *Memorable Doings and Sayings* 3.3.ext. 7.

16. These *exempla*, to name a few, include Horatius Cocles (Valerius Maximus, *Memorable Doings and Sayings* 3.2.1; see 4.7.2); Cloelia, "a girl, holding the light of valour [*virtutis*] before men" (3.2.2); Muncius Scaevola (3.3.1); the self-sacrificing Decii (5.6.5–6); and the numerous exploits of the Scipiones (2.8.5; 2.10.2; 3.2.6; 3.6.1; 5.4.2; 7.2.2). This confirms Marrou's conclusion: "The Roman hero, whatever his name—Horatius Cocles, Camillus, Menenius Agripa, Octavius Augustus—was the man who, by his courage or wisdom, and in the face of great difficulties, saved his country when it was in danger" (Henri Irénée Marrou, *A History of Education in Antiquity*, trans. George Lamb [Madison: University of Wisconsin, 1982], 235).

17. Karl Galinsky, *Augustan Culture* (Princeton: Princeton University Press, 1996), 199. For a succinct description of the main components of the complex, see Martin Spannagel, *Exemplaria principis: Untersuchungen zu Entstehung und Ausstattung des Augustusforums* (Heidelberg: Verlag Archäologie und Geschichte, 1999), 9–13.

18. See Spannagel, *Exemplaria*, 9; see also Galinsky, *Augustan Culture*, 199.

to the population living in Rome during Augustus's reign but extended to the provinces and to the construction projects of subsequent emperors.[19]

In terms of its moral communication, as Martin Spannagel has convincingly argued, the statues most prominently showcased in the forum correspond to Augustus's own martial accomplishments. Romulus (featured in the south apse), for example, points to Augustus's recovery of lost Roman standards from the Parthians. This notion of victory over the east, Spannagel elaborates, advertises Augustus in the honored martial leadership tradition of Alexander the Great.[20] Thus, whether reinforced in memorable ancestral anecdotes or architecturally framing intersections of daily life, courage and martial prowess were not just leadership preferences of a small coterie of Roman statesmen; they were staples in the pedagogical diet of the urban masses.

Josephus's and Philo's Exposure to Roman Politics and Popular Culture

Though hailing from the eastern Mediterranean and claiming Jewish native identities, both Josephus and Philo were no strangers to Roman politics and culture. Josephus, for his part, enjoyed a comfortable position in the Roman capital for well over a decade before beginning his *Antiquities*.[21] There Josephus would regularly have encountered the Roman dis-

---

19. On its replication in the provinces, see Harriet Flower, *Ancestor Masks and Aristocratic Power in Roman Culture* (Oxford: Clarendon, 1996), 229. The Flavians, more ambitiously than the Julio-Claudians, followed Augustus's policy of architecturally advertising military accomplishment. Consider, for example, their Temple of Peace, the Flavian Amphitheatre, and the Arch of Titus.

20. For a review of the literary, numismatic, and iconographic propagation of Augustus's recovery of the standards and his martial fulfillment of both Romulus's legacy as well as the "Alexandernachfolge" motif, see Spannagel, *Exemplaria*, 224–55. On the martial significance of the Aeneas statue (north apse), see ibid., 208–23.

21. On Josephus's semi-elite social position in Rome, see Martin Goodman, "Josephus as Roman Citizen," in *Josephus and the History of the Greco-Roman Period*, ed. Fausto Parente and Joseph Sievers (Leiden: Brill, 1994), 330; John Curran, "Flavius Josephus in Rome," in Pastor, Stern and Mor, *Flavius Josephus: Interpretation and History*, 65–86; and Luuk Huitink and Jan Willem van Henten, "The Publication of Flavius Josephus' Works and Their Audiences," *Zutot* 6 (2009): 49–60. For works arguing for Josephus's social obscurity, however, see Jonathan Price, "The Provincial Historian in Rome," in *Josephus and Jewish History in Flavian Rome and Beyond*, ed. Joseph Sievers and Gaia Lembi (Leiden: Brill, 2005), 101–18; and Hannah M. Cotton and Werner

cursive approaches outlined by Roller as well as those leadership virtues—especially martial prowess—celebrated by politicians and *populus* alike.

While he did not have Josephus's half-lifetime in the capital, Philo did encounter Roman culture in a number of venues. To begin with, his hometown of Alexandria was not untouched by Roman administrative and cultural approaches. Beyond a number of more subtle political and administrative changes, likely only perceptible to more elite Alexandrians, the imperial celebrations and Augustan architecture in Roman Egypt broadcast characteristically Roman values.[22] Additionally, as the leader of an embassy to Caligula, Philo had to remain in Rome for several months.[23] In short, though Philo was not in Rome nearly as long as Josephus, he was in the capital long enough to have, in the words of Maren Niehoff, "imbibed the cultural as well as political climate."[24]

To what degree might both writers' comparative proximity to the widespread Roman discourse of exemplarity have colored their understanding and presentation of Moses's leadership?[25] Starting with the Josephan Moses in *Ant.* 2-4 and then moving to Philo's *Moses* 1-2, I will focus on a narrative sample in each author's work wherein Josephus or Philo takes the most significant liberties with the biblical account to showcase a favored Mosaic leadership quality. Along the way I will consider the narratological shape of the major pericopae in light of Roller's fourfold schema, concluding with a brief comparison of their portrayals of the ancestral hero.

Eck, "Josephus' Roman Audience: Josephus and the Roman Elites," in Edmondson, Mason, and Rives, *Flavius Josephus and Flavian Rome*, 37-52.

22. See Ramsay MacMullen, *Romanization in the Time of Augustus* (New Haven: Yale University Press, 2000), 15-16. For examples of such Romanization, see Naphtali Lewis, "The Romanity of Roman Egypt: A Growing Consensus," in *Atti del XVII Congresso internazionale di Papirologia* (Napoli: Centro Inernazionale per li Studio dei Papiri Ercolanesi, 1984), 1080-84; Dorothy Sly, *Philo's Alexandria* (New York: Routledge, 1996), 36, 87; and Niehoff, *Philo on Jewish Identity*, 19-20.

23. On Philo's longer than expected wait in Rome, see Sly, *Alexandria*, 176-77.

24. Niehoff, *Philo on Jewish Identity*, 88.

25. Maren Niehoff has recently identified the (reciprocal) literary influence of Roman Stoicism on Philo's *Moses* ("Philo's *Exposition* in a Roman Context," *SPhiloA* 23 [2011]: 5-21). While she makes a convincing case with respect to this elite philosophical discourse, my project investigates the imprint of more *popular* Roman pedagogical habits on the Philonic Moses.

Moses as a Leader in *Antiquities* 2–4

While Josephus and Philo are equally eager to paint Moses as a pious *exemplum* of effective leadership,[26] where Josephus most significantly embellishes the biblical account in *Ant.* 2–4, it is to display his Moses as a skilled and daring "general" (στρατηγός).[27] These embellishments, as I will briefly sketch, are frequently colored by the common elements of the Roman discourse of exemplarity.

One important display of martial action occurs in *Ant.* 3.45–51, as Moses skillfully marshals the wandering Hebrews (the episode's primary audience) for battle with the Amalekites, the "most warlike of the peoples in those parts" (*Ant.* 3.40).[28] Preparing for the conflict, Moses personally selects the best warriors (3.49), reorganizes the camp to protect women and children (3.50), passes a "wakeful night, instructing Joshua how to marshal his forces" (3.50), and finally addresses "stirring words to the whole host assembled in arms" (3.52). The text commemorates Moses's actions as efficaciously transforming the Hebrew camp from "a host destitute of everything" (3.43) to an armed force "elated at the peril" and ready for Moses to "lead them instantly and without procrastination against the enemy" (3.48).[29] Finally, though imitation is not explicitly enjoined in the

---

26. Both authors similarly enhance Moses's piety in a number of ways. First, while the LXX only includes two explicit commendations of Moses (Deut 34:10–12 and Num 12:3), both authors unabashedly lavish superlatives on the leader (*Ant.* 4.328–329; *Moses* 1.1, 158–159; 2.192). Second, they carefully exculpate Moses of his killing the Egyptian (Exod 2:11–15). Josephus never mentions the murder, and Philo creatively reinterprets the killing as a well-considered "righteous action" (*Moses* 1.44). Finally, both accounts remove any negative elements associated with Moses's inability to enter the promised land (*Ant.* 4.177 and *Moses* 2.288).

27. Unlike the nomenclature in the LXX or in Philo's *Moses* 1–2, this martial title is the preferred moniker of the Josephan Moses (*Ant.* 2.241, 268; 3.2, 11, 12, 28, 47, 65, 67, 78, 102, 105; 4.82, 194, 329); see Louis Feldman, "Josephus' Portrait of Moses: Part Two," *JQR* 83.1–2 (1992): 13; see also Finn Damgaard, "Brothers in Arms: Josephus' Portrait of Moses in the 'Jewish Antiquities' in the Light of His Own Self-Portraits in the 'Jewish War' and the 'Life,'" *JJS* 59.2 (2008): 221.

28. All English translations of *Ant.* 2–4 rely on H. St. J. Thackeray et al., trans., *Jewish Antiquities*, 10 vols., LCL (Cambridge: Harvard University Press, 1926–1965).

29. Further commemorative activity is noted within the narrative as Moses rewards and eulogizes the military success and those involved (*Ant.* 3.59), erects a commemorative altar (*Ant.* 3.60), and regales "the troops with festivity" (*Ant.* 3.60). On Josephus's *Antiquities* itself serving as a commemorative "inscription in text," see

text, it is certainly implied in the praiseworthy and well-decorated leadership of Joshua—Moses's pupil in the art of war (3.59).[30]

If the above pericope underscores Moses's prowess as a strategist and general, the extrabiblical account of his triumph over the Ethiopians (*Ant.* 2.238–257)—which also corresponds well with Roller's outline of Roman exemplarity—best displays his personal courage on the battlefield.[31] Moses's actions—his "marvelous" military stratagem (στρατήγημα θαυμαστόν) and his personally led attacks—result in the "great carnage of the Ethiopians" (2.248).

At the siege of Saba (2.249–252), in particular, Moses's brave feats take place under the gaze of several carefully mentioned audiences. The Egyptian priests viewing the brave spectacle repent of their desire to kill Moses and "were now not ashamed to crave his succour" (2.242), while Pharaoh "from envy [φθόνου] of Moses's generalship" conspires to murder him (2.255). The Hebrews respond positively, desiring Moses as their general (2.243). Finally, and perhaps most dramatically, "Tharbis, the daughter of the king of the Ethiopians, watching Moses bringing his troops close beneath the ramparts and fighting valiantly [μαχόμενον γενναίως], marveled at the ingenuity of his manoeuvres … [and] fell madly in love with him" (*Ant.* 2.252). If it was anything, Moses's military leadership was eye-catching.

Seth Schwartz, *Were the Jews a Mediterranean Society? Reciprocity and Solidarity in Ancient Judaism* (Princeton: Princeton University Press, 2010), 96.

30. The prizes Moses grants to Joshua and those "whose exploits were attested [μαρτυρούμενον] by the whole army" (*Ant.* 3.59) are not unlike the spoils of war celebrated in Roman triumphs and in monumental architecture such as the Forum Augustum. On Josephus's reluctance to *explicitly* enjoin readers to imitate either Moses's leadership or the Hebrews' desire for such leadership, Reed points out that this reluctance is, in fact, "consistent with the genre conventions of narrative prose history in Roman literary culture of the time." She continues, "Explicit appeals to *exempla* are only sometimes found in the narrative accounts of historical events" ("Construction," 195–96).

31. To be sure, the overall plotline may not be a Josephan original, as Artapanus, to the degree that Eusebius accurately preserves his work (*Praep. ev.* 9.27.1–39), centuries earlier recounts Moses's leadership against the Ethiopians. Nevertheless, Josephus's account is far more detailed and, as Giovanni Frulla notes, particularly affords "the occasion to show everybody [Moses's] military cleverness" ("Reconstructing Exodus Tradition: Moses in the Second Book of Josephus' *Antiquities*," in Pastor, Stern, and Mor, *Flavius Josephus: Interpretation and History*, 116).

Beyond its inscription as text by Josephus,[32] within the narrative Moses's value-laden action is commemorated with his marriage to Tharbis and in his publicly rendering thanks to God for the victory (2.252–253). Finally, like Moses's defeat of the Amalekites reviewed above, this episode does not explicitly enjoin readers to emulate his courage or to share Tharbis's adoration for such a leader; nevertheless, this imitation remains a pervasive subtext in *Ant.* 2–4.[33] In sum, Josephus freely appropriates and redeploys the Roman discourse of exemplarity in an effort to create secondary audiences that could confess with him that Moses "as a general had few to equal him" (4.329).

Philo's Portrayal of Moses's Leadership

Compared with Josephus's *Ant.* 2–4, Philo's presentation of his "beautiful and godlike ... model [παράδειγμα]" (*Moses* 1.158) is far less concerned with Moses's martial ability.[34] Furthermore, though Philo shares many Hellenistic and Roman assumptions about the exemplary use of history, unlike Josephus, his narrative episodes are by and large not structured around the elements of Roman exemplary discourse.[35] Instead, *On the Life of Moses* celebrates above all Moses's philosophical education and eloquence.

To this end, Philo sanitizes embarrassing biblical passages relating to Moses's ineloquence and frames even Moses's exile from Egypt as a season for fruitful philosophical development: "he was ever opening the scroll of philosophical doctrines, digested them inwardly with quick understanding, [and] committed them to memory never to be forgotten" (*Moses* 1.48).[36] In addition to these episodes, both of Philo's most lengthy

---

32. On narratives as commemorations, see Roller, "Exemplarity," 4–5; see also Schwartz, *Were the Jews*, 96.

33. The repeated praise for Moses elsewhere in *Ant.* 2–4 in conjunction with the snapshots of Moses equipping Joshua for military leadership carry strong mimetic implications. For passages directly celebrating Moses's exemplary leadership, see *Ant.* 2.205, 216; 4.312–331.

34. Philo includes only passing mentions of Moses in military leadership. Philo mentions Moses's wisdom as a general (*Moses* 1.249, 257) and includes a brief comment on his offensive against Balak's Moabites (*Moses* 1.306–308).

35. For Philo's presuppositions with respect to the mimetic use of history, see *Abraham* 3–4 and *Moses* 1.158.

36. Redeeming Moses's ineloquence, Philo excludes Exod 6:12 altogether and attributes the hero's hesitation in Exod 4:10 to his pious admiration of God's elo-

emendations to the biblical account celebrate Moses's education and philosophical acumen. The first pericope describes Moses's royal education and unparalleled academic accomplishment while a youth in Egypt. The second extended embellishment frames Moses's rescue of the women at the Midianite well (Exod 2:17) as a marvelous and well-reasoned rhetorical performance (*Moses* 1.54–57). For this article, I will focus on the former episode.

Whereas the biblical account of Moses's upbringing mentions precious little (Exod 2:10), Philo fills in the lacuna with extended details of the remarkable education and character of young Moses. As a youth in Egypt, rather than exploring the sensual pleasures of the kingdom, Moses "with a modest and serious bearing ... applied himself to hearing and seeing what was sure to profit the soul" (*Moses* 1.20). Moreover, Philo tells us:

> Teachers at once arrived from different parts, some unbidden from the neighbouring countries and the provinces of Egypt, others summoned from Greece under promise of high reward. But in a short time he advanced beyond their capacities; his gifted nature forestalled their instruction, so that his seemed a case rather of recollection than of learning, and indeed he himself devised and propounded problems which they could not easily solve. (*Moses* 1.21)

Moses, this "gifted soul" (1.22), received an elite Egyptian education in arithmetic, geometry, meter, rhythm and harmony, music, philosophy conveyed in symbols/Egyptian religion; a Greek education; an Assyrian education in letters; and finally a Chaldean education in astronomy/astrology (1.23–24). In addition to Philo's Platonic portrayal of Moses's learning in terms of recollection, Louis Feldman observes, "it is surely striking that these are the very subjects, indeed in the very order, that Plato (*R*.7.521C–31C) prescribes for the higher education of his philosopher-king."[37]

---

quence—an admiration that provokes God's praise rather than censure (*Moses* 1.83–84).

37. Louis Feldman, *Philo's Portrayal of Moses in the Context of Ancient Judaism*, Christianity and Judaism in Antiquity Series 15 (Notre Dame, IN: University of Notre Dame Press, 2007), 51. Philo's suggestion in *Moses* 2.2 confirms Feldman's observation: "It has been said, not without good reason, that states can only make progress in well-being if either kings are philosophers or philosophers are kings." For more of Philo's praise of Moses's education and cultural competence, see *Moses* 1.27 and 1.32.

In contrast to the content of Josephus's creative biblical elaborations, Philo chooses to leave Moses's military record unadorned in favor of enhancing his hero along the lines of an ideal Platonic (Greek) education. Furthermore, in terms of narrative form, both the above pericope as well as the balance of Philo's *Moses* 1–2 fail to reflect the interacting Roman discursive elements outlined by Roller. In particular, Philo, unlike Josephus, pays almost no attention to primary audience reactions.

Conclusion

As the foregoing study suggests, while Philo's philosophical paragon may reflect a broadly Greco-Roman pedagogical penchant for example or particular Greek moral proclivities shared by the philosophical elite in Rome, it is Josephus's martial Moses—emplotted with attention to actions, audiences, commemoration, and imitation—who bears the conspicuous imprint of popular Roman discourse on exemplary leadership. In sum, whether the Alexandrian foregoes the popular moral idiom due to his comparatively limited time in Rome or as a result of his own Platonic presuppositions and educational experience, with respect to their pedagogical deployments of Moses, it was Josephus, more than Philo, who could have said with conviction, "when in Rome, write as the Romans write."

Are Weeping and Falling Down Funny? Exaggeration in Ancient Novelistic Texts

Jared W. Ludlow

From at least the time of Aristotle, exaggeration has been seen as a tool of comic writers to present humorous tales.[1] In fact some scholars "of the comic consider exaggeration to be a universal comic device."[2] The form of exaggeration may vary by genre, but all rely on the fact that "the easiest way to make things laughable is to exaggerate to the point of absurdity their salient traits."[3] Hyperbole, overboard caricatures, and elaborate wordplays are some examples of exaggeration used for comic purposes. Although crying scenes and falling down in grief or homage are usually signs of sadness, mourning, or respect, they have also been used by ancient writers in exaggerated fashions to signal playfulness within a text. When discussing crying and comedy in Tobit, David McCracken states: "The comic view requires that the suffering be serious but not so serious or pathetic that the affliction eclipses the joy of God's order." Yet the assurance of a happy outcome "does not preclude the tears of the characters."[4] This paper will

---

1. In *Poetics*, Aristotle defines comedy as "mimesis of baser but not wholly vicious characters: rather, the laughable is one category of the shameful. For the laughable comprises any fault or mark of shame which involves no pain or destruction" (*Poet.* 1449a, 31–35). Aristotle's term, "laughable" (γελοῖον), seems to carry the same connotation as "exaggeration" discussed in this paper. Another key comic term for Aristotle is "lampoon" (ἰάμβιζον); see 1448b, 31. According to Aristotle, comedy tends to represent people inferior to existing humans (see 1448a, 16–18).

2. Emil Draitser, *Techniques of Satire: The Case of Saltykov-Scedrin* (Berlin: de Gruyter, 1994), 135.

3. See Max Eastman, *Enjoyment of Laughter* (New York: Simon & Schuster, 1936), 156.

4. David McCracken, "Narration and Comedy in the Book of Tobit," *JBL* 114 (1995): 402, 418.

look at examples where exaggeration of weeping, falling down, and crying out for comedic effect can be found. Since these elements can be serious when viewed in isolation, we will also highlight purposeful creative techniques such as hyperbole, wordplay, and irony that signal when the text is playing with tears and cries.[5] We will focus on three texts as case studies that exhibit many of these techniques: Tobit, Judith, and the Testament of Abraham. It is my assertion that the exaggerated aspects of these ancient texts point toward purposeful playfulness to poke fun at characters and present entertaining stories that teach of God's goodness and protection. Of course, if a few arrogant characters are brought down to earth in the process, then all the better.

Story Beginnings

The beginnings of each of these three texts include clear examples of exaggeration. Tobit is excessively described as pious and righteous in *all* matters but especially in providing proper burials for Jewish dead. In the character's own words:

> I would give my food to the hungry and my clothing to the naked; and if I saw the dead body of any of my people thrown out behind the wall of Nineveh, I would bury it. I also buried any whom King Sennacherib put to death.... For in his anger he put to death many Israelites; but I would

---

5. "The definition of what is 'funny' or 'humorous' can vary from person to person. Indeed, hilarity often depends on the eye, or ear, of the beholder. Additionally, since much of comedy depends on its oral performance, we have difficulties knowing what was said tongue-in-cheek, sarcastically, or with comic voice inflection. Compounding the difficulty are the centuries of distance between the ancient writers and us. What may seem humorous to us now may not have been to them, or what might seem serious to us originally might have been spoken or written with a 'wink of an eye.' Somehow efforts should be made to determine as reasonably as one can the humorous aspects of ancient texts based on what we know about different forms of humor and their existence in the ancient world. The primary concern, of course, is determining that the ancient writers themselves intended to be humorous, rather than misinterpreting their tone. To accomplish this, [one must look] at how comedy, parody, satire, caricature, hyperbole, and irony were used by speakers and authors within the texts to present their messages" (Jared W. Ludlow, *Abraham Meets Death: Narrative Humor in the Testament of Abraham* [Sheffield: Sheffield Academic, 2002], 29–30).

secretly remove the bodies and bury them. So when Sennacherib looked for them he could not find them. (Tob 1:17–18)[6]

Because of his proclivity toward burying the dead and hiding them from Assyrian leaders, Tobit had to hide for his life. Tobit's unique habit of burying the dead is exaggerated in how frequently he does it and the effect it had on his life and family: everything he owned was confiscated. Even when Tobit returned home after Sennacherib's death, and his wife, Anna, and son, Tobias, were restored to him, Tobit could not resist burying the corpse of a Jew who had been murdered and thrown into the market. His late-night burial activity led to his becoming blind from—of all things—sparrow droppings. Surely the author of Tobit set up a whimsical tale about a bumbling, burying, blind Tobit.

The book of Judith will also provide an exaggerated description of a pious Jew, Judith, later in the second part of its story, but the historical blunders at the beginning of the narrative are notorious. Right from the first verse, historical problems abound: "It was the twelfth year of the reign of Nebuchadnezzar, who ruled over the Assyrians in the great city of Nineveh" (Jdt 1:1). Even most casual Bible readers recognize Nebuchadnezzar as the great Babylonian ruler who was responsible for the destruction of the Jerusalem temple, yet here he is the leader of the Assyrians! In addition, he is described as ruling from Nineveh, which was destroyed in 612 BCE, before his reign even began. It would seem that any ancient writer would know these basic facts, so some interpreters have pointed toward these inaccuracies as purposeful intent by the author. Erich Gruen has noted: "The initial jumble of chronology and personnel had to be deliberate—a signal that the tale was fanciful and that the reader was in for some fun."[7] Since the entire story of Judith is filled with irony, these historical mistakes signal playfulness by the author as the fictional storyline is set up. The massive size of the Assyrian army and their dizzying geographical routes continue the exaggerated presentation.

The Testament of Abraham begins with an elaborate description of Abraham's righteousness and hospitality:

---

6. Unless noted otherwise, Apocrypha translations come from *The New Oxford Annotated Apocrypha, New Revised Standard Version*, ed. Bruce M. Metzger and Roland E. Murphy (New York: Oxford University Press, 1991).

7. Erich S. Gruen, *Diaspora: Jews amidst Greeks and Romans* (Cambridge: Harvard University Press, 2002), 163.

> Abraham lived the measure of his life, 995 years. All the years of his life he lived in quietness, gentleness, and righteousness, and the righteous man was very hospitable: ... and welcomed everyone—rich and poor, kings and rulers, the crippled and the helpless, friends and strangers, neighbors and passersby—(all) on equal terms did the pious, entirely holy, righteous, and hospitable Abraham welcome. (A1.1–2)[8]

Hyperbole is evident throughout the Testament of Abraham, beginning right from the start, with Abraham's life coming to a close at the ripe old age of 995 years, well beyond his lifespan in the biblical account. This obvious overexaggeration seems to parallel the similar phenomenon of historical blunders found in Judith. As Lawrence Wills has observed:

> The historical blunders that appear in Daniel and the other novels—not minor inaccuracies but wild flights of mock history—doubtless arise from the nature of the genre as a source of amusement and correspond to a similar tendency in Greek novelistic literature. The humor or satire may vary from the romantic or whimsical (Tobit) to the farcical (Esther), but it seems in every case to be related to the creation of imagined worlds, that is, fiction. The historical blunders do not result from gaps in the authors' knowledge but are an expected part of the experience of reading fiction.[9]

Thus the exaggeration and historical inaccuracies at the beginning of these stories clue the audience into the book's lightheartedness and are important foundations when trying to determine whether weeping scenes and the like are meant to be interpreted comically or seriously.

Having established that the beginnings of these three texts each point toward comic intentions, we can examine examples of exaggeration in the body of these texts, particularly exaggeration related to weeping, crying out, and falling down that leans toward the humorous rather than the tragic.

---

8. English translations for the Testament of Abraham are taken from E. P. Sanders, "The Testament of Abraham," *OTP* 1. We will focus on recension A, which I consider to be the earlier of the two major recensions and which has more intentional comic effects.

9. Lawrence Wills, *The Jewish Novel in the Ancient World* (Ithaca, NY: Cornell University Press, 1995), 218–19. Erich Gruen also points out the significance of "historical howlers" in other Jewish texts: "The author was not composing a work of history and made no pretense of it. He signals his playfulness right at the beginning" (Gruen, "Humor and Irony in Diaspora Texts," in *Diaspora*, 10).

Tobit: Weeping

Almost one-third of the instances of weeping in the Apocrypha are found in Tobit. The first weeping scene in Tobit comes at the beginning of chapter 3 after a confrontation between Tobit and his wife over a kid goat that was given to her as a salary bonus. Inexplicably, Tobit becomes angered by this gift and accuses his wife of stealing the kid goat. His wife snaps back by asking where his acts of charity and righteous deeds are now. At that, Tobit breaks down crying. The Sinaiticus version exaggerates even more Tobit's overblown grief, a consistent characteristic, incidentally, of this longer version:[10] "Then being *grief-stricken* in spirit and *groaning*, I *wept*, and I began to pray with *sighs*" (3:1 NETS, emphasis added). Tobit's prayer leads to a plea to be taken from this earth. In Tobit's words, "it is better for me to die than to see so much distress in my life and to listen to insults" (3:6). Tobit's overblown reaction puts marital discord in new perspective. (Tobit's "woe is me" attitude is reflected again when he first meets Raphael: "What joy is left for me any more? I am a man without eyesight; I cannot see the light of heaven, but I lie in darkness like the dead who no longer see the light. Although still alive, I am among the dead" [5:10]).

The other strand of Tobit's narrative, that of Sarah and Raguel in Ecbatana, immediately follows this episode and includes another potentially tragic scene, but because of its embellishment it never descends to that level. Sarah laments her sad condition after being reproached by one of her father's maids for the loss of her seven husbands, who all had been taken on their wedding night by the demon Asmodeus. She is exceedingly grieved in spirit and weeps, not wanting to hear any further insults or reproaches. She is ready to take her own life, but, being an only child, worries that it will leave her father disgraced and he will enter into Hades with grief. Instead she prays to God that *he* will take her life so she will not listen to reproaches anymore; or if it does not please him to kill her, to at least hear her in her disgrace (see 3:7–15).

---

10. The Codex Sinaiticus version is the longer text form, but almost all the major manuscripts transmit the shorter text form. However, the Old Latin version and Dead Sea Scroll fragments of Tobit were translated from a text form very close to the Sinaiticus version. It seems the shorter form is a reworking of the longer form, and thus most recent translations are based on the longer form. For a fuller discussion of this issue, see Albert Pietersma and Benjamin G. Wright, eds., *A New English Translation of the Septuagint* (New York: Oxford University Press, 2007), 456–57.

These two prayers of Tobit and Sarah, both asking for relief from reproaches through death, are tempered by the next lines that confirm God's hearing their prayers and his solutions to both their plights through the subsequent actions of the angel Raphael (he will provide the means to heal Tobit's blindness and cure Sarah's marriage woes). Thus the tragic potential of these weeping episodes is thwarted by the story's foreshadowing; so although the characters weep, the reader knows all will be well.[11] According to McCracken, "The narrator's repeated undermining of suspense is a comic device that provides assurance of a happy outcome."[12]

The next weeping scene is another one between Tobit and his wife, Anna. In sending off their son, Tobias, to retrieve stored treasure, Anna is certain that he is sent off to his death. Tobit reassures her with the ironic statement that she will see him again because "a good angel will accompany him," even though they do not know Tobias's companion Raphael's true angelic identity (5:18–21). "So she stopped weeping" (5:23).[13] A common feature of these "comic" weeping scenes is the rapidity with which they stop. What seems like a dire situation suddenly dissipates.

Tobit's narrative next jumps to Ecbatana, where Tobias has arrived at the house of Raguel. On introducing himself to Raguel, tears of joy for Tobias's arrival are immediately followed by tears of sadness when hearing about Tobit's blind condition. "Then he [Raguel] fell on the neck of Tobias his kinsman and wept. Also Edna his wife wept for him, and Sarah their daughter likewise wept. Then he slaughtered a ram from the flock and welcomed them very warmly" (7:7–9). Within a few short verses, the Greek verb for weeping, κλαίω, is used four times, and a group weep occurs (similar to a group hug). The sharp jolt from a description of their weeping to a description of receiving Tobias warmly and slaughtering a ram for dinner only adds to the humor. The author seems to be playing with tears here as he sets up the crisis moment of the second narrative strand: the wedding night of Tobias and Sarah, where potentially Tobias could end up dead, like all of Sarah's previous husbands. Before the denouement of the wedding-night scene, there is one more weeping session between mother

---

11. Wills (*Jewish Novel*, 72) compares this predicted happy outcome "with a modern 'romantic comedy' in that a happy ending is so thoroughly guaranteed—there is never any tension—that our interest is focused solely on the various adventures and comic scenes that propel the work forward."

12. McCracken, "Narration and Comedy," 402 n. 5.

13. Or she kept quiet about her crying (Sinaiticus), from the Greek verb σιγάω.

and daughter. The mother wishes her joy in place of sorrow and encourages her daughter to be courageous (7:17). The wedding night turns out to be a success, thanks to the fish parts saved by Tobias under the direction of Raphael. The parents are relieved Tobias has survived the night, and Raguel has his servants quickly fill up the grave he had hastily ordered them to dig just a few hours earlier, thinking he would need to secretly bury Tobias if disaster struck (see 8:9–10, 18)—surely a genius comic touch by the author.

Back in Nineveh, uncertainty about Tobias's fate looms in the parents' minds. This leads to another episode of mourning: Tobit for fear that there is no longer any silver left with his relative, and Tobias's mother for fear that her son must surely be dead by now. This juxtaposition of a father worrying about money while his wife worries about the safety of their child may poke fun at familial stereotypes. Once again Tobit cuts off his wife's weeping and mourning and assures her that Tobias is in good health and will return shortly. This time, however, Hannah is not easily placated and orders him to be quiet while she begins a daily watch for her son, mourning and weeping each night without any sleep (10:7).

The final weeping scene in Tobit occurs at the reunion of Tobias with his parents. Certainly these are tears of joy as all the potential tragedies of the tale are resolved: Tobias has an inheritance, a wife, and a father who can see again.

Judith: To Cry Out and Fall Down

Our discussion of the body of Judith's narrative will focus on its exaggerated use of two Greek roots: πίπτω (to fall down or prostrate oneself; also προσκυνέω) and βοάω (to shout or cry out; also καλέομαι). Over one-third of the instances of "crying out" in the Apocrypha are found in Judith. Both these roots are used many times in various settings and in descriptions of different characters. Due to exaggerated use of these verbs and the comic contexts where they are found, it reaches the point of wordplay rather than mimetic recounting.[14] Although a crisis forms the

---

14. Even in Achior's recounting of Israelite history, the same root for crying out shows up (5:12). In one of Holofernes's speeches, he uses forms of the root "to fall" for expressions meaning something different from prostrating on the ground: "don't let your face drop" and "none of my words will fail [fall down]" (6:9). Also the root is used in describing reclining or lying down to eat (ἀναπίπτω; 12:16).

heart of this story—a siege by a powerful Assyrian army—the craftiness of the main character, the ineptitude of the elders, and the gullibility of the Assyrian general create a lighthearted tale where the crisis is resolved in a most spectacular fashion.[15]

The first episode of crying out in great earnestness comes when the Assyrian army first enters the land. All men, women, children, slaves, resident aliens, and even cattle don sackcloth and humble themselves, crying out to God for deliverance (4:9–10). All those in Jerusalem "threw themselves down facing the shrine and made ashen their heads and spread out their sackcloth in front of the Lord," even draping the altar with sackcloth while calling on God to protect them (4:11–12). While this would seem a very solemn occasion, the text hints at some humor with every possible type of person being listed alongside sack-clothed cattle; and with the singling out of inanimate objects like the altar and the priests' turbans for sackcloth and ashes.

Later, when the villagers of Bethulia hear what Achior told the Assyrians, they throw themselves down and begin crying out to God (6:18). But in the midst of their prayers, they also begin a drinking party (πότος).[16] (This same word will be used later in the story for the drinking party hosted by Holofernes in the Assyrian camp, which lasted so long and was so robust that the servants tired and Holofernes passed out [see 12:10; 13:1].) The transition from petitioning God to a drinking bout humorously calls into question the sincerity of the Israelite penitential actions.

The "crying out" intensifies when the siege is under way, and some become fainthearted (7:19). Besides falling down to pray, some begin falling in the streets from thirst (7:22). The play on the verb "to cry out" continues when the crowd *cries with a loud voice* against the elders for their ineffectiveness, with the crowd's request to the elders to *call upon* the Assyrians to surrender to them, and their promise to the elders that they would *call upon* heaven and earth to witness against the elders' failings. Then in the midst of the assembly "a loud wailing arose with one accord from everyone, and they *cried out* to the Lord God with a loud

---

15. Lawrence Wills describes Judith's humor as a book "about Judith's 'double-dealing.' Irony, double entendre, and humor are the stock-in-trade of the author, and although at first they seem heavy-handed, the text as a whole succeeds as a rousing parody." From "Jewish Novellas in a Greek and Roman Age: Fiction and Identity," *JSJ* 42 (2011): 158.

16. Sometimes translated as orgy or significantly tamed down to a banquet (NRSV).

voice" (7:29). The excessive emphasis on crying out is an exaggeration by the author—perhaps meant to overstate the anxiety of the people and set up the unexpectedness of their deliverance.

As the second part of the story shifts to Judith, the wordplay on calling out and falling down continues. After the exaggerated description of Judith's piousness and her boldness to confront the elders and mandate her plan, which includes the suggestion to *call upon* God for their rescue, Judith begins her wily preparations by falling face down and crying out to the Lord (9:1). When she "ceased crying out to the God of Israel" and "rose from falling," she summons her slave and begins beautifying herself (10:1–2).

The next shouting comes from the Assyrians announcing Judith's arrival because they cannot believe her beauty and come running to encircle her (10:18). In a comic twist on "face," Holofernes and his attendants are "awestruck by the beauty of her *face*, and [Judith] falling *face* forward, she did obeisance to him" (10:23, emphasis added). The next falling forward in the story is done by Holofernes himself: on his bed after drinking too much (13:2). This, of course, gives Judith the opportunity to complete her deadly task.

After Judith returns to her village, it is the Israelites' turn to announce her arrival and come running to encircle her (13:12–13). Judith recounts the previous events and emphasizes the Lord's preservation so that her *face* deceived Holofernes and led to his destruction (13:16). Then the Israelites bend forward and do obeisance to God (13:17). When Achior is brought to Judith and shown the head of Holofernes, "he *fell face down*, and his breathing failed. When they revived him, he *fell* at the feet of Judith and did obeisance to her *face*" (14:6–7).[17] It is noteworthy how frequently wordplays with "face" and "falling down" show up in the narrative interwoven among the various characters with different purposes and results. Then the people "shouted with a loud voice and gave a rousing cry" in good cheer, and Achior becomes circumcised (14:9–10).

Meanwhile back at the Assyrian camp, Holofernes's death is discovered by his steward, who "cried out in a loud voice with wailing and groaning and with a mighty cry, and he tore his clothes" (14:16). Only after check-

---

17. Adolfo Roitman sees a contrast between "Achior's sincere submission to Judith and Judith's hypocritical yielding to Holofernes" in "Achior in the Book of Judith: His Role and Significance," in *"No One Spoke Ill of Her": Essays on Judith*, ed. James C. VanderKam, EJL 2 (Atlanta: Scholars Press, 1992), 44 n. 39.

ing Judith's tent does the steward shout out to the people that their general is lying "on the ground, and his head is not upon him" (14:18). The rulers also begin to tear their tunics, and "there arose from them screaming and an extremely loud cry" (14:19). Instead falling to the ground, "fear and trembling fell upon them," and instead of facing one another, no one is left remaining "to face his neighbor" (15:2). Then the Israelites fall upon them and cut them down (15:5; also 15:6). Following the Israelite victory, one last "running together" scene occurs, with all the women of Israel rushing to see Judith and bless her.

Thus, throughout the text of Judith several wordplays repeat themselves as the story exaggerates the victory of a pious woman over a mighty, evil general. These wordplays are persistent throughout the whole narrative, indicating there is not a separation between the first seven chapters and the last ones, calling into doubt the claims by some that these are two separate tales that have little to do with each other. This conclusion supports the ideas of structural correspondences between the two halves, as argued by Toni Craven in her dissertation on this text.[18]

Testament of Abraham: Weeping

The Testament of Abraham includes several weeping episodes that are used to advance the comic intentions of the narrative. When the archangel first arrives at Abraham's residence, Abraham washes his feet in an act of hospitality, yet two additions by the narrator are noteworthy for their comic effect: first, Michael is described as "the incorporeal one" (3:6)—how can one wash the *feet* of an incorporeal being?; and second, Abraham is washing his feet because he has come from a long journey (3:7)—true, heaven may be far away, but how dirty would Michael's feet get during his descent? While washing Michael's feet, Abraham begins weeping without any explanation. (Recension B resolves this ambiguity by stating that Abraham was given the insight that these would be the last feet he would wash, implying that he will die soon.) Isaac, on seeing his father crying, begins weeping. For good measure, Michael the archangel, on seeing the other two weeping, joins in as well. Michael's tears fall into the wash basin

---

18. Toni Craven, *Artistry and Faith in the Book of Judith*, SBLDS 70 (Chico, CA: Scholars Press, 1983), 53. Craven notes the symmetrical use of πότον (feasts) and the antithetical use of "fear and trembling" falling on characters, and points out some of the wordplay with "face."

and immediately turn into precious stones. Abraham secretly hides these stones, thinking no one else saw them (3:9–12). Later, Abraham shows these stones to Sarah to prove he already knew who Michael really was—an angelic figure (6:6–7). Thus, these tears became integral to the unfolding of the narrative, a narrative that shows many comic features in Recension A, such as Abraham's crafty characterization.

These three male figures weep together again after Isaac has a dream of Abraham's impending death. When Isaac comes out of his bedchamber weeping, Abraham's heart is moved, and he weeps with a loud voice, and then Michael, seeing them weeping, weeps also (see 5:8–10). (Incidentally, Raphael never cried with the characters in Tobit, as Michael does here.) The text certainly seems to be poking fun at a normally exalted figure. When Sarah hears the weeping, she asks what all the crying is about. The scene unfolds with Abraham displaying Michael's stone tears to Sarah, as mentioned earlier.

Later, when Abraham is taken to the heavenly judgment scene, he beholds a man seated on a throne, whom he later learns is Adam. Adam's exaggerated actions on the throne begin the process of judgment for deceased souls. When Adam sees many souls being taken through the broad gate, "that wonderful one tore the hairs of his head and the sides of his beard, and threw himself on the ground from his throne, weeping and lamenting" (11:6). But when a few souls are taken through the narrow gate, "he arose from the ground and sat upon his throne in great joy, rejoicing and exulting." Talk about a tiring eternal assignment: to mourn or rejoice for each group of souls taken through the heavenly gates. Adam's overboard reaction to each soul's fate brings a lighthearted touch to the judgment scene and makes one wonder whether the ancient reader smiled at this scene, or did they believe it depicted the reality of postmortal existence? Considering the tone of the rest of the work, it seems a smile is more in order.

Conclusion

We have reviewed examples of exaggeration from these texts to signal comic intentions even in customarily serious moments such as weeping and falling down in grief. The authors of these texts creatively used these elements to advance their purposes and agendas. But what might have been the purposes for using humor in these ancient texts?

Humor can prod a reader into thinking about issues being cleverly displayed in a comic fashion. Presumably these images will remain with the reader longer than bland exhortations. Comedy, argues J. William Whedbee, is "a serious strategy for dealing with the most profound problems of human existence," since it "can profoundly engage topics that are 'deadly serious' as well as 'very funny.'"[19] In fact, there is a fine line between tragic and comic.[20] Thus according to Conrad Hyers, comedies turn to some of the same issues as tragedies, "but in a different manner and with a different spirit. Those differences represent the comic answer to tragedy."[21] These texts that we have discussed exemplify the ability to comically tackle serious issues such as fear of death, imperial dominion, and life in the diaspora.[22]

When deducing the purposes for humor in ancient Jewish literature, the fact that Jews were often in exile or in bondage to a strong empire are important factors to take into consideration. Often humor in these situations "emerged as a weapon of an oppressed and marginalized people to help its survival amidst the perilous conditions."[23] Tobit and Judith particularly relate how Jews in diaspora could rise above their gentile neighbors and overcome outside threats. As Gruen has stated, "The authors felt free to expose the blemishes of the Jewish leaders and populace, while lampooning the flaws of their enemies."[24] Thus, comedy can attempt to bring down, even if only figuratively, those who seem so powerful and able to take away one's political or religious liberty. Perhaps the comic elements helped defuse fear in such fearful situations. The ability to poke fun at revered figures and produce humorous texts can also indicate the vitality

---

19. J. William Whedbee, *The Bible and the Comic Vision* (Cambridge: Cambridge University Press, 1998), 283, 193.

20. "In tragedy human beings *aspire* to more than they can attain, while in comedy they *pretend* to more, there is also the tragic dimension to Qohelet's portraiture of the Fool. The observer may smile or shed a tear, or, like Qohelet, do both." From Etan Levine, "Qohelet's Fool: A Composite Portrait," in *On Humour and the Comic in the Hebrew Bible*, ed. Yehuda T. Radday and Athalya Brenner (Sheffield: Almond, 1990), 294. (The first line should have been cited as Louis Kronenberger, *The Thread of Laughter* [New York: Knopf, 1952], 5.)

21. Conrad Hyers, *And God Created Laughter: The Bible as Divine Comedy* (Atlanta: Knox, 1987), 113.

22. Wills (*Jewish Novel*, 92) feels that in the case of Tobit, didactic sections (chs. 1, 13–14) were added to a humorous section (chs. 2–12), thus creating a wise and righteous hero while still entertaining the reader.

23. Whedbee, *Bible and the Comic Vision*, 3.

24. Gruen, *Diaspora*, 180–81.

and self-confidence of Jewish life in the diaspora. They felt comfortable enough in their situations that their creative, sometimes irreverent, stories would not cause alienation or disintegration within their community. The humor in these stories seems to make the characters appear needlessly worried: the things they worry about do not happen, and they look a little silly for having worried. Perhaps humor in these stories served to encourage Jews to trust in God rather than panic, because in the end situations can be changed to their favor.

Grotesque and Strange Tales of the Beyond: Truth, Fiction, and Social Discourse

Gerhard van den Heever

"I'm not looking for a theologian. I'm looking for a narrator. Do you know what a religion is, Martín, my friend?... Poetry aside, a religion is really a moral code that is expressed through legends, myths, or any type of literary device in order to establish a system of beliefs, values and rules with which to regulate a culture or a society.... As in literature, or in any other act of communication, what confers effectiveness on it, is the form and not the content," Corelli continued. "What greater challenge for your career than to create a story so powerful that it transcends fiction and becomes a revealed truth?"

— Carlos Ruiz Zafón, *The Angel's Game*

Introduction: Fiction at the Origins of Religious Discourses

Myths and mythical discourses are not "just there." Mythical discourses are mediated through a variety of media, one such medium being literature, more specifically, fiction. Insofar as religion is a species of mythmaking, this essay is concerned with the intersection of fictional literature, mythmaking, and the formation of religious discourses during the first two to three centuries of the Roman imperial era—the crucible in which Christian religious discourses gestated and from which Christian discourses emerged as culturally recognizable phenomena. The underlying assumption of the argument pursued here is the socially foundational function of both religious and mythical discourses and by extension also of fictional literature. The kind of fiction referenced here is of the more fantastical and grotesque kind, the kind of fiction one can, for comparative purposes, define as fantasy literature, science fiction, and Gothic literature.[1]

---

1. This is a popular field of study, and there is by now a vast corpus of scholarly

In a broader theoretical perspective, much has already been said about the role of fiction in the formation of religious discourses, especially in connection with the formation of new religious movements (NRMs).[2] Some NRMs quite explicitly present themselves as constructions informed by fictional literature or other works of fictional cultural production.[3] A particularly instructive example is the figure of L. Ron Hubbard, who, after a career as science fiction writer, created a gnostic-type religion out of concepts derived from his science fiction oeuvre, the religion of Scientology—and then returned in 1982 to science fiction writing in *Battlefield Earth: A Saga of the Year 3000*, a work that reencoded his gnostic religion into fiction. At the other end of the spectrum one finds the Star Wars trilogy with its prequels and sequels, which deliberately incorporate mysticism and Christian, Buddhist, Hinduist, and Manichaean motifs and concepts, constructing a mythology that has been appropriated by the recently manifested Jediism as religion. To these one may add the Church of Jesus Christ of Latter-day Saints, Theosophy, Anthroposophy, varieties of modern paganism, and some new universal religions as instances of the construction of religious discourse and mythology from the interweaving of fiction, fantasy, and fictionalized science.[4]

---

work on popular cultural production and religious discourses. For the purposes of this discussion, I have restricted myself to the following overviews: Edward James and Farah Mendlesohn, eds., *The Cambridge Companion to Fantasy Literature* (Cambridge: Cambridge University Press, 2012); Edward James and Farah Mendlesohn, eds., *The Cambridge Companion to Science Fiction* (Cambridge: Cambridge University Press, 2003); Jerrold E. Hogle, ed., *The Cambridge Companion to Gothic Fiction* (Cambridge: Cambridge University Press, 2002); and David Punter, ed., *A New Companion to the Gothic*, Blackwell Companions to Literature and Culture (Oxford: Blackwell, 2012).

2. Carole M. Cusack, *Invented Religions: Imagination, Fiction and Faith*, Ashgate New Religions (Burlington, VT: Ashgate, 2010).

3. Carole M. Cusack and Alex Norman, eds., *Handbook of New Religions and Cultural Production*, Brill Handbooks on Contemporary Religion 4 (Leiden: Brill, 2012); James R. Lewis and Olav Hammer, eds., *The Invention of Sacred Tradition* (Cambridge: Cambridge University Press, 2007).

4. On Scientology and its fictional mythology, see Adam Possamai and Alphia Possamai-Inesedy, "Battlefield Earth and Scientology: A Cultural/Religious Industry à la Frankfurt School," in *Handbook*, ed. Cusack and Norman, 583–98, esp. 587. On Star Wars: apart from the nonspecific Jediism with its twenty-one Jedi principles, there appear to be two "organized churches" of Jediism, namely, Temple of the Jedi Order: First International Church of Jediism, and the Jedi Church (Cusack, *Invented Religions*, 113–40). On LDS and the other movements referenced, and on religious

This is partly what I am suggesting here, namely, that what we now know as Christianity originated in a historical context through similar processes of cultural bricolage at the intersection of the fictional as contemporary NRMs. Indeed, Christianity was also once a new religious movement, which in its processes of discourse formation exhibited the same kinds of mythologizing discourse assemblages as seen in other (contemporary and ancient) NRMs.[5]

While the works of Spanish novelist Carlos Ruiz Zafón do not in any way constitute a mythology for a NRM as such, they do exemplify the intersection between fantasy, social mythology, and the Gothic, and as such provide a window on the contestations regarding social *imaginaires*—in his case, contemporary Spain. As suggested by the epigraph to this essay, his work forms a suitable comparandum to the issue under consideration here in this essay, namely, the way in which grotesque, strange tales of the beyond define the creative mythologization processes characteristic of the early Roman imperial era, processes that also formed the matrix for the formation of Christian mythology as well as the context for polemical contestations regarding such emerging Christian mythology.

The three novels by Carlos Ruiz Zafón, *The Shadow of the Wind* (2001), *The Angel's Game* (2008), and *The Prisoner of Heaven* (2011),[6] all three mystery novels set in the city of Barcelona in the period from the First World War to the end of the Second World War and slightly after, are late

---

discourse, cultural production, and fiction more generally, see the various essays in Cusack and Norman, *Handbook*. As an aside, the expansion of the Star Wars mythology from a core narrative backwards and forwards in order to complete the mythology represents a case of canon formation similar to that of Christianity, with canonical core writings, plus an extensive expansion of apocryphal material to "fill in the gaps," as it were; simultaneously one finds the development of an authoritative canon of ideas that represent "true" Jediism.

    5. As Olav Hammer and Mikael Rothstein put it: "New religions are just young religions, and tend to resemble all other young religions. And equally: old traditions such as Christianity, Islam, and Buddhism were once young religions" ("Introduction to New Religious Movements," in *The Cambridge Companion to New Religious Movements*, ed. Olav Hammer and Mikael Rothstein, Cambridge Companions to Religion [Cambridge: Cambridge University Press, 2012], 3).

    6. Carlos Ruiz Zafón, *The Shadow of the Wind*, trans. Lucia Graves (London: Weidenfeld & Nicolson, 2005); Ruiz Zafón, *The Angel's Game*, trans. Lucia Graves (London: Weidenfeld & Nicolson, 2009); Ruiz Zafón, *The Prisoner of Heaven*, trans. Lucia Graves (London: Weidenfeld & Nicolson, 2013).

flowerings of the genre of dark, Gothic Spanish fiction that grew in popularity from the mid-nineteenth through twentieth centuries in Spain.[7] From a cultural materialist and new historicist perspective, the rise in popularity of Gothic fiction ran parallel to the traumas of social contestations and redefinitions represented by the Carlist Wars (1833–1840, 1846–1849, 1872–1876) and the Spanish Civil War of 1936–1939, national discords occasioned by the ideological conflict between modernity, liberalism, and republicanism on the one hand, and traditionalism, Catholicism, and authoritarianism on the other. Towards the close of the nineteenth century further impetus to the popularity of Gothic literature came from the rise in fin-de-siècle anxieties occasioned by modernism and the effects of large-scale industrialization. All of these historical factors impacted and centered most strongly on the city of Barcelona and the region of Catalonia, of which it is the capital (issues that reverberate to the modern day, with renewed attempts at Catalonian independence). The recent wave of Spanish Gothic literature, as exemplified by Juan Perucho and Carlos Ruiz Zafón, is a literary manifestation of tapping into these deep anxieties and reimagining a world in the aftermath of these deep traumas.[8] Religio-mythical motifs in Zafón's *The Angel's Game* (the series for which the protagonist David Martin writes is called City of the Damned; he writes at precisely 6.66 pages per day and is enlisted by the mysterious Mr. Corelli from the Éditions de la Lumière, that is, a kind of Lucifer figure, to write the new religion) add poignancy to the title of the book and suggests it is also a kind of religious struggle. So, while the oeuvre of Zafón is, on the one hand, ordinary enjoyable pulp fiction, it is also, on the other, in its grotesquely Gothic darkness an attempt to deal with history and tradition in the aftermath of a convoluted and traumatic history. All three of these novels are about ghostly subterranean depositories of lost books, that is, symbols that invite thinking about the afterlife of suppressed tradition.

---

7. Santiago Díaz Lage, "Afterthoughts on the Spanish Gothic," *European Studies Blog*, January 19, 2015, http://tinyurl.com/SBL4212a.

8. Juan Perucho, *Natural History*, trans. David H. Rosenthal (London: Minerva, 1990); the novel deals with a natural scientist, Antoni de Montpalau, who has to investigate the appearance of a vampire who sometimes appears in the shape of a Carlist guerilla general, Ramon de Cabrera. It is, again, a narrative of the contest between reason and liberalism against reactionary traditionalism. The book originally appeared in 1979, shortly after the death of Generalissimo Franco and the restoration of the monarchy.

It is by framing the argument that follows with attention to fiction, science fiction, and fantasy literature and their role in the formation of new mythologies in NRMs, as well as the tenor of the Gothic as horror fantasy, that I want to suggest a way of interpreting the significance of the rise in fantasy literature, including tales of resurrection, in the context of the Roman Empire and the reactions of some learned men—in this case, Celsus—to these reorderings of the religious world.

Celsus, Origen, and Sensational Tales of Resurrection

In the chapter on resurrection in his book *Fiction as History*, Glen Bowersock famously raised the issue of truth and fiction in his discussion of the literary spat[9] between Middle Platonic philosopher Celsus and Christian theologian-cum-philosopher Origen. The verbal mudslinging centered on the reality of and evidential trustworthiness of Christian resurrection accounts (in this instance, Origen, *Cels.* 2.55–56), specifically on the truthfulness and veracity of early Christian resurrection narratives in the context of long-standing myths of boundary crossing between this world and the underworld, as well as—more significantly—the newly popular literary phenomenon of novelistic fiction.[10]

Celsus sees a literary topos operative in Christian accounts of the life of Jesus Christ, especially the passion, crucifixion, and resurrection accounts, categorizing them among the "juggling tricks" used to "deceive their simple hearers" (2.55) and other similar stories and mythical accounts circulating in antiquity. It is worth citing the passage in full:

> After this the Jew says to his fellow-citizens who believe in Jesus: Come now, let us believe your view that he actually said this. How many others produce wonders like this to convince simple hearers whom they exploit by deceit? They say that Zamolxis (sic), the slave of Pythagoras, also did this among the Scythians and Pythagoras himself in Italy and Rhampsinitus in Egypt. The last-named played dice with Demeter in Hades and returned bearing a gift from her, a golden napkin. Moreover, they say

---

9. I call this a literary spat, although mindful of the fact that the two were not contemporaries: by the time that Origen wrote *Against Celsus*, the antagonist Celsus had already been dead for over half a century. Celsus's lost work Ἀληθὴς λόγος is only preserved through Origen's attack on it.

10. G. W. Bowersock, *Fiction as History: Nero to Julian* (Berkeley: University of California Press, 1994), 99–119, esp. 114–19.

that Orpheus did this among the Odrysians and Protesilaus in Thessaly and Heracles at Taenarum, and Theseus. But we must examine this question whether anyone who really died ever rose again with the same body. Or do you think that the stories of these others really are the legends which they appear to be, and yet that the ending of your tragedy is to be regarded as noble and convincing—his cry from the cross when he expired, and the earthquake and the darkness? While he was alive he did not help himself but after death he rose again and showed the marks of his punishment and how his hands had been pierced. But who saw this? A hysterical female, as you say, and perhaps some other one of those who were deluded by the same sorcery, who either dreamt in a certain state of mind and through wishful thinking had a hallucination due to some mistaken notion (an experience which has happened to thousands), or, which is more likely, wanted to impress the others by telling this fantastic tale, and so by this cock-and-bull story to provide a chance for other beggars. (*Cels.* 2.55)[11]

For Celsus, tales of Jesus's resurrection fit into the same category of tales he encountered in ancient writers—and one should remember that both Celsus and Origen encountered these "events" only as tales narrated in texts of some antiquity, that is, as already mythicized narratives. Celsus recounts the cases of Zalmoxis, the "slave of Pythagoras," in Scythia (Herodotus, *Hist.* 4.95); Pythagoras himself in Italy; Rhampsinitus in Egypt (Herodotus, *Hist.* 2.122), who is said to have played dice with Demeter in Hades and to have returned to the upper world with a golden napkin received from her as gift; Orpheus among the Odrysians (Herodotus, *Hist.* 2.122);[12] Protesilaus in Thessaly; and Hercules at Cape Taenarus (Diodorus Siculus, *Bib. hist.* 4.26.1); and Theseus.

The fact that a good number of the mythical "events" recounted by Celsus are set in the northern wild country of Thrace gives an indication of what he thought of these stories. According to legend, Zalmoxis was a king of Thrace who invented religious rites and inaugurated mysteries, hence the association with Pythagoras, as "slave of Pythagoras." But there is also a slight in this: Zalmoxis, the "slave," having picked up clever and cunning

---

11. I make use of the translation in Origen, *Contra Celsum*, trans. Henry Chadwick (Cambridge: Cambridge University Press, 1965), 109. The introductory sentence is that of Origen; the rest of the passage that follows is a verbal citation from Celsus.

12. Odrysians being a synonym for the Thracians, this is a reference to the myth of Orpheus and Eurydice. Orpheus was associated in mythology with the northern country of Thrace.

tricks among the civilized Athenians, becomes a king among the Thracians, who are so backward that a clever slave can be a king there. That is why they fell for his stories. According to Herodotus (*Hist.* 4.95), Zalmoxis proclaimed loudly to his court that they and their descendants would not die but live forever, all the while building a subterranean chamber into which he disappeared, having "died." After three years, and much mourning from his people, he reappeared, thereby "proving" the veracity of his pronouncements that they would not die. These were exactly the kinds of stories Celsus latched on to when pronouncing on the Christian narrative of resurrection—if they were not even credible in the time of Herodotus, how much less so in his day?[13]

For Celsus these are the detritus of an industry of chicanery, fraud (even if pious), and wholesale deception and rampant superstition mingled with the fictional, for—so Celsus—"the question is, whether anyone who was really dead ever rose with a veritable body," and besides, the only witnesses to this central melodramatic[14] event of Christ's death and resurrection are a "half-frantic woman" and other similarly deluded hyper-imaginative waywards and impostors.

As in any polemic, there is at least a half-truth in Celsus's expressed viewpoint. He would certainly have known of the prevalence of mime and performance as street-theater manifestations of religious myth and discourses. Theatricality and performance was often the way in which to facilitate the epiphany of the gods in religious celebrations.[15] Perhaps the two most famous examples of these, roughly contemporaneous to the times of Celsus and Origen, were the cult of Glykon, inaugurated by Alexander "the false prophet," and Peregrinus, who chose a dramatic moment just after the Olympic Games of 165 CE to immolate himself, a kind of practice run for resurrection, seeing that Peregrinus changed his name

---

13. "Such is the Greek story about him [i.e., Zalmoxis]," ends Herodotus's narration of the story (Herodotus, *The Histories*, trans. A. E. Godley, vol. 2, LCL [Cambridge: Harvard University Press, 1938]), thereby indicating that he, as in other cases, takes some of the legends and myths with some skepticism.

14. Note the details emphasized by Celsus: a crying, unheroic death, an earthquake, darkness, helpless in dying yet showing off his torture marks after rising from the dead.

15. Angelos Chaniotis, "Staging and Feeling the Presence of God: Emotion and Theatricality in Religious Celebrations in the Roman East," in *Panthée: Religious Transformations in the Graeco-Roman Empire*, ed. Laurent Bricault and Nicole Bonnett, RGRW 177 (Leiden: Brill, 2013), 169–89.

from Proteus to Phoenix just before his death in the fire (Lucian, *Peregr.* 27).[16] Often the living context of practiced religion consisted of public performances, processions, and rituals that contributed to the emotional response of the audience.[17] With regard to Christianity, the target of Celsus's invective, it too was thoroughly embedded in the visual and performance culture of the Roman Empire.[18] Thus Harry O. Maier considers the interplay between the visual world of antiquity on the metaphor and message of earlier Christians:

> Vivid representation—in texts, ritual actions, hymns, and confessions—formed a way for believers to visualize the world and their place within it. These forms of visualization cannot be interpreted without reference to the material conditions in which they were formed, nor can they be understood without attention to the visual worlds out of which they were constructed. This becomes all the more clear when we remember that the majority of those who populated earliest Christian communities were probably illiterate and lived in an oral/aural culture as well as one filled with visual images. It is not surprising that biblical traditions were preserved and passed on with the help of both memorable and vivid stories; oral cultures deploy graphic language as a central strategy in performance, persuasion, and the preservation of memory.[19]

One example of Christian theatrical staging is suggested by the beginning of chapter 3 of Paul's Letter to the Galatians, where he tells the audience: "It was before your eyes that Jesus Christ was publicly exhibited as crucified!" (Gal 3:1).[20] "Publicly exhibited" here is the translation of προεγάφη, which recalls vivid performance as a kind of ecphrasis, that is, vivid presentation to make absent things present. Similarly, in 1 Cor 4:9 Paul states, "For I think that God has exhibited us apostles as last of

---

16. Both philosophers were the subjects of scathing sarcasm by Lucian of Samosata, the archsatirist of the Roman imperial era.

17. For a similar point with regard to mystery religions in the Roman Empire in their intersection with ancient Greek fiction, namely, that they all subsisted in a "sea of visual performances," see Gerhard van den Heever, "'Loose Fictions and Frivolous Fabrications': Ancient Fictions and the Mystery Religions of the Early Imperial Era" (DLitt et Phil thesis, University of South Africa, 2005), http://tinyurl.com/SBL4212b.

18. Harry O. Maier, "Vision, Visualisation, and Politics in the Apostle Paul," *MTSR* 27 (2015): 312–32.

19. Ibid., 313–14.

20. Unless otherwise stated, biblical translations follow the NRSV.

all, as though sentenced to death, because we have become a spectacle to the world, to angels and to mortals." Spectacle here translates θέατρον, again a reference to a vivid ecphrastic performance. The effect is to make his sufferings seem more real and to evoke emotions of sympathy in the audience. It is tantalizing to think that this is what the Platonist Celsus had in mind when he spoke of "juggling tricks" used to "deceive their simple hearers."

Celsus, Origen, and the Shadow of Plato

Hidden under Celsus's dismissive language is his Platonizing interpretation of religion—*religiosus platonicus*—according to which gods, or a universalized divinity, are not material, not representable with images, nor do they live in "houses"; that is, religion is concerned with the immaterial (*Cels.* 1.5, 14, 16; 4.36; 6.3, 12–13, 42, 80; 7.28, 53; 8.68). This is, for Celsus, the "true doctrine," the Ἀληθὴς λόγος, the subject of the book that Origen refutes. In his view it has always been the hallmark of all the great religions of his day (and since time immemorial). While Jews and Christians derived their religion from earlier, antecedent religions (the Jews had "fallen away from the Egyptians" [3.5–8; 4.31], and the Christians from the Jews [2.4; 5.33]), they broke with the common tradition of all ancient peoples. They started off with the old doctrine (παλαιὸς λόγος) common to the ancient peoples, and then "lost the plot"[21]—in the case of the Christians, by insisting on the reality of the incarnation and the materiality of the death by crucifixion and subsequent resurrection of Jesus Christ. The argument is that tales of death by crucifixion and resurrection unduly concretized religion and made material whatever Christians thought religion was. Thus, for Celsus, Christian tradition is an invention, and a recent one, and by putting forward his objections the way he does, Celsus acknowledges that the emergence of Christian traditions constitutes a cultural break with the long-enduring past. In effect, Celsus saw Christianity as a new religious movement. To put it differently, Christianity is an epiphenomenon of new discursive formations (new dispositions, new habitus, and a new episteme, to speak in terms derived from Bourdieu and Foucault).[22]

---

21. A play on the remark of Bowersock, *Fiction as History*, 7–8, that "history had simply become the plot."

22. Bowersock argues that the sudden growth of fictional literature with its fascination with resurrection motifs from the middle of the first century CE onwards can

Yet Origen also had an extensive education in classical learning and Pythagorean and Platonic philosophy. Well-versed in the Middle Platonism of Philo of Alexandria, Origen's philosophical training was also steeped in Stoic allegorical text interpretation and emerging Neopythagorean and Neoplatonist thinking: Numenius, Cronius, Apollophanes, Longinus, Moderatus, and Nicomachus. To boot, his fame as a master of Greek philosophy drew a pagan audience into his lecture hall. In fact, Origen's views of the divine are in many ways similar to the views of Celsus. Origen posits a transcendent, incorporeal God and a Trinity of three hypostases, a demiurgic Word, preexistent rational souls, their "fall" into bodies through free will, and their salvation.[23] According to the Neoplatonist philosopher Porphyry of Tyre, in his book *Against the Christians*,[24] Origen was a student of Ammonius Saccas, in his time the most proficient of Greek philosophers. As Eusebius reports it, Porphyry said of Origen:

> 6. For this man was a hearer of Ammonius, who had attained the greatest proficiency in philosophy in our day, and so far as a grasp of knowledge was concerned he owed much to his master; but as regards the right choice in life, he chose the opposite road to him. 7. For Ammonius was a Christian, brought up in Christian doctrine by his parents, yet, when he began to think and study philosophy, he immediately changed his life conformably to the laws; but Origen, a Greek educated in Greek learning drove headlong toward barbarian recklessness [πρὸς τὸ βάρβαρον ἐξώκειλεν τόλμημα]; and making straight for this he hawked himself and his literary skill about; and while his manner of life was Christian and contrary to the law, in his opinions about material things and the Deity he played the Greek, and introduced Greek ideas into foreign fables [τοῖς ὀθνείοις ὑποβαλλόμενος μύθοις]. (Eusebius, *Hist. eccl.* 6.19.6–7)[25]

---

be attributed to the spread of gospel traditions: ibid., 118–19. My issue is not to belabor the point of resurrection as an index of changing social discourse as such; this has been done admirably elsewhere: see Judith Perkins, "Fictive 'Scheintod' and Christian Resurrection," *R&T* 13 (2006): 396–418; and Perkins, *Roman Imperial Identities in the Early Christian Era* (London: Routledge, 2009).

23. *Pace* Mark Edwards's critique of the conventional view; see further the discussion in Alastair H. B. Logan, "Origen (c. 185–254)," in *The Blackwell Companion to the Theologians*, ed. Ian S. Markham (Oxford: Blackwell, 2009), 170–86.

24. In which he claims to have known Origen in his—Porphyry's—youth; the book itself is only preserved in fragments in Eusebius's *Ecclesiastical History*.

25. Translation from Eusebius, *The Ecclesiastical History*, vol. 2, *Books 6–10*, ed.

In Ammonius's judgment, Origen plunged from the heights of Greek philosophy into religious adventurous daring, that is, "barbarian recklessness," by fusing his lofty Greek thinking with "foreign fables." The word μῦθος here has a double entendre: it signifies both Christian discourse (including, in this case, the death and resurrection discourse) and the narratives in which the discourse is embodied, namely the tales of the crucifixion and resurrection. With a little give and take, one can imagine that Porphyry was Celsus contesting with Origen.

Tales, Fiction, History, and Myth

My point is that both Celsus and Origen are aware that the encyclopedia of tales of men who "crossed over" and back are essentially fantastic tales, and while Origen's refutation points to the public nature of the execution of Jesus Christ (therefore, he claims, it does not belong among all the other quick turns and sleights of hand—his death and revivification took place in the open for all to see), already in Origen's defense of the truth of the crucifixion narrative the boundaries between truth and fiction are blurred. Origen's argument is self-defeating: the very same characteristic that gave contemporary history writing and novelistic fiction their power, namely, its *enargeia* or vividness, is precisely that which Origen claims for the gospel account. From Origen's point of view, two hundred years after the fact, there is no longer any living link with the event, only realistic-seeming and dramatic accounts of the life of the "Galilean miracle worker-sage-cum-Cynic peasant" (to use the terminology of John Dominic Crossan[26]).

If it was the vividness (*enargeia*) of the narration (implying the presence of storytelling in history) that compelled belief in the veracity of the historical account, then equally it is the conventions of realism employed in the novel that created the "illusion of belief" in fiction as if it were fact.[27]

---

and trans. J. E. L. Oulton and H. J. Lawlor, LCL (Cambridge: Harvard University Press, 1932).

26. John Dominic Crossan, *The Historical Jesus: The Life of a Mediterranean Jewish Peasant* (New York, N.Y.: HarperCollins, 1991).

27. T. P. Wiseman, "Lying Historians: Seven Types of Mendacity," in *Lies and Fiction in the Ancient World*, ed. Christopher Gill and T. P. Wiseman (Austin: University of Texas Press, 1993), 140–45; J. R. Morgan, "Make-Believe and Make Believe: The Fictionality of the Greek Novels," in Gill and Wiseman, *Lies and Fiction in the Ancient World*, 195–96.

The cluster of rhetorical devices that combine to create the verisimilitude and believed veracity of fiction, called realism, include historiographic form, real geography, authentic detail, pretense to historical authenticity, closeness to social reality, and manner of narration.[28] By the time of the literary dispute between the two Platonic philosophers, the gospel accounts of the extraordinary life events of Jesus Christ had already disappeared under the literary overgrowth of a "sea of similar stories," strange tales from the beyond.[29]

About half a century before Celsus wrote the *True Discourse*, Plutarch decried the same confluence of religion and myth, fiction and popular cultural representations. Plutarch was himself aware of the intersections between myth and fiction. After recounting the myth of Isis and Osiris to his interlocutor, Clea, he turns his nose up at the popular fictions feeding off the myth or repackaging the myth in novelistic fashion:

> That these accounts do not, in the least, resemble the sort of loose fictions [μυθεύμασιν ἀραιοῖς] and frivolous fabrications [διακένοις πλάσμασιν] which poets and writers of prose [λογογράφοι] evolve from themselves, after the manner of spiders, interweaving and extending their unestablished first thoughts, but that these contain narrations of certain puzzling events and experiences, you will of yourself understand. (*Is. Os.* 20)[30]

---

28. For instance of historiographic form, see the titles of novels such as *Aethiopica*, *Ephesiaca*, and *Babyloniaca*, which resemble those of historical works. For this and further examples, see Morgan, "Make-Believe," 197–98. For real geography, see ibid., 198: "The entire geography of the novel's world—distances, directions, sailing times—approximates so closely to reality that there seems nothing odd when the recent Budé Chariton includes a map tracing the fictitious movements of its fictitious characters." For the pretense to historical authenticity, see the deliberately emulating of historians such as Herodotus in style (ibid., 198). For the manner of narration, see not only emulating the diction of Herodotus or Thycidides but also using archaicizing Atticizing diction and declamatory descriptions (ecphrases) (ibid., 205).

29. "Nor is Celsus likely to have been the first to elaborate it. In the hundred years before he composed his treatise, it is obvious, as our review of the literature amply demonstrates, that the theme of bodily resurrection was all too familiar to pagan readers and even audiences in the theatre. For a sage like Apollonius or for a hero like Protesilaus, a resurrection of this kind could be presented in total seriousness and enjoyed, if not necessarily believed" (Bowersock, *Fiction as History*, 118).

30. Plutarch, *Isis and Osiris*, in vol. 5 of *Moralia*, trans. Frank Cole Babbitt, LCL (Cambridge: Harvard University Press, 1936).

By arguing for a qualitative difference between his recounted version of the myth and the other, fictional versions of it (διακένοις πλάσμασιν, "empty/idle concoctions"), Plutarch actually witnesses to the existence of story plots that encapsulate or imitate the mythic narrative. Given the contents and the setting, one might surmise that Plutarch was thinking of the very similarity in plot and setting between the Isis and Osiris myth and Achilles Tatius's novel *Leucippe and Clitophon*. It had already begun to be impossible to properly distinguish between fact and fiction, and as the cases of Celsus and Plutarch demonstrate, the wish to distinguish at all is a function of the ideology embedded in social positionality.[31]

It is not as if members of the literate high society (most pointedly the "consumers" and producers of literature, but also the class of people who had a stake in determining the difference between [philosophical] truth and fiction) could not distinguish between truth and fiction. The difference, and confusion of the two, could by the same token easily be the source of merriment and fun. Lucian of Samosata's *True History*, for example, is a veritable (self-confessed) send-up of history, epic, and myth.[32] But when Lucian provides merriment with his tales of sky journeys, sun and moon empires, strange events in the belly of a giant whale, a visit to the underworld and council of the gods and heroes, spicing up his accounts with truly weird and wonderful creatures and events, he is moving in a world not dissimilar to the world of Jewish-Christian apocalypses and hagiographies.

In a genre that takes itself extremely seriously (*vide* Rev 22:18–19), we move among grotesque sky-beings wreaking havoc on earth; gory, blood-spattering punishments meted out and cosmic wars being fought; stunning scenes of bejeweled celestial cities and fiery heavenly throne rooms; wailing and wrestling in burning, sulphury mud pits—the Left Behind corpus of antiquity. Indeed, apocalyptic literature has been called the science fiction of antiquity.[33] This is not a view of little consequence: science

---

31. Witness the wholesale rewriting of history and myth in the period, see Gerhard van den Heever, "Novel and Mystery: Discourse, Myth and Society," in *Ancient Fiction: Matrix of Early Christian and Early Jewish Narrative*, ed. Jo-Ann A. Brant, Charles W. Hedrick, and Christine Shea, SBLSymS 32 (Atlanta: Society of Biblical Literature, 2005), 89–114; and van den Heever, "Loose Fictions," especially ch. 4.

32. Virtually the entire work reflects on the fuzzy boundaries between history and fiction, but see especially Lucian, *Ver. hist.* preface; 1.13, 26; and 2.31.

33. Catherine Hezser, "'Ancient Science Fiction': Journeys into Space and Visions

fiction is the literature of expansion of vision and imagination of different worlds (thus its social-critical function), hence often the foundation for the mythology of NRMs. If the genre of apocalypticism left room for the imagination and the speculative, descriptions of pilgrimage shrines and the wonders encountered there are given with deadpan seriousness, as, for example, Jerome's *Letter to Eustochium* 108 (ca. 414) describing Paula's life. Especially noteworthy is his account of her visit to the *martyrium* of Elisha, Obadiah, and John the Baptist in Samaria/Sebaste (13):

> There lie the prophets Elisha and Obadiah and John the Baptist than whom there is not a greater among those that are born of women. And here she was filled with terror by the marvels she beheld; for she saw demons screaming under different tortures before the tombs of the saints, and men howling like wolves, baying like dogs, roaring like lions, hissing like serpents and bellowing like bulls. They twisted their heads and bent them backwards until they touched the ground; women too were suspended head downward and their clothes did not fall off. (*NPNF* 2/6:201)[34]

Even allowing for the popular appeal and novelistic character evinced by the apocryphal acts, still the hagiographic function of these texts—and they are effectively constructing a class of divine men-mediator figures for a new kind of embodied religiosity—suggests a tone of seriousness amid the wonderment elicited by these texts. At the climax of the Acts of Peter (ch. 12 onwards), when the contest between the apostle and Simon the magus comes to a head in the city of Rome, a dog speaks to the apostle, a broken statue of the emperor is repaired by "baptizing" it with water, a dead sardine is thrown into a swimming pool and revives and swims away, followed by a miracle contest between Simon and Peter in front of the city prefect in the forum.

---

of the World in Jewish, Christian, and Greco-Roman Literature of Antiquity," in *Christian Origins and Hellenistic Judaism: Social and Literary Contexts for the New Testament*, ed. Stanley E. Porter and Andrew W. Pitts, TENTS 10 (Leiden: Brill, 2013), 397–438.

34. This was a tradition noted also by other authorities for these strange phenomena: Hilary, Sulpicius, and Paulinus. For strange features of other pilgrimage sites, see Joachim Jeremias, *Heiligengräber in Jesu Umwelt (Mt. 23,29; Lk. 11,47): Eine Untersuchung zur Volksreligion der Zeit Jesu* (Göttingen: Vandenhoeck & Ruprecht, 1958).

Perhaps one should stand back and listen to the gospel account itself as Celsus would have heard it (that is, distanced from our theological presuppositions), and then one might see the following: a chorus of light beings in a dark sky; a band of ruffians rushing in from the veld to a cavern stable; a bright star portending impending momentous events in the sky; a party of gift-bearing wise men, a scheming king, and a massacre of infants; booming voices from heaven and a dove alighting on a man in a river; the paralyzed getting up and walking off; the dead getting up; screaming demons in uncanny places; a herd of swine rushing lemming-like off a cliff; a man walking, ghostlike, half-floating, above the water surface, and storms miraculously calmed; two fish and five loaves of bread miraculously feeding a crowd of thousands; bright lights on a mountain with swirling mists and celestial visitors; a man screaming on a cross that is set on a hill that looks like a skull; an earthquake that opens graves, letting the dead walk free; a curtain tearing of its own accord; a tomb for which the stone had rolled away and is empty; a story that ends with people running away in fear in one version, in another a man walking through a locked door and showing his torture wounds; a cloud settling on a man on a hill, who then disappears.

Veering between the amazing and the astonishing, dark horror and terror, the Christian story is a kind of Gothic of the Greco-Roman world, precisely the kind of narrative that, when offered as divine revelation history, would elicit Celsus's protest that this is not the manifestation of the divine. But then, the world was changing around him.

Fiction, Social Discourse, and Remythologizing the Roman Empire

If we may return to Origen's verbal duel with Celsus, the thrust of Origen's counterargument in *Cels.* 2.55 is that if the accounts of Moses are so similar to that of Jesus and Zalmoxis and Pythagoras, then Celsus as a Jew should at least concede that, if you accept the veracity of the life of Moses, then the narrative of Jesus is credible as well. But if you find the Christian account of Jesus Christ incredible, that is because, well, you just do not believe. To pose the question in this manner, as a choice pro and con, is to misrepresent the issue, for the work of both Celsus and Origen subsists in the same discourse, namely the redefinition of the cosmos effected by the arrival of the Roman Empire, a redefinition in which the wholesale fictionalizing and remythologizing that was the Roman Empire played a significant part.

If novelistic fiction is a product of empire,[35] then the interpretive task should be to historicize the emergence of fiction as a social discourse and let the light shine on the social discursivity of the production of literature. Arguably one of the main motivations for empire building has been to include the new and the exotic in the boundaries of the empire even as the horizons opened up.[36] Fiction was a well-suited vehicle to satisfy the flowering interest in other peoples and places, for ancient fiction (like its modern counterpart) entextualized a betraveled cosmos, either into other faraway and exotic places or into the weirdly exotic imaginary space of fantasy. Imperial fiction is concerned with the inhabitants and events on the margins, with going away (by choice or through force), and with confrontation with the unknown.[37] The bizarre characters that populate imperial fiction from Petronius's *Satyricon* to Antonius Diogenes's *The Wonders beyond Thule* to Lucian's *True History* testify, alongside the combination of travel to faraway and fantasy destinations with romantic plots, to a growing fascination with the fictional and the marvelous from the first century onwards.[38] But the implicit social discourse embodied in the tall tales of the beyond is one of imperial spatiality—the cosmos has been conquered and been made accessible for travel, even if this is only in the imagination, and what is more, the beyond now appears here on earth. It was exactly the appearance of wholesale fictionalizing that created the problem of truth, of what constituted true history.[39] In this, a world redolent with the marvelous fictional, "truth" becomes stranger than fiction. The overwhelming rise of the fictional created the sense of the Saturnalian character of the Roman Empire as *paradoxon*, a marvel.[40]

Much was therefore at stake for Celsus and Origen, and others. How we classify the narratives—as myths, deluded tales, as fantasy—allows a

---

35. Van den Heever, "Loose Fictions," 98, a reference to Edward Said.
36. Bowersock, *Fiction as History*, 31–33.
37. Ibid., 33.
38. Ibid., 37.
39. There is an exact parallel in the seventeenth century when the philosophy, or science, of history was newly conceived as the endeavor to "check sources, eliminate hearsay, and destroy superstition, lies, and credulity," Percy G. Adams, *Travel Literature and the Evolution of the Novel* (Lexington: University Press of Kentucky, 1983), 12. The trouble arose from the use in fiction of such narrative ruses as calling the fictional works "adventures of," "life of," "history of," "the travels of," "the memoirs of," "the journal of," or "the confessions of." See ibid., 8.
40. Van den Heever, "Loose Fictions," 103.

reader to negotiate these social ideological issues. The majority of modern scholars of ancient fiction prefer to read them as harmless stories for private enjoyment and see the function of fiction in an untheorized "narrative pleasure," or "entertainment," or "fantasy," and so on.[41] The stance taken here assumes a political role for fictional narratives, a stance influenced by Fredric Jameson's call to "always historicize!"[42] In his discussion of the politics of myth, Bruce Lincoln devised a taxonomy for adjudicating fable, legend, history and myth according to their truth claims, credibility, and authority.[43] The genres of history and myth both claim truth and credibility, but myth exercises authority as the foundation for social formation that has been elevated to an unassailable position from culture to nature. As such, how we categorize narratives—as fables, as history, as myth (or as religion)—opens a contended space in which the rhetoric of social definition plays out. In the making of a Christian Roman Empire, this is what was at stake in the verbal dual between Origen and Celsus.

---

41. "We might argue, for example, that fiction in general answers to a universal human need for narrative pleasure." J. R. Morgan, "Introduction," in *Greek Fiction: The Greek Novel in Context*, ed. J. R. Morgan and Richard Stoneman (London: Routledge, 1994), 3.

42. *The Political Unconscious: Narrative as a Socially Symbolic Act* (Ithaca, NY: Cornell University Press, 1981), 9.

43. Bruce Lincoln, *Discourse and the Construction of Society: Comparative Studies of Myth, Ritual, and Classification* (New York: Oxford University Press, 1989), 25.

Part 3
Pedagogies Ancient and Modern

Origen and Hypatia:
Parallel Portraits of Platonist Educators

Ilaria Ramelli

What I Set Out to Argue

In a recent book, Arthur Urbano has shown how intellectual biographies were a field for religious competition in late antiquity.[1] He examines sets of two biographies at a time, usually a biography of a Christian by a Christian author, and another biography of a pagan by a pagan: for instance, Origen's biography by Eusebius and Plotinus's biography by Porphyry, or Macrina's biography by Gregory Nyssen and Sosipatra's by Eunapius. Instead, I intend to analyze the portraits that the Christian Socrates delineates of both Origen of Alexandria—the extremely learned Christian Platonist who ran a university-level school first in Alexandria and later in Caesarea[2]—and Hypatia, the extremely learned Neoplatonist and expert in philosophy as well as astronomy and mathematics, who likewise ran a university-level school in Alexandria. Socrates of Constantinople was active in the first half of the fifth century under Theodosius II, but he was not a court historian. He strongly admired Origen and knew

---

1. Arthur Urbano, *The Philosophical Life: Biography and the Crafting of Intellectual Identity in Late Antiquity* (Washington, DC: Catholic University of America Press, 2013).

2. See Ilaria L. E. Ramelli, "Origen, Patristic Philosophy, and Christian Platonism: Re-Thinking the Christianization of Hellenism," *VC* 63 (2009): 217–63; Christoph Markschies, *Hellenisierung des Christentums: Sinn und Unsinn einer historischen Deutungskategorie* (Leipzig: Evangelische Verlagsanstalt, 2012); Ramelli, "Origen the Christian Middle/Neoplatonist," *Journal of Early Christian History* 1 (2011): 98–130; and Ramelli, "*Ethos* and *Logos*: A Second-Century Apologetical Debate between 'Pagan' and Christian Philosophers," *VC* 69.2 (2015): 123–56. A monograph will eventually appear with Cambridge University Press.

the Origenian Evagrius's work, from which he quoted passages.[3] Socrates is not the only Christian historian with a penchant for Origen and his tradition; others were Eusebius, Rufinus, Sozomen, and Palladius.

I will point out that—apparently oddly enough, given that Origen was a Christian and Hypatia a pagan—Socrates, who was an admirer and a strong defender of Origen as well as of serious and free intellectual investigation, and who opposed violence,[4] constructed his biographical narratives concerning Origen and Hypatia respectively as parallel portraits. This parallel between the two was certainly intended. The main points of contact between Origen and Hypatia are their intellectual brilliance and exceptional learning, especially their excellence in philosophy (Platonism) and the liberal arts; their dedication to education; their high asceticism, depicted as one with their philosophical vocation; their having been envied by mediocre people and misunderstood and persecuted by ignorant people; and their lives' having been sealed by martyrdom at the end.

Socrates's Description and Praise of Origen

Unlike Eusebius, Socrates did not devote a full book to a panegyric-style biography of Origen. Nevertheless Socrates, who esteemed Origen no less than Eusebius did, managed to praise him highly and repeatedly throughout his *Historia ecclesiastica*, insisting especially on denouncing envy as

---

3. Socrates, *Hist. eccl.* 3.7; 4.23.

4. For Socrates's defense of Origen, see Michel Fédou, "L'historien Socrate et la controverse origéniste," in *L'historiographie de l'Église des premiers siècles*, ed. Bernard Pouderon and Yves-Marie Duval (Paris: Beauchesne, 2001), 271–80; Bernhard Neuschäfer, "Zur Bewertung des Origenes bei Sokrates," in *Die Welt des Sokrates von Konstantinopel*, ed. Balbina Bäbler and Heinz-Gunther Nesselrath (Munich: Saur, 2001), 71–95; Peter van Nuffelen, *Un héritage de paix et de piété* (Leuven: Peeters, 2004), 37–42; Nuffelen, "Two Fragments from the Apology for Origen in the Church History of Socrates Scholasticus," *JTS* 56 (2005): 103–14. Socrates in *Hist. eccl.* 3.7.5–10 and 4.27.3–6 quotes two fragments from Pamphilus's and Eusebius's apology, but he may have had an interpolated Origenistic version thereof. For Socrates's opposition to violence, see Nuffelen, *Un héritage*. See also Martin Wallraff, *Der Kirchenhistoriker Sokrates: Untersuchungen zu Geschichtsdarstellung, Methode und Person* (Göttingen: Vandenhoeck & Ruprecht, 1997); Theresa Urbainczyk, *Socrates of Constantinople: Historian of Church and State* (Ann Arbor: University of Michigan Press, 1997); Hartmut Leppin, *The Church Historians I*, in *Greek and Roman Historiography: Fourth to Sixth Century*, ed. Gabriele Marasco (Leiden: Brill, 2003), 219–54.

the main factor that brought about his persecution—the same factor that Socrates denounces in the case of Hypatia. As Socrates declares in *Hist. eccl.* 7.45, "envy has been vented against Origen since his death."

Indeed, Socrates in *Hist. eccl.* 6.13 proposes an explanation centered on envy for the first attacks on Origen: "Those who have poor capabilities and are unable to make themselves illustrious by means of their own faculties wish to acquire fame by criticizing those who are better than they are. This passion affected first Methodius…, then Eusthatius…, then Apollinaris, and finally Theophilus. This is the quartet of defamers who slandered Origen."[5] Indeed, Pamphilus, Eusebius, Jerome, and Rufinus confirm that an important role in the opposition to Origen was played by envy, hostilities, and misunderstandings. Origen himself, in his letters and in other works, even homilies, lamented that he was misunderstood, envied, and hated.[6] In *Ep.* 33.5 to Paula, from 385, Jerome dubs *rabidi canes* those who claimed that Origen was condemned for dogmatic reasons and averred that hostility toward Origen was rather the fruit of mere envy for Origen's extraordinary learning, eloquence, and success—the same that led to hostility against Hypatia, as will be pointed out: *Roma ipsa contra hunc cogit senatum, non propter dogmatum novitatem, ut nunc adversus eum rabidi canes simulant, sed quia gloriam eloquentiae eius et scientiae ferre non poterant, et illo dicente omnes muti putabantur!* This envy against Origen, his learning, eloquence, and dialectic vigor (such that, when he opened his mouth, all the others instantly seemed mute) is the same motive that was individuated by Pamphilus in his apology and later by Socrates to explain the hostility with which Origen was immediately and enduringly targeted. Remarkably, Jerome reserved the same appellation, *rabidi canes*, for the enemies of Origen and for the enemies of Christ.[7]

Both Origen's greatness and the misunderstandings of which he was the object are highlighted by Socrates in *Hist. eccl.* 4.25, where, after praising the Origenian Didymus as extremely learned and a defender of

---

5. Socrates, however, also attests that Methodius in his last work, *Xenon*, expressed admiration for Origen (*Hist. eccl.* 6.13). Indeed, Socrates presents this late work of Methodius's as a withdrawal of previous criticism, a recantation.

6. See Ilaria Ramelli, "Decadence Denounced in the Controversy over Origen: Giving Up Direct Reading of Sources and Counteractions," in *Décadence: "Decline and Fall" or "Other Antiquity"?*, ed. Therese Fuhrer and Marco Formisano (Heidelberg: Winter, 2014), 263–83.

7. *Rabidi adversum Christum canes* (Jerome, *Vir. ill.* pr. 7).

orthodoxy, he observes that he wrote ὑπομνήματα devoted to the defense and clarification of Origen's *First Principles* because Origen's philosophical masterpiece was widely misinterpreted, as is also attested by Pamphilus. Readers "could not understand what that great man meant" (4.25). Didymus's commentary is also quoted by Jerome as *commentarioli Didymi* (Jerome, *Ruf.* 1). This was a remarkable, unique intellectual enterprise, the first Christian commentary on a work of a Christian author outside the Bible. The exceptional character of this work points to the exceptional value of Origen's masterpiece in Didymus's view and in that of his readership, to its difficulty, and to the attacks launched on it by adversaries either because of a lack of understanding or out of sheer hostility (the reasons already pointed out by Pamphilus: ignorance or envy).

Socrates points out also elsewhere the difficulty of Origen's books, again in the context of a defense and praise of him. In *Hist. eccl.* 6.17 he reports that Theophilus of Alexandria was criticized for returning to the reading of Origen's works after condemning—or pretending, ostentatiously, to condemn—Origen's errors,[8] but he defended himself by claiming that it was possible to pick flowers among Origen's writings while avoiding thorns. Socrates observes that Theophilus did not consider that the words of wise people are like a spur, and those who are pricked by their hidden meanings should not be disobedient toward them. With this, Socrates means, once more, that Origen's works are difficult to understand and have hidden senses, like Scripture—note again the assimilation of Origen's oeuvre to Scripture itself! Thus, Socrates implies, one should not simply reject these profound meanings in a selective manner, as Theophilus claimed he did, but rather try to penetrate them. This amounts to a claim that there are no bad doctrines among Origen's teachings; rather, those criticized are in fact misunderstood due to their difficulty.

Socrates in 4.26 speaks at length of Basil's and Gregory Nazianzen's predilection for Origen. He recounts that, shortly after their approach to philosophy, they began to collect and read Origen's work, and they took over from him "the exegetical method of the holy Scriptures," that is, allegorical/spiritual exegesis. Socrates remarks that at that time Origen enjoyed "a great fame throughout the inhabited world" (μέγα γὰρ κλέος τὸ Ὠριγένους καθ' ὅλης τότε τῆς οἰκουμένης). Socrates also sides with Origen's followers

---

8. See Ilaria L. E. Ramelli, *The Christian Doctrine of Apokatastasis: A Critical Assessment from the New Testament to Eriugena* (Leiden: Brill, 2013), 584–91.

in 6.9–10, which, together with Palladius, represents an important source concerning the Origenian monks called "Tall Brothers," exiled from Egypt by Theophilus in the years in which he needed to show hostility against Origen's doctrine. Socrates describes Theophilus's anti-Origenistic activity as animated by politico-ecclesiastical reasons (6.7, 10). Socrates depicts Theophilus as an Origenian who rejected anthropomorphic notions of God and for this reason was threatened with death by simpler monks, who scared him and demanded that he anathematize Origen's works. In general, according to Socrates, Theophilus's purpose in the Origenistic business was to deprive John Chrysostom of his episcopal dignity—and Socrates had sympathy for John, who received and helped the Origenian monks exiled by Theophilus, as Socrates himself narrates (6.7–9). It is indicative not only of Socrates's views but also of people's solidarity with the Origenian monks, as Socrates narrates in 6.17, that when Dioscorus—one of the Tall Brothers—died, shortly after being exiled by Theophilus, he "was honored with a magnificent burial and tomb." Socrates represents the Tall Brothers, whom Theophilus initially admired, as philosophical ascetics, true followers of Origen and like him "distinguished both for the holiness of their lives and the extent of their erudition," and adds that "for these reasons their reputation was very high at Alexandria" (6.7), as that of Origen was in the whole world. Socrates notes that their aversion to divine anthropomorphisms came especially from Origen's arguments and contrasts their learning with the uncultivated minds of the monks whom Theophilus stirred up against them. Likewise, Origen had been persecuted by ignorant and envious people. Socrates emphasizes the association with Origen by remarking that the Tall Brothers were dubbed "Origenists" by their more ignorant fellow monks, instigated by Theophilus (6.7).

Socrates denounces Theophilus's opportunistic behavior and exalts Origen and his orthodoxy, observing that Theophilus "wrote to all the bishops of the various cities, and concealing his real motive, ostensibly condemned therein the books of Origen merely—which Athanasius, his predecessor, had used in confirmation of his own faith, frequently appealing to the testimony and authority of Origen's writings, in his orations against the Arians" (6.9).[9] Socrates also unmasks Theophilus's opportunism when he (Theophilus) induced Epiphanius to convene a synod to

---

9. On Athanasius's use of Origen in his anti-Arian works see Ilaria L. E. Ramelli, "Origen's Anti-subordinationism and Its Heritage in the Nicene and Cappadocian Line," *VC* 65 (2011): 21–49.

condemn Origen's writings "almost two centuries after his death," and moreover summoned a synod himself for the same professed purpose—but "rather his purpose was revenge" on the Origenian monks, as well as an attempt "to divest John of his bishopric" (6.10).

Socrates in 6.12 narrates that, instigated again by Theophilus, Epiphanius went to Constantinople, bringing along a document containing the condemnation of Origen's works. He summoned the bishops in Constantinople and read them this paper. Socrates, who appreciated rational argument, as befits his admiration for Origen and his followers, points out that Epiphanius could produce no reason for that condemnation, apart from saying that Theophilus and he himself wanted it—which is no reason but an argument from authority. Some bishops agreed, but many did not. Among those who resisted was Theotimus, bishop of Tomi, a friend of John Chrysostom and an Origenian. Socrates reports the speech of Theotimus, who refused to attack Origen, stating that the latter had died in peace long since, had been never condemned by the church, and taught pious doctrines. Theotimus, a convert from "paganism," was a professional philosopher;[10] this is why he valued rational argument and, like Pamphilus,[11] defended Origen by means of Origen's own words, reading them in public:

> "I do not intend, O Epiphanius, to insult this man, who died long ago in sanctity. Nor do I dare attempt a blasphemous thing, condemning what our predecessors did not reject, especially since I know that there is no bad teaching in Origen's works." And putting forward a book of Origen, he read a passage from it, and indicated in it the expositions good for the church. After which, he added: "Those who abuse these thoughts do not realize that they also abuse the things on which these discourses focus." This is how Theotimus, famous for his piety and the rectitude of his life, replied to Epiphanius. (6.12)

Socrates sides with Theotimus's defense of Origen and consistently, in the immediately following chapter (6.13), puts forward his own defense of Origen, dictated by the circumstance that "carping detractors have imposed upon many people and have succeeded in deterring them from

---

10. Sozomen attests that Theotimus "had been brought up in the practice of philosophy" and "always kept the long hair he wore when he first devoted himself to the practice of philosophy" (*Hist. eccl.* 7.26).

11. See Ramelli, "Decadence Denounced."

reading Origen, as though he were a blasphemous writer." Here Socrates inserts his abovementioned remark that the detractors of Origen were worthless characters, destitute of ability to attain eminence themselves, who therefore sought to get into notice by decrying those who excelled them, namely, Origen. But these revilers were not in agreement about what fault to find with Origen. Socrates accuses them of incoherence and thereby inconclusiveness, even drawing therefrom a praise of Origen:

> One found one cause of accusation against him, and another another; and thus each has demonstrated that what he has taken no objection to, he has fully accepted. For since one has attacked one opinion in particular, and another has found fault with another, it is evident that each has admitted as true what he has not assailed.... *But I affirm that from the censure of these men, greater commendation accrues to Origen.* For those who have sought out whatever they deemed worthy of reprobation in him, and yet have never charged him with holding unsound views regarding the holy Trinity, are in this way most distinctly shown to bear witness to Origen's orthodoxy: and by not reproaching him on this point, they commend him by their own testimony. (emphasis added)

As already in 6.9, here, too, Socrates appeals to Athanasius's use of Origen as an authority:

> Athanasius, the defender of the doctrine of consubstantiality, in his discourses against the Arians continually cites Origen as a witness of his own [Nicene] faith, interweaving his words with his own, and saying, "The most admirable and hard-worker Origen by his own testimony confirms our doctrine concerning the Son of God, affirming him to be coeternal with the Father." Consequently, those who load Origen with opprobrium overlook the fact that their maledictions fall at the same time on Athanasius, who praised Origen. So much will be enough for the *vindication of Origen.* (emphasis added)

Likewise, in 2.21 Socrates defends Origen, like Eusebius, from accusations of subordinationism—as he does again in 7.6—expressing once more his admiration for Origen's genius and his arduous writings, as well as his indignation at the calumnious charges of which Origen was the victim, by

> those who have slanderously attempted to traduce and criminate him. Neither can they prove that Eusebius attributes a beginning of subsis-

> tence to the Son of God ... especially because he was an emulator and admirer of Origen's works, in which *those who are able to comprehend the depth of Origen's writings*, will perceive it to be everywhere stated that the Son was begotten of the Father. (emphasis added)

Socrates defends Origen's doctrines also in 3.7, where he once more highlights that—like Hypatia—he was unjustly attacked by ignorant, and praises his apologists: Origen

> accepts that the Incarnate God took on himself a human soul.... That holy man Pamphilus, and Eusebius who was surnamed after him, are trustworthy witnesses on this subject: both these witnesses in their joint life of Origen, *an admirable defense of him in answer to such as were prejudiced against him*, prove that he was not the first who made this declaration, but that in doing so he was the mere expositor of the mystical tradition of the church. (emphasis added)

Socrates especially lauds Origen—precisely like Hypatia—both for his activity as an educator and for his extraordinary and wide-ranging learning: "Origen most commonly taught in the church on those days. He was an extremely learned teacher in the holy Scripture," of which he propounded "a spiritual interpretation" (5.22). Similarly, in 2.35 Socrates praises Origen, with Clement and Julius Africanus, as "eminent for his information in every department of literature and science." Origen, indeed, thought that the Spirit, the inspirer of Scripture, deliberately hid in the holy writ meanings to be discovered by exegetes not only thanks to God's assistance but also by means of specific scientific competences: grammatical, linguistic, historical, or coming from other liberal disciplines, and above all philosophical. Especially in his letter to Gregory Thaumaturgus, Origen points out the value of the liberal arts and of philosophy as paramount for biblical hermeneutics. As Origen recommends at the end of the letter, Christian theology must be grounded in biblical exegesis, but the "zetetic" exegesis theorized and practiced by Origen was a philosophical exegesis supported by the contributions of the liberal disciplines, of which philosophy was the pinnacle. Only this could attain the spiritual meanings of Scripture.[12]

---

12. See Ilaria L. E. Ramelli, "Patristic Exegesis' Relevance to Contemporary Biblical Hermeneutics," *R&T* 22 (2015): 100–132.

Socrates's Description and Praise of Hypatia

Winrich Löhr observes[13] that there were philosophical schools, both pagan and Christian, in the second–third centuries CE, but at the beginning of the fifth century only pagan philosophical schools were left, because of the strengthening of bishops in the church, which damaged schools and free research. I add, however, that still Nyssen and Nazianzen, Synesius and Theotimus were true Christian philosophers, albeit being also bishops. The line was set by the Christian philosopher-presbyter Origen, who in turn legitimated his position by adducing the examples of the philosophers-presbyters Pantaenus and Heraclas.[14] Meaningfully, Origen himself, Plotinus, Hypatia, and Ammonius of Alexandria had both pagan and Christian disciples at their philosophical school-universities. Moreover, not only Christian universities, but even pagan philosophical universities, could not survive in the Christian empire: that of Hypatia was terminated with her murder in 415 CE and the Platonic school of Athens closed about one century later by order of Justinian, who disliked both pagan and Origen's Christian Platonism.[15]

The biography of the pagan Neoplatonist Hypatia of Alexandria is closely connected with those of two Christian bishops: Synesius, who was a pagan Neoplatonist himself and became bishop of Ptolemais (409–415 CE) and was Hypatia's disciple, and Cyril, Theophilus's relative, who was bishop of Alexandria when Hypatia was murdered by Christian fanatics in 415. In 380 Theodosius had proclaimed "orthodox" Christianity the official religion of the empire and in 392 proscribed pagan cults (Codex Theodosianus 16.10.12).[16]

Synesius, who remained a Neoplatonist also as a bishop—as Origen had remained a Middle-Neoplatonist as a presbyter—continued to vener-

---

13. Winrich Löhr, "Christianity as Philosophy: Problems and Perspectives of an Ancient Intellectual Project," *VC* 64 (2010): 160–88.
14. Analysis in Ramelli, "Origen's Anti-Subordinationism."
15. See Ramelli, *Apokatastasis*, 724–38.
16. Hypatia's historical background is analyzed by Maria Dzielska, *Hypatia of Alexandria* (Cambridge: Harvard University Press, 1995); Dzielska, "Once More on Hypatia's Death," in *Divine Men and Women in the History and Society of Late Hellenism*, ed. Maria Dzielska and Kamilla Twardowska (Krakow: Jagiellonian University Press, 2013), 1–74: like Socrates, Hypatia went back into the cave and tried to orient a larger audience toward the Good, but was killed; Edward J. Watts, *Hypatia: The Life and Legend of an Ancient Philosopher* (Oxford: Oxford University Press, 2017).

ate his professor, to whom he wrote letters. In *Letter* 16 he reverently calls her "mother, sister, professor and benefactor together, the sum of whatever one can honor in words and deeds." Synesius, who interpreted the Trinity in the light of the Neoplatonic Triad, wrote to his brother (*Letter* 105) that even as a bishop he would keep rejecting the preexistence of bodies to souls, upholding the eternity of the world, and affirming a spiritual notion of resurrection. As for Origen, the allegorical-spiritual exegesis of Scripture for Synesius paralleled the hermeneutics of Plato's myths (as the prologue to *De insomniis* suggests).[17] His bishopric was offered him by Theophilus in 410: so, long after exiling the Origenian monk-philosophers, Theophilus wanted a Neoplatonist as a bishop!

According to the Neoplatonist Damascius, Hypatia was more of a genius than her father, Theon, the philosopher and mathematician at whose school she had studied. According to Henri-Irénée Marrou,[18] she may have occupied one of the imperial chairs of philosophy in Alexandria. She was an expert in astronomy, mathematics,[19] geography, geometry, mechanics (to which she contributed inventions), and philosophy—like Origen, who highly valued liberal arts and philosophy. She wrote an *Astronomy Canon*, according to the *Suda*, and commentaries, now lost, on classical works of geometry by Euclides and Apollonius, geography by Ptolemy, and mathematics by Diophantus. At her school she taught especially philosophy—Neoplatonism.

Socrates, in his portrait of Hypatia, parallel to that of Origen, praises her as "superior to all the philosophers of that time" and as a successor of Plotinus as a Platonist scholarch, admired for her learning and virtue—just as Origen was a fellow disciple of Plotinus, one of the best Platonists, admired for his learning and virtue. Many came from far away

---

17. See Ilaria L. E. Ramelli, "Origen's Allegoresis of Plato's and Scripture's Myths," in *Religious Competition in the Greco-Roman World*, ed. Nathaniel P. Desrosiers and Lily C. Vuong, WGRWSup 10 (Atlanta: SBL Press, 2016), 85–106; Jay Bregman, "Synesius of Cyrene," in *The Cambridge History of Philosophy in Late Antiquity*, ed. Lloyd P. Gerson (Cambridge: Cambridge University Press, 2010), 1:520–37; Ramelli, *Apokatastasis*, 602–3; see Helmut Seng and Lars Hoffmann, eds., *Synesios von Kyrene: Politik, Literatur, Philosophie* (Turnhout: Brepols, 2013).

18. Henri-Irénée Marrou, "Synesius of Cyrene and Alexandrian Neoplatonism," in *The Conflict of Paganism and Christianity in the Fourth Century*, ed. Arnaldo Momigliano (Oxford: Clarendon, 1963), 126–50.

19. Michael Deakin, "Hypatia and Her Mathematics," *American Mathematical Monthly* 101.3 (1994): 234–43.

to attend Hypatia's classes as well as Origen's (Socrates himself in *Hist. eccl.* 4.27 lingers on Gregory Thaumaturgus, who, like many others, came from far away to study with Origen). Hypatia, like Origen, was famous and respected among both pagans and Christians. "Neither did she feel abashed in coming to an assembly of men. For all men, on account of her extraordinary dignity and virtue, admired her the more" (7.15). Hypatia, as a good Neoplatonist and Alexandrian, probably knew Origen's works—all the more so if Origen the Christian was, as is likely, the same as Origen the Neoplatonist. Like Origen, Hypatia conducted a life of a philosopher and ascetic; according to Damascius, she always remained a virgin. Again like Origen, she was eloquent, brilliant, and successful—therefore, tragically, she was the object of envy and hostility, as Origen was. Both of them concluded their life with martyrdom, Origen at the hands of pagans (although he was hated and envied by Christians no less), Hypatia at the hand of Christians unworthy of this name, as Socrates makes clear.

The prefect of Alexandria, Orestes, was a pagan and a friend of Hypatia, who was his informal adviser. Bishop Cyril was in conflict with Orestes due to disorders that occurred shortly before Hypatia's murder.[20] Socrates, who wrote twenty years after this murder, is the earliest source concerning it (*Hist. eccl.* 7.15).[21] According to him, the cause of Hypatia's murder was envy, the same that he denounced as a cause for hostility against Origen. Out of envy, "it was calumniously reported among the Christian populace that it was she who prevented Orestes from being reconciled to the bishop." In March 415, during Lent, a mass of people, "hurried away by a fierce and bigoted zeal"—Socrates does not even speak of monks—led by Peter Anagnostes (a collaborator of Cyril, but Socrates does not draw a connection between him and Cyril), seized Hypatia while she was returning

---

20. See Jean Rougé, "La politique de Cyrille d'Alexandrie et le meurtre d'Hypatie," *CNS* 11 (1990): 485–504; Luigi Canfora, *Un mestiere pericoloso: La vita quotidiana dei filosofi greci* (Palermo: Sellerio, 2000), 196–203; Edward Watts, "The Murder of Hypatia: Acceptable or Unacceptable Violence?," in *Violence in Late Antiquity: Perceptions and Practices*, ed. Harold Drake (Burlington, VT: Ashgate, 2006), 333–42.

21. Besides Damascius and Palladas, examined below, other sources on Hypatia are Philostorgius, *Historia Ecclesiastica* 8.9; John Malalas, *Chron.* 359; John of Nikiu, *Chronicle* 84.100–102; Theophanes, *Chronicle* 5906. Sinesius, Socrates, Cassiodorus—who depends on Socrates—Damascius, Palladas, Philostorgius, Hesychius, and Malalas are commented on by Henriette Harich-Schwarzbauer, *Hypatia: Die spätantiken Quellen* (Bern: Lang, 2011).

home and dragged her out of her carriage. They took her to the Kaisareion church, where they stripped and murdered her with tiles. After tearing her body into pieces, they took her mangled limbs to a place called Kinaron and there burned them. Socrates comments: "This affair brought not the least opprobrium, not only upon Cyril, but also upon the whole church of Alexandria. Surely nothing can be farther from the spirit of Christianity than the allowance of massacres, fights, and transactions of that sort." Socrates's spirit was also the spirit of Origen.

Unlike Socrates, the pagan Neoplatonist Damascius, in his *Life of Isidore*,[22] directly attaches to Cyril the responsibility for the murder, albeit admitting that the crime was perpetrated by "bestial men." The motivation individuated by Damascius is the same indicated by Socrates for both Hypatia and Origen: "envy," for Damascius that of Cyril before Hypatia's many admirers and followers, who revered her, and before her teaching not only at school but also publicly—like Origen in his public debates—addressing anyone who wished to listen to her elucidations of Plato, Aristotle, or other philosophers. According to Damascius, Theodosius II himself would have avenged this crime, if Aedesius had not bribed the emperor's friends; however, a descendant of his—perhaps Valentinian—paid for the injustice of his predecessor. Damascius remarks that the memory of these events was still alive among the Alexandrians in his day, almost one century later.

Like Socrates and Damascius, the *Suda* also adduces envy as the cause of Hypatia's murder: envy for the outstanding learning and wisdom, especially her competence in astronomy. The *Suda* also attributes the responsibility for her murder either to Cyril, "according to some" (among whom Damascius), or to the Alexandrians, "according to others" (among whom perhaps Socrates). Cyril was Theophilus's nephew. He had received an ascetic formation in Egyptian desert monasticism, with intense study of Scripture, Athanasius, Eusebius, and Basil, all authors profoundly influenced by Origen. At the outbreak of the Origenian controversy, which ended up with the exile of the Origenian monks from the Egyptian desert, Cyril was called back from the desert by his uncle, who was probably aware that Cyril's teacher was an Origenian. Cyril was well acquainted with Origen's and Didymus's works; he probably met the latter when Didymus was

---

22. Damascius, *On the Life of the Philosopher Isidore* 166; see Photius, *Bibliotheca* 181.

the head of the Didaskaleion, appointed by Athanasius. Cyril knew and cited the Cappadocians, admirers of Origen, Peter of Alexandria, Origen's follower, and the early Jerome, who also praised Origen to the skies. As his commentary on John, written about a decade before his episcopate, shows, Cyril followed Origen's spiritual exegesis. In what is often considered a refutation of Origen, Cyril in fact neither cites him nor refutes his true thought. Actually, Cyril's Origenian pedigree might be one reason why Socrates, who also admired Origen, refrained from directly blaming Cyril for the tragedy of Hypatia.

Socrates, like Synesius, testifies to the admiration that many, including many Christians, felt toward Hypatia, the learned philosopher and ascetic. Similarly, a Greek epigram by Palladas (Anth. Pal. 9.400) calls her "venerable" and "purest star of wise learning." At the beginning, the epigrammatist plays on a double entendre based on the double possible syntactical dependence of both σε and τῆς παρθένου, so that one way to understand the opening is "When I see you, I adore you and your words, the words of the virgin," whose acts were all "turned toward heaven." This, too, bears a double meaning, both because Hypatia was a great scholar in astronomy and because she was, like Origen, a great theologian. As Synesius observed, the study of heaven was a means to elevate the mind "to the ineffable theology" (*De dono* 4).

Conclusive Reflections

Socrates revered and defended Origen as much as he respected Hypatia, as a supporter of serious, free intellectual research and a denouncer of violence. His narratives concerning these two Alexandrian Platonist educators, victims of stupidity and violence, and incarnations of learning and philosophical investigation, are in many ways parallel portraits, albeit of a Christian and a pagan. For both Origen and Hypatia Socrates emphasizes their intellectual brilliance; their excellence in philosophy (Platonism) and the liberal arts; their dedication to education; their asceticism, represented as inseparable from their philosophical life; and their having been envied, misunderstood, slandered, and persecuted by the ignorant; both their lives were terminated by martyrdom. Socrates was building on Pamphilus's and Eusebius's portrait of Origen as a most learned philosopher-ascetic and teacher (*magister ecclesiae*, Pamphilus, *Apol.* 16). These traits are all common to Hypatia. That both are portrayed as philosophers-ascetics is particularly interesting, in the light of the role, pointed out in a recent monograph,[23] of philosophical asceticism (especially in the Origenian tradition) in the rejection of violence and oppression, the same that Socrates too denounces in his narratives about Origen and Hypatia.

---

23. Ilaria L. E. Ramelli, *Social Justice and the Legitimacy of Slavery: The Role of Philosophical Asceticism from Ancient Judaism to Late Antiquity* (Oxford: Oxford University Press, 2017).

Teaching Fiction, Teaching Acts: Introducing the Linguistic Turn in the Biblical Studies Classroom

Shelly Matthews

Helping students of biblical narrative to recognize that the boundaries between the genres of ancient historiography, fiction, and rhetoric are porous, and that authors of biblical narratives were not simply compiling records of the past "as it really was," is a perennial challenge in the biblical studies classroom.[1] It seems a particularly crucial task in a historical moment that witnesses to a resurgence of religious fundamentalism, in which positivist readings of ancient narratives deemed sacred are employed to fuel fear, and even hatred, for those outside the fundamentalist's own reading community.

In classrooms populated predominantly with students identified, however loosely, with Western Christian traditions, recognizing the fictive nature of the Acts of the Apostles poses a particular challenge. Differently from the canonical gospels, which can be set aside one another in columns, so that redactional interests can be illuminated, contradictions noted, and the historical certainty of any one narrative readily called into question, Acts is the single canonical narrative of events in the postresurrection *ekklēsia*. The singularity of the narrative, along with factors such as its structural coherence, and the professed interest of the implied author in matters of accuracy and eyewitness testimony (see Luke 1:1–4; Acts 1:1), has resulted in widely held assumptions that Acts may be treated as

---

1. Several brief reflections on this pedagogical challenge are contained within the volume by Mark Roncace and Patrick Gray, eds., *Teaching the Bible: Practical Strategies for Classroom Instruction*, RBS 49 (Atlanta: Society of Biblical Literature, 2005).

a relatively straightforward and "reliable" window onto the history of the early church.²

My own approach to teaching Acts is influenced by the work of Richard I. Pervo, who taught us several years ago that the Acts of the Apostles shares a multitude of features with ancient novels.³ It is also heavily indebted to the work of Todd Penner, who demonstrated that even if Acts is classified under the genre of ancient history—*historia*—this genre shares significant overlap with ancient rhetoric, especially in the Roman period, insofar as its purveyors understood historical composition as a "moral and political act" in the service of *paideia*.⁴ Finally, it is influenced by currents in poststructuralist historiography, which recognize that (1) language, rather than providing a transparent window onto the past, instead plays a constitutive role in creating the past;⁵ (2) insofar as historians represent past events through emplotting them in narrative form, the practice of writing historical narratives is identical to the practice of writing fiction;⁶

---

2. Arguments have been made for thematic parallels between Acts and ancient epic, and it might be said that had the author of Acts adopted the actual form of ancient epic, with its characteristic poetic meter, students might more readily acknowledge this author's poetic license. Consider Karen Ní Mheallaigh, who speaks of meter as equipping ancient poetry with "lie-signals" that are lacking in ancient prose narrative, making the truth value of the latter more difficult to ascertain. See *Reading Fiction with Lucian: Fakes, Freaks and Hyperreality* (Cambridge: Cambridge University Press, 2014), 81. As Todd C. Penner has shown, this desire to treat Acts, or at least large swaths of Acts, as historical narrative in the modern sense, faithfully representing the reality of past events, is not uncommon, even among biblical scholars. See *In Praise of Christian Origins: Stephen and the Hellenists in Lukan Apologetic Historiography* (New York: T&T Clark, 2004), esp. 1–69.

3. Richard I. Pervo, *Profit with Delight: The Literary Genre of the Acts of the Apostles* (Philadelphia: Fortress, 1987); see also his discussion of the genre of Acts, in *Acts: A Commentary*, ed. Harold W. Attridge, Hermeneia (Minneapolis: Fortress, 2009), 14–18.

4. Penner, *In Praise of Christian Origins*, 104–222.

5. This turn to the poststructuralist acknowledgement of the constitutive role of language for the past is referred to by historians as the "linguistic turn."

6. Which is often misconstrued to mean that postmodern historians think that "nothing happened" in the past, or that facts do not exist. As Fred W. Burnett clarifies, "Postmodern historians believe that the world is real and that events really happened. Their point is not so much the old question of history (reality) versus fiction as it is that the non-fictive and the fictive are never fully separable." See his "Historiography," in *Handbook of Postmodern Biblical Interpretation*, ed. A. K. M. Adam (St. Louis: Chalice, 2000), 111. The fictive nature of historical narrative is an argument often associ-

and (3) because there is no necessary correlation between ancient events and how they are emplotted in language, decisions about how to write historical narrative are perspectival and value laden and can be judged according to ethical criteria.[7]

In what follows, I first share a pedagogical exercise for helping students to see the fictive nature of biblical narrative in general and of Acts in particular. The overarching aim of this exercise is recognition that the criteria of ideological fittingness factors much more into ancient historical projects than concerns for accurate representation of historical events. In this sense it could be said that my pedagogical aim is deconstructive. But this deconstructive move is only a first step. After helping them to recognize that ancient history blurs with ancient fiction and serves ideological or political ends, I wish to underscore similar understandings in postmodern historical projects as a means to help them navigate the linguistic turn in our own time. To this end, the essay concludes with an example of how to engage students in the ethical implications of the "fiction" of historical narrative. But let us turn now to the first component of the pedagogical exercise.

Employing Extrabiblical Fictions in Bible Courses

As a means to assist students in recognizing that biblical authors employ criteria other than "achieving historical accuracy" for constructing narratives, I commonly invite them to compare extrabiblical narratives from the ancient world, which they would regard as obviously fictional, with beloved biblical narratives. In certain introductory course settings, when the primary source is short and the biblical narrative is reasonably well known, these comparisons can be invited in classroom settings with little advance preparation. Thus, I often include the reading of excerpts from Suetonius's account of the birth of Caesar (*Aug.* 94) in the first class session

---

ated with the work of Hayden White. See, for instance, "The Discourse of History," in *The Fiction of Narrative: Essays on History, Literature, and Theory 1957–2007*, ed. Robert Doran (Baltimore: Johns Hopkins University Press, 2010), 187–202.

7. A concise and accessible account of the differences between modern and postmodern historiography is offered in Burnett, "Historiography," 106–12. For reflection by historians on the ethics of history writing after the linguistic turn, see David Carr, Thomas R. Flynn, and Rudolf A. Makkreel, *The Ethics of History* (Evanston, IL: Northwestern University Press, 2004).

of a New Testament introduction, both as a means to prompt discussion of the similarities between it and the infancy narratives of Matthew and Luke and to foreshadow the sorts of critical comparisons that will be introduced as the course proceeds.

In situations when reading can be assigned in advance of class discussion, scholarship aiding in the understanding of the primary sources can be added. Among successful secondary sources for eliciting comparison between biblical and extrabiblical fictions are David Gowler's chapter-length treatment of the *chreia* and Saundra Schwartz's comparison between trial scenes in Greek novels and Acts.[8]

In ancient compositional handbooks, the *chreia* is defined as a brief remembrance of a saying or action attributed to a person, often providing a "useful" instance of exemplary behavior. Gowler's chapter introduces exercises contained in the *Progymnasmata* of Theon and Hermogenes to show how students at all educational levels in antiquity learned to manipulate *chreiai*, through processes including recitation, inflection, commentary, expansion, and condensation. He then supplies pericopes from the Synoptic Gospels that seem to exhibit the *chreia* form, accounting for variations within the synoptic parallels as owing to the flexibility of the form. Schwartz's study is more straightforward. She undertakes a typological study of trial scenes in ancient fiction, focusing on thirteen trial scenes within the five extant complete Greek novels, and then considers how the tropes in these trial scenes compare with trial scenes in Acts.

I have assigned the Gowler article in courses on the gospels, and Schwartz in courses on Luke-Acts, settings in which I am often suggesting, with various levels of firmness, that these particular narratives are not instances of historical writing in the modern sense. These two pieces of scholarship generally bring students to this recognition in ways that my lectures and discussion prompts alone do not. Gowler invites students to think about the actual educational processes that might have formed the gospel authors. For virtually all students I encounter, this is a field of inquiry that is utterly new to them but also quite compelling. Schwartz

---

8. David B. Gowler, "The Chreia," in *The Historical Jesus in Context*, ed. Amy-Jill Levine, Dale C. Allison Jr., and John Dominic Crossan, Princeton Readings in Religion (Princeton: Princeton University Press, 2006), 132–48; Saundra Schwartz, "The Trial Scene in the Greek Novels and in Acts," in *Contextualizing Acts: Lukan Narrative and Greco-Roman Discourse*, ed. Todd C. Penner and Caroline Vander Stichele, SBLSymS 20 (Atlanta: Society of Biblical Literature, 2003), 105–33.

draws attention to the poetics of trial narratives that have implications for not only the Acts narrative but also the gospel narratives of the trial of Jesus. Both supply useful comparative charts as part of their conclusions.[9]

I have had similar success in raising questions concerning the historicity of the story of the stoning of Stephen in Acts, through introducing students to the comparable story told of the martyrdom of James, the brother of Jesus, as preserved by Hegesippus, an early Christian author of the late second century. While the former is often considered as a straightforward historical account, the Hegesippus account contains details that even the most literally minded reader might concede are products of a symbolic imagination. In courses of instruction, I first invite students to identify and analyze the significance of parallels through their own close reading of these primary texts, before supplying them with my own analysis, which comes from an extended study of these two narratives and the possible relationships between them.[10] That analysis is shared here.

Thematic Similarity between Hegesippus's James and Acts's Stephen

The Temple as Locus of Conflict

When both Stephen and James confront hostile opponents, the temple plays a central role in the conflict. In the Acts narrative, Stephen faces accusations of having spoken against the temple and threatened its destruction

---

9. I highlight the contributions of Gowler and Schwartz because they are short and contained studies, well suited for the typical hourlong session of an introductory course in biblical literature. Of course, a number of studies could be cited that do similar comparative work. Consider, for instance, Rubén R. Dupertuis, "The Summaries of Acts 2, 4, and 5 and Plato's Republic," in *Ancient Fiction: The Matrix of Early Christian and Jewish Narrative*, ed. Jo-Ann A. Brant, Charles W. Hedrick, and Chris Shea, SBLSymS 32 (Atlanta: Society of Biblical Literature, 2005), 275–95; John Byron, "Ancient Historiography and the Book of Acts," in Roncace and Gray, *Teaching the Bible*, 336–38. Monographs with this comparative emphasis on biblical literature and Greek fiction include Pervo's *Profit* as well as several studies of Dennis R. MacDonald pointing to patterns between Homeric myth and biblical narrative. See for example, Dennis R. MacDonald, *Does the New Testament Imitate Homer? Four Cases from the Acts of the Apostles* (New Haven: Yale University Press, 2003).

10. Shelly Matthews, *Perfect Martyr: The Stoning of Stephen and the Construction of Christian Identity* (Oxford: Oxford University Press, 2010), 85–89.

(Acts 6:13–14). This accusation appears to be borne out when Stephen speaks with apparent disdain for the temple cult (7:47–50).[11] Hegesippus underscores James's link with the temple more heavily, noting that James was set apart for temple service from his mother's womb. In an assertion that flies in the face of what can be gleaned from other ancient sources concerning the high priesthood (and which most students can recognize as a decidedly nonliteral detail), Hegesippus positions James himself as high priest, interceding incessantly for the people within the temple. Furthermore, James's conflict with his opponents is depicted in spatial terms as literally *over* the temple, in that he gives testimony while standing on the temple's pinnacle and is thrown down from that pinnacle to his death.[12]

The High Christological Claim as the Tipping Point

In both narratives, the violent mob action is ignited by a high christological claim professed by the martyr. After his speech prompts the angered crowd to gnash their teeth, Stephen announces that he sees "the Son of Man standing at the right hand of God." This is the provocation that leads the crowd to drag him out of the city and stone him (Acts 7:56–58a). Hegesippus's martyrdom account has a similar structure. It is James's acclamation of the Son of Man "sitting in heaven on the right hand of the great power, who will come on the clouds of heaven" that prompts the scribes and Pharisees to throw him from the temple's pinnacle (Eusebius, *Hist. eccl.* 2.23.13–14).[13] Thus, both Hegesippus and the author of Acts communicate that the urge to kill the martyr is the direct result of the high

---

11. I disagree with those who argue that Stephen's speech is not antitemple. Designating the temple as a house made with "human hands" in 7:48, on the heels of equating idolatry with the work of "human hands" in 7:41, tars the temple as a place of idolatry.

12. In accounting for the similarities between Hegesippus and Acts concerning the centrality of the temple, students might be pointed to traditions concerning Jesus's own conflicts concerning the temple and temple authorities. It might be further noted that inasmuch as temple and Torah function as twin pillars of early Judaism (see Seth Schwartz, *Imperialism and Jewish Society 200 B.C.E. to 640 C.E.* [Princeton: Princeton University Press, 2001], 59–69), situating the conflict in terms of the temple functions metonymically: this is a crisis of Jesus believers concerning one of Judaism's pillars.

13. Eusebius, *Ecclesiastical History*, vol. 1, trans. Kirsopp Lake, LCL (Cambridge: Harvard University Press, 1926). Mutual dependence on the synoptic accounts of the trial of Jesus seems the best explanation for this common structure. Hegesippus fol-

christological claim that Jesus, as the exalted Son of Man, participates in the unique divine identity of God, sharing God's throne and his judgment over his enemies.[14]

Mock Trial; Lynch Justice; Death by Stoning

In both stories mob behavior leads to the martyr's death. While accusations against Stephen are first lodged in a judicial setting, before a council, in which [false] witnesses provide testimony, this formal juridical process collapses as the crowd interrupts his speech.[15] The scene shifts quickly from courtroom to mob riot, thus confirming the barbarous nature of Stephen's enemies. According to Hegesippus, James's death is also ignited by an "uproarious crowd [ἦν θόρυβος] of Jews, scribes and Pharisees" (Eusebius, *Hist. eccl.* 2.23.10 [Lake, modified]). These leaders subject James to an investigative inquiry at the pinnacle of the temple, but as in the case of Stephen, the death of James is not the result of a formal judicial process ending with the pronouncement of the death penalty as his deserved reward. Rather, it is the outcome of a series of impulsive and violent actions that, when taken together, depict a chaotic execution: First James's opponents hurl him down from the temple's pinnacle, then they stone him (despite the cry of the interceding Rechabite), and then one from among them pulls out his club to strike the final death blow.

---

lows more closely synoptic structure and terminology. Compare Eusebius, *Hist. eccl.* 2.23.13–14 with Mark 14:62–64.

14. In their formulation of the high christological claim—Jesus at the right hand of God as God's throne partner in judgment—these two authors accept a widespread early Christian exegesis of Ps 110:1 ["The LORD says to my lord, 'Sit at my right hand until I make your enemies your footstool'"] as prophecy of Jesus's uniquely exalted and divine status. On the significance of Ps 110:1 to early Christian christological claims, see Martin Hengel, "'Sit at My Right Hand,'" in *Studies in Early Christology*, ed. Martin Hengel (Edinburgh: T&T Clark, 1995), 119–225; Richard Bauckham, "The Throne of God and the Worship of Jesus," in *The Jewish Roots of Christological Monotheism*, ed. Carey C. Newman, James R. Davila, and Gladys S. Lewis (Leiden: Brill, 1999), 43–69. All English translations of biblical texts follow the NRSV unless otherwise noted.

15. For recent analysis of the rhetorical significance of the interruptions in the Stephen speech, see Daniel Lynwood Smith, *The Rhetoric of Interruption: Speech-Making, Turn-Taking, and Rule-Breaking in Luke-Acts and Ancient Greek Narrative*, BZNW 193 (Berlin: de Gruyter, 2012), 223–27.

The superhuman endurance exhibited by James in this narrative—surviving the plunge from the temple heights *and* a stoning, before being felled by the fuller's club—defies verisimilitude and aligns this tale with stories of the endurance of other early Jewish and Christian martyrs (consider 4 Maccabees or the Letter of the Churches of Vienne and Lyons to the Churches of Asia and Phrygia). Richard Bauckham has suggested that the third manner of execution, the blow by the fuller's club, might be an exegetical reference. The death of James "through wood" aligns his fate with the death of Isaiah, sawn in half with a wooden saw, according to the Ascension of Isaiah, and, of course, with the wood of the cross.[16]

In spite of his recognition of exegetical method at play in this particular feature of the James narrative, Bauckham resorts to a historicist argument when assessing the matter of the stonings of both Stephen and James. He proposes that because stoning is the Levitical punishment for blasphemy (Lev 24:16), both of these historical figures must have been formally charged with committing blasphemy in Sanhedrin-like settings.[17] This proposal ignores how in both narratives the councils dissolve quickly into chaos, which seems important to painting the martyrs' opponents in a lawless manner, as noted above. I suggest a different resonance for the stoning, looking to exegetical tropes as the source of the narrative. In the literary topos of the persecuted prophet, stoning is the typical means of inflicting punishment. Second Chronicles preserves the tradition that the prophet Zechariah was stoned (24:21); stoning is also integral to the lament pertaining to prophet persecution in the oracle of Luke/Q 13:34: "Jerusalem, Jerusalem, the city that kills the prophets and stones those who are sent to it!" That is, it is possible to see both the clubbing with wood and the stoning as part of a process of exegetical reflection on how prophets/martyrs appropriately meet their fates.

---

16. Richard Bauckham, "For What Offence Was James Put to Death?," in *James the Just and Christian Origins*, ed. Bruce D. Chilton and Craig A. Evans, NovTSup 98 (Leiden: Brill, 1999), 199–232.

17. See ibid., 218–32; and Richard Bauckham, "James and the Jerusalem Community," in *Jewish Believers in Jesus*, ed. Oskar Skarsaune and Reidar Hvalvik (Peabody, MA: Hendrickson, 2007), 64, 76. On the difficulties in accounting for first-century incidents of stoning with references to prescriptions in the Torah, see James S. McLaren, "Ananus, James, and Earliest Christianity: Josephus' Account of the Death of James," *JTS* 52 (2001): 1–25, esp. 16–17.

The Hypermerciful Victim

Both Stephen and James respond to the barbaric violence with a prayer that is striking for the extent of its mercy. Stephen paraphrases the dying forgiveness prayer of Jesus in Luke, "Lord, do not hold this sin against them" (Acts 7:60b). James echoes the prayer of his brother more precisely, "I beseech thee, O Lord, God and Father, forgive them, for they know not what they do" (Eusebius, *Hist. eccl.* 2.23.16 [Lake]; see Luke 22:34a). In the same way that Hegesippus underscores more heavily than Acts the first martyr's association with the temple, so here he underscores more centrally the merciful nature of the martyr: James's dying prayer of mercy is but an extension of his lifelong and merciful intercession on behalf of the Jews: "He used to enter alone into the temple and be found kneeling and praying for the forgiveness of the people [αἰτούμενος ὑπερ τοῦ λαοῦ ἄφεσιν], so that his knees grew hard like a camel's because of his constant worship of God, kneeling and asking forgiveness for the people [αἰτεῖσθαι ἄφεσιν τῷ λαῷ]" (Eusebius, *Hist. eccl.* 2.23.6 [Lake]). The dying forgiveness prayer receives further emphasis in the James narrative, as the Rechabite draws attention to it during the stoning through his interjection: "Stop! What are you doing [τί ποιεῖτε]? The just is praying for you" (Eusebius, *Hist. eccl.* 2.23.17 [Lake]).[18]

Shared Allusions to Zechariah ben Jehoiada

As noted above, the narrative detail that Stephen and James are stoned aligns their fate with that of the persecuted prophets, exemplified by the death of Zechariah son of Jehoiada. Further links are noted here. According to 2 Chr 24:17–25, Zechariah is a priest who indicts King Joash and the

---

18. The question τί ποιεῖτε also draws attention to (and perhaps calls into question?) the explanatory clause in James's prayer, "forgive them, *for they know not what they do.*" See Karlmann Beyschalg, "Das Jacobsmartyrium und seine Verwandten in der frühchristlichen Literatur," *ZTK* 56 (1965): 149–78. For further consideration of the role of the forgiveness prayer in early Christian martyrdom narratives, see Matthews, *Perfect Martyr*, 99–130; for discussion of the significance of this forgiveness prayer linked to the version of the First Apocalypse of James from the recently discovered Tchacos Codex, see Karen King, "Martyrdom and Its Discontents in the Tchacos Codex," in *The Codex Judas Papers: Proceedings of the International Congress on the Tchacos Codex Held at Rice University, Houston, Texas*, ed. April D. DeConick (Leiden: Brill, 2009), 23–42.

people for sins relating to law and temple. As he is subsequently stoned by a defiant people in the court of the temple, his dying words are a cry for vengeance, "May the LORD see and avenge!" (2 Chr 24:22). Vengeance is quickly executed, as in the next episode Jerusalem is destroyed and King Joash is killed by servants who conspire against him "because of the blood of [Zechariah]" (2 Chr 24:25).

The dying words of Zechariah become a touchstone for meditations on prophet persecution, the destruction of Jerusalem, and the need for blood vengeance, both in early Jewish and Christian literature. For instance, in the Protoevangelium of James a witness in search of Zechariah enters the sanctuary and discovers his blood next to the altar while a disembodied voice clarifies, "Zechariah has been murdered! His blood will not be cleaned up until his avenger appears" (Prot. Jas. 24:4–5 SV).[19]

It is possible to trace a chain of allusions to the fate of Zechariah in the narrative leading up to Stephen's death in Acts. Jesus delivers an oracle pertaining to prophet persecution with direct reference to Zechariah's blood at Luke/Q 11:49–51:

> Therefore also the Wisdom of God said, "I will send them prophets and apostles, some of whom they will kill and persecute," so that this generation may be charged with the blood of all the prophets since the foundation of the world, from the blood of Abel to the blood of Zechariah, who perished between the altar and the sanctuary. Yes, I tell you, it will be charged against this generation.

The climax of Stephen's speech in Acts 7:51–53, before he is dragged out to be stoned, includes an accusation that his audience persecuted the prophets and killed "the Righteous One." Thus, Stephen's words and fate serve as an exemplum of the prophet persecution described in Luke/Q 11:49–51. Moreover, Luke's introduction to this prophet-persecution oracle at Luke 11:48, "So you are witnesses [μάρτυρες] and approve of [συνευδοκεῖτε] the deeds of your ancestors," is echoed in the introduction of Saul/Paul at Stephen's death: "and the witnesses [οἱ μάρτυρες] laid their coats at the feet of

---

19. In this instance, the Zechariah of Chronicles has been conflated with Zechariah the father of John the Baptist. For rabbinic references to the blood of Zechariah, which needs requiting, consider b. Git. 57b; Midr. Num. 30:15; b. Sanh. 96b; Eccl. Rab. 3:16; 10:4.

a young man named Saul.... And Saul approved [ἦν συνευδοκῶν] of their killing him" (Acts 7:58–8:1).

In the Hegesippus narrative of James the links to Zechariah are not so tightly knit as they are in Luke-Acts, yet James resembles Zechariah in that both are stoned in the court of the temple by the people in response to their speech. A possible allusion to James speaking from the pinnacle of the temple may pertain in the fact that Zechariah is said to stand *above* the people to pronounce his prophetic oracle.

A further indication that the Stephen narrative and the James narrative may both be evoking the Zechariah story, if to counter it rather than to mirror it, lies in the forgiveness prayer. The prayer for vengeance, Zechariah's last utterance according to the Chronicler, and the subsequent elaboration of a tradition that the blood of this prophet must be avenged, are countered rhetorically with the dying words of Stephen and James (and the Lukan Jesus before them), praying forgiveness on their persecutors.

Jewish Rejection Leading to Cosmic Vindication

One distinction between the narratives of Luke-Acts and Hegesippus is that in the former the rejection of Jesus (rather than Stephen) is linked to Jerusalem's destruction, while for Hegesippus, the city's defeat is tied explicitly to the death of James. In the Third Gospel, as Jesus weeps over the impending destruction of the city, he accounts for it as a consequence of Jerusalem's failure to recognize their "visitation from God" (Luke 19:44).[20] Hegesippus makes the consequences of the killing of James both swift and clear in his summary sentences: "He became a true witness both to Jews and to Greeks that Jesus is the Christ, and at once Vespasian began to besiege them [μάρτυς οὗτος ἀληθὴς Ἰουδαίοις τε καὶ Ἕλλησιν γεγένηται ὅτι Ἰησοῦς ὁ Χριστός ἐστιν. Καὶ εὐθὺς Οὐεσπασιανὸς πολιορκεῖ αὐτούς]" (Eusebius, *Hist. eccl.* 2.23.18 [Lake]). These two narratives share the view that Rome is the ultimate agent of God's retribution, but the violence of the imperial situation is treated more like a footnote than as a primary cause.

---

20. For further consideration of this lament with respect to Luke's understanding of the destruction of Jerusalem as cosmic vindication, see Shelly Matthews, "The Weeping Jesus and the Daughters of Jerusalem: Gender and Conquest in Lukan Lament," in *Doing Gender—Doing Religion: Fallstudien zur Intersektionalität im frühen Judentum, Christentum und Islam*, ed. Christine Gerber, Ute E. Eisen, and Angela Standhartinger, WUNT 302 (Tübingen: Mohr Siebeck, 2013), 385–403.

The central conflict is not the momentous calamity of the Roman destruction of Jerusalem, but rather the murderous attack on the innocent martyr by Jews who reject messianic claims for Jesus.

It might also be noted that in spite of how the vector of the dying prayers of Jesus, Stephen, and James differ from that of Zechariah—asking forgiveness rather than vengeance—the resolution in all cases is one of vengeance—a city destroyed as a consequence of having rejected the prophet/martyr. That is, in the worldview of these texts, Zechariah's prayer seems to be answered in ways that the merciful prayers of James and Stephen are not.[21]

Summary

The figure of the first Christian martyr in both Hegesippus and Acts is drawn thus: the prophet/martyr stands in conflict over the temple; the high christological acclamation serves as the point of decision, leading resistors to kill; the tumultuous crowd conforms to prophet-persecutors of old, through stoning the righteous one sent by God; the prophet/martyr responds in a hypermerciful way, praying forgiveness on undeserving and unrepentant persecutors; the prayer for forgiveness has no effect, as the author of the martyrdom narrative makes clear through accounting for the destruction of Jerusalem as God's vengeance on these persecutors.

Differences in emphases may also be underscored. Hegesippus, through featuring James as first martyr, situates the conflict between Jesus believers and other Jews more centrally within "Judaism," as James is treated in early Christian sources as law observant[22] and is depicted here as having assumed the central religious role of the cult, the high priesthood. In contrast Acts, through introducing a character otherwise unknown in early Christian tradition—Stephen, the Greek-speaking Hellenist, and the bridge between Jesus and Paul the apostle to the gentiles—situates the conflict slightly off center and in the direction of the gentile mission.

As noted more than once above, Hegesippus, unlike the author of Acts, seems less concerned with verisimilitude and more prone to employ narrative details with obvious symbolic resonance. James does not merely pray

---

21. This phenomenon is treated under the category of the "grammatical intransitivity" of the forgiveness prayers in Matthews, *Perfect Martyr*, 117–21.

22. A point famously made by Paul in Gal 3:12 and elaborated in the Pseudo-Clementine tradition.

forgiveness at the point of his death but is the very embodiment of merciful intercession, wearing the linen and acquiring calluses through kneeling perpetually in the sanctuary to offer his high-priestly prayers on the people's behalf. His death involves not only stoning but a threefold manner of execution with suggestive exegetical allusions. He is not merely *debating* over the temple; he is debating, literally, *over* the temple. Though the Acts narrative is not devoid of symbolic touches—for instance, offering up a martyr whose Greek name translates literally as "Crown" (*Stephanos*)—on the whole its story of the martyr's death possesses more verisimilitude. Of course, the verisimilitude of Acts also accounts for the common assumption of students that when reading it they have landed upon a historical account, in the modern sense of the word. Yet, laying out the common structure of these two narratives prompts awareness that even verisimilitude might be accounted for on other grounds than historical accuracy.

While a comparative chart of relationships among these texts, constructed by students themselves in conversation and debate, may be more effective than a chart provided to them by their professor, an organizational chart is provided as a visual aid to the summary (see pp. 226–27).

Ethical Evaluation

I then raise specific ethical problems that arise from a history of early Christianity drawn from a straightforward reading of Acts, particularly owing to the proper names it employs for social groups and the causal relationships it emplots among them. These ethical problems relate to pressing questions in our own time: the violent effects of imperial rule and the violent history of Jewish-Christian relations.

The book of Acts, with only a few exceptions, depicts Jews who do not believe in Jesus as committing acts of violence or desiring to commit acts of violence against Jesus's followers at a high rate of frequency. Jews who reject Jesus are singled out in a large number of speeches as responsible for the crucifixion; Jews who reject messianic claims for Jesus are depicted as desiring the deaths of the heroic apostles and missionaries in Acts and going to great pains to bring about these deaths.[23] Jesus believ-

---

23. Consider, for instance, the elaborate plot to take Paul's life described in Acts 23:12–15. More than forty *Ioudaioi* take an oath not to eat or drink until Paul is killed, and the chief priests and elders apparently sanction the plot.

	Place of Temple in the Conflict	High Christological Confession	Means of Death	Dying Prayer	Prophet Persecution Motif	Consequence
Zechariah ben Jehoiada	Indicts king and people of Judah for transgressions relating to law and temple Dies in the temple court		Stoning in the court of the temple by Judeans	"May the LORD see and avenge!" (2 Chr 24:22)	Zechariah's death becomes a touchstone for reflection on blood vengeance in multiple Jewish and Christian sources	Jerusalem destroyed (2 Chr 24:23–25)
Jesus	Accused of speaking against temple	"But from now on the Son of Man will be seated at the right hand of the power of God" (Luke 22:69)	Crucified by Romans	"Father, forgive them; for they know not what they are doing" (Luke 23:34a)	Indicts Jerusalem for killing prophets and apostles (Luke 13:34) and for witnessing and approving murderous deeds of ancestors (Luke 11:48) Foretells that the blood, from Abel to Zechariah, will be required of this generation (Luke 11:51)	Destruction of Jerusalem foretold in reflection on prophet persecution (Luke 11:35) Destruction of Jerusalem predicted, for not having recognized time of visitation (Luke 19:44)

Stephen	Accused of speaking against the temple; depicted as speaking against the temple	"Look, I see the heavens opened and the Son of Man standing at the right hand of God!" (Acts 7:56)	Stoned to death outside the city; intra-Jewish affair; no Roman participation	"Lord, do not hold this sin against them" (Acts 7:60)	Indicts the people as prophet persecutors and murderers; is dragged out and stoned Saul witnesses and approves	Spread of the gentile mission (Acts 8:1; 11:19)
James (Hegesippus)	Interrogated on the pinnacle of the temple Thrown down from the temple to death	"Why do you ask me concerning the Son of Man? He is sitting in heaven on the right hand of the great power" (Hegesippus, *Hist. eccl.* 2.23.13 [Lake])	Hurled down; stoned in the court of the temple; clubbed; intra-Jewish affair; no Roman participation	"I call upon you, O Lord, God and Father, forgive them, for they know not what they do" (Hegesippus, *Hist. eccl.* 2.23.16)	This prophet and son of a priest meets death in the court of the temple; stoned as Zechariah is also stoned	Destruction of Jerusalem commences "immediately" on the death of James (Hegesippus, *Hist. eccl.* 2.23.18)

ers are always depicted as victims of this violence and never as agents of violence themselves.

The story of the stoning of Stephen epitomizes this dualistic framing of agents and victims of violence. Aside from the death of James, the brother of John, which is mentioned in passing in Acts 12, the story of Stephen's martyrdom is the only story in Acts in which a Jesus believer is executed by opponents. He is stoned by an angry mob of Jews in Jerusalem, while he stands in a position of merciful prayer for those who murder him. Luke has assigned only two social positions in this pericope—violent Jews and the merciful Jesus believer.[24] In Luke's telescopic narrative, only one death of a Jesus believer is treated at any length, and because of the weight of the canon in Christian understanding of historical events, this narrative has considerable impact on how Christians over the centuries have understood Jewish-Christian relations.

Moreover, while the violence of Roman imperial rule is sometimes glimpsed—in the beating and jailing at Philippi (16:22–38), or the preparations made for Paul to be flogged in the Roman barracks in Jerusalem (22:24–25)—the force of this rule is largely used for benign purpose in Acts, most notably to rescue Paul from his Jewish persecutors (for instance, at 21:31–36; 23:17–31). In the case of the execution of Stephen, no Romans at all are reported to be on the scene.

Students invited to plot out the series of relationships between Jews who accepted messianic claims for Jesus and those who did not, and then to overlay Roman involvement in key scenes from Acts, might recognize that the intra-Jewish relationships are too simplistically depicted and the portrait of Roman rule unrealistically benign.

---

24. The term *Christian* is used only twice in Acts (11:26; 26:28) and is never asserted emphatically by characters in the story who make messianic claims for Jesus. Yet, the followers of the Way are regarded as a distinct grouping in Acts. For one discussion of the issue of proper names for social groups in Acts, see Matthews, *Perfect Martyr*, 6–8. See also, for the argument that Luke writes for Christians and constructs Paul as a Christian (without frequent reference to the term Christian), Christopher Mount, "Constructing Paul as a Christian in the Acts of the Apostles," in *Engaging Early Christian History: Reading Acts in the Second Century*, ed. Rubén R. Dupertuis and Todd Penner (Durham, UK: Acumen, 2013), 141–52.

Writing a Better History

A classroom exercise demonstrating the blurred lines between ancient history and fiction and the ideological underpinnings of such narratives might lead at least some students to question the project of writing ancient history altogether. If one cannot tell whether it was Stephen or James—or both, or neither—who was killed in the manner so described, then what can be known about the deaths of these heroes at all? If historical narrative is not a faithful mirror onto ancient events, and if authors—including biblical authors—employ fictional tropes in the service of their ideologically interested and ethically problematic narratives of past events, why not regard the entire enterprise with cynicism or apathy?

To this question, one engaged in history writing after the linguistic turn might respond as follows. It is true that separating reality from fiction is impossible, as is objectivity in translating past events into language. Yet, there remain compelling ethical reasons to write history, both for the sake of the dead and for the sake of the future.[25] It is fruitful to inquire about the ethics of historical narrative, asking, for instance, what are the proper names assigned to persons and social groups in the narrative? What are the causal links and explanatory relationships that are emplotted between these persons and social groups? Because the choice to privilege one historical narrative necessarily involves the suppression of other possible tellings, it may be asked how one might do justice to submerged voices and alternate versions of past human experiences and events. Because historical narratives are written in the service of the present and have material effects, one might ask who benefits from a particular telling and who is harmed by it. Are there alternative histories that might be told with better effects—histories that do "less harm"?

To head off the conclusion that such questions give license simply to make things up and are not disciplined by studied consideration of the ancient sources, I offer one possible solution to the ethical problems of the

---

25. For reflections on the ethical component of history writing, see Carr, Flynn, and Makkreel, *Ethics of History*; Shelly Matthews, *Acts of the Apostles: Taming the Tongues of Fire*, Sheffield Guides to the New Testament 5 (Sheffield: Sheffield Phoenix, 2013), 74–75. The approach to history writing suggested here appears not to be in view in Fernando F. Segovia's critique of historical-critical approaches to biblical texts in his essays on pedagogy collected in *Decolonizing Biblical Studies: A View from the Margins* (Maryknoll, NY: Orbis Books, 2000).

Acts narrative, drawn from another ancient text. As an aid to imagining a more complex set of relationships, both intra-Jewish and between Jews and Romans, during the violent years of imperial rule of Judea, Josephus's narrative of the death of James may be introduced, as preserved in the *Ant.* 20.197–203.

Josephus's story of the death of James, in contrast to the story of the death of Stephen in Acts, includes a complex web of relationships. James, identified as the brother of Jesus, is killed by the high priest Ananias while there is a power vacuum in Judea owing to a transition in the Roman procuratorship. The circumstances of his death are murky. James is killed "and others with him" on the vague charge of having "transgressed the law." No indication is given whether association with Jesus has anything to do with the execution of either James or the others. Curiously, those identified as strict in observance of the law are "burdened with grief" at this death. This group turns their grief into political action, working to discredit Ananus. They send a delegation to the newly appointed procurator, Albinus, arguing that Ananus's actions prove him unfit for office. King Agrippa in turn deposes Ananus.

True to our understanding of how ancient historical narrative functions elaborated above, it should not be assumed that Josephus's narrative is an objective and reliable account of the actual events surrounding the death of James. Josephus is certainly crafting his narrative according to his own interests, assigning character traits and motives in ways that other interested parties might have disputed. The Sadducees and their supporters would certainly have bristled at his characterization of them as "savage" with respect to their judgments (*Ant.* 20.199). Moreover, the vagueness of the charges make it impossible to draw precise conclusions about even what Josephus himself understands to be the reason for the death of Jesus's brother.

Yet, it may be argued that Josephus provides a "better" historical source for thinking about relationships among Jews who made messianic claims for Jesus and Jews who did not than the narrative of Stephen in Acts, for the following reasons. Josephus does not know of the great parting that will come to take place among these two kinds of Jews and thus has no basis for providing a dualistic narrative of violent Jews killing a merciful Christian. His narrative contains a more complex web of relationships between social groups that have more nuanced proper names. This provides a better model for a historical understanding of relations between various agents in the first century leading up to the Jewish war with Rome and beyond.

Students invited to identify the proper names and chart the relationships among various groups might come up with some the following observations: the text introduces a Jewish high priest, a Roman imperial government system, a Jewish client king, a Roman procurator, and a number of Jews, including at least one Jew associated with Jesus, who was killed with other Jews—perhaps Jesus believers, but perhaps not—leading still another group of Jews characterized by strict observance for the law to grief and to political action. It is especially this last image, that of strictly law-observant Jews mourning the loss of someone within the Jewish community who held familial ties to Jesus of Nazareth, that I wish to underscore for my students. Here Josephus evokes an alliance among parties that is remarkably out of sync with canonical narratives of relationships between them. Focusing on this narrative of solidarity and communal grief enriches the historical imagination concerning possible relationships among Jesus believers and other Jews in the past, which in turn makes possible richer and more complex relationships in the present and future.

Signature Pedagogies for Ancient Fiction? Thecla as a Test Case

B. Diane Lipsett

Thecla gets around these days. Beast-fighter that she is, she moves through the academic arena from baptism to bulls, as more and more scholars are thinking *with* Thecla, thinking *beyond* Thecla, or, thinking *of* Thecla.[1] Itinerant teacher, she enters many classrooms. Anecdotal evidence suggests that not only graduate students but undergraduates and seminarians meet Thecla often in their courses in New Testament or early Christian studies. Sometimes she shows up with Paul, but often with other women. The Acts of Thecla suits so many syllabi because it sharpens attention to canonical texts and the Pauline traditions and because of its pertinence for studying women, gender, the body, marriage, households, asceticism, martyrdom, ancient novelistic texts, and more.

Signature Pedagogies

So how does one teach the Acts of Paul and Thecla well, particularly outside the doctoral seminar? Are there ways of teaching that particularly reflect ways ancient fiction and narrative are studied? Within the scholarship of teaching and learning, I find intriguing the concept of signature pedagogies. While a generic pedagogy may be practiced across many academic fields, a *signature* pedagogy is one that draws students into distinctive ways

---

1. With Thecla: Kate Cooper, *The Virgin and the Bride: Idealized Womanhood in Late Antiquity* (Cambridge: Harvard University Press, 1996), 55, 65. Beyond Thecla: Caroline Vander Stichele and Todd Penner, *Contextualizing Gender in Early Christian Discourse: Thinking beyond Thecla* (London: T&T Clark, 2009). Of Thecla: Shelly Matthews, "Thinking of Thecla: Issues in Feminist Historiography," *JFSR* 17 (2001): 29–55. (See also her contribution to the present volume.)

of knowing, doing, and valuing in a particular discipline. The premise is that students' learning is improved when it reflects "disciplinary habits of mind," "the ways of thinking and doing of disciplinary experts."[2]

In an essay on signature pedagogies within literary studies, Nancy Chick insists that the notion does not (indeed cannot) ignore or flatten theoretical or methodological variety.[3] Nor does it assume that students have the knowledge necessary to do quite what their professors do, albeit in some attenuated way.[4] Rather, Chick suggests that literature professors, for all their theoretical and methodological diversities, do have considerable agreement about what they do and what they aim to guide students to do: "reading…, interpretation…, and criticism (determining the greater implications, significance, and value of texts with results most often presented in writing)."[5] She also describes a long discussion within the Modern Language Association on "teaching the conflicts"—that is, exposing students to "the way intellectual work in the field is done" by "engaging them in the conversations, questions, and debates central to what we do professionally,"[6] rather than merely offering students the results of scholars' intellectual work. Other writers on signature pedagogies suggest a further goal should be to teach students not just to accept multiple points of view but "to distinguish between unfounded opinions and well-supported conclusions."[7]

Perhaps the Acts of Thecla can provide a test case for elucidating how "disciplinary habits of mind" in the study of ancient fiction and related narratives might shape our teaching. How do we invite students into our

---

2. Nancy L. Chick, Aeron Haynie, and Regan A. R. Gurung, "From Generic to Signature Pedagogies: Teaching Disciplinary Understandings," in *Exploring Signature Pedagogies: Approaches to Teaching Disciplinary Habits of Mind*, ed. Regan A. R. Gurung, Nancy L. Chick, and Aeron Haynie (Sterling, VA: Stylus, 2009), 1–16, esp. 3.

3. Nancy L. Chick, "Unpacking a Signature Pedagogy in Literary Studies," in Gurung, Chick, and Haynie, *Exploring Signature Pedagogies*, 36–55.

4. Ibid., 45.

5. Ibid., 38.

6. Chick, "Unpacking," 47. For the discussion within the Modern Language Association, see Gerald Graff's response in "Teaching the Conflicts at Twenty Years," *Pedagogy* 3 (2003): 245–73; and Gerald Graff, *Beyond the Culture Wars: How Teaching the Conflicts Can Revitalize American Education* (New York: Norton, 1992).

7. Joel M. Sipress and David J. Voelker, "From Learning History to Doing History: Beyond the Coverage Model," in Gurung, Chick, and Haynie, *Exploring Signature Pedagogies*, 30–31.

"peculiar constellation of knowledge- and meaning-making activities"?[8] I offer four preliminary examples, the first and last bearing on reading, interpretation, and criticism, the middle two on teaching the questions or conflicts in the Acts of Thecla.

Reading for Form and Structure

One obvious, preliminary, yet challenging pedagogical goal is to teach students to read attentively. The Acts of Thecla in its ancient two-part form is particularly inviting when guiding students to attend to narrative structure and pattern in ways that can then bear fruit in interpretation and criticism. With little prompting, students can identify the many doublets—both repetitions and contrasts—that take place in the action in Iconium and the action in Antioch. Simply tabulating parallels encourages close reading: naming and comparing the maternal figure in each episode; naming and comparing the "frustrated lover [who] secures her death sentence from the local Roman authority";[9] noting contrasting details in the attempted executions and reactions from onlookers. Students benefit from identifying repetitions and contrasts within episodes also: Antioch's men and male animals *versus* its women and lioness. So, too, in the frame narratives—students may analyze how the opening welcome of the bandy-legged, unibrowed Paul by Onesiphorus is answered by the closing reunion in which the elusive apostle belatedly authorizes Thecla's teaching. This particular early Christian tale quickly rewards formal analysis of narrative symmetries, inversions, and patterns. Formal analysis may be merely preliminary to interpretation and criticism, but students who can precisely identify and describe structural patterns are prepared to offer interpretations that more fully engage the narrative textures and particularities of the story.

---

8. Jan Parker et al., "Editorial: Boundaries, Signature Pedagogies and Theorizing," *Arts & Humanities in Higher Education* 7 (2008): 115–16.

9. Dennis MacDonald's perceptive, compressed summaries of "the law of repetition" and "the law of contrast" in the stories remain concise guides to key features of the story. Dennis R. MacDonald, *The Legend and the Apostle: The Battle for Paul in Story and Canon* (Philadelphia: Westminster, 1983), 28–31.

Composition History: Teaching the Questions

Unlike teacher-scholars of authors such as George Eliot or Alice Munro, scholars of ancient novelistic texts grapple with textual traditions that are fluid, sometimes in the extreme. When we grant a presumption of coherence to a particular form of the text for purposes of interpretation, the variability of ancient manuscripts and versions and the complexities of composition history keep confronting us with our presumption. Outside doctoral seminars, only some courses teach technical disciplines of composition history or textual criticism. Students nevertheless may grapple with how such disciplinary practices matter for interpretation.

As one example, several scholars, including Richard Pervo, propose that the Antioch episode, with its vocal, active Thecla, prolonged arena scene, cast of supporting female characters, and absent Paul, came first, with the Iconium scene added later, creating a more passive heroine, a dependence on Paul, and a place within the larger Acts of Paul.[10] This current scholarly question and proposal can undergird a constructive teaching exercise. Whether or not students know enough to argue cogently for or against the proposal, they can consider a "so what" question. How would the representation of Thecla be different if all the reader had is what happens in Antioch—no love-at-first-hearing motif, no silent, still Thecla, no prison assignation, no frame stories with Paul? How would those differences bear on larger issues of the representation of women, gender, marriage, households, the body, asceticism, or martyrdom? A proposal about composition history turns to redaction criticism. If the Antioch episode did come first, what might have motivated a subsequent editor to add the Iconium and frame stories or to place the Acts of Thecla into the larger Acts of Paul? Scholarly divergence about the proposal helps communicate to students that they are engaging a current scholarly question.

---

10. See Richard I. Pervo, *The Acts of Paul: A New Translation with Introduction and Commentary* (Eugene, OR: Cascade Books, 2014), 87, 146–47, and Richard Pervo, "Thecla Wove This Web, or, Some Things I Learned from Attempting to Write a Commentary on the Acts of Paul" (paper presented at the Annual Meeting of the Society of Biblical Literature, Chicago, November 17, 2012). See also Elisabeth Esch-Ermeling, *Thekla—Paulusschülerin wider Willen? Strategien der Leserlenkung in den Theklaakten*, NTAbh 53 (Münster: Aschendorff, 2008); Anne Jensen, *Thekla die Apostolin: Ein apokrypher Text neu entdeckt* (Freiburg: Herder, 1995); and Margaret P. Aymer, "Hailstorms and Fireballs: Redaction, World Creation, and Resistance in the *Acts of Paul and Thecla*," Semeia 75 (1997): 43–61.

Textual Emendation and Fluidity: Teaching the Questions

The complex and fascinating textual transmission of the Acts of Paul and Thecla also provides pedagogical entry points. As with composition history, whether or not they are learning the technical disciplines of textual criticism, students can be exposed to how scribes and translators rewrote Thecla and consider with what motives and effects. Kim Haines-Eitzen's *The Gendered Palimpsest* offers provocative examples and discussion.[11] Students could analyze, for example, Paul's climactic beatitude (3.13) as it is modified in later manuscripts. "Blessed are the bodies of the virgins for they shall be well-pleasing to God and shall not lose the reward of their purity."[12] Or, as it appears in several eleventh- and twelfth-century Greek manuscripts: "Blessed are the bodies and spirits/souls/breath of the virgins, for they shall be well-pleasing." How is the striking blessing on bodies affected by the scribal addition of spirits, souls, or breath of the virgins? What tension about blessing "bodies" may have led to such additions?

Alternatively, one may invite students to explore the ways later versions alter the prison scene, where Thecla's devotion to Paul is vividly depicted. Thecla goes to the prison to see Paul, sits at his feet, kisses his fetters, and is discovered "bound with him, in a manner of speaking, in affection" (3.19). The feet, the kisses, and the affection are details that invite many later variants, as Haines-Eitzen details:

Latin versions:
"as though joined to his feet"
"sitting by Paul's feet"
"listening to God's teaching from Paul"
"Sitting at the feet of Paul, joined in the desire of Christ"

Syriac version:
"And they went, as the doorkeeper told them, and found her sitting at Paul's feet, she and many persons, and they were listening to the great things of the Most High."

---

11. Kim Haines-Eitzen, *The Gendered Palimpsest: Women, Writing, and Representation in Early Christianity* (New York: Oxford University Press, 2012), 95–112, esp. 101.

12. Trans. R. McL. Wilson (*NTApoc* 2:240).

Armenian version:
"So they went and found her as the doorkeeper told them; they came and found her sitting at the feet of Paul, and saw several other people as well who were listening to the great things of Christ."[13]

Students can, in my experience, perceptively analyze such examples and reflect on what scribal concerns or anxieties may have motivated change. Such evidence provides access, narrow yet stimulating, into the reception history of Thecla's story. Moreover, textual criticism of a fluid apocryphal text may not provoke student anxieties in the same way that encountering a malleable canonical text sometimes does. So Thecla and the changes to her story may help prepare students more constructively to engage the complexities of textual transmission in New Testament texts.

Reading, Interpretation, Criticism, and Bliss

As scholarship informs pedagogy, teaching may refresh our own reading practices. One gift of teaching texts such as the Acts of Thecla is witnessing how first-time readers react: amusement and laughter, distress or indignation, perplexity or confusion. For Thecla's is not a text that, in Roland Barthes's words, "comes from culture and does not break with it, is linked to a comfortable practice of reading"; it is not a nondisruptive "text of pleasure."[14] As we work to situate Thecla's tale within the larger corpus of ancient novelistic texts and within articulations of ancient values and virtues our students may not know,[15] we nonetheless should respect how unsettling it can be to encounter a starkly unfamiliar expression of ancient Christianity. We do well to validate, not merely manage, student readers' responses: amusement at a valiant woman rescued by other women's perfume and fainting, or indignation at an apostle who blesses virgins' bodies but disappears when one such body is molested. Perhaps we may also encourage students to feel a tingle—to slow down and savor how a

---

13. For these examples, carefully analyzed, see ibid., 102–3.

14. Roland Barthes, *The Pleasure of the Text*, trans. Richard Miller (New York: Hill & Wang, 1975), 14.

15. For a reading of Thecla that perceptively highlights not gender disruption but ancient virtues of modesty and female agency, see Susan E. Hylen, *A Modest Apostle: Thecla and the History of Women in the Early Church* (New York: Oxford University Press, 2015), esp. 71–91.

consuming infatuation is represented, however paradoxical its object. The Acts of Thecla may then be, in Barthean terms, a "text of bliss": "the text that imposes a state of loss, the text that discomforts…, unsettles the reader's historical, cultural, psychological assumptions, the consistency of his tastes, values, memories, brings to a crisis his relation with language."[16] In the narrative turns of the Acts of Thecla and in its cultural disruptions and discomforts, might we find a signature pedagogy that allows for bliss?

---

16. Barthes, *Pleasure of the Text*, 14.

Teaching Mimesis as a Criterion for Textual Criticism: Cases from the Testament of Abraham and the Gospel of Nicodemus

Dennis R. MacDonald

Introduction

Textual criticism of ancient fiction suffers from a major shortcoming: the reluctance to use literary imitation to evaluate varying recensions. This is especially the case when the only witnesses are in multiple languages or wildly varying recensions, which applies to many if not most apocrypha. But it stands to reason that if one can establish an author's mimetic engagement with a targeted model, what one might call an antetext, one can better assess which textual variants are more likely to have appeared in the prototype. I first became aware of the contributions of mimesis to textual criticism when reconstructing the Acts of Andrew, where the author's repeated imitations of Homer, Euripides, and Plato often were crucial for deciding the best readings among competing versions.[1] This symbiosis between mimesis criticism and textual criticism by no means trumps other canons of philology; even so, literary imitation may contribute to internal considerations of the author's compositional project.

The imitation of Greek classics by no means exhausts the mimetic intertextuality in ancient religious fiction. With respect to Jewish literature I would note recent interests in rewritten Scripture. With respect to Christian apocrypha I would note the widely recognized imitations of the New Testament. Just as important is the mimetic intertextuality among

---

1. Dennis R. MacDonald, *The Acts of Andrew and the Acts of Andrew and Matthias in the City of the Cannibals*, SBLTT 33, Christian Apocrypha 1 (Atlanta: Scholars Press, 1990).

apocrypha. For example, the Acts of Andrew became a model for later apocryphal acts, including the Acts of Thomas, the Acts of Mark, and the Acts of John by Prochorus. Insofar as many works of Jewish and Christian fiction survive in multiple recensions, it often is useful to understand what antetexts likely informed the original work, in order to determine which of the recensions is the most reliable.

Plato's Myth of Er

The study at hand presents two examples, one Jewish and one Christian, both of which imitate Plato's famous Myth of Er at the end of the *Republic*. Plato's Socrates claimed that a slain soldier came back to life after having been given a tour of the netherworld (*Resp.* 386a–387c). According to Er's account, when the dead first arrive in Hades, they are judged; the righteous ascend through a chasm into the sky, while the wicked descend through a chasm below. The most evil are thrown into Tartarus for eternal tortures. He saw two more chasms: from one the righteous descend after a thousand years of bliss, but from the other the wicked emerge, showing the wear of their torments. After issuing from these chasms, the souls assemble to reenter bodies and cast lots to decide in what order they will choose their new lives. Er and these other souls then "went to the Field of Lethe ['Forgetfulness'], through heat and a terrible choking, for it was devoid of trees and all that the earth produces. At dusk they set up tents by the River Ameleta ['Unconsciousness']." After drinking from the waters of amnesia, the other souls "suddenly were transported upward ... into birth, like shooting stars" for their various reincarnations (621b). Er, however, was not allowed to drink, so that he might be a messenger to mortals.

The Testament of Abraham

The Testament of Abraham survives in two Greek recensions, conventionally called A, the longer of the two, and B, but only A contains sustained imitation of Socrates's myth. Here is a translation of B:

> Michael took Abraham bodily on a cloud and brought him to the River Oceanus. And Abraham looked and saw two ways [δύο ὁδούς], one small, and one large. And in-between the two gates a man sat [ἐκάθητο] on a throne of great glory. ...He was weeping, and then laughing [ἦν κλαίων, καὶ πάλιν γελῶν].... [Michael:] "So when you see him weeping [κλαίοντο],

know that he saw many souls being brought to destruction. And when you see him laughing, he saw souls being brought to life." Behold, an angel of the Lord drove sixty thousand souls of sinners to destruction.

Recension A is both longer and closer to the Myth of Er.

Resp. 614c–615a	T. Ab. 11 (recension A)
[Er said that he traveled among the souls of many others of the dead to] a certain preternatural place in which there were two chasms [δύ' ... χάσματα] on the ground opposite each other and two others in heaven opposite them above.	And Michael turned the chariot and brought Abraham to the east at the first gate of heaven. And Abraham saw two ways [δύο ὁδούς]. One way was narrow and difficult, and the other was wide and broad. He also saw there two gates [δύο πύλας], one wide gate at the wide way, and one narrow gate at the narrow way.
Judges were sitting [καθῆσθαι] between these. Whenever they rendered their judgment, they commanded the righteous to go to the right and up through the sky,… and the unjust to the left and down.	There outside the two gates they saw a man sitting [καθήμενον] on a gilded throne. And he saw many souls being driven by angels through the wide gate, and they saw a few other souls carried by angels through the narrow gate.
[Er then said that he also saw souls emerging from the other two chasms and gathering in a meadow where they spoke about what they had experienced.]	And when the amazing one who sat [καθήμενος] on the throne of gold saw the few souls passing through the narrow gate and the many passing through the wide gate, immediately that amazing man ripped hair from his head and the beard on his cheek, threw himself from his throne to the ground
"Some lamenting and weeping [ὀδυρομένας τε καὶ κλαιούσας]" [when they recalled their sufferings. The others narrated] "their delights and extraordinary visions of the beautiful."	weeping and lamenting [κλαίων καὶ ὀδυρόμενος].
He [Er] said that there stood wild men, fiery to behold [διάπυροι ἰδεῖν].… [They]	And whenever he observed many souls entering through the narrow gate, he then rose from the ground, sat on his throne with great delight, rejoicing and exulting. Behold, two angels with fiery appearance [πύρινοι τῇ ὄψει], merciless mind, and severe visage

grabbed them and took them away. But Ardiaeus and others they bound hand, feet, and head, threw them down,… dragged them along outside along the road,… and led them to drop into Tartarus.	drove ten thousand souls, beating them mercilessly with fiery whips. And the angel seized one soul. And they brought all the souls into the wide gate of destruction.

Recension A clearly wins the prize for greater fidelity to the imitation of the *Republic*.

- Only recension A uses the expression κλαίων καὶ ὀδυρόμενος, which resembles Plato's ὀδυρομένας τε καὶ κλαιούσας. Recension B reads only κλαίων (B 8).
- Recension B says nothing about torturers with a fiery appearance.
- Only recension A states that the fates of the dead are eternal and inalterable, likely a response to Plato's metempsychosis. "Righteous Abraham, this is a perfect judgment and reward [of the dead], eternal and inalterable; one that no one can question" (A 13).
- It also may be worth noting, on the other hand, that only recension B states that Michael transported Abraham on a cloud "and brought him to the River Oceanus" (B 8), an echo of *Od.* 11.13. Although it is possible that the B redactor created this reference to evoke Odysseus's *nekyia*, it is more likely that in this one particular B witnesses to the original. If this is the case, both recensions have a claim on preserving the original author's mimetic efforts.

The Gospel of Nicodemus

Here is my second example. Among the significant contributions of Series Apocryphorum of Corpus Christianorum is Rémi Gounelle's *Les Recensions byzantines de l'Évangile de Nicodème*,[2] in which he argues that the

---

2. Rémi Gounelle, *Les Recensions byzantines de l'Évangile de Nicodème*, Corpus Christianorum: Series Apocryphorum, Instrumenta 3 (Turnhout: Brepols, 2008).

author of the Byzantine recension M of the Gospel of Nicodemus translated and incorporated a Latin Descensus Christi as an alternative to the ending of the much earlier recension A. Surely Gounelle is correct that the redactor radically transformed the ending of the Gospel of Nicodemus and that the text of the Descensus known as Latin A represents an earlier textual stratum than the Greek recension, but I hope to show that the famous story of Jesus's harrowing of Hades never existed before the composition of recension M and certainly was not composed in Latin. I make this claim because of the symbiosis between mimetic and textual criticisms. Just to be clear, Jesus's descent into the netherworld per se is well attested already in the second century; the Descensus at the end of recension M as told in Latin A, however, displays reliance on Plato.

Plato, *Resp.* 614b–621d	Descensus 1–2, 11; Latin A (Passion and Resurrection of Jesus by Aeneas 17–18 and 27:1–3)
Er, the son of Armenius, died in battle and on the twelfth day, after his corpse had been taken home for burial, he came back to life.	Karinus and Leucius, sons of Simeon, died and not long afterward came back to life. Their tombs were found to be empty; the risen twins had gone to Arimathea but spoke to no one. [The Greek recension speaks of the twins but never names them. There also is no reference to their silence.] According to both recensions, the chief priests, Annas, Caiaphas, Joseph, Nicodemus, and Gamaliel went to Arimathea, brought the twins to Jerusalem, and adjured them to tell the truth about how they came back to life.
"Once revived, he told what he had seen there" in the world beyond. (614b–c)	The boys said: "Give us each a book of papyrus, and we will write what we saw and heard." [Greek: The boys said, "Give us a papyrus, ink, and a pen."]
Er said that he arrived at the realm of the dead with many others and saw throngs of souls being judged and then departing for a millennium of punishment or reward.	[The lads wrote that they were in Hades with "all our fathers" (Greek), or with "all who ever had fallen asleep from the beginning of time" (Latin). Both recensions then narrate how Christ emptied Hades of all the

When Er himself came to the judges, they told him that he had been designated as an *angelos* to mortals about what happened there, and "commanded him to hear and observe everything." (614d)	dead and brought them to paradise. (The author's model for this section above all is the nekyia in Homer, *Od.* 11.)] (27.1) "*These* are the divine and sacred mysteries, which we saw and heard, I, Karinus, and Leucius."
	[Greek: "When we had seen and heard these things, we identical twins,…"]
Er narrated what he heard and saw. Most of the dead were not permitted to remember their experiences in their previous afterlives.	"We are not permitted to disclose additional mysteries of God, because Michael the archangel adjured us: 'On returning with your brothers, you will be in Jerusalem offering prayers and glorifying the resurrection of the Lord Jesus Christ, who resuscitated you with him from the dead. And you will speak with no one; you will sit tight like mutes until the hour comes when the Lord permits you to mention his divine mysteries.' [Greek: … who were sent by Michael the archangel and were ordered to preach the resurrection of the Lord.]"
They then "went to the Field of Lethe through heat and a terrible choking, for it was devoid of trees and all that the earth produces. At dusk they set up tents by the River Ameleta."	For the archangel Michael ordered us to walk to the Jordan, to a fertile and luxuriant place, where there were many who had risen with us, as a witness of the resurrection of Christ the Lord. We who had risen from the dead were permitted for only three days to celebrate the Lord's Pascha *in Jerusalem* with our living relatives as a witness of the resurrection of Christ the Lord; we were baptized in the holy Jordan River, and each one received a white robe. And after three days of the Lord's Pascal celebration, all who had been resurrected with us were led across the Jordan. [Greek: … and first to go out to the

"They suddenly were transported upward here and there into birth [φέρεσθαι ἄνω εἰς τὴν γένεσιν], like shooting stars." (621b)	Jordan and be baptized. So we left there and were baptized together with the other dead who had risen. And then we went into Jerusalem and completed the Pascha of the resurrection.]"
	... were caught up into the clouds [*rapti sunt in nubibus*] and were no longer seen by anyone."
"The story just might save us, if we are convinced of it.... We will always hold to the upward way and in every way attend to righteousness with wisdom." (621c)	(27:2) "We, however, were ordered to persist in prayer in Arimathea. The Lord ordered us to relate to you these things to this extent. Give him praise and confession; perform penance, so that he may have mercy on you. Peace to you from the Lord Jesus Christ himself and savior of *all of you*. Amen." [Greek: "So now, having left Hades, we are not able to travel back there. And the love of God and Father, the grace of the Lord Jesus Christ, and the fellowship of the Holy Spirit be with all of you."]

Here is a comparison of the ending of the two recensions of the Descensus:

Latin	Greek
(27.3) And after they completed *writing* all these things in individual books of papyrus, they rose up; Karinus gave what he had written to the hands of Annas, Caiaphas, and Gamaliel. Likewise, Leucius gave what he had written to the hands of Nicodemus and Joseph. And immediately they were transfigured and made exceedingly bright, and became invisible.[3]	After they had written these things and sealed the books, they gave half to the chief priests and half to Joseph and Nicodemus. And immediately they became invisible,

---

3. In the Myth of Er, the fates "wear white clothing" (*Resp.* 617c).

	for the glory of our Lord Jesus Christ. Amen.
Their writings were discovered to be identical, not a single letter more or less. [The Latin recension continues.]	[The Greek recension ends here.]

Before comparing these recensions with the *Republic*, I would note a glaring narrative incongruity in both. The twins have just narrated in detail how Jesus led *all* the dead out of Hades into paradise. Only the brothers were ordered to witness to the event, but in both versions they inexplicably join "many who had risen" with them (Latin) or "the other dead who had risen" (Greek). In the Latin text they celebrate the Passover with their "living relatives," and then "all who had been resurrected" with them ascended into the clouds; Karinus and Leucius, however, are left behind so that they can narrate what they saw while dead. After doing so, they, too, disappeared. The author apparently was unaware that the harrowing of hell left no room for a resurrection of anyone other than the Symeon's sons who alone were designated as witnesses. The incongruity most likely derived from mimesis of the Myth of Er, where Er shoots up into the world with those being reincarnated.

If the author of the Descensus wrote Christ's harrowing of hell as an imitation of the *Republic*, the Latin text surely is a more reliable witness to it than the Greek.

- Plato's Socrates names the witness to life after death: "Er, the son of Armenius." Only the Latin recension names Simeon's sons: "Karinus and Leucius." The Greek recension likely omitted the names because of their association with texts precious to Manicheans. A Leucius Charinus was variously associated with the Acts of John and a collection of five apocryphal acts.
- According to Er's testimony, all of the dead were forbidden to remember their previous afterlives, but the judges ordered him "to hear and observe everything" so that he could recall them for the living. Similarly, in the Latin (but not the Greek) of the Descensus Karinus and Leucius at first were ordered to be silent but later broke their silence by composing their accounts.
- Er recounts that the souls about to be reincarnated gathered at "the Field of Lethe ['Forgetfulness'], through heat and a ter-

rible choking, for it was devoid of trees and all that the earth produces. At dusk they set up tents by the River Ameleta ['Unconsciousness']." Only the Latin Descensus states that the place near the Jordan River was "fertile and luxuriant," apparently a meaningful transform of the barren Field of Lethe.
- Only the Latin recension states that those who had been raised with the twins "were caught up into the clouds," apparently an echo of Socrates's statement that those who were to be reincarnated "were transported upward here and there into birth, like shooting stars."

From these data I would make the following observations.

- The author of the Descensus used the Myth of Er as his model for the framework for the twins' narrative; the intervening chapters, however, owe more to the Odyssean *nekyia*.
- Insofar as the Latin recension is closer to the ending of the *Republic*, it witnesses to a textual stratum anterior to the surviving Greek recension. Gounelle thus was correct about its priority.
- Unlike Gounelle, however, I propose that the author of the Latin recension translated a Greek text that no longer survives. First, it is more likely that the imitation of the Greek antetext was the accomplishment of a Greek author than of a Latin one. Second, in several respects the Greek text contains variants that have a stronger claim on being the prototype than the Latin. Here then we have alternating primitivity.
- Finally, recension M of the Gospel of Nicodemus repeatedly redacted recension A by imitating the death and burial of Hector at the end of the *Iliad*. In other words, as James Rendel Harris suggested long ago, the gospel is a Christian *Iliad-Odyssey*, narrating the death and burial of Jesus, à la Hector, and then his resurrection and visit to Hades, à la Odysseus.[4] In fact, this recension calls itself "An Exposition about the

---

4. James Rendel Harris, *The Homeric Centones and the Acts of Pilate* (London: Clay, 1898).

Passion of Our Lord Jesus Christ and His Holy Resurrection Written by a Jew Named Aeneas."

Conclusion

The two imitations of the Myth of Er—one in the Testament of Abraham and one in the Descensus in recension M (preserved in Latin A) of the Gospel of Nicodemus—suggest that when reconstructing the text of ancient fictions one effective way of assessing variants is to identify the antetexts that the author targeted for imitation, including biblical texts and other apocrypha. Ancient rhetoricians considered mimesis an essential part of philology and literary criticism. It is a pity that it often plays such a modest role among modern critics.

A New Subjectivity?
Teaching Ἔρως through the Greek Novel
and Early Christian Texts

David Konstan

There survive five ancient Greek novels, that is, book-length prose fictions, and all five center on love or, more precisely, on ἔρως. Their structure takes the form of a young couple's initial enamorment, a subsequent separation or other obstacle to the fulfillment of their passion, and their final reunion, culminating in marriage. The significance of this pattern has been variously interpreted, as we shall see. I wish to suggest, however, that love in the novels represents what we may think of as a new kind of subjectivity—a grand word that smacks of Michel Foucault's historical investigations[1] but strictly applicable, I believe, to the representation of ἔρως in these texts. For the lovers in the novels maintain an undying fidelity to each other, based on the absolute freedom of their will and their consequent ability to withstand any degree of trial or torture. In this respect, moreover, the protagonists of the novels are similar to Christian martyrs and saintly types who remain loyal to their love of God despite the most extreme pressures to abandon their faith. To fully appreciate the novels, we must in fact see them as representing a new inflection of the self in the first centuries of the Christian era. The purpose of this paper is thus to encourage courses in

---

This paper is a revised and expanded version of a talk delivered in the Ancient Fiction and Early Christian and Jewish Narrative section at the 2012 Annual Meeting of the Society of Biblical Literature. Rather than provide extensive footnotes and references, I have referred the reader to other studies by me and others that offer further discussion of the points made here and provide full bibliographies.

1. See, for example, Michel Foucault, *On the Government of the Living: Lectures at the Collège de France 1979–1980*, trans. Graham Burchell (New York: Palgrave Macmillan, 2014).

which the novels are read alongside early Jewish and Christian literature, with a view to eliciting common themes and structures of feeling as well as indicating where the traditions part company, for example, in relation to the idea of sin and forgiveness. Two features that especially reward attention are precisely ἔρως and free will.

I have argued in the past that the narrative pattern of Greek novels corresponds to a new ideal of matrimony, based on a reciprocal erotic attraction between a young man and woman.[2] No doubt, mutual desire culminating in marriage defines the narrative trajectory of the hero and heroine in the novels; nevertheless, scholars disagree on whether the apparent equivalence of the protagonists—both alike fall in love, both are active in their erotic desire—is meant to signal a new model for adult relations or is rather presented as a juvenile phenomenon, which is understood to give way ultimately to the traditional hierarchy within the family, with the husband clearly the dominant partner and the wife reduced to a subservient or at all events more domestic position. On this latter reading, the adventures of the protagonists, while they are apart, serve as a kind of liminal stage, in Arnold Van Gennep's terms, marking a transition from the relatively undifferentiated sexual roles of adolescents to the unequal relation characteristic of marriage in the classical world.[3]

Within the novels themselves, alternative arrangements for marriage are represented, which suggests that the experience of the hero and heroine is not necessarily being promoted as a universal ideal. Three of the novels, for example, conclude with an arranged marriage that takes place alongside that of the main couple, and in these cases the woman has scarcely even been consulted, never mind fallen in love. What is more, the space in which the principal lovers are most equal and autonomous lies outside their home cities: it is in this no-man's land that their mutual passion is allowed to play itself out and be tested against trials and temptations. As is well known, the physical movement or orbit of the hero and heroine in the Greek novels tends to be circular, as they journey away from their hometown and finally return to the original place of departure. This is evident, for example, in Xenophon of Ephesus's tale, the *Ephesiaca*, where the couple start out in Ephesus and end up there in the finale. Again, in

---

2. David Konstan, *Sexual Symmetry: Love in the Ancient Novel and Related Genres* (Princeton: Princeton University Press, 1994).

3. See Sophie Lalanne, *Une éducation grecque: Rites de passage et construction des genres dans le roman grec ancien* (Paris: Éditions La Découverte, 2006).

Chariton's novel, *Callirhoe*, the hero and heroine are from leading families in Syracuse and return there in triumph at the end of the story. So too, in Achilles Tatius's novel, Clitophon is from Tyre and Leucippe from Byzantium: in the end, they return first to Byzantium, then to Tyre (8.18.5). Yet, although the two lovers do, in each case, come home in the end, they are actually reunited elsewhere, and sometimes the final terminus of their journey seems almost an afterthought. This is especially clear in Xenophon's *Ephesiaca*, where the resolution takes place mainly on Rhodes, and there is only the briefest mention of the return to Ephesus (5.15.1), and again in Achilles Tatius, where the reunion and dramatic trial are located in Ephesus, rather than in Byzantium or Tyre. In Chariton's novel, Chaereas and Callirhoe recognize each other on the island of Arados, and only then make the voyage to Syracuse.[4]

What is the significance of this pattern? We may take the case of Xenophon's novel. By placing the reunion of the couple in Rhodes rather than in Ephesus, Xenophon can allow Habrocomes and Anthia to meet as faithful lovers, without taking into consideration the structured social relations of their home city. A sign of this relaxation of civic constraints, I suggest, is the couple's relationship with their slaves, Leucon and Rhode. They are separated from Habrocomes and Anthia earlier in the novel and sold abroad (2.9.2); they end up in Xanthus, a city in Lycia, where the old man who purchased them treated them as his own children (2.10.4). When their new master (δεσπότης, 5.6.3; see 5.10.11) dies, he leaves them his fortune, and they set sail for Ephesus, where they supposed that their original masters (δεσποτῶν) were alive and well. However, they stop first in Rhodes, where they learn that Habrocomes and Anthia are still missing and that their parents have died; with this, they decide to stay in Rhodes for a while, until they can learn something about the fate of their masters (δεσποτῶν, 5.6.4). Still in the role of slaves (οἰκετῶν, 5.10.7), they dedicate memorials to Habrocomes and Anthia.

When Anthia arrives in Rhodes, she laments that she is now a slave rather than a free woman (δούλη ... ἀντ' ἐλευθέρας, 5.11.4), and she sets up a stele. Leucon and Rhode recognize the names of their masters (δεσποτῶν, 5.12.1), and when they finally see Anthia, they acknowledge her as their mistress (δέσποινα) and themselves as her slaves (οἰκέται, 5.12.5). Then

---

4. Niall Slater, "Space and Displacement in Apuleius's *Golden Ass*," in *Space in the Ancient Narrative*, Ancient Narrative Supplementum 1 (Groningen: Berkhuis Publishing and the University Library Groningen, 2002), 161–76.

Habrocomes, Anthia, and Hippothous, their bandit friend, move into Leucon's quarters. In the end, Habrocomes and Anthia, along with Hippothous and his boyfriend Clisthenes, return to Ephesus where, we are told in the final paragraph of the novel, Leucon and Rhode share in everything with their agemates and companions from birth (συντρόφοις, 5.15.4).

What, we may ask, will be the status of Leucon and Rhode when they return to Ephesus? With the death of their kind master in Lycia and the disappearance of Habrocomes and Anthia, they have been prosperous and independent; they are instrumental in reuniting their old masters and entertain them in their own home. For all that they, and the text, acknowledge their servile status in respect to Habrocomes and Anthia, they seem more like their equals, and indeed, far better off. Anthia's lament about her own loss of freedom reflects, in turn, her diminished social position. All this can pass in Rhodes, where the reader does not have to reflect on what the ultimate domestic arrangements will be. Back in Ephesus, Habrocomes and Anthia might have given them their freedom and would in any case have treated them with the affection they deserve. But status rules and roles would have snapped back into place as the primary couple in the narrative set up house and established their position as heads of *oikoi*. I am suggesting, then, that Rhodes continues to serve as a liminal space in respect to wider social relations, which are partially suspended as masters become slaves and slaves achieve the liberties of free people. It is in such an environment that the love that binds the protagonists of the novel finds its least trammeled expression. Even if the norms or conventions of society reimpose themselves in the end—and this is more noticeable in Chariton's novel than it is in Xenophon's—there is a prior closure to the romance in which the leveling that takes place in the liminal space is preserved.[5]

There is a late antique Christian novella known as the Acts of Xanthippe and Polyxena, in which Polyxena travels a route that is similarly cyclic. Polyxena, a beautiful young woman, is carried off from her native Spain by a vicious man who is a rival to her suitor, who plans to take her to Babylonia; en route, however, they meet the apostle Peter, who deflects their ship to Greece, where Philip rescues Polyxena and hands her over to the care of a holy man. The abductor raises an army of eight thousand men to recapture Polyxena, but they are defeated by thirty servants.

---

5. For further discussion, see David Konstan, "*Erôs* and *Oikos*," in *Narrative, Culture and Genre in the Ancient Novel*, ed. Stephen Harrison and Stavros Frangoulidis (Berlin: de Gruyter, 2012), 217–24.

Polyxena escapes and takes shelter in the cave of a lioness, which spares her because she is still unbaptized (she is subsequently baptized by the apostle Andrew). An evil prefect seizes her, captivated by her beauty, but his son, who has been converted to Christianity by Paul and Thecla, conspires to escape with her to Spain. Their plan is discovered, however, and the prefect orders both to be thrown to the lions, but the savage creature merely licks their feet, at the sight of which the prefect and the whole populace convert to Christianity. The prefect arranges to have Polyxena and his son transported back to Spain, where she is reunited with the apostle Paul and with her sister Xanthippe; the violent kidnapper, who intends to carry Polyxena off yet again, also is baptized by Paul, along with Polyxena's original suitor.[6] Out in the adventure space, Polyxena manages to keep her virginity intact against all threats; once she is back home, she is safe in the bosom of a surrogate Christian family.

The heroic ability of men and women to resist both temptations and open violence in defense of their chastity is evidence of their courage, canniness, and commitment, though sometimes too it is simply a matter of luck, as rescuers appear at critical moments. But the novels also intimate what I believe is a new kind of confidence in the spiritual autonomy of the self, which serves to gird up and confirm the ability of ἔρως to prevail against all odds. The novelistic protagonists themselves assert the invulnerability of the soul in respect to any and all pressures from outside, including threats of the most excruciating torture. At the end of Xenophon's novel, for example, Anthia embraces her husband and declares:

> Husband and master, I have recovered you after wandering much land and sea, having escaped the threats of bandits, the designs of pirates, the outrages of brothel-keepers, bonds, graves, manacles, poisons and ditches, and I come to you, despite all, O Habrocomes lord of my soul, as I was when I first went from Tyre to Syria, and no one induced me to sin, not Moeris in Syria, nor Perilaus in Cilicia, nor Psammis and Polyidus in Egypt, nor Anchialus in Ethiopia, nor my master in Tarentum, but I have remained holy [ἁγνός] for you, having practiced every device of chastity [σωφροσύνη]. (5.14.1–2)

---

6. For a more detailed discussion, see David Konstan, "Reunion and Regeneration: Narrative Patterns in Ancient Greek Novels and Christian Acts," in *Fiction on the Fringe: Novelistic Writing in Late Antiquity*, ed. Grammatiki Karla and Ingela Nilsson, Mnemosyne Supplements Series 310 (Leiden: Brill, 2009), 105–20.

Anthia is here asserting her unalterable devotion, to be sure, but she is the same time affirming a sense of control over herself and her destiny that seems transcendental. Earlier in the novel, Habrocomes, when he is threatened with torture by Manto, who is in love with him, asserts: "I am a slave, but I know how to keep my promises. They have power over my body, but I have a soul that is free. Let Manto threaten me, then, if she wishes, with swords and nooses and fire and everything that can compel the body of a slave; I will never be persuaded willingly to wrong Anthia" (2.4). In the anonymous epistolary novel about the tyrannicide Chion of Heraclea, Chion declares (14.4): "Know that I have become the kind of man, thanks to philosophy, whom Clearchus will never make a slave, even if he ties me up, even if he does the most terrible things to me; for he will never conquer my soul, in which slavishness and freedom reside, since the body is always at the mercy of fortune, even if it is not subject to a tyrannical man." Some years ago, Brent Shaw called attention to Leucippe's response, in Achilles Tatius's novel, when she is threatened with rape:

> Take up all your instruments of torture, and at once; bring out against me the whips, the wheel, the fire, the sword.... I am naked, and alone, and a woman. But one shield and defense I have, which is my freedom, which cannot be struck down by whips, or cut by the sword, or burned by fire. My freedom is something I will not surrender—burn as you might, you will find that there is no fire hot enough to consume it. (6.21)[7]

These bold declarations are reminiscent, as Shaw pointed out, of the Christian martyrs and the Christian ideal of inalterable fidelity to God. To mention just a few examples, in the *Passio Anastasiae*, the soon-to-be-martyred Irene declares: "Just as my flesh would endure beasts, fire, beatings, or any other punishment, so too it will endure a fornicator, a dog, a bear, or a serpent.... For the soul cannot be faulted for impurities to which it does not consent.... Willingness brings with it punishment, but necessity brings the crown" (17.10–20). And fifth-century rhetorician Choricius of Gaza asserts in his third *Oration* (3.2.13): "So how did you [sc. Aratius] correct those who were so blind to the duties of subjects? You knew that phalanxes of hoplites, light troops, and arrays of cavalry, physical force and the nature of war in general can perhaps conquer bodies, but

---

7. Brent Shaw, "Body/Power/Identity: Passions of the Martyrs," *JECS* 4 (1996): 269–312.

not the mind" (trans. David Westberg). In the third poem in Prudentius's *Peristephanon* (91–95), Eulalia declares: "Come on, torturer, burn and cut, split my limbs compacted of clay. It's easy to break so fragile a thing, but my inner spirit [*animus*] will not be penetrated, though pain torment it." In the Passio Perpetuae et Felicitatis, the narrator reports: "Perpetua, that she might taste some pain, being pierced between the ribs, cried out loudly, and she herself placed the wavering right hand of the youthful gladiator to her throat."[8] Felicitas cries out when experiencing birth pangs (she was pregnant when arrested), but she declares that when it comes to her actual execution, "there will be another in me, who will suffer for me, because I also am about to suffer for Him" (trans. Wallis). Additional such bold proclamations of the invincible freedom of the self will no doubt occur to readers of this chapter.

What are we to make of these extraordinary affirmations, both pagan and Christian? One might have thought that enough pain could coerce the will of even the most dauntless hero, and all the more so that of the innocent adolescents who are the protagonists of the novels and, often enough, of the various martyr tales as well.[9] Christian faith, to be sure, was presumed to grant exceptional power to the believer, who was under God's dispensation. But the heroes and heroines of the novels are motivated by another kind of fidelity, one that is inspired solely by ἔρως—a passion that was regarded in the classical period as being notoriously fickle. Might there be something in common between the absolute commitment of the lovers to each other in the Greek novels and the unshakable fidelity to God—itself describable as the deepest kind of love—that Christians professed? It is just when faithfulness, whether to one's beloved or to one's deity, is understood as an inner disposition, pertaining to the soul or mind as distinct from the body, that it begins to appear to be invulnerable to physical vicissitudes. It may be worth observing that the hero or heroine in the novels may, under certain circumstances, be induced to have sex with a person other than the beloved, for example, when Callirhoe, in Chariton's novel, remarries in the belief that her original husband is dead (and, further, the male protagonist has sex with a woman other than his destined

---

8. Trans. R. E. Wallis (*ANF* 3:292).

9. For a more extended discussion of attitudes toward torture, see David Konstan, "Torture and Identity: Paganism, Christianity and Beyond," in *Christian Body, Christian Self: Concepts of Early Christian Personhood*, ed. Clare K. Rothschild and Trevor W. Thompson (Tübingen: Mohr Siebeck, 2011), 283–98.

bride in Longus's *Daphnis and Chloe* and Achilles Tatius's novel). However, they are never represented as experiencing ἔρως toward another—another sign that purity in the novels has to do not with sex per se but with an inward sensibility. The combination of enduring devotion with a sense of the interior self as impervious to external violence suggests an attitude toward personal identity in the novels that is analogous to the way the self is represented in Christian texts.[10]

Although they are young and vulnerable, the protagonists of the novels—both male and female—are heroes of the self. Their sufferings are brought on not by some internal flaw or failing but by circumstances, and their resolution never falters. In this respect, they resemble Christians who are steadfast despite the severest tortures, like Perpetua and Felicitas, and who boldly declare to their pagan persecutors, "*Christianus sum*." But there is another story, that of sin and redemption, which situates the struggle for fidelity within the soul itself and looks to God's grace for forgiveness and salvation. This narrative is perhaps implicit in the martyr tales, insofar as the victims of persecution appeal to God for strength and place their confidence in him: to put their faith entirely in their own will might smack of pride. The novels' characters are more self-reliant: ἔρως alone seems sufficient motive or guarantee of integrity. They may summon the gods to pity them and put an end to their misfortunes, reuniting them with their beloveds, but they do not doubt their capacity to endure on their own.

At the beginning of the *Ephesiaca*, Xenophon explains that the outstanding physical beauty of the protagonist, Habrocomes, inclined him to despise the attractions of others and to deny that Eros was even a god (1.1.5). This is the kind of rivalry with a deity that readily invites punishment, and Eros, duly furious (1.2.1), causes the youth to fall in love with Anthia. The situation would seem to be tailor-made for a plea for forgiveness on Habrocomes's part. Yet, the first time either of the two protagonists offers supplication to a deity, it is Anthia, and she appeals to Isis rather than to Eros: she declares that she has remained chaste and kept her marriage to Habrocomes pure, and prays that she either be restored to her husband, if he is alive, or else that she remain faithful to his corpse (4.3.3–4; see the

---

10. For intersections between the novels and Christian narratives, see David Konstan and Ilaria Ramelli, "The Novel and Christian Narrative," in *The Blackwell Companion to the Ancient Novel*, ed. Shannon Byrne and Edmund Cueva (Hoboken, NJ: Wiley & Sons, 2014), 180–97.

similar plea at 5.4.6). When Habrocomes is bound to a cross as a result of the false testimony of a woman who is in love with him, he does not hesitate to proclaim his innocence as he prays to the god of the Nile: if he has done any wrong, he declares, let him die a miserable death (4.2.4), but let the gracious Nile not look on indifferently at the death of a man who has committed no injustice. The god at once takes pity on him (4.2.6; see Anthia's appeal to Apis at 5.4.10). At no point do Habrocomes and Anthia even hint that they might be guilty of some offense against the gods, and hence there is no question of repentance or forgiveness. They have proved their mutual fidelity in the course of their sufferings and in the end express gratitude for their deliverance.

By way of contrast, we may consider a novelistic work in the Judeo-Christian tradition (there is some doubt as to its provenience, but the consensus is that it is Christian). According to the so-called Life of Adam and Eve, after the first couple was driven from Eden, Eve gave birth to Cain and Abel, and after the murder of Abel, to Seth. When Adam was on the point of death, at 930 years of age, he gathered around him his thirty sons and thirty daughters, and explained the origin of the curse of death, when he, at Eve's instigation, tasted the forbidden fruit, with the result that "God became angry at us" (8). Adam instructs Eve to seek out paradise together with Seth, bidding them weep and beg God to have pity on him. When they return to Adam's tent, Adam asks her to relate the story of the fall, and her responsibility for it, to their children (14). He then begs Eve to pray to God, and she intones: "I have sinned, God, I have sinned, Father of all, I have sinned against you, I have sinned against your chosen angels, I have sinned against the Cherubim, I have sinned against your unshakable throne, I have sinned, Lord, I have sinned greatly, I have sinned before you, and all sin in creation has arisen through me" (32). At this, an angel approaches her and announces, "Arise, Eve, from your repentance" (32). He grants her a vision of a chariot descending to Adam, and the angels beseeching the Lord to yield (33), since Adam is made in his image. Adam and Cain are buried together in a secret place, as God declares that he will resurrect Adam on the final day together with all humankind. Eve supplicates the Lord to bury her next to Adam, even though she is unworthy and sinful (42), and her wish is granted.

As in the Greek novels and in the Acts of Polyxena, the protagonists of this narrative are driven from home—here it is paradise—and in the end return there, if we take heaven in this context to represent the state of things before the fall.[11] But the cause of their exile is not kidnapping or persecution but resides entirely in their own actions: it is sin that banishes them, and their liminal space is earth itself. Throughout, Eve insists on her guilt and is full of remorse; it is because of this realization and confession of culpability that God is prepared to grant the couple reprieve and resurrection. The protagonists of the novels, by contrast, suffer terrible hardships, but they are not really being punished: sin has no place in these narratives, nor has apology. They fall in love, but there is no fall; they are tested but not tempted.

The new subjectivity (if it was indeed entirely new) of freedom and fidelity developed in tandem with a sense of sin, guilt, and the need for confession.[12] But while both conceptions might exploit a similar narrative framework of exile and return, the psychological dynamics are deeply different—and this distinction is evident within Christian texts themselves (martyrs too typically declare their innocence). A thoroughgoing exploration of subjectivity in pagan and Judeo-Christian narratives has still to be written, but a good starting point would be the ideal of love and commitment in the novels as the manifestation of an autonomous and invulnerable self. Good translations and commentaries for the relevant texts are now available and can form the basis of courses on the literature of the Roman Empire that look across the divide between pagan and Jewish or Christian writings. Such courses would provide the chance for stimulating classroom discussion and genuine discovery, and would at the same time be a novel way to teach the topic of ἔρως in antiquity.

---

11. Whether the text intimates the doctrine of *apokatastasis* is moot, but it appears that all of humanity will be saved; see Ilaria Ramelli, *The Christian Doctrine of Apokatastasis: A Critical Assessment from the New Testament to Eriugena* (Leiden: Brill, 2013), 76–77.

12. See Foucault, *On the Government*.

Bibliography

Achilles Tatius. *Leucippe and Clitophon*. Translated by S. Gaselee. Rev. ed. LCL 45. Cambridge: Harvard University Press, 1984.
Adams, Percy G. *Travel Literature and the Evolution of the Novel*. Lexington: University Press of Kentucky, 1983.
Althusser, Louis. *Lenin and Philosophy*. Translated by Ben Brewster. New York: Monthly Review Press, 1971.
Aretaeus. *The Extant Works of Aretaeus, the Cappadocian*. Edited by Francis Adams. London: Sydenham Society, 1856.
Aristotle. *Poetics*. Edited by Stephen Halliwell. Cambridge: Harvard University Press, 1995.
Ashcroft, Bill, Gereth Griffiths, and Helen Tiffin. *Post-colonial Studies: The Key Concepts*. 2nd ed. London: Routledge, 2007.
Attridge, Harold W., and Robert A. Oden Jr. *Philo of Byblos: The Phoenician History; Introduction, Critical Text, Translation, Notes*. CBQMS 9. Washington, DC: Catholic Biblical Association, 1981.
Aymer, Margaret P. "Hailstorms and Fireballs: Redaction, World Creation, and Resistance in the *Acts of Paul and Thecla*." *Semeia* 75 (1997): 43–61.
Bal, Mieke. "Lots of Writing." *Semeia* 54 (1991): 77–102.
Balsdon, J. P. V. D. "Gaius and the Grand Cameo of Paris." *JRS* 26 (1936): 152–60.
Bar-Efrat, Shimon. *Narrative Art in the Bible*. Translated by Dorothea Shefer-Vanson. Sheffield: Almond, 1989.
Barnes, Timothy D. *Early Christian Hagiography and Roman History*. Tübingen: Mohr Siebeck, 2010.
Barrier, Jeremy W. *The Acts of Paul and Thecla: A Critical Introduction and Commentary*. Tübingen: Mohr Siebeck, 2009.
Barthes, Roland. *The Pleasure of the Text*. Translated by Richard Miller. New York: Hill & Wang, 1975.

———. *S/Z: An Essay*. Translated by Richard Miller. New York: Hill & Wang, 1974.

Bauckham, Richard. "The Beloved Disciple as Ideal Author." *JSNT* 49 (1993): 21–44.

———. "For What Offence Was James Put to Death?" Pages 199–232 in *James the Just and Christian Origins*. Edited by Bruce D. Chilton and Craig A. Evans. NovTSup 98. Leiden: Brill, 1999.

———. "James and the Jerusalem Community." Pages 55–95 in *Jewish Believers in Jesus*. Edited by Oskar Skarsaune and Reidar Hvalvik. Peabody, MA: Hendrickson, 2007.

———. "The Throne of God and the Worship of Jesus." Pages 43–69 in *The Jewish Roots of Christological Monotheism*. Edited by Carey C. Newman, James R. Davila, and Gladys S. Lewis. Leiden: Brill, 1999.

Beal, Timothy K. *The Book of Hiding: Gender, Ethnicity, Annihilation, and Esther*. London: Routledge, 1997.

Beard, Mary. "The Triumph of Flavius Josephus." Pages 543–58 in *Flavian Rome: Culture, Image, Text*. Edited by A. J. Boyle and W. J. Dominik. Leiden: Brill, 2003.

Bechtel, Carol. *Esther*. IBC. Louisville: Westminster John Knox, 2002.

Bennett, E. N. "James, *Apocrypha Anecdota*." *Classical Review* 8 (1894): 101–3.

Berg, Sandra Beth. *The Book of Esther: Motifs, Themes and Structure*. SBLDS 44. Missoula, MT: Scholars Press, 1979.

Berlin, Adele. *The JPS Bible Commentary: Esther*. Philadelphia: Jewish Publication Society of America, 2001.

Berman, Joshua A. "Hadassah Bat Abihail: The Evolution from Object to Subject in the Character of Esther." *JBL* 120 (2001): 647–69.

Betz, Monika. "Die betörenden Worte des fremden Mannes: Zur Funktion der Paulusbeschreibung in den Theklaakten." *NTS* 53 (2007): 130–45.

Beyschalg, Karlmann. "Das Jacobsmartyrium und seine Verwandten in der frühchristlichen Literatur." *ZTK* 56 (1965): 149–78.

Blank, Josef. *Das Evangelium nach Johannes*. Geistliche Schriftlesung: Erläuterungen zum Neuen Testament für die geistliche Lesung 4.2. 2nd ed. Düsseldorf: Patmos, 1986.

Bond, Shelagh M. "The Coinage of the Early Roman Empire." *GR* 4.2 (1957): 149–59.

Bonnet, Max. "Sur les Actes de Xanthippe et Polyxène." *Classical Review* 8 (1894): 336–41.

Borges, Jorge Luis. "Befragungen." Pages 7–204 in *Gesammelte Werke*. Vol. 5.2. Translated by Karl August Horst. Munich: Hanser, 1981.
Boring, Eugene. "Mark 1:1–15 and the Beginning of the Gospel." *Semeia* 52 (1990): 451–71.
Bovon, François. "Canonical and Apocryphal Acts of Apostles." *JECS* 11 (2003): 165–94.
Bowersock, Glen W. *Fiction as History: Nero to Julian*. Berkeley: University of California Press, 1994.
Bowie, Ewen. "Philostratus: Writer of Fiction." Pages 181–99 in *Greek Fiction: The Greek Novel in Context*. Edited by J. R. Morgan and Richard Stoneman. London: Routledge, 1994.
Bradley, Keith. "On Captives under the Principate." *Phoenix* 58 (2004): 298–318.
Braun, Martin. *History and Romance in Graeco-Oriental Literature*. Oxford: Blackwell, 1938.
Bregman, Jay. "Synesius of Cyrene." Pages 520–37 in *The Cambridge History of Philosophy in Late Antiquity*. Vol. 1. Edited by Lloyd P. Gerson. Cambridge: Cambridge University Press, 2010.
Bremmer, Jan N. "The Acts of Thomas: Place, Date, and Women." Pages 74–90 in *The Apocryphal Acts of Thomas*. Edited by Jan Bremmer. Leuven: Peeters, 2001.
———. "Magic, Martyrdom and Women's Liberation in the Acts of Paul and Thecla." Pages 36–59 in *The Apocryphal Acts of Paul and Thecla*. Edited by Jan Bremmer. Kampen: Kok, 1996.
———. "Man, Magic, and Martyrdom in the Acts of Andrew." Pages 15–34 in *The Apocryphal Acts of Andrew*. Edited by Jan Bremmer. Leuven: Peeters, 2000.
———. "Why Did Early Christianity Attract Upper-Class Women?" Pages 35–47 in *Fructus centesimus: Mélanges offerts à Gerard J.M. Bartelink à l'occasion de son soixante-cinquième anniversaire*. Edited by A. Bastiaensen, A. Hilhorst, and C. Kneepkens. Instrumenta Patristica 19. Dordrecht: Kluwer, 1989.
———. "Women in the Apocryphal Acts of John." Pages 37–56 in *The Apocryphal Acts of John*. Edited by Jan Bremmer. Kampen: Kok, 1995.
Bretzigheimer, Gerlinde. "Dares Phrygius: *Historia ficta*; Die Präliminarien zum Trojanischen Krieg." *Rheinisches Museum* 151 (2008): 365–99.
———. "Dares Phrygius: Transformationen des Trojanischen Kriegs." *Rheinisches Museum* 152 (2009): 63–95.

Brooten, Bernadette J. *Love between Women: Early Christian Responses to Female Homoeroticism.* Chicago: University of Chicago Press, 1998.

Brunt, Peter A. Review of *Die Aussenpolitik des Augustus und die augusteische Dichtung*, by H. D. Meyer. *JRS* 53 (1963): 170–76.

Burnett, Fred W. "Historiography." Pages 106–12 in *Handbook of Postmodern Biblical Interpretation*. Edited by A. K. M. Adam. St. Louis: Chalice, 2000.

Burrus, Virginia. *Chastity as Autonomy: Women in the Stories of Apocryphal Acts.* Studies in Women and Religion. Lewiston, NY: Mellen, 1987.

———. "Gender, Eros, and Pedagogy: Macrina's Pious Household." Pages 167–81 in *Ascetic Culture: Essays in Honor of Philip Rousseau*. Edited by Blake Leyerle and Robin Darling Young. Notre Dame: University of Notre Dame Press, 2013.

———. "Mimicking Virgins: Colonial Ambivalence and the Ancient Romance." *Arethusa* 38 (2005): 49–88.

———. *The Sex Lives of Saints: An Erotics of Ancient Hagiography.* Divinations: Rereading Late Ancient Religion. Philadelphia: University of Pennsylvania Press, 2004.

Byron, John. "Ancient Historiography and the Book of Acts." Pages 336–38 in *Teaching the Bible: Practical Strategies for Classroom Instruction*. Edited by Mark Roncace and Patrick Gray. RBS 49. Atlanta: Society of Biblical Literature, 2005.

Caelius Aurelianus. *On Acute Diseases and On Chronic Diseases.* Edited by I. E. Drabkin. Chicago: University of Chicago Press, 1950.

Camery-Hoggatt, Jeremy. *Irony in Mark's Gospel: Text and Subtext.* Cambridge: Cambridge University Press, 1992.

Campbell, David A., trans. *Greek Lyric.* LCL. Cambridge: Harvard University Press, 1982.

Canfora, Luigi. *Un mestiere pericoloso: La vita quotidiana dei filosofi greci.* Palermo: Sellerio, 2000.

Carey, Holly J. "Judas Iscariot: The Betrayer of Jesus." Pages 249–68 in *Jesus among Friends and Enemies: A Historical and Literary Introduction to Jesus in the Gospels*. Edited by Chris Keith and Larry Hurtado. Grand Rapids: Baker Academic, 2011.

Carr, David, Thomas R. Flynn, and Rudolf A. Makkreel, eds. *The Ethics of History.* Evanston, IL: Northwestern University Press, 2004.

Chaniotis, Angelos. "Staging and Feeling the Presence of God: Emotion and Theatricality in Religious Celebrations in the Roman East." Pages

169–89 in *Panthée: Religious Transformations in the Graeco-Roman Empire*. Edited by Laurent Bricault and Nicole Bonnett. RGRW 177. Leiden: Brill, 2013.

Charles, R. H. *The Greek Versions of the Testaments of the Twelve Patriarchs*. Oxford: Clarendon, 1908.

———. *The Testaments of the Twelve Patriarchs Translated from the Editor's Greek Text*. London: Black, 1908.

Chick, Nancy L. "Unpacking a Signature Pedagogy in Literary Studies." Pages 36–55 in *Exploring Signature Pedagogies: Approaches to Teaching Disciplinary Habits of Mind*. Edited by Regan A. R. Gurung, Nancy L. Chick, and Aeron Haynie. Sterling, VA: Stylus, 2009.

Chick, Nancy L., Aeron Haynie, and Regan A. R. Gurung. "From Generic to Signature Pedagogies: Teaching Disciplinary Understandings." Pages 1–16 in *Exploring Signature Pedagogies: Approaches to Teaching Disciplinary Habits of Mind*. Edited by Regan A. R. Gurung, Nancy L. Chick, and Aeron Haynie. Sterling, VA: Stylus, 2009.

Clarke, Howard. *Homer's Readers: A Historical Introduction to the "Iliad" and "Odyssey."* Newark: University of Delaware Press, 1980.

Clines, David J. A. *Ezra, Nehemiah, Esther*. NCB. Grand Rapids: Eerdmans, 1984.

Collins, John J. *The Apocalyptic Imagination: An Introduction to Jewish Apocalyptic Literature*. 2nd ed. Grand Rapids: Eerdmans, 1998.

Cooper, Kate. *The Virgin and the Bride: Idealized Womanhood in Late Antiquity*. Cambridge: Harvard University Press, 1996.

Cotton, Hannah M., and Werner Eck. "Josephus' Roman Audience: Josephus and the Roman Elites." Pages 37–52 in *Flavius Josephus and Flavian Rome*. Edited by Jonathan Edmondson, Steve Mason, and James Rives. New York: Oxford University Press, 2005.

Craig, Kenneth. *Reading Esther: A Case for the Literary Carnivalesque*. Literary Currents in Biblical Interpretation. Louisville: Westminster John Knox, 1995.

Craigie, W. A., trans. "Acts of Xanthippe and Polyxena." *ANF* 9:205–17.

Craven, Toni. *Artistry and Faith in the Book of Judith*. SBLDS 70. Chico, CA: Scholars Press, 1983.

Crenshaw, James L. "The Expression *mî yōdēaʿ* in the Hebrew Bible." *VT* 36 (1986): 274–88.

Crossan, John Dominic. *The Historical Jesus: The Life of a Mediterranean Jewish Peasant*. New York: HarperCollins, 1991.

———. *In Search of Paul: How Jesus's Apostle Opposed Rome's Empire with God's Kingdom; A New Vision of Paul's Words and World*. San Francisco: HarperSanFrancisco, 2004.

Curran, John. "Flavius Josephus in Rome." Pages 65–86 in *Flavius Josephus: Interpretation and History*. Edited by Jack Pastor, Pnina Stern, and Menahem Mor. Leiden: Brill, 2011.

Curtius, Ernst Robert. *European Literature and the Latin Middle Ages*. Translated by Willard R. Trask. New York: Harper, 1962.

Cusack, Carole M. *Invented Religions: Imagination, Fiction and Faith*. Ashgate New Religions. Burlington, VT: Ashgate, 2010.

Cusack, Carole M., and Alex Norman, eds. *Handbook of New Religions and Cultural Production*. Brill Handbooks on Contemporary Religion 4. Leiden: Brill, 2012.

Damgaard, Finn. "Brothers in Arms: Josephus' Portrait of Moses in the 'Jewish Antiquities' in the Light of His Own Self-Portraits in the 'Jewish War' and the 'Life.'" *JJS* 59.2 (2008): 218–35.

Dandamaev, Muhammed A., and Vladimir G. Lukonin. *The Culture and Social Institutions of Ancient Iran*. Translated by Philip L. Kohl. Cambridge: Cambridge University Press, 1989.

D'Angelo, Mary Rose. "Abba and 'Father': Imperial Ideology and the Jesus Traditions." *JBL* 111 (1992): 611–30.

Dannemann, Irene. "Die Akten der Xanthippe, Polyxena und Rebekka oder: Drei Frauen und zwei Löwinnen." Pages 748–56 in *Kompendium: Feministische Bibelauslegung*. Edited by Luise Schottroff and Marie-Theres Wacker. Gütersloh: Gütersloher Verlagshaus, 1999.

Davidson, James N. *The Greeks and Greek Love: A Bold New Exploration of the Ancient World*. New York: Random House, 2007.

Day, Linda M. *Esther*. AOTC. Nashville: Abingdon, 2005.

Deakin, Michael. "Hypatia and Her Mathematics." *American Mathematical Monthly* 101.3 (1994): 234–43.

Dio Chrysostom. *Dio Chrysostom*. Vol. 1. Translated by J. W. Cohoon. LCL. Cambridge: Harvard University Press, 1932.

Donahue, John, and Daniel Harrington. *The Gospel of Mark*. SP 2. Collegeville, MN: Liturgical Press, 2002.

Doody, Margaret Anne. *The True Story of the Novel*. New Brunswick, NJ: Rutgers University Press, 1996.

Döpp, Siegmar. "Metalepsen als signifikante Elemente spätlateinischer Literatur." Pages 431–65 in *Über die Grenze: Metalepse in Text- und*

Bildmedien des Altertums. Edited by Ute E. Eisen and Peter von Möllendorff. Berlin: de Gruyter, 2013.
Dover, Kenneth James. *Greek Homosexuality*. Cambridge: Harvard University Press, 1978.
Draitser, Emil. *Techniques of Satire: The Case of Saltykov-Scedrin*. Berlin: de Gruyter, 1994.
Dube Shomanah, Musa. *Postcolonial Feminist Interpretation of the Bible*. St. Louis: Chalice, 2000.
Dunn, Peter W. "Women's Liberation, the Acts of Paul, and Other Apocryphal Acts of the Apostles: A Review of Some Recent Interpreters." *Apocrypha* 4 (1994): 245–62.
Dupertuis, Rubén R. "The Summaries of Acts 2, 4, and 5 and Plato's Republic." Pages 275–95 in *Ancient Fiction: The Matrix of Early Christian and Jewish Narrative*. Edited by Jo-Ann A. Brant, Charles W. Hedrick, and Chris Shea. SBLSymS 32. Atlanta: Society of Biblical Literature, 2005.
Dzielska, Maria. *Hypatia of Alexandria*. Cambridge: Harvard University Press, 1995.
———. "Once More on Hypatia's Death." Pages 1–74 in *Divine Men and Women in the History and Society of Late Hellenism*. Edited by Maria Dzielska and Kamilla Twardowska. Krakow: Jagiellonian University Press, 2013.
Eastman, Max. *Enjoyment of Laughter*. New York: Simon & Schuster, 1936.
Edmonson, Jonathan, Steve Mason, and J. B. Rives, eds. *Flavius Josephus and Flavian Rome*. New York: Oxford University Press, 2005.
Eisen, Ute E. "Metalepsis in the Gospel of John—Narration Situation and 'Beloved Disciple' in New Perspective." Pages 318–45 in *Über die Grenze: Metalepse in Text- und Bildmedien des Altertums*. Edited by Ute E. Eisen and Peter von Möllendorff. Berlin: de Gruyter, 2013.
———. *Die Poetik der Apostelgeschichte: Eine narratologische Studie*. NTOA 58. Göttingen: Vandenhoeck & Ruprecht, 2006.
Eisen, Ute E., and Peter von Möllendorff, eds. *Über die Grenze: Metalepse in Text- und Bildmedien des Altertums*. Narratologia 39. Berlin: de Gruyter, 2013.
Eisen, Ute E., and Peter von Möllendorff. "Zur Einführung." Pages 1–9 in *Über die Grenze: Metalepse in Text- und Bildmedien des Altertums*. Narratologia 39. Berlin: de Gruyter, 2013.
Eisenhut, Werner. *Dictys Cretensis*. 2nd ed. Leipzig: Teubner, 1973.
Emerton, J. A. "The Meaning of *šēnā'* in Psalm CXXVII 2." *VT* 24 (1974): 15–31.

Erim, Kenan T. *Aphrodisias: A Guide to the Site and Its Museum*. Istanbul: NET Turistik Yayınlar, 1990.

———. "A New Relief Showing Claudius and Britannia from Aphrodisias." *Britannia* 13 (1982): 277.

———. "Recentes decouvertes à Aphrodisias en Carie, 1979–1980." *RAr* 8 (1982): 167.

Esch-Ermeling, Elisabeth. *Thekla—Paulusschülerin wider Willen? Strategien der Leserlenkung in den Theklaakten*. NTAbh 53. Münster: Aschendorff, 2008.

Eusebius, *The Ecclesiastical History*. Vol. 1. Translated by Kirsopp Lake. LCL. Cambridge: Harvard University Press, 1926.

———. *The Ecclesiastical History*. Vol. 2, *Books 6–10*. Edited and translated by J. E. L. Oulton and H. J. Lawlor. LCL. Cambridge: Harvard University Press, 1932.

Fédou, Michel. "L'historien Socrate et la controverse origéniste." Pages 271–80 in *L'historiographie de l'Église des premiers siècles*. Edited by Bernard Pouderon and Yves-Marie Duval. Paris: Beauchesne, 2001.

Feldman, Louis H. "Josephus' Portrait of Moses: Part Two." *JQR* 83 (1992): 7–50.

———. *Philo's Portrayal of Moses in the Context of Ancient Judaism*. Christianity and Judaism in Antiquity Series 15. Notre Dame: University of Notre Dame Press, 2007.

Ferrand, Jacques. *A Treatise on Lovesickness*. Translated by Donald A. Beecher and Massimo Ciavolella. Syracuse, NY: Syracuse University Press, 1990.

Flower, Harriet. *Ancestor Masks and Aristocratic Power in Roman Culture*. Oxford: Clarendon, 1996.

Formisano, Marco. "Toward an Aesthetic Paradigm of Late Antiquity." *Antiquité Tardive* 15 (2007): 277–84.

Foucault, Michel. *The Care of the Self*. Translated by Robert Hurley. Vol. 3 of *The History of Sexuality*. New York: Vintage, 1988.

———. *An Introduction*. Vol. 1 of *The History of Sexuality*. Translated by Robert Hurley. New York: Pantheon, 1978.

———. *On the Government of the Living: Lectures at the Collège de France 1979–1980*. Translated by Graham Burchell. New York: Palgrave Macmillan, 2014.

———. *The Use of Pleasure*. Translated by Robert Hurley. Vol. 2 of *The History of Sexuality*. New York: Vintage, 1985.

Fox, Michael V. *Character and Ideology in the Book of Esther*. 2nd ed. Studies on Personalities of the Old Testament. Grand Rapids: Eerdmans, 2001.
Frazer, R. M., Jr. *The Trojan War: The Chronicles of Dictys of Crete and Dares the Phrygian*. Bloomington: Indiana University Press, 1966.
Friesen, Steven J. "Poverty in Pauline Studies: Beyond the So-Called New Consensus." *JSNT* 26 (2004): 323–61.
Frulla, Giovanni. "Reconstructing Exodus Tradition: Moses in the Second Book of Josephus' *Antiquities*." Pages 111–24 in *Flavius Josephus: Interpretation and History*. Edited by Jack Pastor, Pnina Stern, and Menahem Mor. Leiden: Brill, 2011.
Galinsky, Karl. *Augustan Culture*. Princeton: Princeton University Press, 1996.
Gardner, Percy. "Countries and Cities in Ancient Art." *JHS* 9 (1888): 47–81.
Genette, Gérard. *Métalepse: De la figure à la fiction*. Paris: Editions du Seuil, 2004.
———. *Narrative Discourse: An Essay in Method*. Translated by Jane E. Lewin. Ithaca, NY: Cornell University Press, 1980.
———. *Narrative Discourse Revisited*. Translated by Jane E. Lewin. Ithaca, NY: Cornell University Press, 1988.
Gilbert, William S., and Arthur S. Sullivan. *The Complete Plays of Gilbert and Sullivan*. New York: Modern Library, 1936.
Giuliani, Luca, and Gerhardt Schmidt. *Ein Geschenk für den Kaiser: Das Geheimnis des grossen Kameo*. Munich: Beck, 2010.
Goldhill, Simon. *Foucault's Virginity: Ancient Erotic Fiction and the History of Sexuality*. Cambridge: Cambridge University Press, 1995.
Goodacre, Mark. "Scripturalization in Mark's Crucifixion Narrative." Pages 33–47 in *The Trial and Death of Jesus: Essays on the Passion Narrative of Mark*. Edited by Geert van Oyen and Tom Shepherd. Leuven: Peeters, 2006.
Goodman, Martin. "Josephus as Roman Citizen." Pages 329–38 in *Josephus and the History of the Greco-Roman Period*. Edited by Fausto Parente and Joseph Sievers. Leiden: Brill, 1994.
Gorman, Jill. "Reading and Theorizing Women's Sexualities: The Representation of Women in the *Acts of Xanthippe and Polyxena*." PhD diss., Temple University, 2003.
———. "Thinking with and About 'Same-Sex Desire': Producing and Policing Female Sexuality in the *Acts of Xanthippe and Polyxena*." *Journal of the History of Sexuality* 10 (2001): 416–41.

Gounelle, Rémi. *Les Recensions byzantines de l'Évangile de Nicodème.* Corpus Christianorum: Series Apocryphorum, Instrumenta 3. Turnhout: Brepols, 2008.

Gowler, David B. "The Chreia." Pages 132–48 in *The Historical Jesus in Context.* Edited by Amy-Jill Levine, Dale C. Allison Jr., and John Dominic Crossan. Princeton Readings in Religion. Princeton: Princeton University Press, 2006.

Graff, Gerald. *Beyond the Culture Wars: How Teaching the Conflicts Can Revitalize American Education.* New York: Norton, 1992.

———. "Teaching the Conflicts at Twenty Years." *Pedagogy* 3 (2003): 245–73.

Grossman, Jonathan. *Esther: The Outer Narrative and the Hidden Reading.* Sifrut 6. Winona Lake, IN: Eisenbrauns, 2011.

Gruen, Erich S. *Diaspora: Jews amidst Greeks and Romans.* Cambridge: Harvard University Press, 2002.

———. "Polybius and Josephus on Rome." Pages 149–62 in *Flavius Josephus: Interpretation and History.* Edited by Jack Pastor, Pnina Stern, and Menahem Mor. JSJSup 146. Leiden: Brill, 2011.

Haines-Eitzen, Kim. *The Gendered Palimpsest: Women, Writing, and Representation in Early Christianity.* New York: Oxford University Press, 2012.

Halperin, David M. "Is There a History of Sexuality?" *History and Theory* 28 (1989): 257–74.

Hammer, Olav, and Mikael Rothstein, eds. *The Cambridge Companion to New Religious Movements.* Cambridge Companions to Religion. Cambridge: Cambridge University Press, 2012.

Harich-Schwarzbauer, Henriette. *Hypatia: Die spätantiken Quellen.* Bern: Lang, 2011.

Harrelson, Walter. "Patient Love in the Testament of Joseph." Pages 29–35 in *Studies on the Testament of Joseph.* Edited by George W. E. Nickelsburg. SCS 5. Missoula, MT: Scholars Press, 1975.

Harris, James Rendel. *The Homeric Centones and the Acts of Pilate.* London: Clay, 1898.

Haynes, Katharine. *Fashioning the Feminine in the Greek Novel.* London: Routledge, 2003.

Heever, Gerhard A. van den. "'Loose Fictions and Frivolous Fabrications': Ancient Fiction and the Mystery Religions of the Early Imperial Era." DLitt et Phil thesis. University of South Africa, 2005. http://tinyurl.com/SBL4212b.

———. "Novel and Mystery: Discourse, Myth and Society." Pages 89–114 in *Ancient Fiction: Matrix of Early Christian and Early Jewish Narrative*. Edited by Jo-Ann A. Brant, Charles W. Hedrick, and Christine Shea. SBLSymS 32. Atlanta: Society of Biblical Literature, 2005.
Hengel, Martin. "'Sit at My Right Hand.'" Pages 119–225 in *Studies in Early Christology*. Edited by Martin Hengel. Edinburgh: T&T Clark, 1995.
Herodotus. *The Histories*. Translated by A. E. Godley. Vol. 2. LCL. Cambridge: Harvard University Press, 1938.
Hezser, Catherine. "'Ancient Science Fiction': Journeys into Space and Visions of the World in Jewish, Christian, and Greco-Roman Literature of Antiquity." Pages 397–438 in *Christian Origins and Hellenistic Judaism: Social and Literary Contexts for the New Testament*. Edited by Stanley E. Porter and Andrew W. Pitts. TENTS 10. Leiden: Brill, 2013.
Highet, Gilbert. *The Classical Tradition: Greek and Roman Influences on Western Literature*. New York: Oxford University Press, 1949.
Hogle, Jerrold E., ed. *The Cambridge Companion to Gothic Fiction*. Cambridge: Cambridge University Press, 2002.
Hölkeskamp, Karl-Joachim. "*Exempla* und *mos maiorum*: Überlegungen zum kollektiven Gedächtnis der Nobilität." Pages 301–38 in *Vergangenheit und Lebenswelt: Soziale Kommunikation, Traditionsbildung und historisches Bewusstsein*. Edited by Hans Joachim Gehrde and Astrid Möller. Tübingen: Narr, 1996.
Hollander, Harm W. "The Ethical Character of the Patriarch Joseph: A Study in the Ethics of the Testaments of the XII Patriarchs." Pages 47–104 in *Studies on the Testament of Joseph*. Edited by George W. E. Nickelsburg. SCS 5. Missoula, MT: Scholars Press, 1975.
———. *Joseph as an Ethical Model in the Testaments of the Twelve Patriarchs*. SVTP 6. Leiden: Brill, 1981.
Hollander, Harm W., and Marinus de Jonge. *The Testaments of the Twelve Patriarchs: A Commentary*. Leiden: Brill, 1985.
Hölscher, Tonio. "Images of War in Greece and Rome: Between Military Practice, Public Memory, and Cultural Symbolism." *JRS* 93 (2003): 1–17.
Hölter, Achim. "Das Eigenleben der Figuren: Eine radikale Konsequenz der neueren Metafiktion." Pages 29–53 in *Komparatistik: Jahrbuch der Deutschen Gesellschaft für Allgemeine und Vergleichende Literaturwissenschaft 2007*. Edited by Christiane Dahms. Heidelberg: Synchron, 2008.

Holzberg, Niklas. "The Genre Novels Proper and the Fringe." Pages 11–28 in *The Novel in the Ancient World*. Edited by Gareth Schmeling. Rev. ed. Leiden: Brill, 2003.
Horsley, Richard A. *Hearing the Whole Story: The Politics of Plot in Mark's Gospel*. Louisville: Westminster John Knox, 2001.
———. *Jesus and Empire: The Kingdom of God and the New World Disorder*. Minneapolis: Fortress, 2003.
Howard, Cameron B. R. "Writing Yehud: Textuality and Power under Persian Rule." PhD diss., Emory University, 2010.
Hughes, Jessica. "Personifications and the Ancient Viewer: The Case of the Hadrianeum 'Nations.'" *Art History* 32 (2009): 1–20.
Huitink, Luuk, and Jan Willem van Henten. "The Publication of Flavius Josephus' Works and Their Audiences." *Zutot* 6 (2009): 49–60.
Hunter, Richard. "The Trojan Oration of Dio Chrysostom and Ancient Homeric Criticism." Pages 43–62 in *Narratology and Interpretation: The Content of Narrative Form in Ancient Literature*. Edited by Jonas Grethlein and Antonios Rengakos. Berlin: de Gruyter, 2009.
Hyers, Conrad. *And God Created Laughter: The Bible as Divine Comedy*. Atlanta: Knox, 1987.
Hylen, Susan E. *A Modest Apostle: Thecla and the History of Women in the Early Church*. New York: Oxford University Press, 2015.
Jackson, Stanley W. *Melancholia and Depression: From Hippocratic Times to Modern Times*. New Haven: Yale University Press, 1986.
Jacobs, Andrew S. "A Family Affair: Marriage, Class, and Ethics in the Apocryphal Acts of the Apostles." *JECS* 7 (1999): 105–38.
James, Edward, and Farah Mendlesohn, eds. *The Cambridge Companion to Science Fiction*. Cambridge: Cambridge University Press, 2003.
James, Edward, and Farah Mendlesohn, eds. *The Cambridge Companion to Fantasy Literature*. Cambridge: Cambridge University Press, 2012.
James, Montague Rhodes, ed. *Apocrypha Anecdota: A Collection of Thirteen Apocryphal Books and Fragments*. 2 vols. Texts and Studies: Contributions to Biblical and Patristic Literature. Cambridge: Cambridge University Press, 1893.
Jameson, Fredric. *The Political Unconscious: Narrative as a Socially Symbolic Act*. Ithaca, NY: Cornell University Press, 1981.
———. "Third-World Literature in the Era of Multinational Capitalism." *Social Text* 15 (1986): 65–88.

Jenkinson, Edna. "Nepos—An Introduction to Latin Biography." Pages 1-15 in *Latin Biography*. Edited by Thomas A. Dorey. New York: Basic Books, 1967.
Jensen, Anne. *Thekla die Apostolin: Ein apokrypher Text neu entdeckt*. Freiburg: Herder, 1995.
Jeremias, Joachim. *Heiligengräber in Jesu Umwelt (Mt. 23,29; Lk. 11,47): Eine Untersuchung Zur Volksreligion der Zeit Jesu*. Göttingen: Vandenhoeck & Ruprecht, 1958.
Jobling, J'Annine, and Alan Roughley. "The Right to Write: Power, Irony, and Identity in the Book of Esther." Pages 317-33 in *Sacred Tropes: Tanakh, New Testament, and Qur'an as Literature and Culture*. Edited by Roberta Sterman Sabbath. BibInt 98. Leiden: Brill, 2009.
Jong, Irene de. "Metalepsis in Ancient Greek Literature." Pages 87-115 in *Narratology and Interpretation: The Content of Narrative Form in Ancient Literature*. Edited by Jonas Grethlein and Antonios Rengakos. Berlin: de Gruyter, 2009.
Jonge, Marinus de. "The Future of Israel in the Testaments of the Twelve Patriarchs." *JSJ* 17 (1986): 196-211.
———. "Die Paränese in den Schriften des Neuen Testaments und in den Testamenten der Zwölf Patriarchen." Pages 538-50 in *Neues Testament und Ethik: Für Rudolf Schnackenburg*. Edited by Helmut Merklein. Freiburg: Herder, 1989.
———, ed. *Studies on the Testaments of the Twelve Patriarchs: Text and Interpretation*. Leiden: Brill, 1975.
———. *The Testaments of the Twelve Patriarchs: A Critical Edition of the Greek Text*. Leiden: Brill, 1978.
———. "The Testaments of the Twelve Patriarchs and the 'Two Ways.'" Pages 179-94 in *Biblical Traditions in Transmission: Essays in Honour of Michael A. Knibb*. Edited by Charlotte Hempel and Judith M. Lieu. Leiden: Brill, 2006.
———. "The *Testaments of the Twelve Patriarchs*: Central Problems and Essential Viewpoints." Pages 359-420 in *Principat 20, 1: Religion*. Edited by Wolfgang Haase. Berlin: de Gruyer, 1987.
Josephus. *Jewish Antiquities*. Translated by H. St. J. Thackeray et al. 10 vols. LCL. Cambridge: Harvard University Press, 1926-1965.
Junod, Eric. "Vie et conduite des saintes femmes Xanthippe, Polyxène, et Rébecca (BHG 1877)." Pages 83-106 in *Oecumenica et patristica: Festschrift für Wilhelm Schneemelcher zum 75. Geburtstag*. Edited by

Damaskinos Papandreou, Wolfgang A. Bienert, and Knut Schäferdiek. Stuttgart: Kohlammer, 1989.

Kaestli, Jean-Daniel. "L'usage du narratif dans le Testament de Joseph." Pages 201-12 in *Narrativity in Biblical and Related Texts*. Edited by George J. Brooke and Jean-Daniel Kaestli. Leuven: Leuven University Press, 2000.

Kähler, Heinz. *Die Augustusstatue von Primaporta*. Cologne: DuMont Schauberg, 1959.

Kee, H. C. "The Testaments of the Twelve Patriarchs." Pages 775-828 in *Apocalyptic Literature and Testaments*. Edited by James H. Charlesworth. Vol. 1 of *The Old Testament Pseudepigrapha*. Garden City, NY: Doubleday, 1983.

Keith, Alison. *Engendering Rome: Women in Latin Epic*. Cambridge: Cambridge University Press, 2000.

King, Karen. "Martyrdom and Its Discontents in the Tchacos Codex." Pages 23-42 in *The Codex Judas Papers: Proceedings of the International Congress on the Tchacos Codex Held at Rice University, Houston, Texas*. Edited by April D. DeConick. Leiden: Brill, 2009.

Klimek, Sonja. *Paradoxes Erzählen: Die Metalepse in der phantastischen Literatur*. Paderborn: Mentis, 2010.

Konstan, David. "Acts of Love: A Narrative Pattern in the Apocryphal Acts." *JECS* 6 (1998): 15-36.

———. *Before Forgiveness: The Origins of a Moral Idea*. Cambridge: Cambridge University Press, 2010.

———. "*Erôs* and *Oikos*." Pages 217-24 in *Narrative, Culture and Genre in the Ancient Novel*. Edited by Stephen Harrison and Stavros Frangoulidis. Berlin: de Gruyter, 2012.

———. "Reunion and Regeneration: Narrative Patterns in Ancient Greek Novels and Christian Acts." Pages 105-20 in *Fiction on the Fringe: Novelistic Writing in Late Antiquity*. Edited by Grammatiki Karla and Ingela Nilsson. Mnemosyne Supplement Series 310. Leiden: Brill, 2009.

———. *Sexual Symmetry: Love in the Ancient Novel and Related Genres*. Princeton: Princeton University Press, 1994.

———. "Torture and Identity: Paganism, Christianity and Beyond." Pages 283-98 in *Christian Body, Christian Self: Concepts of Early Christian Personhood*. Edited by Clare K. Rothschild and Trevor W. Thompson. Tübingen: Mohr Siebeck, 2011.

Konstan, David, and Ilaria Ramelli. "The Novel and Christian Narrative." Pages 180–97 in *The Blackwell Companion to the Ancient Novel*. Edited by Shannon Byrne and Edmund Cueva. New York: Wiley & Sons, 2014.
Kraemer, Ross S. "The Conversion of Women to Ascetic Forms of Christianity." *Signs* (1980): 298–307.
Kronenberger, Louis. *The Thread of Laughter*. New York: Knopf, 1952.
Kugler, Robert A. *The Testaments of the Twelve Patriarchs*. Guides to the Apocrypha and Pseudepigrapha. Sheffield: Sheffield Academic, 2001.
Kuttner, Ann L. "Culture and History at Pompey's Museum." *TAPA* 129 (1999): 343–73.
———. *Dynasty and Empire in the Age of Augustus: The Case of the Boscoreale Cups*. Berkeley: University of California Press, 1995.
Lage, Santiago Díaz. "Afterthoughts on the Spanish Gothic." *European Studies Blog*, January 19, 2015. http://tinyurl.com/SBL4212a.
Lalanne, Sophie. *Une éducation grecque: Rites de passage et construction des genres dans le roman grec ancien*. Paris: Éditions La Découverte, 2006.
Leppin, Hartmut. "The Church Historians I." Pages 219–54 in *Greek and Roman Historiography: Fourth to Sixth Century*. Edited by Gabriele Marasco. Leiden: Brill, 2003.
Lessing, Gotthold Ephraim. "On the Proof of the Spirit and of Power." Pages 83–88 in *Philosophical and Theological Writings*. Edited and translated by H. B. Nisbet. Cambridge: Cambridge University Press, 2005.
Levenson, Jon. *Esther: A Commentary*. OTL. Louisville: Westminster John Knox, 1997.
Levi, Annalina Caló. *Barbarians on Roman Imperial Coins and Sculpture*. New York: American Numismatic Society, 1952.
Levine, Amy-Jill. "Introduction." Pages 1–17 in *A Feminist Companion to the New Testament Apocrypha*. Edited by Amy-Jill Levine and Maria Mayo Robbins. London: Continuum, 2006.
Levine, Etan. "Qohelet's Fool: A Composite Portrait." Pages 277–94 in *On Humour and the Comic in the Hebrew Bible*. Edited by Yehuda T. Radday and Athalya Brenner. Sheffield: Almond, 1990.
Lewis, James R., and Olav Hammer, eds. *The Invention of Sacred Tradition*. Cambridge: Cambridge University Press, 2007.
Lewis, Naphtali. "The Romanity of Roman Egypt: A Growing Consensus." Pages 1077–84 in *Atti del XVII Congresso internazionale di Papirologia*. Napoli: Centro Inernazionale per li Studio dei Papiri Ercolanesi, 1984.

Lieu, Judith M. "The 'Attraction of Women' in/to Early Judaism and Christianity: Gender and the Politics of Conversion." *JSNT* 21.72 (1999): 5–22.

Liew, Tat-Siong. *The Politics of Parouisa: Reading Mark Inter(Con)textually.* Leiden: Brill, 1999.

Lincoln, Bruce. *Discourse and the Construction of Society: Comparative Studies of Myth, Ritual, and Classification.* New York: Oxford University Press, 1989.

Logan, Alastair H. B. "Origen (c. 185–254)." Pages 170–86 in *The Blackwell Companion to the Theologians*. Edited by Ian S. Markham. Oxford: Blackwell, 2009.

Löhr, Winrich. "Christianity as Philosophy: Problems and Perspectives of an Ancient Intellectual Project." *VC* 64 (2010): 160–88.

Lopez, Davina C. *Apostle to the Conquered: Reimagining Paul's Mission.* Minneapolis: Fortress, 2008.

Ludlow, Jared W. *Abraham Meets Death: Narrative Humor in the Testament of Abraham.* Sheffield: Sheffield Academic, 2002.

Luke, Trevor S. "The Parousia of Paul at Iconium." *R&T* 15.3 (2008): 225–51.

MacDonald, Dennis R. *The Acts of Andrew and the Acts of Andrew and Matthias in the City of the Cannibals.* SBLTT 33. Christian Apocrypha 1. Atlanta: Scholars Press, 1990.

———. *Christianizing Homer: The Odyssey, Plato, and the Acts of Andrew.* Oxford: Oxford University Press, 1994.

———. *Does the New Testament Imitate Homer? Four Cases from the Acts of the Apostles.* New Haven: Yale University Press, 2003.

———. *The Legend and the Apostle: The Battle for Paul in Story and Canon.* Philadelphia: Westminster, 1983.

MacLean, Jennifer K. Berenson, and Ellen Bradshaw Aitken. *Flavius Philostratus: Heroikos.* WGRW 1. Atlanta: Society of Biblical Literature, 2001.

MacMullen, Ramsay. *Romanization in the Time of Augustus.* New Haven: Yale University Press, 2000.

Maier, Harry O. "Vision, Visualisation, and Politics in the Apostle Paul." *MTSR* 27 (2015): 312–32.

Makowski, John F. "Greek Love in the Greek Novel." Pages 490–501 in *A Companion to the Ancient Novel*. Edited by Edmund P. Cueva and Shannon N. Byrne. Chichester, UK: Wiley-Blackwell, 2014.

Marcus, Joel. *Mark 1–8: A New Translation with Introduction and Commentary.* AB 27. New York: Doubleday, 2000.
Markschies, Christoph. *Hellenisierung des Christentums: Sinn und Unsinn einer historischen Deutungskategorie.* Leipzig: Evangelische Verlagsanstalt, 2012.
Marrou, Henri-Irénée. *A History of Education in Antiquity.* Translated by George Lamb. Madison: University of Wisconsin Press, 1982.
———. "Synesius of Cyrene and Alexandrian Neoplatonism." Pages 126–50 in *The Conflict of Paganism and Christianity in the Fourth Century.* Edited by Arnaldo Momigliano. Oxford: Clarendon, 1963.
Marshall, John W. "Sexual Violence—Roman World." Pages 360–66 in vol. 2 of *Oxford Encyclopedia of Bible and Gender Studies.* Oxford: Oxford University Press, 2014.
Mason, Steve. "Figured Speech and Irony in T. Flavius Josephus." Pages 244–88 in *Flavius Josephus and Flavian Rome.* Edited by Jonathan Edmondson, Steve Mason, and James Rives. New York: Oxford University Press, 2005.
———. "Flavius Josephus in Flavian Rome: Reading on and between the Lines." Pages 559–90 in *Flavian Rome: Culture, Image, Text.* Edited by A. J. Boyle and W. J. Dominik. Leiden: Brill, 2003.
Matthews, Shelly. *Acts of the Apostles: Taming the Tongues of Fire.* Sheffield Guides to the New Testament 5. Sheffield: Sheffield Phoenix, 2013.
———. *Perfect Martyr: The Stoning of Stephen and the Construction of Christian Identity.* Oxford: Oxford University Press, 2010.
———. "Thinking of Thecla: Issues in Feminist Historiography." *JFSR* 17 (2001): 29–55.
———. "The Weeping Jesus and the Daughters of Jerusalem: Gender and Conquest in Lukan Lament." Pages 385–403 in *Doing Gender—Doing Religion: Fallstudien zur Intersektionalität im frühen Judentum, Christentum und Islam.* Edited by Christine Gerber, Ute E. Eisen, and Angela Standhartinger. WUNT 302. Tübingen: Mohr Siebeck, 2013.
May, Regine. "Medicine and the Novel: Apuleius' Bonding with the Educated Reader." Pages 105–24 in *The Ancient Novel and the Frontiers of Genre: Fluid Texts.* Edited by Marília P. Futre-Pinheiro, Gareth Schmeling, and Edmund Cueva. Ancient Narrative Supplementum 18. Groningen: Barkhuis, 2014.
McCracken, David. "Narration and Comedy in the Book of Tobit." *JBL* 114 (1995): 401–18.

McLaren, James S. "Ananus, James, and Earliest Christianity: Josephus' Account of the Death of James." *JTS* 52 (2001): 1–25.

McWhirter, Jocelyn. "Messianic Exegesis in Mark's Passion Narrative." Pages 69–97 in *The Trial and Death of Jesus: Essays on the Passion Narrative of Mark*. Edited by Geert van Oyen and Tom Shepherd. Leuven: Peeters, 2006.

Meggitt, Justin J. *Paul, Poverty and Survival*. Edinburgh: T&T Clark, 1998.

Meister, Ferdinand. *Daretis Phrygii De Excidio Troiae Historia*. Leipzig: Teubner, 1873.

Merkle, Stefan. "'Artless and Abrupt'? Bemerkungen zur 'Ephemeris belli Troiani' des Diktys von Kreta." Pages 79–90 in vol. 3 of *Groningen Colloquia on the Novel*. Edited by Heinz Hofmann. Groningen: Forsten, 1990.

———. *Die Ephemeris belli Troiani des Diktys von Kreta*. Studien zur klassischen Philologie 44. Frankfurt am Main: Lang, 1989.

———. "News from the Past: Dictys and Dares on the Trojan War." Pages 155–66 in *Latin Fiction: The Latin Novel in Context*. Edited by Heinz Hofmann. London: Routledge, 1999.

———. "Telling the True Story of the Trojan War: The Eyewitness Account of Dictys of Crete." Pages 183–96 in *The Search for the Ancient Novel*. Edited by James Tatum. Baltimore: Johns Hopkins University Press, 1994.

———. "*Troiani belli verior textus*. Die Trojaberichte des Dictys und Dares." Pages 491–522 in *Die deutsche Trojaliteratur des Mittelalters und der frühen Neuzeit: Materialien und Untersuchungen*. Edited by Horst Brunner. Wiesbaden: Reichert, 1990.

———. "The Truth and Nothing but the Truth: Dictys and Dares." Pages 563–80 in *The Novel in the Ancient World*. Edited by Gareth Schmeling. Rev. ed. Leiden: Brill, 2003.

Metzger, Bruce M., and Roland E. Murphy, eds. *The New Oxford Annotated Apocrypha, New Revised Standard Version*. Oxford: Oxford University Press, 1991.

Moore, Stephen D. *Empire and Apocalypse: Postcolonialism and the New Testament*. Sheffield: Sheffield Phoenix, 2006.

Moreland, Milton. "Jerusalem Destroyed: The Setting of Acts." Pages 17–44 in *Engaging Early Christian History: Reading Acts in the Second Century*. Edited by Rubén R. Dupertuis and Todd Penner. Durham, UK: Acumen, 2014.

Morgan, John R. "Introduction." Pages 1–12 in *Greek Fiction: The Greek Novel in Context*. Edited by J. R. Morgan and Richard Stoneman. London: Routledge, 1994.

———. "Lucian's *True Histories* and the *Wonders beyond Thule* of Antonius Diogenes." *CQ* 35 (1985): 475–90.

———. "Make-Believe and Make Believe: The Fictionality of the Greek Novels." Pages 175–229 in *Lies and Fiction in the Ancient World*. Edited by Christopher Gill and T. P. Wiseman. Austin: University of Texas Press, 1993.

Morgan, Teresa. *Popular Morality in the Early Roman Empire*. Cambridge: Cambridge University Press, 2007.

Mosala, Itumeleng J. "The Implications of the Text of Esther for African's Women's Struggle for Liberation in South Africa." *Semeia* 59 (1992): 129–37.

Mount, Christopher. "Constructing Paul as a Christian in the Acts of the Apostles." Pages 141–52 in *Engaging Early Christian History: Reading Acts in the Second Century*. Edited by Rubén R. Duptertuis and Todd Penner. Durham, UK: Acumen, 2013.

Naumann, R., Kenan T. Erim, Hatice Gonnet, Jacques Cauvin, Olivier Aurenche, H. Vetters, Selahattin Erdemgil, et al. "Recent Archaeological Research in Turkey." *Anatolian Studies* 31 (1981): 177–208.

Nauta, Ruurd. "The Concept of 'Metalepsis': From Rhetoric to the Theory of Allusion and to Narratology." Pages 469–82 in *Über die Grenze: Metalepse in Text- und Bildmedien des Altertums*. Edited by Ute E. Eisen and Peter von Möllendorff. Berlin: de Gruyter, 2013.

Neuschäfer, Bernhard. "Zur Bewertung des Origenes bei Sokrates." Pages 71–95 in *Die Welt des Sokrates von Konstantinopel*. Edited by Balbina Bäbler and Heinz-Gunther Nesselrath. Munich: Saur, 2001.

Ní Mheallaigh, Karen. *Reading Fiction with Lucian: Fakes, Freaks and Hyperreality*. Cambridge: Cambridge University Press, 2014.

Nickelsburg, George W. E. "Introduction." Pages 1–14 in *Studies on the Testament of Joseph*. Edited by George W. E. Nickelsburg. SCS 5. Missoula, MT: Scholars Press, 1975.

Niehoff, Maren. "Philo and Plutarch as Biographers: Parallel Responses to Roman Stoicism." *GRBS* 52 (2012): 361–92.

———. *Philo on Jewish Identity and Culture*. TSAJ 86. Tübingen: Mohr Siebeck, 2001.

———. "Philo's *Exposition* in a Roman Context." *SPhiloA* 23 (2011): 1–21.

———. "The Symposium of Philo's Therapeutae: Displaying Jewish Identity in an Increasingly Roman World." *GRBS* 50 (2010): 95–117.
Nuffelen, Peter van. "Two Fragments from the Apology for Origen in the Church History of Socrates Scholasticus." *JTS* 56 (2005): 103–14.
———. *Un héritage de paix et de piété*. Leuven: Peeters, 2004.
Omerzu, Heike. "The Portrayal of Paul's Outer Appearance in the Acts of Paul and Thecla: Re-Considering the Correspondence between Body and Personality in Ancient Literature." *R&T* 3.4 (2008): 252–79.
Origen. *Contra Celsum*. Translated by Henry Chadwick. Cambridge: Cambridge University Press, 1965.
Östenberg, Ida. *Staging the World: Spoils, Captives, and Representations in the Roman Triumphal Procession*. Oxford: Oxford University Press, 2009.
Ostrowski, Janusz A. "Personifications of Countries and Cities as a Symbol of Victory in Greek and Roman Art." Pages 264–72 in *Griechenland und Rom: Vergleichende Untersuchungen zu Entwicklungstendenzen und- Hohenpunkten der antiken Geschichte, Kunst und Literatur*. Edited by Manfred Fuhrmann, Rismag Gordesiani, Christian Meier, and Ernst Gunther Schmidt. Tbilisi: Universitatsverlag Tbilissi in Verbindung mit der Palm & Enke, 1996.
———. "Simulacra Barbarorum: Some Questions of Roman Personifications." Pages 566–67 in *Akten des XIII Internationalen Kongresses für Klassische Archäologie Berlin 1988*. Mainz: von Zabern, 1990.
Overbeck, Franz. *Das Johannesevangelium: Studien zur Kritik seiner Erforschung*. Tübingen: Mohr, 1911.
Parker, Jan, Ellie Chambers, Mary Huber, and Alison Phipps. "Editorial: Boundaries, Signature Pedagogies and Theorizing." *Arts & Humanities in Higher Education* 7.2 (2008): 115–16.
Paton, Lewis B. *A Critical and Exegetical Commentary on the Book of Esther*. ICC. Edinburgh: T&T Clark, 1908.
Penner, Todd C. *In Praise of Christian Origins: Stephen and the Hellenists in Lukan Apologetic Historiography*. New York: T&T Clark, 2004.
Percy, William Armstrong. *Pederasty and Pedagogy in Archaic Greece*. Urbana: University of Illinois Press, 1996.
———. "Reconsiderations about Greek Homosexualities," Pages 13–62 in *Same-Sex Desire and Love in Greco-Roman Antiquity and in the Classical Tradition of the West*. Edited by Beert C. Verstraete and Vernon Provencal. Binghamton, NY: Haworth, 2006.

Perkins, Judith. "Fictive 'Scheintod' and Christian Resurrection." *R&T* 13 (2006): 396–418.

———. *Roman Imperial Identities in the Early Christian Era*. London: Routledge, 2009.

Perry, Ben E. *The Ancient Romances: A Literary-Historical Account of Their Origins*. Berkeley: University of California Press, 1967.

Perucho, Juan. *Natural History*. Translated by David H. Rosenthal. London: Minerva, 1990.

Pervo, Richard I. *Acts: A Commentary*. Edited by Harold W. Attridge. Hermeneia. Minneapolis: Fortress, 2009.

———. *The Acts of Paul: A New Translation with Introduction and Commentary*. Eugene, OR: Cascade Books, 2014.

———. "Dare and Back: The Stories of Xanthippe and Polyxena." Pages 161–204 in *Early Christian and Jewish Narrative: The Role of Religion in Shaping Narrative Forms*. Edited by Ilaria Ramelli and Judith Perkins. WUNT 348. Tübingen: Mohr Siebeck, 2015.

———. *Dating Acts: Between the Evangelists and the Apologists*. Santa Rosa, CA: Polebridge, 2006.

———. *Profit with Delight: The Literary Genre of the Acts of the Apostles*. Philadelphia: Fortress, 1987.

———. "Thecla Wove This Web, or, Some Things I Learned from Attempting to Write a Commentary on the Acts of Paul." Paper presented at the Annual Meeting of the Society of Biblical Literature. Chicago, November 17, 2012.

Pesch, Rudolf. *Das Markusevangelium. I. Teil: Einleitung und Kommentar zu Kap. 1,1–8,26*. HThKNT 2.1. Freiburg: Herder, 1980.

Philo. *On the Life of Abraham*. Translated by F. H. Colson. LCL. Cambridge: Harvard University Press, 1935.

———. *On the Life of Moses*. Translated by F. H. Colson. LCL. Cambridge: Harvard University Press, 1935.

Pietersma, Albert, and Benjamin G. Wright, eds. *A New English Translation of the Septuagint*. Oxford: Oxford University Press, 2007.

Plato. *Lysis; Symposium; Gorgias*. Vol. 3 of *Plato*. Translated by W. R. M. Lamb. LCL 166. Cambridge: Harvard University Press, 1925.

———. *Plato's Phaedrus*. Translated by R. Hackforth. Cambridge: Cambridge University Press, 1952.

Pliny the Younger. *Letters and Paegyricus*. Translated by Betty Radice. 2 vols. LCL. Cambridge: Harvard University Press, 1969.

Plutarch. *Isis and Osiris*. Vol. 5 of *Moralia*. Translated by Frank Cole Babbitt. LCL. Cambridge: Harvard University Press, 1936.
Possamai, Adam, and Alphia Possamai-Inesedy. "Battlefield Earth and Scientology: A Cultural/Religious Industry à la Frankfurt School." Pages 583–98 in *Handbook of New Religions and Cultural Production*. Edited by Carole M. Cusack and Alex Norman. Brill Handbooks on Contemporary Religion 4. Leiden: Brill, 2012.
Price, Jonathan J. "The Provincial Historian in Rome." Pages 101–18 in *Josephus and Jewish History in Flavian Rome and Beyond*. Edited by Joseph Sievers and Gaia Lembi. Leiden: Brill, 2005.
Punter, David, ed. *A New Companion to the Gothic*. Blackwell Companions to Literature and Culture. Oxford: Blackwell, 2012.
Quint, David. *Epic and Empire: Politics and Generic Form from Virgil to Milton*. Princeton: Princeton University Press, 1993.
Ramelli, Ilaria L. E. *The Christian Doctrine of Apokatastasis: A Critical Assessment from the New Testament to Eriugena*. Leiden: Brill, 2013.
———. "Decadence Denounced in the Controversy over Origen: Giving Up Direct Reading of Sources and Counteractions." Pages 263–83 in *Décadence: "Decline and Fall" or "Other Antiquity"?* Edited by Therese Fuhrer and Marco Formisano. Heidelberg: Winter, 2014.
———. "*Ethos* and *Logos*: A Second-Century Apologetic Debate between 'Pagan' and Christian Philosophers." *VC* 69 (2015): 123–56.
———. "Origen, Patristic Philosophy, and Christian Platonism: Re-thinking the Christianization of Hellenism." *VC* 63 (2009): 217–63.
———. "Origen the Christian Middle/Neoplatonist." *Journal of Early Christian History* 1 (2011): 98–130.
———. "Origen's Allegoresis of Plato's and Scripture's Myths." Pages 85–106 in *Religious Competition in the Greco-Roman World*. Edited by Nathaniel P. Desrosiers and Lily C. Vuong. WGRWSup 10. Atlanta: SBL Press, 2016.
———. "Origen's Anti-subordinationism and Its Heritage in the Nicene and Cappadocian Line." *VC* 65 (2011): 21–49.
———. "Patristic Exegesis' Relevance to Contemporary Biblical Hermeneutics." *R&T* 22 (2015): 100–132.
———. *Social Justice and the Legitimacy of Slavery: The Role of Philosophical Asceticism from Ancient Judaism to Late Antiquity*. Oxford: Oxford University Press, 2017.

Ramsby, Teresa R., and Beth Severy-Hoven. "Gender, Sex, and the Domestication of the Empire in Art of the Augustan Age." *Arethusa* 40 (2007): 43–71.

Reed, Annette Yoshiko. "The Construction and Subversion of Patriarchal Perfection: Abraham and Exemplarity in Philo, Josephus, and the *Testament of Abraham*." *JSJ* 40 (2009): 185–212.

Rehak, Paul. *Imperium and Cosmos: Augustus and the Northern Campus Martius*. Madison: University of Wisconsin Press, 2009.

Reiser, Marius. "Der Alexanderroman und das Markusevanelium." Pages 131–64 in *Markus-Philologie*. Edited by Hubert Cancik. Tübingen: Mohr Siebeck, 1984.

———. *Syntax and Stil des Markusevangeliums im Licht der hellenistichen Volksliteratur*. Tübingen: Mohr Siebeck, 1984.

Resch, Robert P. *Althusser and the Renewal of Marxist Social Theory*. Berkeley: University of California Press, 1992.

Reynolds, Joyce M. "Further Information on Imperial Cult at Aphrodisias." *Studii clasice* 24 (1986): 109–17.

———. "New Evidence for the Imperial Cult in Julio-Claudian Aphrodisias." *ZPE* 43 (1981): 317–27.

Rhoads, David, Joanna Dewey, and Donald Michie. *Mark as Story: An Introduction to the Narrative of a Gospel*. 2nd ed. Minneapolis: Fortress, 1999.

Richlin, Amy. *The Garden of Priapus: Sexuality and Aggression in Roman Humor*. New Haven: Yale University Press, 1983.

Rimmon-Kenan, Shlomith. *Narrative Fiction: Contemporary Poetics*. London: Routledge, 2002.

Roemer, Michael. *Telling Stories: Postmodernism and the Invalidation of Traditional Narrative*. Lanham, MD: Rowman & Littlefield, 1995.

Roitman, Adolfo. "Achior in the Book of Judith: His Role and Significance." Pages 31–46 in *"No One Spoke Ill of Her": Essays on Judith*. Edited by James C. VanderKam. EJL 2. Atlanta: Scholars Press, 1992.

Roller, Matthew. "The Consul(ar) as *exemplum*: Fabius Cunctator's Paradoxical Glory." Pages 182–210 in *Consuls and "Res Publica": Holding High Office in the Roman Republic*. Edited by Hans Beck, Antonio Duplá, Martin Jehne, and Francisco Pina Polo. Cambridge: Cambridge University Press, 2011.

———. "Exemplarity in Roman Culture: The Cases of Horatius Cocles and Cloelia." *CP* 99 (2004): 1–56.

———. "The Exemplary Past in Roman Historiography and Culture: The Case of Gaius Duilius." Pages 214–30 in *The Cambridge Companion to Roman Historiography and Culture*. Edited by Andrew Feldherr. Cambridge: Cambridge University Press, 2009.

Roncace, Mark, and Patrick Gray, eds. *Teaching the Bible: Practical Strategies for Classroom Instruction*. RBS 49. Atlanta: Society of Biblical Literature, 2005.

Rougé, Jean. "La politique de Cyrille d'Alexandrie et le meurtre d'Hypatie." *CNS* 11 (1990): 485–504.

Ryan, Marie-Laure. *Avatars of Story*. Minneapolis: University of Minnesota Press, 2006.

Schäferdiek, Knut. "The Acts of John." Pages 152–212 in *Writings Related to the Apostles, Apocalypses and Related Subjects*. Vol. 2 of *New Testament Apocrypha*. Edited by Wilhelm Schneemelcher. Louisville: Westminster John Knox, 1992.

Scaffai, Marco. "Aspetti e problemi dell'"Ilias Latina."" *ANRW* 32.3:1926–42.

Scheidel, Walter, and Steven J. Friesen. "The Size of the Economy and the Distribution of Income in the Roman Empire." *JRS* 99 (2009): 61–91.

Schetter, Willy. "Beobachtungen zum Dares Latinus." *Hermes* 116 (1988): 94–109.

———. "Dares und Dracontius über die Vorgeschichte des Trojanischen Krieges." *Hermes* 115 (1987): 211–31.

Schneemelcher, Wilhelm. "Introduction: Second and Third Century Acts of the Apostles." Pages 75–86 in *Writings Related to the Apostles, Apocalypses and Related Subjects*. Vol. 2 of *New Testament Apocrypha*. Edited by Wilhelm Schneemelcher. Louisville: Westminster John Knox, 1992.

———, ed. *Writings Related to the Apostles, Apocalypses and Related Subjects*. Vol. 2 of *New Testament Apocrypha*. Loiuseville: Westminster John Knox, 1992.

Scholz, Peter. *Den Vätern folgen: Sozialisation und Erziehung der republikanischen Senatsaristokratie*. Berlin: Verlag Antike, 2011.

Schwartz, Saundra. "From Bedroom to Courtroom: The Adultery Type-Scene and the Acts of Andrew." Pages 267–312 in *Mapping Gender in Ancient Religious Discourses*. Edited by Todd C. Penner and Caroline Vander Stichele. Leiden: Brill, 2007.

———. "The Trial Scene in the Greek Novels and in Acts." Pages 105–33 in *Contextualizing Acts: Lukan Narrative and Greco-Roman Discourse*.

Edited by Todd C. Penner and Caroline Vander Stichele. SBLSymS 20. Atlanta: Society of Biblical Literature, 2003.

Schwartz, Seth. *Imperialism and Jewish Society 200 B.C.E. to 640 C.E.* Princeton: Princeton University Press, 2001.

———. *Were the Jews a Mediterranean Society? Reciprocity and Solidarity in Ancient Judaism.* Princeton: Princeton University Press, 2010.

Schwiebert, Jonathan D. "Jesus' Question to Pilate in Mark 15:2." *JBL* 136 (2017): 937–47.

Scott, Joan W. "Gender: A Useful Category of Historical Analysis." *AHR* 91 (1986): 1053–75.

Sebesta, Judith Lynn, and Larissa Bonfante. *The World of Roman Costume.* Madison: University of Wisconsin Press, 2001.

Segovia, Fernando F. *Decolonizing Biblical Studies: A View from the Margins.* Maryknoll, NY: Orbis Books, 2000.

Seng, Helmut, and Lars Hoffmann, eds. *Synesios von Kyrene: Politik, Literatur, Philosophie.* Turnhout: Brepols, 2013.

Shapira, Yona. "A Postmodernist Reading of the Biblical Book of Esther: From Cultural Disintegration to Carnivalesque Texts." PhD diss., SUNY Stony Brook, 1996.

Shepherd, Tom. "The Irony of Power in the Trial of Jesus and the Denial by Peter: Mark 14:53–72." Pages 229–45 in *The Trial and Death of Jesus: Essays on the Passion Narrative of Mark.* Edited by Geert van Oyen and Tom Shepherd. Leuven: Peeters, 2006.

Sipress, Joel M., and David J. Voelker. "From Learning History to Doing History: Beyond the Coverage Model." Pages 19–35 in *Exploring Signature Pedagogies: Approaches to Teaching Disciplinary Habits of Mind.* Edited by Regan A. R. Gurung, Nancy L. Chick, and Aeron Haynie. Sterling, VA: Stylus, 2009.

Slater, Niall. "Space and Displacement in Apuleius's *Golden Ass.*" Pages 161–76 in *Space in the Ancient Narrative.* Ancient Narrative Supplementum 1. Groningen: Barkhuis Publishing and the University Library Groningen, 2002.

Sly, Dorothy. *Philo's Alexandria.* New York: Routledge, 1996.

Smid, Harm Reinder. *Protevangelium Jacobi: A Commentary.* Assen: Van Gorcum, 1965.

Smith, Daniel Lynwood. *The Rhetoric of Interruption: Speech-Making, Turn-Taking, and Rule-Breaking in Luke-Acts and Ancient Greek Narrative.* BZNW 193. Berlin: de Gruyter, 2012.

Smith, R. R. R. "The Imperial Reliefs from the Sebasteion at Aphrodisias." *JRS* 77 (1987): 88–138.

———. "Myth and Allegory in the Sebasteion." Pages 89–100 in *Aphrodisias Papers: Recent Work on Architecture and Sculpture*. Edited by Kenan T. Erim and Charlotte Roueché. Journal of Roman Archaeology Supplement Series. Ann Arbor: University of Michigan Press, 1990.

———. "Simulacra Gentium: The Ethne from the Sebasteion at Aphrodisias." *JRS* 78 (1988): 50–77.

Smith, Stephen H. *A Lion with Wings: A Narrative-Critical Approach to Mark's Gospel*. Sheffield: Sheffield Academic, 1996.

Snyder, Glenn E. *Acts of Paul: The Formation of a Pauline Corpus*. WUNT 2/352. Tübingen: Mohr Siebeck, 2013.

Söder, Rosa. *Die apokryphen Apostelgeschichten und die romanhafte Literatur der Antike*. Stuttgart: Kohlhammer, 1932.

Spannagel, Martin. *Exemplaria principis: Untersuchungen zu Entstehung und Ausstattung des Augustusforums*. Heidelberg: Verlag Archäologie und Geschichte, 1999.

Speyer, Wolfgang. *Bücherfunde in der Glaubenswerbung der Antike*. Hypomenemata 24. Göttingen: Vandenhoeck & Ruprecht, 1970.

Stoneman, Richard. "The Alexander Romance: From History to Fiction." Pages 117–29 in *Greek Fiction: The Greek Novel in Context*. Edited by J. R. Morgan and Richard Stoneman. London: Routledge, 1994.

Szepessy, Tibor. "Narrative Model of the *Acta Xanthippae et Polyxenae*." *Acta Antiqua Academiae Scientiarum Hungaricae* 44 (2004): 317–40.

Temelini, Mark A. "Pompey's Politics and the Presentation of His Theatre-Temple Complex, 61–52 BCE." *Studia Humaniora Tartuensia* 7 (2006): 1–14.

Thomas, Christine. *The Acts of Peter, Gospel Literature, and the Ancient Novel*. Oxford: Oxford University Press, 2003.

Thurman, Eric. "Novel Men: Masculinity and Empire in Mark's Gospel and Xenophon's An Ephesian Tale." Pages 185–230 in *Mapping Gender in Ancient Religious Discourses*. Edited by Todd Penner and Caroline Vander Stichele. Leiden: Brill, 2007.

Toit, David du. "Entgrenzungen: Zu metaleptischen Strategien in der frühchristlichen Erzählliteratur." Pages 292–317 in *Über die Grenze: Metalepse in Text- und Bildmedien des Altertums*. Edited by Ute E. Eisen and Peter von Möllendorff. Berlin: de Gruyter, 2013.

Tolbert, Mary Ann. *Sowing the Gospel: Mark's World in Literary-Historical Perspective*. Minneapolis: Fortress, 1989.

Toohey, Peter. "Love, Lovesickness, and Melancholia." *Illinois Classical Studies* 17 (1992): 265–86.

———. *Melancholy, Love, and Time: Boundaries of the Self in Ancient Literature*. Ann Arbor: University of Michigan Press, 2004.

Toynbee, Jocelyn M. C. *The Hadrianic School: A Chapter in the History of Greek Art*. Cambridge: Cambridge University Press, 1934.

Urbainczyk, Theresa. *Socrates of Constantinople: Historian of Church and State*. Ann Arbor: University of Michigan Press, 1997.

Urbano, Arthur. *The Philosophical Life: Biography and the Crafting of Intellectual Identity in Late Antiquity*. Washington, DC: Catholic University of America Press, 2013.

Valerius Maximus. *Memorable Doings and Sayings*. Translated by Shackleton Bailey. 2 vols. LCL. Cambridge: Harvard University Press, 2000.

Vander Stichele, Caroline, and Todd Penner. *Contextualizing Gender in Early Christian Discourse: Thinking beyond Thecla*. London: T&T Clark, 2009.

Vermeule, Cornelius. "The Colossus of Porto Raphti: A Roman Female Personification." *Hesperia* 45 (1976): 67–76.

Vines, Michael. *The Problem of Markan Genre: The Gospel of Mark and the Jewish Novel*. Atlanta: Society of Biblical Literature, 2002.

Waddell, Helen. *The Wandering Scholars: The Life and Art of the Lyric Poets of the Latin Middle Ages*. Garden City, NY: Doubleday, 1961.

Wallraff, Martin. *Der Kirchenhistoriker Sokrates: Untersuchungen zu Geschichtsdarstellung, Methode und Person*. Göttingen: Vandenhoeck & Ruprecht, 1997.

Walter, Uwe. *Memoria und Res Publica: Zur Geschichtskultur im republikanischen Rom*. Studien zur alten Geschichte 1. Frankfurt am Main: Verlag Antike, 2004.

Watts, Edward J. *Hypatia: The Life and Legend of an Ancient Philosopher*. Oxford: Oxford University Press, 2017.

———. "The Murder of Hypatia: Acceptable or Unacceptable Violence?" Pages 333–42 in *Violence in Late Antiquity: Perceptions and Practices*. Edited by Harold Drake. Burlington, VT: Ashgate, 2006.

Whedbee, J. William. *The Bible and the Comic Vision*. Cambridge: Cambridge University Press, 1998.

White, Hayden. "The Discourse of History." Pages 187–202 in *The Fiction of Narrative: Essays on History, Literature, and Theory 1957–2007*. Edited by Robert Doran. Baltimore: Johns Hopkins University Press, 2010.

Whitmarsh, Tim. *Narrative and Identity in the Ancient Greek Novel: Returning Romance.* Cambridge: Cambridge University Press, 2011.

Williams, Craig. *Reading Roman Friendship.* Cambridge: Cambridge University Press, 2012.

Wills, Lawrence. *The Jewish Novel in the Ancient World.* Ithaca, NY: Cornell University Press, 1995.

———. "Jewish Novellas in a Greek and Roman Age: Fiction and Identity." *JSJ* 42 (2011): 158.

———. *The Quest for the Historical Gospel: Mark, John, and the Origins of the Gospel Genre.* London: Routledge, 1997.

Wiseman, T. P. "Lying Historians: Seven Types of Mendacity." Pages 122–46 in *Lies and Fiction in the Ancient World.* Edited by Christopher Gill and T. P. Wiseman. Austin: University of Texas Press, 1993.

Xenophon of Ephesus. *Longus: Daphnis and Chloe and Xenophon of Ephesus; Anthia and Habrocomes.* Edited and translated by Jeffrey Henderson. LCL 69. Cambridge: Harvard University Press, 2009.

Zafón, Carlos Ruiz. *The Angel's Game.* Translated by Lucia Graves. London: Weidenfeld & Nicholson, 2009.

———. *The Prisoner of Heaven.* Translated by Lucia Graves. London: Weidenfeld & Nicolson, 2013.

———. *The Shadow of the Wind.* Translated by Lucia Graves. London: Weidenfeld & Nicolson, 2005.

Contributors

Virginia Burrus (mvburrus@syr.edu) is The Bishop W. Earl Ledden Professor of Religion at Syracuse University, where she has taught since 2013; prior to that, she taught for twenty-two years at Drew Theological School. Her publications engage late ancient Christian literature and theology and include *The Sex Lives of Saints: An Erotics of Ancient Hagiography* (2004); *Saving Shame: Martyrs, Saints, and Other Abject Subjects* (2008); *Seducing Augustine: Bodes, Desires, Confessions* (with Mark Jordan and Karmen MacKendrick) (2010); *The Life of Saint Helia: Critical Edition, Translation, Introduction, and Commentary* (with Marco Conti) (2014); and *Ancient Ecopoetics* (forthcoming). Burrus is past president of the North American Patristics Society and coeditor of the Penn Press series Divinations: Rereading Late Ancient Religion.

Christy Cobb (c.cobb@wingate.edu) is Assistant Professor of Religion at Wingate University in North Carolina. She holds a PhD from Drew University, where she focused on New Testament and Early Christianity. Her research interests include ancient fiction, slavery in the Greco-Roman world, and gender and sexuality in early Christianity. In addition to serving on the steering committee of the Ancient Fiction section of the Society of Biblical Literature, Christy is a member of the editorial board for the *Journal of Feminist Studies in Religion*. She is currently completing a book on female slaves in Luke-Acts and other ancient narratives.

Rubén R. Dupertuis (rdupertu@trinity.edu) is Associate Professor of Religion in the Religion Department at Trinity University. He is the author of several essays and articles and the coeditor of *Engaging Early Christian History: Reading Acts in the Second Century* (2013).

Ute E. Eisen (eisen@evtheologie.uni-giessen.de) is Professor of Old and New Testament at the Institute for Protestant Theology at Justus-Liebig-

University Giessen (Germany). She is author of *Women Officeholders in Early Christianity: Epigraphic and Literary Studies* (2000) and *Die Poetik der Apostelgeschichte: Eine narratologische Studie* (2006), and coeditor of *Doing Gender—Doing Religion: Fallstudien zur Intersektionalität im frühen Judentum, Christentum und Islam* (2013), *Über die Grenze: Metalepse in Text- und Bildmedien des Altertums* (2013), and *Gott als Figur: Narratologische Analysen biblischer Texte und ihrer Rezeption* (2016). Currently she is coediting *Schrift im Streit—Jüdische, christliche und muslimische Perspektiven: Auf dem Weg zu einer interrelgiösen Hermeneutik* (2018).

Scott S. Elliott (selliott@adrian.edu) is Associate Professor in the Department of Philosophy and Religion at Adrian College. He is the author of *Reconfiguring Mark's Jesus: Narrative Criticism after Poststructuralism* (2011) and has contributed to *The Oxford Handbook of Biblical Narrative*, edited by Danna Nolan Fewell (2016), and to *The Oxford Handbook to the Bible in American Popular Culture*, edited by Dan W. Clanton Jr. and Terry Ray Clark (forthcoming). He is currently writing a book on biographical narratives in the letters of Paul in conversation with the work of Roland Barthes that will be published by Bloomsbury T&T Clark.

Gerhard van den Heever (vdheega@unisa.ac.za) is Professor of New Testament and Early Christian Studies at the University of South Africa, Pretoria. His graduate training was in Religious Studies (specifically history of religion) with a master's thesis on the motif of conflagration as index of syncretistic patterns between Zoroastrian, early Jewish, and early Christian apocalypticism. His PhD thesis investigated ancient Greek romances and mystery religions of the early imperial era. He is also long-standing editor of *Religion and Theology: A Journal of Contemporary Religious Discourse* and is current chair of the Greco-Roman Religions Section of the Society of Biblical Literature. Recent research interests include transdisciplinary and cross-cultural comparative theorizing of cult foundations and new religious movements with reference to Christian origins, critical spatiality theory and religious literature, comparative theorizing of religious violence, and conversion in mystery religions.

Sara R. Johnson (sara.johnson@uconn.edu) is Associate Professor of Classics and Ancient Mediterranean Studies in the Department of Literatures, Cultures, and Languages at the University of Connecticut. Her publications include *Historical Fictions and Hellenistic Jewish Identity: Third*

Maccabees in Its Cultural Context (2004). Her current long-term project is a comparative study of historical fictions in the Greek-speaking Mediterranean and Heian Japan.

David Konstan (david_konstan@brown.edu) is Professor of Classics at New York University. His interests embrace classical Greek and Roman literature and philosophy, with a special focus on comedy and the novel, Epicureanism, Aristotle, and the history of emotions and value concepts. Among his publications are *Sexual Symmetry: Love in the Ancient Novel and Related Genres* (1994); *Greek Comedy and Ideology* (1995); *Friendship in the Classical World* (1997); *Pity Transformed* (2001); *The Emotions of the Ancient Greeks: Studies in Aristotle and Classical Literature* (2006); *"A Life Worthy of the Gods": The Materialist Psychology of Epicurus* (2008); *Before Forgiveness: The Origins of a Moral Idea* (2010); and *Beauty: The Fortunes of an Ancient Greek Idea* (2014). He is a past president of the American Philological Association (now the Society for Classical Studies) and a vice president of the Bristol Institute of Greece, Rome and the Classical Tradition. He is a fellow of the American Academy of Arts and Sciences and an honorary fellow of the Australian Academy of the Humanities.

B. Diane Lipsett (diane.lipsett@salem.edu) is Associate Professor of Religion at Salem College. She is the author of *Desiring Conversion: Hermas, Thecla, Aseneth* (2011) and coeditor with Phyllis Trible of *Faith and Feminism: Ecumenical Essays* (2014). Current teaching interests include early Christian narrative texts and their reception, the Bible and literature, and refugees and immigrants in religious texts and communities. Current research interests include representations of early Christian bodies, of households, and of places and forms of sanctuary in early Christian apocrypha and hagiography.

Jared W. Ludlow (jared_ludlow@byu.edu) is Professor of Ancient Scripture and Ancient Near Eastern Studies at Brigham Young University, where he has taught since 2006. Previously he spent six years teaching religion and history at BYU Hawaii; he also taught two years at the BYU Jerusalem Center for Near Eastern Studies. He received his bachelor's degree from BYU in Near Eastern Studies, his master's degree from the University of California-Berkeley in Biblical Hebrew, and his PhD in Near Eastern Religions from University of California-Berkeley and the Graduate Theological Union. His primary research interests are with texts related to ancient

Judaism and early Christianity. He has published various articles and a book, *Abraham Meets Death: Narrative Humor in the Testament of Abraham* (2002), on narratological topics. He is also the author of a world history textbook, *Revealing World History to 1500 CE* (2016).

Dennis R. MacDonald (dmacdon@cst.edu) is Research Professor of New Testament and Christian Origins at the Claremont School of Theology. His is the author of a dozen books and scores of articles devoted to the Synoptic problem, gospels, and Acts, canonical and apocryphal. He is best known as a pioneer of mimesis criticism and the influence of classical Greek poetry on the gospels and Acts. These publications include *The Gospels and Homer* (2014), *Luke and Vergil* (2014), *Mythologizing Jesus: From Jewish Teacher to Epic Hero* (2014), and *The Dionysian Gospel: The Fourth Gospel and Euripides* (2017). Soon he will complete two more books: *From the Lost Gospel (Q/Q+) to the Gospel of Mark: Solving the Synoptic Problem with Mimesis Criticism*, and *Luke and the Politics of Homeric Imitation: Luke-Acts as a Rival to Vergil's Aeneid*.

John W. Marshall (john.marshall@utoronto.ca) is Associate Professor in the Department for the Study of Religion at the University of Toronto. He is the author of *Parables of War: Reading John's Jewish Apocalypse* (2001) and coeditor (with John Kloppenborg) of *Apocalypticism, Anti-Semitism and the Historical Jesus: Subtexts in Criticism* (2005) as well as articles on Paul, Marcion, postcolonial interpretation, Revelation, Ignatius, and pseudepigraphy. His current focus is on concepts of authorship in the Greco-Roman world.

Shelly Matthews (s.matthews@tcu.edu) is Professor of New Testament at the Brite Divinity School, on the campus of Texas Christian University. Her recent publications include *The Acts of the Apostles: Taming the Tongues of Fire* (2017); *Perfect Martyr: The Stoning of Stephen and the Construction of Christian Identity* (2010); and several articles on early Christian resurrection. She is coeditor, with Melanie Johnson-DeBaufre, of the Feminist Studies in Religion Book Series; and the cofounder and cochair, with Tat-Siong Benny Liew, of the Society of Biblical Literature consultation on Racism, Pedagogy, and Biblical Studies. She is currently working on two book-length projects: a feminist biblical theology of resurrection and a coauthored feminist commentary on the Gospel of Luke.

CONTRIBUTORS 293

Richard I. Pervo devoted his career to studying the early Christian and Jewish writings in their larger cultural contexts. He taught at Seabury-Western Theological Seminary and the University of Minnesota. He is the author of many books, including *Profit with Delight: The Literary Genre of the Acts of the Apostles* (1987), *Dating Acts: Between the Evangelists and the Apologists* (2006), *Acts: A Commentary* (2008), *The Gospel of Luke* (2014), and *The Pastorals and Polycarp* (2016). He passed away on May 20, 2017.

James M. Petitfils (james.m.petitfils@biola.edu) is Assistant Professor of New Testament and Early Christianity at Biola University. His research focuses on Roman spectacles of violence, ancient Christian martyrdom, and discourse on exemplary leadership in the Roman Mediterranean. He is the author of Mos Christianorum: *The Roman Discourse of Exemplarity and the Jewish and Christian Language of Leadership* (2016). He is currently working on a project studying appearance and physiognomic discourse in Roman novels and early Christian martyr texts.

Donald C. Polaski (donaldpolaski@rmc.edu) is Assistant Professor of Religious Studies at Randolph-Macon College in Ashland, Virginia. He is the author of *Authorizing an End: The Isaiah Apocalypse and Intertextuality* (2000) and coauthor of *An Introduction to the Hebrew Bible: A Thematic Approach* (2008). His main interests include the book of Daniel, Persian-period literature, and the development of authoritative textuality in early Judaism. He has published several essays on that subject, including the one in this volume, as well as ones found in *Approaching Yehud: New Approaches to the Study of the Persian Period* (2007), *New Perspectives on Ezra-Nehemiah: Story and History, Literature and Interpretation* (2012), and *Worlds That Could Not Be: Constructing Utopia in Chronicles, Ezra and Nehemiah* (2016).

Ilaria Ramelli (iramelli@princeton.edu) is Full Professor of Theology and K. Britt Chair at the Graduate School of Theology, Sacred Heart Major Seminary, Thomas Aquinas University "Angelicum" (Detroit), and currently holds the position of Senior Fellow at Princeton, at the Institute for Advanced Study (Central European University), and at Oxford University, Christ Church (Fowler Hamilton fellowship). Further positions held have included Professor of Roman Near Eastern History and Fellow in Ancient Philosophy (Catholic University, Milan); Senior Fellow in Ancient and Patristic Philosophy (Durham), in Religion (Erfurt, Max Weber Centre), and in Patristics (Oxford University, Corpus Christi); and Onassis Senior Visiting Professor of Greek Thought (Harvard University and Boston University). She has authored numerous books, articles, and reviews on ancient and patristic philosophy and theology, early Christianity, Jewish-Christian relations, ancient religions, and the relationship between theology and philosophy in "pagan," Jewish, and Christian thought. Among her books are *Hierocles the Stoic* (2009), *Bardaisan of Edessa* (2009), *The Christian Doctrine of Apokatastasis* (2013), *Evagrius' Kephalaia Gnostika* (2015), and *Social Justice and the Legitimacy of Slavery* (2016).

Christine Shea (cshea@bsu.edu) is Professor of Classics in the Department of Modern Languages and Classics at Ball State University. Her publications include, among others, works on the canonical Acts, the Greek romances as models for Christian narratives, and Roman epic and Christian identity.

Brian O. Sigmon (bosigmon@gmail.com) is editor of United Methodist resources at The United Methodist Publishing House, where he edits books, Bible studies, and official resources. Brian is the editor of the *Daily Christian Advocate* and managing editor of the *Book of Discipline* and *Book of Resolutions*. He has a PhD in Hebrew Bible from Marquette University, where he has taught courses in theology. His research interests include the Pentateuch, family conflict in the Bible, Wesleyan approaches to biblical interpretation, and mythic structures in ancient and modern narratives. His passion is making the biblical text accessible to a broad audience and helping people of all backgrounds deepen their understanding of the Bible.

Eric Thurman (etthurma@sewanee.edu) is Associate Professor of Religious Studies at Sewanee: The University of the South. His current research and teaching interests include the reception history of Jesus and the New Testament gospels, the Bible and popular culture, feminist and queer hermeneutics, masculinity studies, postcolonial theory, gender in early Christian literature and Roman imperial culture, and ancient narrative. He has published several essays and chapters on masculinity and male characters in the Bible and is working on a book on the masculinity of Jesus in Mark's Gospel.

Ancient Sources Index

Hebrew Bible/Old Testament

Genesis
24:13	21
24:15–16 LXX	21
27:42	21 n. 28
27:45	21 n. 28
37	139
37:23	151
37:31–33	151
40:14–15	141–42

Exodus
2:10	163
2:11–15	160 n. 26
2:17	163
4:10	162 n. 36
6:12	162 n. 36

Numbers
12:3	160 n. 26

Deuteronomy
34:10–12	160 n. 26

Leviticus
24:16	220

Ruth
1:16 LXX	22

2 Chronicles
24:17–25	221–22
24:21	220
24:22	222, 226
24:23–25	226
24:25	222

Esther
1:1	120
1:8	111 n. 17
1:13	110
1:16–22	114
1:19	108
1:19–20	110
1:20	114
1:22	110, 113–14, 118
2:1	111
2:3	112, 114, 115 n. 30, 116
2.4	115
2:8	115
2:8–9	117
2:9	112 n. 20
2:10	114 n. 29
2:12	112, 116
2:14	116
2:15	117
2:17	115
2:20	115
2:21	109
2:22	109
3:8	112, 119
3:9, 11	112, 113
3:10–15	119–20
3:12	116, 118
3:12–13	113–14
3:14	117
4:1	118
4:3	116, 118
4:8	116

Esther (cont.)		12:6	171 n. 14
4:11	117	12:10	172
6:1–2	109	13:1	172
6:2	117	13:2	173
7:3	119	13:12–13	173
8:8	108 n. 7, 119	13:16	173
8:9	114, 118 n. 41, 120	13:17	173
8:9–14	119	14:6–7	173
8:11	120	14:9–10	173
8:17	120	14:16	173
9:10	121	14:18	174
9:13–14	120	14:19	174
9:14–15	119	15:2	174
9:15, 16	121	15:5, 6	174
9:20–32	108, 119, 121–122		
F:11 LXX	108 n. 8	Tobit	
		1–2	176 n. 22
Psalms		1:17–18	166–67
37:6	18	3	169–70
41:10	81	3:1	169
55:10–11	81	3:6	169
110:1	83, 219 n. 14	3:7–15	169
142:4	18	5:10	169
		5:18–21	170
Daniel		5:23	170
6:8	108 n. 7	7:7–9	170
6:15	108 n. 7	7:17	171
7:13	83	8:9–10	171
		8:18	171
Deuterocanonical Books		10:7	171
		13–14	176 n. 22
Judith			
1:1	167	**Pseudepigrapha**	
4:9–10	172		
4:11–12	172	Joseph and Aseneth	24
5:12	171 n. 14	24–28	139 n. 5
6:9	171 n. 14		
6:18	172	Jubilees	
7:19	172	25:14	21 n. 28
7:22	172		
7:29	172–173	Life of Adam and Eve	
9:1	173	8	259
10:1–2	173	14	259
10:18	173	32	259
10:23	173	33	259

42	259	4.2	143, 148

Testament of Abraham 242–44
1.1–2   167–68
3.6   174
3.7   174
3.9–12 175
5.8–10 175
6.6–7   175
B8   244
A11   242–43
11.6   175
A13   244

Testament of Benjamin
2.1–5   142–43
2.3–5   143

Testament of Dan
1.4–9   141
1.4   145
1.5   139
1.6–8   144

Testament of Gad
1.4–2.5 141
1.4   148–49
1.6–8   146, 148
1.6–9   144–45
2.3   145

Testament of Joseph
3.1–9.5 141
9.4   142
11.2–16.6 141–42
16.5–6   151

Testament of Naphtali
7.2–4   140

Testament of Simeon
2.5–9   139
2.6–13   139–40
2.10–12 146–47
4.1–3   139–40

Testament of Zebulun
1.5–4.13 140–41
1.5   139, 150
1.6–7   148
2.1   143
2.4–6   146–47
4.7–10   143
4.8–13   151
4.11–12   147–48

New Testament

Matthew
9:13   21 n. 27
24:15   94

Mark
1:1–15   77–80, 84 n. 27, 86
2:1–12   6, 92–93
2:10   93 n. 26
2:28   93 n. 26
5:27–28 13
8:27   84
8:29   84
8:31   81, 93 n. 26
8:38   93 n. 26
9:7   84 n. 27
9:9   93 n. 26
9:12   93 n. 26
9:31   81, 93 n. 26
10:32–34 78, 81, 93 n. 26
10:45   93 n. 26
11:27–33 84
12:6   84 n. 27
12:13–17 84
13:3–37 94
13:10   78
13:14   93–94
13:26   93 n. 26
14:1–15 80–86
14:34   94
14:37   94
14:39   80–86

Mark (cont.)		21:24	99–102, 130
14:62–64	219 n. 13		
		Acts	
Luke		1:1	95–96, 213
1:1–4	95–96, 213	6:13–14	217–18
1:4	103	7:41	218 n. 11
11:35	226	7:47–50	218
11:48	222–23, 226	7:51–53	222
11:49–51	222	7:56	227
11:51	226	7:56-58	218
13:34	220, 226	7:58–8:1	222–223
14:16–24	96–97	7:60	227
16:1–9	6	7:60	221
19:44	223–26	8:1	227
21:20	94	11:19	227
22:34	221	11:26	228 n. 24
22:69	226	12	228
23:34	226	16:10–17	95–96
		16:22–38	228
John		20:5–15	95–96
1:1–18	99	21:1–18	95–96
1:14	103	21:31–36	228
1:14–16	98	22:24–25	228
1:17	103	23:12–15	225 n. 23
1:18	100	23:17–31	228
1:21	98	26:28	228 n. 24
3:1–21	97–99	27:1–28	95–96
3:11	98–99		
4:6–7	21	1 Corinthians	
12:3	13	4:9	186–87
13:23	99–100		
13:25	99–100	Galatians	
19:26	100	3:1	186
19:27	100	3:12	224 n. 22
19:33–34	100		
19:35	99–101	Colossians	
20:1–10	101	4:7	14 n. 11
20:2	100		
20:4	102	2 Timothy	
20:15	132	1:16–18	14 n. 11
20:29–31	100	4:19	14 n. 11
20:30	99		
21:1–23	99, 102	2 Peter	
21:7	100	1:16–21	130
21:20	100		

Revelation
7:9   68
22:18–19   191

Rabbinic Works

b. Gittin
576   222 n. 19

b. Sanhedrin
96b   222 n. 19

b. Sotah
13a   21 n. 28

Ecclesiastes Rabbah
3:16   222 n. 19
10:4   222 n. 19

Genesis Rabbah
67:9   21 n. 28

Midrash Numbers
30:15   222 n. 19

Targum Neofiti
49   139 n. 5

Targum Pseudo-Jonathan
37:19   139 n. 5

Greco-Roman Literature

Achilles Tatius, *Leucippe and Clitophon*
30, 36, 257–58
1.13   37
1.14.1   38
6.21   256
8.18.5   253

Antonius Diogenes, *The Wonders beyond Thule* 194

Aretaeus of Cappadocia, *De causis et signis acutorum morborum*   31, 32
1.5   32

Aristotle, *Poetics*
1448b.16–18   165 n. 1
1448b.31   165 n. 1
1449a.31–35   165 n. 1

Arrian, *Anabasis*
1.26   129 n. 26
7.4.4–5.6   55

Chariton, *Chaereas and Callirhoe* 257–58
1.1.5   134 n. 49

Chion of Heraclea (Anonymous)
14.4   256

Choricius of Gaza, *Orationes*
3.2.13   256–57

Cicero, *De provinciis consularibus*
10   55

Codex Theodosianus
16.10.12   207

Damascius, *Life of Isidore*
181   210 n. 22

Dares the Phrygian, *Acta diurna belli Troiani*
1–5   133–34
4.11   134
22   135 n. 57
23   135 n. 57
25   135 n. 57
26   135 n. 57
27   134 n. 49
29   135 n. 57
31   135 n. 57
32   135 n. 57
34   134 n. 50, 135 n. 57
44   129, 135

ANCIENT SOURCES INDEX

Dictys of Crete, *Ephemeris belli Troiani*
1.7	135 n. 53
1.13	128
2.30	129
3.10	135 n. 53
3.15	135
3.17	135 n. 53
3.23	135 n. 53
4.3	135
4.12	135 n. 53
5.6	135 n. 53
5.17	129
6.7	129
6.10	129

Dio Chrysostom, *Orationes*
11.19–21 (*Trojana*)	131
11.88–90	132

Diodorus Siculus, *Bibliotheca historica*
4.26.1	184

Diogenes Laertius, *Vitae philosophorum*
8.4	131 n. 33

Eusebius, *Historia ecclesiastica*
2.23.6	221
2.23.10	219
2.23.13–14	218–19
2.23.16	221
2.23.17	221
2.23.18	223
6.19.6–7	288

Eusebius, *Praeparatio evangelica*
9.27.1–39	161 n. 31

Galen, *On the affected parts*   30, 31

Gregory of Nyssa, *Life of Macrina*   26

Hegesippus, *Historia ecclesiastica*
2.23.13	227
2.23.16	227
2.23.18	227

Heliodorus, *Aethiopica*   24

Herodotus, *Histories*
2.3–4	129 n. 26
2.122	184
3.111–119	117 n. 38
4.95	184–85

Homer, *Iliad*
8	132
16.805–817	131

Homer, *Odyssey*   35
11	246
11–13	244

Jerome, *Adversus Rufinum*
1	202

Jerome, *De viris illustribus*
prologue 7	201

Jerome, *Epistulae*
22.13 (*Eustochium*)	192
33.5	201
108.13	192

John Malalas, *Chronographia*
359	209 n. 21

John of Nikiu, *Chronicle*
84.100–102	209 n. 21

Josephus, *Jewish Antiquities*
2–4	159–62
2.238–257	161–62
2.241	160 n. 27
2.268	160 n. 27
2.347–348	129 n. 26
3.2	160 n. 27
3.11	160 n. 27
3.12	160 n. 27
3.28	160 n. 27
3.45–51	160
3.47	160 n. 27

3.52	160	1.14	187
3.59	161 n. 30	1.16	187
3.65	160 n. 27	2.4	187
3.67	160 n. 27	2.55–56	183–84, 193
3.78	160 n. 27	3.5–8	187
3.102	160 n. 27	4.31	187
3.105	160 n. 27	4.36	187
4.82	160 n. 27	5.33	187
4.177	160 n. 26	6.3	187
4.194	160 n. 27	6.11–13	187
4.328–329	160 n. 26	6.42	187
4.329	160, 162	6.80	187
20.197–203	230	7.28	187
20.199	230	7.53	187
		8.68	187

Justin, *Apologia ii*   44

Lactantius, *Institutiones*
1.22   126 n. 13

Livy
7.6   157 n. 15
40.29.3–14   126 n. 13

Longus, *Daphnis and Chloe*   25, 257–58

Lucian, *De morte Peregrini*
27   185–86

Lucian, *Somnium*
17   131

Lucian, *Vera historia*
  preface   191 n. 32
  1.13   191 n. 32
  1.26   191 n. 32
  2.31   191 n. 32

Lucretius, *De rerum natura*   55

Ovid, *Metamorphoses*
15.160–175   131 n. 33

Origen, *Contra Celsum*
1.5   187

Palladas, *Anthologia graeca*
9.400   211

Pamphilus, *Apologia*
16   211

Passio Anastasiae
17.10–20   256

Passio Perpetuae et Felicitatis   257

Petronius, *Satyricon*   194

Philo, *Moses*
1–2	159–62, 164
1.20	163
1.22	163
1.23–24	163
1.27	163 n. 37
1.32	163 n. 37
1.44	160 n. 26
1.48	162
1.54–57	163
1.83–84	162 n. 36
1.158	162 n. 35
1.158–159	153, 160, 162
1.163–180	129 n. 26
1.249	162 n. 34
1.257	162 n. 34

ANCIENT SOURCES INDEX

Philo, *Moses* (cont.)
1.306–308	162 n. 34
2.2	163 n. 37
2.192	160 n. 26
2.288	160 n. 26

Philostorgius, *Historia ecclestiastica*
8.9	209 n. 21

Philostratus, *Heroicus*
24	132
26.17	131 n. 33
26.33	131 n. 33
26.39	131 n. 33
26.41	131 n. 33
42.1–2	131 n. 33
43.3	131 n. 33
52	134 n. 50
138–139	132 n. 40

Philostratus, *Historia ecclesiastica*
8.9	209 n. 21

Photius, *Bibliotheca*
166, 1111a–b	127 n. 17

Plato, *De insomniis*
prologue	208

Plato, *Phaedrus*
	35
244b	36

Plato, *Republic*
386a-387c	242
614b–621d	245–47
614c–615a	243–44
617c	247 n. 3
621b	242
7.521c–531c	163

Plato, *Symposium*
217c	40
215e	40

Pliny the Elder, *Naturalis historia*
13.84–87	126 n. 13

Pliny the Younger, *Panegyricus*
45.6	153

Plutarch, *De Iside et Osiride*
20	190

Plutarch, *Numa*
22	126

Prudentius, *Peristephanon*
3.91–95	257

Pseudo-Callisthenes, *Alexander Romance*
	68–69
1.41	69
2.10	69
2.17	69

Sappho of Lesbos
Frag. 31	29, 32, 35

Sextus Empiricus, *Adversus mathematicos*
1.263–269	132

Socrates of Constantinople, *Historia ecclesiastica*
2.21	205–6
2.35	206
3.7	200 n. 3, 206
3.7.5–10	200 n. 4
4.23	200 n. 3
4.25	201–2
4.26	202
4.27	209
4.27.3–6	200 n. 4
5.22	206
6.7	209
6.7–9	203
6.9	203
6.9–10	202–3
6.10	203–4
6.12	204–5

6.13	201, 204–5	Virgil, *Aeneid*	55
6.17	202–3		
7.6	205	Xenophon, *Cyropedia*	135–36
7.15	209		
7.45	201	Xenophon of Ephesus, *Ephesiaca*	30, 39
		1.1.5	258
Soranus of Ephesus, *On Acute and*		1.2.1	258
Chronic Illnesses	30, 31, 32	2–4	256
		2.9.2	253
Sozomen, *Historia ecclesiastica*		2.10.4	253
7.26	204 n. 10	3.2.2	38
		3.2.3–4	38
Suda	210–11	4.2.4	259
		4.2.6	259
Suetonius, *Augustus*		4.3.3–4	258–59
31.5	157	5.4.6	258–59
94	215	5.4.10	259
		5.6.3	253
Synesius, *De dono*		5.6.4	253
4	211	5.10.7	253
		5.10.11	253
Synesius, *Epistulae*		5.11.4	253
Letter 16	208	5.12.1	253
Letter 105	208	5.12.5	253
		5.14.1–2	255
Theophanes, *Chronographia*		5.15.1	253
5906	209, n. 21	5.15.4	254

Valerius Maximus, *Memorable Deeds and Sayings*

2.7 praef.	156
2.8.5	157 n. 16
2.10.2	157 n. 16
3.2.1	157 n. 16
3.2.2	157 n. 16
3.2.6	157 n. 16
3.3 ext 7	157 n. 15
3.3.1	157 n. 16
3.6.1	157 n. 16
4.7.2	157 n. 16
5.4.2	157 n. 16
5.6.2	156–157
5.6.5–6	157 n. 16
7.22	157 n. 16

Modern Authors Index

Adams, Percy G.	194	Bretzigheimer, Gerlinde	123,125, 128, 134–35
Althusser, Louis	75, 115		
Ashcroft, Bill	115	Brooten, Bernadette J.	54
Attridge, Harold W.	127	Brunt, Peter A.	54
Aymer, Margaret P.	236	Burnett, Fred W.	214–15
Bal, Mieke	110	Burrus, Virginia	2, 29, 37, 43
Balsdon, J. P. V. D.	65	Byron, John	217
Bar-Efrat, Shimon	138–39, 145	Camery-Hoggatt, Jeremy	81
Barnes, Timothy D.	60	Canfora, Luigi	209
Barrier, Jeremy W.	47	Carey, Holly J.	81
Barthes, Roland	78, 238, 239	Carr, David	215, 229
Bauckham, Richard	102, 219, 220	Chambers, Ellie	235
Beal, Timothy K.	110–12, 120	Chaniotis, Angelos	185
Beard, Mary	154	Chick, Nancy L.	234,
Bechtel, Carol	112–13, 116, 118–19	Clarke, Howard	124
Bennett, E. N.	10–11	Clines, David J. A.	115, 121
Berg, Sandra Beth	113	Collins, John J.	138
Berman, Joshua A.	114–17	Cooper, Kate	45, 233
Betz, Monika	48	Cotton, Hannah M.	158
Beyschalg, Karlmann	221	Craig, Kenneth	107, 108
Blank, Josef	101	Craven, Toni	174
Bond, Shelagh M.	64	Crenshaw, James L.	112
Bonfante, Larissa	62	Crossan, John Dominic	56, 189, 216
Bonnet, Max	9–11	Curran, John	158
Borges, Jorge Luis	88	Curtius, Ernst Robert	124
Boring, Eugene	77	Cusack, Carole M.	180–81
Bovon, François	44–45, 53,	Damgaard, Finn	160
Bowersock, Glen W.	132–33, 183, 187, 190,194	Dandamaev, Muhammed A.	113
		D'Angelo, Mary Rose	85
Bowie, Ewen	132	Dannemann, Irene	16–17, 20–21
Bradley, Keith	80	Davidson, James N.	37
Braun, Martin	71–74	Day, Linda M.	116
Bregman, Jay	208	Deakin, Michael	208
Bremmer, Jan N.	44–45, 50–51	Dewey, Joanna	75
		Donahue, John	81–82

Doody, Margaret Anne	24	Harich-Schwarzbauer, Henriette	211
Döpp, Siegmar	91	Harrelson, Walter	151
Dover, Kenneth James	33	Harrington, Daniel	81–82
Draitser, Emil	165	Harris, James Rendel	249
Dube Shomanah, Musa	55	Haynes, Katharine	38
Dunn, Peter W.	43	Haynie, Aeron	234
Dupertuis, Rubén R.	217	Heever, Gerhard A. van den	5, 191
Dzielska, Maria	207	Hengel, Martin	102, 219
Eastman, Max	165	Henten, Jan Willem van	158
Eck, Werner	158	Hezser, Catherine	191–92
Eisen, Ute E.	3, 5–6, 89, 95, 97, 99, 103	Highet, Gilbert	124
Eisenhut, Werner	123, 125	Hoffmann, Lars	208
Emerton, J. A.	112	Hogle, Jerrold E.	180
Erim, Kenan T.	56	Hölkeskamp, Karl-Joachim	154
Esch-Ermeling, Elisabeth	236	Hollander, Harm W.	138, 140–43, 146, 148, 150–51
Fédou, Michel	200		
Feldman, Louis H.	160, 163	Hölscher, Tonio	65
Ferrand, Jacques	31	Hölter, Achim	88
Flower, Harriet	158	Holzberg, Niklas	132
Flynn, Thomas R.	215, 229	Horsley, Richard A.	74, 81, 85–86
Formisano, Marco	10	Howard, Cameron B. R.	109, 121
Foucault, Michel	33, 53, 187, 251, 260	Huber, Mary	235
Fox, Michael V.	108–9, 111, 119	Hughes, Jessica	61
Friesen, Steven J.	45	Huitink, Luuk,	158
Frulla, Giovanni	161	Hunter, Richard	131
Galinsky, Karl	157	Hyers, Conrad	76
Gardner, Percy	65, 67	Hylen, Susan E.	238
Genette, Gérard	71, 76, 87–89	Jackson, Stanley W.	31
Gilbert, William S.	107	Jacobs, Andrew S.	43, 45–47
Goldhill, Simon	53	James, Edward	180
Goodacre, Mark	84, 86	James, Montague Rhodes	9, 127
Goodman, Martin	158	Jameson, Fredric	71–74, 195
Gorman, Jill	10–11, 15, 17, 19, 21, 23–24, 27	Jenkinson, Edna	128
		Jensen, Anne	236
Gounelle, Rémi	244–45, 249	Jeremias, Joachim	192
Gowler, David B.	216–217	Jobling, J'Annine	107, 114
Graff, Gerald	234	Jong, Irene de	89–91, 94
Gray, Patrick	213	Jonge, Marinus de	138, 140–43, 146
Griffiths, Gereth	115	Junod, Eric	9–11, 15–16
Grossman, Jonathan	107	Kaestli, Jean-Daniel	142
Gruen, Erich S.	154, 167–68, 176	Kähler, Heinz	62
Gurung, Regan A. R.	234	Kee, H. C.	143
Haines-Eitzen, Kim	237	Keith, Alison	55
Halperin, David M.	53, 54	King, Karen	221
Hammer, Olav	180, 181	Klimek, Sonja	87, 89

Konstan, David   5, 12, 37–39, 43, 255, 257–58
Kraemer, Ross S.   47, 53
Kronenberger, Louis   176
Kugler, Robert A.   138–41, 145–47
Kuttner, Ann L.   62, 65, 67, 68
Lage, Santiago Díaz   182
Lalanne, Sophie   252
Leppin, Hartmu   200
Lessing, Gotthold Ephraim   103
Levenson, Jon   107–8, 111–13, 117, 119
Levi, Annalina Caló   64
Levine, Amy-Jill   45, 46
Levine, Etan   176
Lewis, James R.   180
Lewis, Naphtali   159
Lieu, Judith M.   44
Liew, Tat-siong   85
Lincoln, Bruce   195
Logan, Alastair H. B.   188
Löhr, Winrich   207
Lopez, Davina C.   56
Ludlow, Jared W.   4
Luke, Trevor S.   48, 70
Lukonin, Vladimir G.   113
MacDonald, Dennis R.   5, 32–36, 40, 217, 235
MacMullen, Ramsay   159
Maier, Harry O.   186
Makkreel, Rudolf A.   215, 229
Makowski, John F.   12
Marcus, Joel   73
Markschies, Christoph   199
Marrou, Henri-Irénée   157, 208
Marshall, John W.   2
Mason, Steve   154
Matthews, Shelly   5, 133, 217, 223, 229
May, Regine   32
McCracken, David   165, 170
McLaren, James S.   220,
McWhirter, Jocelyn   83, 86
Meggitt, Justin J.   45
Meister, Ferdinand   124
Mendlesohn, Farah   180
Merkle, Stefan   125, 128, 133–35

Metzger, Bruce M.   167
Michie, Donald   75
Möllendorff, Peter von   89, 103
Moore, Stephen D.   85
Moreland, Milton   64
Morgan, John R.   127, 136, 189–90, 195
Morgan, Teresa   154–56,
Mosala, Itumeleng J.   121
Mount, Christopher   228
Murphy, Roland E.   167
Naumann, R.   56
Neuschäfer, Bernhard   200
Ní Mheallaigh, Karen   214
Nickelsburg, George W. E.   142
Niehoff, Maren   154, 159
Norman, Alex   180–81
Nuffelen, Peter van   200
Oden, Robert A., Jr.   127
Omerzu, Heike   48
Östenberg, Ida   68
Ostrowski, Janusz A.   64
Overbeck, Franz   100
Parker, Jan   235
Paton, Lewis B.   110, 112, 115, 118
Penner, Todd C.   214, 233
Percy, William Armstrong   33
Perkins, Judith   188
Perry, Ben E.   134
Perucho, Juan   182
Pervo, Richard I.   9–11, 14–15, 19, 22, 47, 214, 217, 236
Pesch, Rudolf   92
Phipps, Alison   235
Pietersma, Albert   169
Possamai, Adam   180
Possamai-Inesedy, Alphia   180
Price, Jonathan J.   158
Punter, David   180
Quint, David   55
Ramelli, Ilaria L. E.   3, 201, 203, 206–7, 212, 258, 260
Ramsby, Teresa R.   46
Reed, Annette Yoshiko   153
Rehak, Paul   161
Reiser, Marius   73

Resch, Robert P. 115
Reynolds, Joyce M. 56, 58–59
Rhoads, David 75
Richlin, Amy 53
Rimmon-Kenan, Shlomith 138, 143, 149, 151
Roemer, Michael 76, 80
Roitman, Adolfo 173
Roller, Matthew 155–56, 159, 161–62, 164
Roncace, Mark 213
Rothstein, Mikael 181
Roughley, Alan 107, 114
Ryan, Marie-Laure 91
Schäferdiek, Knut 49, 67
Scaffai, Marco 124
Scheidel, Walter 45
Schetter, Willy 124
Schneemelcher, Wilhelm 11, 43–44
Scholz, Peter 155
Schwartz, Saundra 34–35, 216–17
Schwartz, Seth 161–62, 218
Schwiebert, Jonathan D. 83–84
Scott, Joan W. 46, 70
Sebesta, Judith Lynn 62
Segovia, Fernando F. 229
Seng, Helmut 208
Severy-Hoven, Beth 46
Shapira, Yona 107
Shaw, Brent 256
Shepherd, Tom 82
Sipress, Joel M. 234
Slater, Niall 253
Sly, Dorothy 159
Smid, Harm Reinder 130
Smith, Daniel Lynwood 219
Smith, R. R. R. 56, 58–60, 62, 68,
Smith, Stephen H. 77,
Snyder, Glenn E. 47
Söder, Rosa 130
Spannagel, Martin 157, 158
Speyer, Wolfgang 126
Stoneman, Richard 69
Sullivan, Arthur S. 107
Szepessy, Tibor 11, 15–16

Temelini, Mark A. 67
Thomas, Christine 73
Thurman, Eric 82, 85
Tiffin, Helen 115
Toit, David du 92–93, 96, 99, 103
Tolbert, Mary Ann 73
Toohey, Peter 29–31
Toynbee, Jocelyn M. C. 62, 68
Urbainczyk, Theresa 200
Urbano, Arthur 199
Vander Stichele, Caroline 233
Vermeule, Cornelius 67
Vines, Michael 89
Voelker, David J. 234
Waddell, Helen 124
Wallraff, Martin 200
Walter, Uwe 154–55
Watts, Edward J. 207, 209
Whedbee, J. William 176
White, Hayden 215
Whitmarsh, Tim 37
Williams, Craig 24
Wills, Lawrence 73, 168, 170, 172, 176
Wiseman, T. P. 136, 189
Wright, Benjamin G. 169
Zafón, Carlos Ruiz 179, 181, 182

Subject Index

Abraham
    Philo, *On the Life of Abraham*, 162
    Sarah, wife of, 175
    slave of, 21
    Testament of. *See also* ancient sources index; *see* Testament: of Abraham
Achilles (in Homer), 131, 134–35
Achilles Tatius, 2, 30, 36–38, 191, 253, 256, 258. *See also* ancient sources index
Achior, 171–73
Acts. *See also* ancient sources index, apostles, disciples, Luke-Acts
    apocryphal, 1, 9–10, 12, 15–16, 24, 43–53, 56, 61, 68, 70, 192, 242, 248
    canonical, 1, 5–6, 44, 53, 65, 68, 92, 95–99, 102–3, 126, 130, 213–31, 236
    of Andrew, 2, 10, 29–36, 40, 46, 50–51, 241–42
    of John, 17, 46, 49–50, 67, 242, 248
    of Mark, 242
    of Paul (and Thecla), 5, 10, 13–14, 17, 22, 43, 46, 47–48, 52, 123, 136, 233–39, 255
    of Peter, 10, 48–49, 73, 192
    of Philip, 10
    of Pilate, 249
    of Thomas, 10, 51–53, 242
    of Xanthippe and Polyxena, 9–11, 14–15, 17, 19, 21–22, 27, 254–55, 259
Adam, 50, 175, 259
adultery. *See* sexual morality
Aeneas. *See also* Virgil
    in Virgil, 55, 132, 157–58
    Jew named, 245, 250

Ahasuerus, 109–10, 113, 116, 120–21
Ajax, 131
Alexander Romance, 68–69, 73, 123
Alexander Severus, 132
Alexander the false prophet, 185
Alexander the Great, 55, 68–69, 71–72, 123, 127, 158
Alexandria, 3–4, 153, 159, 164, 188, 199, 202–3, 207–11. *See also* Cyril, Hypatia, Origen, Philo, Theophilus
Ammonius Saccas, 188–89
Ammonius of Alexandria, 207
anachronism/anachronistic, 30
Andrew. *See* Acts of
angel(s), 127–28, 170, 174, 187, 242–46, 259. *See also* messenger(s)
    Angelos/Er, 246. *See also* Er, Myth of
    Angel's Game, 179–82. *See also* Carlos Ruiz Zafón
    Michael, 174–75, 242–46
    Raphael, 170
animal(s), 20, 25, 52, 141, 143, 235. *See also* bear, bull, dog, lion, lioness, serpent, snake, talking animals, wolves
Antioch, 48, 235–36
Antonius Diogenes. *See Wonders beyond Thule*
Aphrodite, 56, 65, 132. *See also* Venus
apocalypse(s), 85, 191
    of James, 221
    of Paul, 127–28
apocalyptic, 2, 83, 93–94, 138, 191–92
apocryphal acts. *See* Acts: apocryphal
Apollo, 129, 134
apostasy. *See* idolatry, idolaters

apostles, 2, 10, 12–17, 19–24, 27, 30, 33–34, 40–41, 43–46, 48–53, 56, 61, 68, 70, 128, 186, 192, 213–14, 217, 222–26, 228, 229, 235, 238, 254–55. *See also* disciples, Acts
apostrophe, 90, 94
Apuleius, 32, 253
archangel. *See* angel(s)
Aretaeus of Cappadocia, 30–32
Ascension of Isaiah, 220
ascetic(ism), 2, 11–13, 15–18, 26–27, 30, 33, 47, 200, 203, 209–12, 233, 236
Assyria. *See* Syria
Athens, 124, 185, 207
authority, 4, 48–49, 79, 82, 84–85, 90–93, 96, 100–01, 103, 108, 111–12, 119, 126–27, 195, 203–5, 235
autopsy, 91, 100, 103, 128. *See also* eyewitness, authority
Bakhtin, Mikhail, 107
bear, 146, 150, 256. *See also* animals.
beloved disciple. *See* love: beloved disciple
Benjamin. *See* Testament of
Bethulia, 172
biography (genre), 4, 16, 128, 150, 154, 199–200, 207
blending of narrative voices/worlds, 6, 90–91, 93, 96–98, 101, 103
blessing, 101, 237
bottom up, 88, 90–91, 94
brother(s), 18, 21, 51, 137–52, 160, 203, 208, 217, 221, 228, 230, 246, 248. *See also* sister(s), sibling
bulls, 192, 233. *See also* animals
Caesarea, 199
Carlos Ruiz Zafón, 179–82
carnival(esque), carnivalization, 3, 107–10, 114, 119–22
Celsus, 183–95. *See also* Origen
characterization (method), 40, 45, 52, 74–77, 81, 83, 97–98, 134, 136, 141, 145–48, 152, 175, 230
chastity. *See* sexual morality
Chaucer, 124
chreia, 216

Chrysostom. *See* Dio Chrysostom, John Chrysostom
city, 13, 32, 47, 50, 65, 120, 127, 156, 167, 181–82, 192, 218, 220, 223–24, 227, 241, 253. *See also* civic, Jerusalem
civic. *See also* city
  constraints, 253
  officials, 45, 47
  order, 47–48
Codex Sinaiticus, 169
Codex Theodosianus, 207
Codex, Tchacos, 221
colonial
  ambivalence, 24, 37
  colonialism, 52, 55, 69
  context, 115
  decolonization, 72, 229
  discourse, 117
  domination, 44–45, 51, 69–70
  ideology, 52
  postcolonial(ism), 3, 55, 69, 72, 74, 85, 115
  Roman colonial model, 44, 85
  rule, 48
  subject, 80, 115–17
  subjectivity, 116–17
comedy, 4, 165–66, 170, 176. *See also* funny, humor, parody, satire
conversion (converted, converts), 2, 12–17, 27, 33, 44–53, 68, 204, 255
Corinth 65, 67
Cornelius Nepos. *See* Nepos
court(s)
  law court, 34–35, 219. *See also* law
  royal/imperial, 107–08, 114–16, 185, 199. *See also* empire, imperial, kingdom, royal
  Temple Court, 222–23, 226–27. *See also* temple(s): in Jerusalem
creativity (creative), 10, 73, 160, 164, 166, 175, 177, 180–81. *See also* fiction, invention
crowds, 13, 79, 84, 172, 193, 218–19, 224. *See also* mob, masses
Cyril, 207. *See also* Alexandria

SUBJECT INDEX 311

Cyropaedia, 135
Dan. *See* Testament: of Dan
Daniel (biblical), 168
Daniel Defoe, 136
Dares, 3, 123–25, 128–36
Darius I, 113
Darius III, 68–69
death. *See also* tomb
   in ancient novel, 15, 37, 254, 259
   in apocryphal acts, 13–15, 18, 23–27, 49, 235
   in Esther, 107–8, 117–20
   in Socrates's history, 201, 203–4
   in Tobit, 166–67, 170
   of Darius, 69
   of Dinias, 127
   of Er, 248
   of Holofernes, 173
   of Hypatia, 207
   of James, 218–30
   of Jesus, 80–86, 93, 100, 184–89, 249
   of patriarchs, 21, 141, 166, 175–76, 259
   of Peregrinus, 186
   of Trojan heroes, 131, 249
   of Stephen, 218–19, 222, 227–28, 230
   of Zechariah, 221
Descensus, 245–50. *See also* Er, Gospel of Nicodemus, Hades
destiny, 71–72, 119, 256. *See also* fate
dialogue
   Heroicus, 131–32. *See also* Philostratus
   in narrative, 84, 97, 10
   Plato, 36
diaspora, 167–68, 176–77. *See also* exile
Dictys, 3, 123–25, 128–36
didactic, 176. *See also* education, paideia, pedagogy
Dio Chrysostom, 131–32. *See also* ancient sources index
Diogenes, Antonius. *See* Wonders beyond Thule
Diogenes Laertius, 131. *See also* ancient sources index

disciples, 12, 14, 19, 22–26, 30, 34, 36, 77, 90, 94, 97–102, 207–8. *See also* apostles
discourse, 34, 45, 51, 69–71, 76, 78–79, 81–85, 88–91, 94, 108, 110–11, 114, 117–18, 120–21, 153–56, 159–60, 162, 164, 179–81, 185, 188–91, 193–95, 204–5, 215–16, 233
divination. *See* prophecy
doctors, 30–31, 34. *See also* Greek physicians, healing, health
dog(s), 51, 192, 256. *See also* animals
dream(s), 13, 18, 74, 175, 184. *See also* oracles, predictions, prophecy, visions
ecphrasis (ecphrastic performance), 186–87, 190
education (educated), 32, 95, 132–33, 155, 162–64, 188, 199–200, 206, 211–12, 216, 234–35, 252. *See also chreia*, didactic, exemplary, Greek education, paideia, pedagogy, philosphy, Plato, progymnasmata
Egypt(ian), 2, 58, 89, 108, 141–43, 148, 159, 161–63, 183–84, 187, 203, 210, 255. *See also* Alexandria
   empire, province, language, 2, 58, 89, 159
   patriarchs in, 141–43, 148, 160, 161
empire, 2, 4, 45–52, 55–56, 60–65, 68, 71–74, 78–82, 85, 108–21, 136, 154, 156–57, 176, 183–86, 191–95, 207, 260. *See also* authority, colonial, court, Egypt(ian), kingdom, imperial(ism), Persian, Roman, royal
empty tomb motif. *See* tomb of Jesus
enargeia, 189
epic (genre), 55, 103, 124, 131–33, 191, 214
Er, Myth of, 242–50. *See also* Plato
erastes, 17, 24, 30, 33, 35, 38–40
eromenos, erōmenē, 18, 24, 30, 33, 35–36, 40
Eros, 26, 37, 254, 258. *See also erôs*, love, lovesick(ness)
erôs, 31, 251–52, 255, 257–58, 260

SUBJECT INDEX

Esther, 3, 107–23, 168
ethnic(ity), ethnographic, ethnos, 22, 54–56, 58, 110–14, 118, 122, 153. *See also* peoples/nations
Euphorbus, 131. *See also* Homer, Pythagoras
Euripides, 241
Eusebius, 161, 188, 199–201, 205–6, 210–11, 218–19, 221, 223. *See also* ancient sources index
exaggeration, 4, 112, 128, 131, 165–29, 171, 173–75. *See also* comedy, humor, hyperbole, parody, satire
exegesis, 11, 83, 202, 206, 208, 211, 219
exemplary/exemplarity, 4, 153–62, 164, 216
exemplum/exempla, 154–61, 222
exile(d), 23–24, 162, 176, 203, 210, 260. *See also* diaspora
eyewitness, 95–96, 99–101, 103, 128, 134, 213. *See also* autopsy
fable, 188–89, 195. *See also* fiction, myth
fade-out. *See* loose-end technique
family/families, 2, 43–47, 56, 69, 114–15, 139, 142, 167, 252–53, 255. *See also* brother, sister, sibling
fantasy/fantastic, 25, 88, 179–84, 189, 194–95
fate, 20, 81, 111, 121, 171, 175, 220–22, 244, 247, 253. *See also* destiny
feminist (feminism), 1, 16, 17, 45, 55, 233. *See also* women
fiction, 1–6, 24, 45, 51–55, 69, 71–73, 76, 88–89, 123–24, 127–38, 143, 149, 151, 167–68, 172, 179–95, 213–17, 229, 233–34, 241–42, 250–51, 255. *See also* creativity, history and fiction, novel, romance
fidelity
    romantic/sexual, 251, 257, 259. *See also* sexual morality
    to God, 256–58, 260. *See also* loyalty, obedience, pious, piety
first person narration. *See* narration, first person

forgiveness, 6, 92–93, 221, 223–27, 252, 258–59
friend(ship), 22–24, 33, 36, 45–49, 81, 168, 204, 209–10, 254
funny, 165–66, 176. *See also* comedy, exaggeration, humor, hyperbole, parody, satire
Gad. *See* Testament: of Gad
Galen, 30–31
genre, 5, 10, 12, 16, 19, 26, 32, 38, 55, 73, 132, 136, 155, 161, 165, 168, 182, 191–92, 195, 213–14, 252, 254. *See also* apocalypse, epic, *exemplum*, gospel (genre), gothic literature, history (genre), novel, romance, Testament, tragedy
gentile, 22, 24, 176, 224, 227
geography/geographical, 71, 129, 167, 190, 208
Glykon, cult of, 185
God, 2, 14, 20, 22, 43, 48, 50, 52, 68, 74–75, 78–82, 84, 86, 93, 97–98, 101, 140, 151, 162–63, 165–66, 169–70, 172–73, 176–77, 186, 188, 203, 205–6, 218–19, 221–27, 237, 246–46, 251, 256–60
god(s), 36–37, 52, 65, 129–31, 185, 187, 191, 258–59
godlike, 153, 162
gospel. *See also* ancient sources index, John, Luke, Mark, Matthew, Nicodemus
    genre, 73–75, 77, 93, 95, 97, 99–100, 188–90, 193, 213, 216, 249
    message, 43, 47–50, 52–53, 70, 77–78
Gospel of Nicodemus. *See* Nicodemus
gothic literature, 179–83, 193
Greece, 14, 19–21, 163, 254. *See also* Athens
Greek
    art, 62–65
    culture, 153, 188
    education, 163–64, 188. *See also* education, paideia, pedagogy
    evidence, 56. *See also* sources

Greek (cont.)
history, 200
Homeric, 132. *See also* Homer
homosexuality, 33, 37, 54. *See also* homoerotic, same-sex, pederasty
influence, 124
language, 11, 15, 32, 34, 126–27, 170–71, 224–25
literature, 4, 29, 36, 73, 89, 103, 185, 211, 241
manuscript/recension, 9, 142, 237, 242, 245–49
novel. *See* novel, ancient; romance
original, 124
philosophy, 55, 164, 188–89. *See also* Hypatia, Origen, Plato
physicians, 30–32, 34. *See also* healing, health
rule, 72. *See also* empire, imperial
title, 20
traditions, 78
versions/Testament, 78, 111, 219. *See also* Septuagint, Testament
world, 89
Greek(s), 23–24, 105, 125, 135, 188, 223
greeting(s), 20
guilt, 37, 147, 150, 259–60
Hades, 169, 183–84, 242, 245–49. *See also* Descensus, underworld
hagiography, 15–16, 26, 60, 191–92
Haman, 111–13, 116–21
healing, health 6, 12–13, 33, 92, 170–71. *See also* Greek: physicians
medical, 2, 30–32, 34
physicians, 12, 16, 30–31
Hebrew Bible, 85, 112, 176. *See also* Tanak, Torah, Testament: OT
Hector, 132, 134, 135, 249
Hecuba, 131, 134
Hegesippus, 217–19, 221, 223–24, 227
Heliodorus, 24
hero (heroes, heroic), 24, 71–86, 124, 131–34, 157, 159, 162, 164, 176, 185, 190–91, 225, 229, 252–58. *See also* heroine, national hero

Herodotus, 117, 129, 184–85, 190. *See also* ancient sources index
Heroicus, 131–34. *See also* ancient sources index, dialogue, Philostratus
Herodotus, 184–85, 190. *See also* ancient sources index
heroine, 12, 19, 21, 236, 252–53, 257. *See also* hero
historical(ly), 1, 46, 55, 69, 73–77, 81–82, 123–36, 154, 161, 167–68, 181–82, 189–90, 206–07, 213–17, 220, 225, 228–31, 239, 251. *See also* history
historicity, 9, 217. *See also* history, verisimilitude
historiography, 89, 123, 125, 155, 190, 200, 213–15, 217, 233. *See also* history
history
and fiction, 1, 3, 55, 68–69, 71–73, 76, 123–36, 168, 183, 187, 189–95, 214–15, 229–31
genre, 128–29, 136, 161, 168, 189, 191, 195, 213–15, 234, 236–38
Christian/of the church, 60, 65, 188, 199, 214, 218, 225, 228
in Josephus, 154, 158, 161–62
Israelite/Jewish, 85, 121, 171
of art, 61–62, 67
of scholarship, 44
of sexuality, 11, 33, 53–54
of Socrates of Constantinople, 199–212
of Spain, 182
postmodern approach, 3, 5
reception history, 3, 5
Holofernes, 171–73
Homer, 36, 40, 124, 125, 131–33, 135, 217, 241, 246, 249. *See also* ancient sources index, *Iliad*, *Odyssey*, Trojan, Troy
homoerotic(ism), 11–12, 18, 23, 25–26, 30, 34, 36, 38–39, 54
homosexual, 33, 54. *See* Greek: homosexuality, homoerotic(ism), same-sex love

humor(ous), 5, 53, 109–11, 165–72, 175–77. *See also* comedy, exaggeration, funny, hyperbole, parody, satire
Hypatia, 4, 199–201, 206–12
hyperbole, 4, 119, 165–66, 168. *See also* exaggeration
identity
　Christian, 71, 75, 79, 217, 256–57
　divine/of God, 219
　Greco-Roman, 37. *See also* Greek
　constructed, construction, fictional, imagined, invented, 75, 83
　Jewish, 115–17, 120, 154, 159, 174
　national, collective, group, 3, 74, 79–80, 107, 114. *See also* national hero
　of Jesus, 84–84, 86
　of the self, 258
　politics, 2, 71–72
　philosophical, 199
　social status, 85, 115, 257
　true/hidden, 109, 114–17, 151, 170
ideology/ideological, 5, 52, 55, 73, 75–76, 79–80, 85–86, 108, 115, 118, 121, 182, 191, 195, 215, 229. *See also* politics
idolater(s), 21–23
idolatry, 218
Iliad, 124, 129, 249. *See also* Achilles, ancient sources index, Homer, Troy
imperial(ism), 3, 43, 47–49, 54–64, 68, 70–71, 78, 85, 89, 107–10, 112–22, 176, 179, 181, 186, 188, 194, 208, 218, 223–25, 228, 230–31. *See also* colonial, empire, Persia(n), Roman
intertextual(ity), 21, 241
invention, 103, 135, 180, 187. *See also* creativity, fiction, identity
irony (literary, dramatic), 81–85, 107, 128, 154, 166–68, 172. *See also* comedy, humor, reversal
Isaac, 174–75
Isaiah. *See* Ascension of. *See also* ancient sources index
Isis (and Osiris), 190–91, 258

James. *See also* ancient sources index, Josephus
　apocalypse of, 221
　Protoevangelium of, 222
　in Hegesippus, 217–21, 223–24, 227
　disciple, 94
　brother of John, 228–29
　Josephus's narrative of, 230
Jerome, 192, 201–02, 211
Jerusalem
　Christian community 128, 220, 223–24, 227, 245–46
　destruction of, 64, 167, 222–28
　foreign rule, 228
　in NT, 78, 220, 223–28
　Jewish community, 108, 172
　Targum, 21
　temple, 167. *See also* temple(s): in Jerusalem
Jesus Christ
　descent into underworld, 245–50. *See also* Descensus, underworld
　in apocryphal acts, 43–48, 51–53, 217–28
　in Celsus/Origen, 183–90, 193
　in Josephus, 230–31
　in NT, 6, 13, 21–22, 73–86, 92–102, 186, 216–28
　James, brother of, 217, 224, 227, 230–31
John
　Acts of. *See* Acts: of John, and *See also* ancient sources index
　Baptist, 78–79, 99, 192, 222
　brother of James, 228
　Chrysostom, 203–04
　Gospel of, 6, 9, 92, 97–103. *See also* ancient sources index
　Malalas, 125, 209
Joseph. *See also* ancient sources index, Testaments of Twelve Patriarchs, Testament of Joseph
　and Aseneth, 24
　in Gospel of Nicodemus, 245–47

Joseph (*cont.*)
  in Testaments of Twelve Patriarchs, 3, 137–52
  Testament of. *See* Testament: of Joseph
Josephus, 4, 153–54, 158–62, 164, 220, 230–31. *See also* ancient sources index
Judith, 4, 166–68, 171–176
Justin Martyr, 44
kingdom(s)
  of God, 56, 74
  of the world, 48, 110, 121, 163. *See also* court, empire, imperial, royal
law
  Greco-Roman, 52, 120, 188
  Jewish, 222, 224, 226, 230–31. *See also* Torah
  of Medes and Persians, 3, 108–120. *See also* Persia(n): law of the Medes and Persians
Leucippe and Clitophon, See Achilles Tatius, ancient sources index
Life of Adam and Eve, 259
liminal, 252, 254, 260. *See also* margin(s)
lion(s), 22, 142–43, 192, 255. *See also* animals, lioness
lioness, 14, 20, 22–25, 27, 235, 255. *See also* animals, lion(s)
literate/literacy 3, 86, 113, 126, 186, 191
loose-end (fade-out) technique, 90–91, 94, 103
love
  beloved disciple, 90, 97–102
  divine, 247
  familial, 13–27, 140–44, 147–48, 151–52. *See also* family, brother, sister, sibling
  Jesus as beloved son, 79
  romantic, 5, 12–20, 23–45, 48–49, 52, 54, 134–35, 161, 235–36, 251–60. *See also* passion
lovesick(ness), 2, 13, 17, 29–36, 39–41
loyalty, 52. *See also* empire, fidelity, obedience, piety
Lucian, 125, 127, 131, 186, 191, 194, 214. *See also* ancient sources index, satire

Luke. *See also* ancient sources index; Acts: canonical
  Acts, 213, 228
  Gospel of, 6, 22, 94, 99, 213, 216, 220–23, 226
  Luke-Acts, 92, 95–97, 99, 102–3, 216, 219, 223
lyric, 29, 124. *See also* meter, music, poetry, poetics
magic 46
making present, 87, 92, 99, 101, 103
margin(s), 71, 176, 194, 229. *See also* liminal
Mark. *See also* ancient sources index
  acts of, 242
  Gospel of, 2–3, 6, 13, 71–86, 92–95, 102–3, 123, 219
marriage, 5, 17, 23–25, 37, 43, 46–52, 55, 114, 129, 162, 170, 233, 236, 251–52, 257–58. *See also* sexual morality
martyr(dom), 4–5, 12, 46, 52, 192, 200, 209, 211, 217–21, 224–25, 228, 233, 236, 251, 256–58, 260. *See also* Justin Martyr, Stephen
masses, 71–72, 132, 158, 209. *See also* crowd, mob
medicine. *See* healing, health, Greek physicians
memorial, 58, 253
memory, 60, 65, 154–55, 162, 186, 210, 239
messenger(s), 21, 242. *See also* angel(s)
metalepsis (metaleptic), 5–6, 87–103
metalepsis, ontological, 91, 102
meter, 214. *See also* lyric, music, poetry
Michael. *See* angel(s): Michael
Middle Platonic. *See* Plato: Middle Platonic
mimesis (mimetic), 5, 76, 80, 162, 165, 171, 241, 244–45, 248, 250
mimetic stabilization, 91
miracle (miraculous), 16, 48, 51, 92, 133, 189, 192–93
mob, 47, 218–19, 228. *See also* crowd, masses

modesty. *See* sexual morality
Mordecai, 108–10, 114, 116–22
Moses, 4, 153–54, 159–64, 193
music, 163. *See also* lyric, meter, poetry
mysteries, divine, 246
mystery cults, 184, 186, 191
mystery novel, 181
mysticism, 180, 206
myth (mythology)
  and religion, 179–95. *See also* religion
  and fiction, 179–95. *See also* fiction
  Christian, 181
  (de)mythologize, 131, 181, 193
  of Er, 242–50
  of Isis and Osiris. *See* Isis
  of Israel's origins, 77
  Homeric, 131, 217. *See also* Homer
  in Celsus/Origen, 183–86, 208. *See also* Celsus, Origen
  in NRMs, 180–183, 192. *See also* NRMs
  in Plato, 208, 242–3
  mythical founding figures, 73. *See also* national hero (romance)
  mythmaking, 179
  Roman, 56, 58
Naphtali. *See* Testament of
narrative/narration/narrate, *passim*
narrative metalepsis, 5–6, 87–103
narrative pathology, 87, 102
narration, first person, 3, 14, 89, 95–101, 130, 137–52
narrator (narrative voice), 6, 18–19, 24, 51 n.19, 75, 77–79, 83–84, 87, 90–103, 116, 120–22, 131, 135, 137–52, 170, 174, 179, 257
narrator, reliability of the, 137–152
national hero (romance), 71–86. *See also* hero, identity, romance (genre)
Nebuchadnezzar, 167
Neoplatonic. *See* Plato: Neoplatonic
Nepos, Cornelius, 124, 128
new religions. *See* religion
New Testament. *See* Testament: NT
Nicodemus
  Gospel of, 5, 241, 244–50

Nicodemus (*cont.*)
  in John, 97–99
novel, ancient, 1, 5, 12, 15, 17, 19, 24, 27, 30, 32, 36–40, 50, 69, 71–73, 82, 125, 128, 130, 132, 134–36, 168–76, 189–95, 214, 216, 251–60. *See also* fiction, romance
novel, gothic/Spanish, 181–82. *See also* *Angel's Game*, Carlos Ruiz Zafón
novelistic (texts), 10–11, 19, 73, 134, 165, 168, 183, 189–95, 233, 236, 238, 255, 259
NRMs (new religious movements). *See* religion
obey/obedience, 23, 112, 114–17, 202. *See also* fidelity, loyalty, religion, piety, worship
Odyssey/Odysseus, 36, 124, 244, 249. *See also* ancient sources index, Homer
  of Christ, 73, 80–83, 183, 245, 250, 256
  romantic, 16, 36, 39, 134, 201, 251–52, 256–57. *See also* love
Old Testament. *See* Hebrew Bible, Testament: OT, Torah, Tanak
oracles, 156, 220–23. *See also* dreams, prophecy, predictions, visions
orality, 91, 94, 103
Origen, 3–4, 183–89, 193–95, 199–212. *See also* ancient sources index, Celsus
outer space. *See* space
Ovid, 131
paideia, 214. *See also* education, Greek education, pedagogy
papyrus/papyri, 124–25, 245–47. *See also* ancient sources index
parable, 6, 96–97. *See also* fable
paradox/paradoxical(ly), 11, 24, 78–79, 82, 85–89, 96, 98, 155, 194, 239
parody (parodic), 14, 78, 108, 111–14, 119, 122, 166, 172. *See also* humor, satire, comedy
passion. *See also* love, martyr(dom), suffering(s)
  of Jesus, 73, 80–83, 183, 245, 250

passion (*cont.*)
  of martyrs, 256
  romantic, 36, 39, 251–52, 256–57
Paul. *See also* ancient sources index; apocryphal acts; canonical Acts; Acts: of Paul (and Thecla); apostle(s)
  Acts of Paul (and Thecla), 5, 10, 13–14, 17, 22, 43, 46, 47–48, 52, 123, 136, 233–38, 255
  Apocalypse of, 127
  apostle, 56, 224
  in canonical Acts, 95–96, 222, 225, 228
  in Acts of Xanthippe, 12–27, 255
  letters of 14, 186, 224
  tomb of, 128
Paula, 192, 201
pedagogy, 5, 26, 33, 133, 153–59, 164, 197, 213–31, 233–39. *See also* education
pederasty/pederastic, 30, 33, 37–39. *See also* homoerotic, same-sex
peoples/nations, 53–56, 58–59, 61, 65, 67–68, 70, 72, 78, 114, 116–20, 160, 187, 194. *See also* ethnic, identity, national hero
Peregrinus, 185
Persia(n). *See also* court, Darius, empire, imperial, law, royal
  book of annals, 109
  court, 107–9, 113
  daughters of Darius, 55, 69
  empire/rule, 2, 109, 120–21
  Esther queen of, 115, 117
  individuals, 117, 120
  language, 113, 120–21
  law of the Medes and Persians, 3, 108–20
perspective
  feminist, 17
  narrative, 75, 137, 139, 143–45, 147–48, 152. *See also* first-person narration
  new historicist, 182
  theoretical, 180

Peter
  Acts of. *See* Acts: of Peter
  apostle, 14, 19, 82, 94, 101–02, 192, 254
Petronius, 194
Philip. *See* Acts: of Philip
Philo of Alexandria, 4, 153–54, 158–60, 162–64, 188. *See also* Alexandria, ancient sources index, philsophy
Philo of Byblos, 127
philosophy, 4, 33, 35, 55, 75, 103, 115, 127, 159, 162–64, 183, 186, 188–91, 199–212, 256. *See also* Greek philosophy, Hypatia, Origen, Philo, Plato, Pythagoras
Philostratus, 131–132. *See also Heroicus*
Phoenix (name), 186
physicians. *See* Greek physicians, healing, health
piety, 12, 160, 204. *See also* obedience, pious, fidelity, religion
Pilate. *See* Acts: of Pilate
pious, 26, 129, 160, 162, 166–68, 173–74, 185, 204. *See also* obedience, piety, fidelity, religion
pity (mercy, compassion), 20, 38, 140, 147, 258–59
Plato. *See also* ancients sources index, dialogue
  Christian Platonism, 207–08
  Middle Platonic, 183, 187–90
  Myth of Er, 242–50
  Neoplatonic, 188, 190, 199, 207–11
  philosopher/works, 2, 35–36, 163, 187, 217, 241–45, 248
  Platonist education, 163–64, 199, 207. *See also* education
  Platonist tradition, 3, 163–64, 199, 207
plot, 10–15, 17, 19–20, 23–24, 27, 33, 73–74, 76, 79–80, 83, 91, 96, 110, 112–13, 118, 133–36, 155, 161, 164, 187, 191, 194, 214–15, 225, 228–29
Plotinus, 199, 207–08
Plutarch, 3, 126–28, 133, 154, 190–91. *See also* ancient sources index

poet(ry), 32, 131–33, 190, 214. *See also* lyric, meter, music, poetics
poetics, 95, 99, 138, 165, 217. *See also* lyric, meter, music, poetry
polemic, 50, 181, 185
politics/political, 2, 44, 53–55, 59, 65, 67, 71–79, 81, 84–86, 127, 158–59, 176, 186, 195, 203, 214–15, 230–31. *See also* identity politics
Polybius, 154
Polydamas, 129
polysemia, 74
polytheist, 4
Polyxena, daughter of Hecuba, 134
Polyxena, sister of Xanthippe, 9–27, 134, 254–55, 259. *See also* Acts of Xanthippe and Polyxena
Porphyry, 188–89, 199
postcolonial. *See* colonial: postcolonial(ism)
prayer
  Christian, 19, 22, 25, 49, 51, 81, 221–28, 246–47
  Jewish, 169–70, 172, 223–28
predictions, 84, 226. *See also* dreams, oracles, visions, prophecy
Priam, 135
private (versus public), 47, 71–73, 131, 195
progymnasmata, 216. *See also chreia*, education, exemplary
property, 121
prophecy (prophetic), 18, 21, 79–80, 185, 192, 219–27. *See also* dreams, oracles, predictions, visions
Protoevangelium of James, 222. *See also* ancient sources index, James
Ptolemy the geographer, 208
public (versus private), 65, 71–73, 154–55, 162, 186, 189, 204, 210. *See also* private (versus public)
Purim, 3, 108, 121–22
Pythagoras (Pythagorean), 127, 131, 183–84, 188, 193. *See also* Euphorbus
Raguel, 169–71. *See also* Tobit

Raphael. *See* angel(s): Raphael
Rebecca, in Acts of Xanthippe and Polyxena 9, 14–16, 19–27
Rebecca, wife of Isaac, 21
religion. *See also* mystery cults, worship and myth. *See* myth
  Christianity as official, 207
  Egyptian, 163. *See also* Egypt
  in Celsus, 187. *See also* Origen
  in Plutarch, 190
  NRMs (new religious movements), 179–82
  Roman, 126, 186
Republic
  of Plato, 217, 242, 244, 248–49. *See also* ancient sources index, Plato
  Roman, 155, 182
resurrection, 47–48, 93, 183–90, 208, 213, 245–50, 259–60
Reuben, 140, 146–47, 152. *See also* Testaments of the Twelve Patriarchs
reversal (reversed, the reverse), 30, 36, 40, 79, 90, 107–8, 113, 122. *See also* carnival; paradox
rhetoric(al), 16, 68, 87, 91, 96, 102, 113, 129, 155, 163, 190, 196, 213–14, 219, 223, 250, 256
romance (genre), 11–12, 14–15, 19–27, 37, 48, 68–69, 71–73, 82, 123–24, 134, 254. *See also* fiction, novel
romantic. *See* love; novel; romance (genre); passion
Rome/Roman. *See also* empire
  art, 46, 58–59, 61–62, 64–65, 67
  Augustan, 46
  city of, 12, 18, 128, 158, 192
  empire/power/culture, 53–55, 61, 73, 80, 126, 136, 154–55, 223, 231
  Josephus and, 154–55, 158–59, 164
  Philo and, 154–55, 159, 164
royal, 109–11, 114–16, 119, 121, 163. *See also* court(s), empire, kingdom(s), Persia(n).
Sallust, 124, 128

same-sex love, 2, 9–27, 33. *See also* homoerotic, homosexual, love, pederasty
Sappho, 29
Sarah
    in Tobit, 169–70. *See also* Raguel
    wife of Abraham, 175. *See also* Abraham
satire, 165–66, 168, 186. *See also* comedy, exaggeration, hyperbole, humor, Lucian, parody
science fiction, 179–80, 183, 191. *See also* fiction
Scientology, 180
Sebaste, 192
Sebasteion, 56–61, 65. *See also* Theoi Sebastoi
Septuagint, 169. *See also* Greek: versions/Testament
serpent, 192, 256. *See also* animals, snake
sexual morality. *See also* marriage
    adultery, 34, 49
    chastity, 2, 12, 43–45, 47, 50, 52, 68, 255, 258
    fidelity (faithful), 49, 251, 253, 257–59
    modesty, 163, 238
    virginity, 14–16, 19–27, 35, 43, 45, 47, 112, 115, 134, 209, 211, 233, 237–38, 255
Shakespeare, 4, 124
sibling, 24. *See also* brother, sister
Simeon. *See* Testament of
simultaneity, 90–91, 96–97, 103
sin(s) (sinful, sinners), 6, 21, 50, 92–93, 140, 221–22, 227, 243, 252, 255, 258–60
sister(s), 13, 15, 18, 22–27, 208, 255. *See also* brother, sibling
snake, 50. *See also* animals, serpent
Socrates (of Constantinople), 3–4, 199–212
Socrates (the philosopher), 36, 40
sophistic (novel), 1
Soranus of Ephesus, 30–32
source-critical, 92, 94–95, 102

sources (ancient, historical, literary), 3, 55–56, 62, 95, 98, 124–26, 138, 194, 201, 203, 209, 215–16, 218, 224, 226, 229–30
space
    cognitive, 54
    domestic, 2, 18, 26, 46, 155, 252, 254
    geographical, 56, 116–17, 252–55, 260. *See also* geography/geographical
    imperial, 194
    literary, 75, 195
    outer, 191, 194
    ritual, 157
spatiality, 194
spectacle, 187
speech with double relevance, 90, 93, 97–98, 103
subversion/subversive, 101, 103, 108–09, 154. *See also* paradox, reversal
suffering(s), 16, 18, 27, 29, 31–32, 84, 165, 187, 243, 258–59. *See also* ascetic(ism), passion (of Christ)
Star Wars, 180–81
Syracuse, 253
Syria (Assyria, Syriac), 51, 55, 163, 167, 172–73, 237, 255
talking animals/objects, 14, 23–24, 52, 192. *See also* animals
Tall Brothers, 203
Tanak, 107. *See also* Hebrew Bible, Torah, Testament: OT
temple(s)
    body as, 51
    destruction of, 167. *See also* Jerusalem
    Greco-Roman, 56, 67, 134, 157–58. *See also* Greek, religion
    in Jerusalem, 81, 167, 217–27
    in NRMs, 180
    Second Temple period, 62
Testament (biblical). *See also* ancient sources index
    NT, 21, 68, 78, 94, 99, 103, 130, 216–17, 233, 238, 241
    OT, 21–22. *See also* Hebrew Bible, Torah, Tanak

Testament. *See also* ancient sources index, Testaments of the Twelve Patriarchs
  of Abraham, 4, 154, 166–68, 174–75, 241–44, 250
Testament (cont.)
  of Benjamin, 137, 139, 142–43, 151
  of Dan, 137, 139, 145
  of Gad, 137, 139, 145–46, 148
  of Joseph, 137, 139, 141–42, 148, 151–52
  of Naphtali, 140
  of Simeon, 137, 139–40, 143, 146
  of Zebulun 137, 139–40, 143, 146–47, 150–51
Testaments of the Twelve Patriarchs, 1, 3, 137–52. *See also* ancient sources index
Thecla. *See* Acts of Paul (and Thecla)
Theoi Sebastoi, 56. *See also* Sebasteion
Theophilus, 202. *See also* Alexandria
Thomas. *See* Acts: of Thomas
Thule. *See* Wonders beyond Thule
tomb
  books found in, 126–27
  in Dares/Dictys, 126
  in Descensus, 245
  of Dinias, 127
  of Jesus, 101, 193
  of Numa, 126
  of Paul, 128
  of Protesilaus, 130
  of saints, 192
  of Tall Brothers, 203
top down, 88, 90–91, 95. *See also* bottom up
Torah, 108, 218, 220. *See also* Hebrew Bible, Tanak, Testament: OT
tragedy
  genre, 176, 184
  tragic(ally), 12, 23, 27, 37, 81, 168–69, 170–71, 176, 209, 211
travel(s)
  between worlds, 102
  of Er, 243. *See also* Er, Myth of
  of Paul, 96
  plot element, 12, 14–15, 24, 194, 254

travel(s) (cont.)
  to Hades/underworld, 247. *See also* Descensus
Trojan War, 3, 123–36
Troy, 123–24, 131
True Doctrine (Celsus, Ἀληθὴς λόγος), 183. *See also* ancient sources index, Celsus, Origen
True History (Lucian, Ἀληθῆ διηγήματα), 191, 194. *See also* ancient sources index, Lucian
underworld, 183, 191. *See also* Descensus, Er, Hades
Vashti, 110–12
Venus, 62, 65. *See also* Aphrodite
Vergil. *See* Virgil
verisimilitude, 132–33, 135, 190, 220, 224–25. *See also* historicity
Virgil, 55
virginity. *See* sexual morality
vision(s), 13, 17–18, 27, 83, 191, 243, 259. *See also* dreams, oracles, prediction, prophecy
wisdom, 157, 162, 210, 222, 247
wolves, 192. *See also* animals
women, 1–2, 9–23, 26–27, 37, 43–48, 50–51, 53–56, 61–62, 65, 68–69, 110, 112, 114–16, 121, 134, 160, 163, 172, 174, 192, 207, 233, 235–38, 255
Wonders beyond Thule, 127, 194
wordplay, 165–66, 171, 173–74. *See also* comedy, humor
worship, 221. *See also* religion, piety, obedience
Xanthippe, sister of Polyxena, 9–13, 15–27, 254–55. *See also* Acts: of Xanthippe and Polyxena
Xanthippe, wife of Albinus, 49
Zebulun. *See* Testament: of Zebulun
Zechariah, 220–24, 226–27

www.ingramcontent.com/pod-product-compliance
Lightning Source LLC
Chambersburg PA
CBHW020110010526
44115CB00008B/765